Cambridge Studies in Islamic Civilization

Men of modest substance

Cambridge Studies in Islamic Civilization

Editorial Board

Titles in the series

Men of modest substance

House owners and house property in seventeenth-century Ankara and Kayseri

SURAIYA FAROQHI

Middle East Technical University,
Ankara

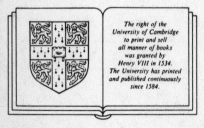

The right of the
University of Cambridge
to print and sell
all manner of books
was granted by
Henry VIII in 1534.
The University has printed
and published continuously
since 1584.

Cambridge University Press

Cambridge
London   New York   New Rochelle
Melbourne   Sydney

Published by the Press Syndicate of the University of Cambridge
The Pitt Building, Trumpington Street, Cambridge CB2 1RP
32 East 57th Street, New York NY 10022, USA
10 Stamford Road, Oakleigh, Melbourne 3166, Australia

First published 1987

Printed in Great Britain at the University Press, Cambridge

British Library cataloguing in publication data

Faroqhi, Suraiya
Men of modest substance : house owners
and house property in seventeenth-century
Ankara and Kayseri. – (Cambridge studies
in Islamic civilization)
1. Home ownership – Turkey – History –
17th century
I. Title
333.3′23   HD7287.82.T9

Library of Congress cataloguing-in-publication data

Faroqhi, Suraiya, 1941–
Men of modest substance.
(Cambridge studies in Islamic civilization)
Bibliography.
Includes index.
1. Housing – Turkey – Ankara – History – 17th century.
2. Housing – Turkey – Kayseri – History – 17th century.
3. Architecture, Domestic – Turkey – History – 17th
century. 4. Housing – Religious aspects – Islam – History
– 17th century.   5. Home ownership – Turkey – History –
17th century.   I. Title.   II. Series.
HD7358.25.A53F37 1987   307.3′36   86–13618

ISBN 0 521 32629 X

To Elisabeth Hesse – in gratitude for many things

Contents

Tables

Graphs

Illustrations

Figures

Abbreviations

AKS	Ankara kadı sicilleri, Etnoğrafya Müzesi, Ankara.
Ankara Evleri	Edip Kömürcüoğlu, *Ankara Evleri*, İTÜ, Mimarlık Fakültesi Yayınları (İstanbul, 1950).
'Ankara'nın Eski bir Resmi'	Semavi Eyice, 'Ankara'nın Eski bir Resmi', *Atatürk Konferansları*, IV (1972), pp. 61–124.
'Ankara'nın Yerleşim Durumu'	Özer Ergenç, 'XVII Yüzyıl Başlarında Ankara'nın Yesleşim Durumu Üzerine Bazı Bilgiler,' *Osmanlı Araştırmaları-J1 of Ottoman Studies* I (1980), 85–108.
'Askerî Kassam,'	Ömer L. Barkan, 'Edirne Askerî Kassamına Ait Tereke Defterleri, (1545–1659),' *Belgeler*, III, 5–6 (1966), 1–479.
AÜ	Ankara Üniversitesi
BA	Başbakanlık Arşivi, Istanbul.
Celâlî	Mustafa Akdağ, *Celâlî İsyanları* 1550–1603 (Ankara, 1963).
Civilisation matérielle	Fernand Braudel, *Civilisation matérielle, économie et capitalisme, XVᵉ–XVIIIᵉ Siècle*, 3 vols (Paris, 1979)
'1600–1615 Yılları'	Özer Ergenç, '1600–1615 Yılları Arasında Ankara İktisadî Tarihine Ait Araştırmalar,' in: *Türkiye İktisat Tarihi Semineri*, ed. Osman Okyar, Ünal Nalbantoğlu (Ankara, 1975), pp. 145–168.
Démographie	Roger Mols, *Introduction à la*

	démographie historique des villes d'Europe du XIV*au XVIII* siècle, 3 vols. (Louvain, 1955).
Divriği	Necdet Sakaoğlu, Divriği'de Ev Mimarisi (Istanbul, 1978)
EI	Encyclopedia of Islam, 2nd edition.
Great Arab Cities	André Raymond, The Great Arab Cities in the 16th–18th Centuries. An Introduction (New York, 1984).
Habitat	J. C. Garcin, 'Habitat médiéval et histoire urbaine à Fusṭāṭ et au Caire,' in: J. C. Garcin, Bernard Maury, Jacques Revault, Mona Zakarya, Palais et maisons du Caire, vol. 1 Époque mamelouke (XIIIᵉ–XVIᵉ siècles) (Paris 1982)
IJMES	International Journal of Middle Eastern Studies.
Introduction	Joseph Schacht, An Introduction to Islamic Law (Oxford, 1964).
Introduction à l'histoire	Antoine Abdel Nour, Introduction à l'histoire urbaine de la Syrie ottomane (XVIᵉ–XIXᵉ siècle). Publications de l'Université Libanaise, Section des Etudes historiques (Beirut, 1982).
'Islamic City'	Albert H. Hourani, 'Introduction: The Islamic City in the Light of Recent Research,' in: The Islamic City, ed. A. H. Hourani, S. M. Stern (Oxford, 1970), pp. 9–24.
İA	İslam Ansiklopedisi.
İFM	İstanbul Üniversitesi İktisat Fakültesi Mecmuası.
İTÜ	İstanbul Teknik Üniversitesi.
İÜ	İstanbul Üniversitesi.
Jerusalem	Amnon Cohen, Jewish Life under Islam, Jerusalem in the Sixteenth Century (Cambridge, Mass., London, 1984).
JESHO	Journal of the Economic and Social History of the Orient.
'Kadi, Court, and Legal Procedure'	Ronald Jennings, 'Kadı, Court and Legal Procedure in 17th Century

	Ottoman Kayseri,' *Studia Islamica* XLVIII (1978), 133–172.
Kapukulu Ocakları	İsmail Hakkı Uzunçarşılı, *Osmanlı Devletinde Kapukulu Ocakları*, 2 vols. Türk Tarih Kurumu Yayınlarından Seri, VIII–12 (Ankara, 1943, 1944).
Kayseri Evleri	Jíü Mimarlık Fakültesi Yayınlerı Necibe Çakiroğlu, *Kayseri Evleri* (İstanbul, 1951).
KKS	Kayseri kadı sicilleri, Etnoğrafya Müzesi, Ankara.
Konut	Ayda Arel, *Osmanlı Konut Geleneğinde Tarihsel* Sorunlar, Ege Üniversitesi Güzel Sanatlar Fakültesi Yayınları, No. 11 (İzmir, 1982).
'Limitations'	Ronald Jennings, 'Limitations of the Judicial Powers of the *Kadı* in 17th century Ottoman Kayseri,' *Studia Islamica* L (1979), 151–184.
'Loans'	Ronald Jennings, 'Loans and Credit in Early 17th Century Judicial Records, The Sharia Court of Ottoman Kayseri,' *JESHO*, XVI, 2–3 (1973).
MD	Mühimme defterleri.
'Men, Women, and Property'	Abraham Marcus, 'Men, Women, and Property,' JESHO, XXVI, 2 (1983), 137–163.
METU	Middle East Technical University.
M.M.	Maliyeden müdevver.
Monuments	Albert Gabriel, *Monuments turcs d'Anatolie*, 2 vols. (Paris, 1931, 1934), Vol. 1, *Kayseri, Niğde*
Narh	Mübahat S. Kütükoğlu, *Osmanlılarda Narh Müessesesi ve 1640 Tarihli Narh Defteri* (İstanbul, 1983).
ODTÜ	Orta Doğu Teknik Üniversitesi
'Osmanlı Para Tarihinde'	Halil Sahillioğlu, 'Osmanlı Para Tarihinde Dünya Para ve Maden Hareketlerinin Yeri,' *Türkiye İktisat Tarihi Üzerinde Araştırmalar, Gelişme Dergisi* (special issue 1978–79), 1–38.

Plan Tipleri	Sedad Eldem, *Türk Evi Plan Tipleri*, İstanbul Teknik Üniversitesi Mimarlık Fakültesi (İstanbul, 1968)
'15. Asır'	Halil Inalcık, '15. Asır Türkiye İktisadî ve İçtimaî Tarihi Kaynakları,' *İFM*, 15, 1–4 (1953–54), 51–75.
Seyahatnamesi	Evliya Çelebi, *Seyahatnamesi*, 10 vols. (Istanbul, 1314/1896–97 to 1938).
Tagebuch	Hans Dernschwam, *Tagebuch einer Reise nach Konstantinopel und Kleinasien (1553–1555)*, ed. Franz Babinger (Munich, 1925).
TK	Tapu ve Kadastro Genel Müdürlüğü, Kuyudu kadime archive, Ankara.
Towns	Suraiya Faroqhi, *Towns and Townsmen of Ottoman Anatolia, Trade, Crafts and Food Production in an Urban Setting* (Cambridge, England, 1984).
TT	Başbakanlık Arşivi, section Tapu Tahrir.
'Urban Population'	Ronald Jennings "Urban Population in Anatolia in the Sixteenth Century. A Study of Kayseri, Amasya, Trabzon and Erzurum," *IJMES*, VII, 1 (1976), 21–57.
'Usurious Piety'	Jon Mandaville, 'Usurious Piety: The Cash Waqf Controversy in the Ottoman Empire,' *IJMES*, X, 3 (1979), 289–308.
'Vekil'	Ronald Jennings, 'The Office of *Vekil (Wakil)* in 17th Century Ottoman Sharia Courts,' *Studia Islamica*, XLII (1975), 147–169.
Vier Briefe	*Vier Briefe aus der Türkei* von Ogier Ghiselin von Busbeck, tr. and commented by Wolfram von den Steinen, Der Weltkreis 2 (Erlangen, 1926).
Wohnhaus	Edip Kömürcüoğlu, *Das alttürkische Wohnhaus* (Wiesbaden, 1966).

'Women'

Ronald Jennings, 'Women in Early 17th Century Ottoman Judicial Records – the Sharia Court of Ottoman Kayseri,' *JESHO*, XVIII, 1 (1975), 53–114.

'Women of Bursa'

Haim Gerber, 'Social and Economic Position of Women in an Ottoman City, Bursa 1600–1700,' *IJMES*, 12 (1980), 231–244.

'Zimmis'

Ronald Jennings, 'Zimmis (non-Muslims) in 17th Century Ottoman Judicial Records: the Sharia Court of Ottoman Kayseri,' *JESHO*, XXI, 3 (1978), 225–293.

Preface

At some point in their careers, most historians become sensitive to the manner in which the craft they exercise might be of use in the 'real world'. For the present author, growing consciousness in this respect has led to an interchange of ideas with architects, urban planners and restoration specialists at Middle East Technical University in Ankara, where I have been teaching for the past fourteen years. If an attempt was to be made to protect certain historical environments, it was obviously necessary to learn as much as possible about the environment to be protected. When referring to the contribution which might be made by a historian working mainly on the sixteenth and seventeenth centuries, this boiled down to three simple questions: how did Anatolian towns of this period function? what kinds of buildings did they contain? and how were the latter used? With an optimism largely due to inexperience, I set about finding the answers to these questions.

During the early stages, I was mainly concerned with the manner in which townsmen made a living. Translated into urban space, this involved a study of how the 'business districts' of Anatolian towns came into being. But peoples' lives do not solely consist of earning a living and, if one studies the scene on which Ottoman townsmen acted when they were not working, one's attention is automatically drawn to the often handsome houses which still exist in the more 'traditional' quarters of certain Anatolian towns. Thus the present study may be regarded as a companion volume to my *Towns and Townsmen of Ottoman Anatolia: Trade, Crafts and Food Production in an Urban setting, 1520–1650* (Cambridge, 1984) but oriented toward the residential neighbourhoods whereas the previous volume focused on shops and market places. However, the present study can in no way claim to cover Anatolian urban society in its totality; many of its facets remain to be considered in further studies.

The source material used in this instance consists of documents on sales, inheritances and disputes as contained in the *kadı* registers of Ankara and Kayseri. The data contained in these documents have been tabulated for easier analysis. As a result it has not usually been possible to give references

xx Preface

for individual texts, and very rarely is a conclusion based on one or two documents alone. An attempt to give individual references would have resulted in notes so voluminous and confusing as to be virtually useless. As it stands, the present study is based upon the fifty-odd tables which appear in different chapters; the references concern mainly the secondary literature and a few individual archive documents.

Both the *Towns and Townsmen* study and the present one have been a long time in the making. But in a sense the present one, although written later, is the older of the two; for I began to think about it at the time, now more than ten years ago, when Dr Leila Bisharat (Erder) involved me in the work of her fourth-year city planning students on nineteenth-century Bursa. It must have been about this time that I first became aware of the use that urban planners and restoration specialists might make of a reconstitution of an important Anatolian city, based upon Ottoman archival documents.

Other contacts were to follow. Dr Emine Caner, equally from Middle East Technical University's Faculty of Architecture, will remember heated discussions, over innumerable cups of tea, about the validity of certain restoration projects in particular, and the right of every generation to manipulate the historical environment in general. Dr Sevgi Aktüre and Dr Ömür Bakırer were both, along with myself, involved in a series of seminars concerning the city of Ankara; both of them also taught me a great deal in the course of informal conversations. Ms Latife Bayraktar generously shared her knowledge of old Kayseri and its domestic architecture and allowed me to use the photographs she had taken, while Ms Tülay Artan not only drew several maps and graphs, but also pointed out secondary literature that it would have taken me a long time to discover on my own. Dr Huri İslamoğlu-İnan's encouragement led me to formulate my assumptions more clearly than I might otherwise have done. Moreover, I am much indebted to Mr Necati Yurtsever who took great care in printing and developing the photographs. Several of the graphs were ably drawn by Mr Haluk Cangökçe. The Dean of Istanbul Technical University, Prof. Gündüz Atalık, and Profs. Necife Gakıroğlu and Eyüp A. Kömürcü kindly permitted the use of house plans originally established by Profs. Gakıroğlu and Kömürcüoğlu and published in their respective books, *Kayoeri Evleri* (Istanbul, 1951) and *Ankara Evleri* (Istanbul, 1950). I am deeply grateful to them all. But needless to say, none of these people are in the least responsible for any errors of fact and judgment that the present book may contain.

The data upon which this study is based were collected at the Etnoğrafya Müzesi in Ankara. Mr Osman Aksoy, the director, and his staff provided hospitality over a long period of time; without their kindness and understanding, my work would have been impossible. Certain supporting data were collected at the Başbakanlık Arşivi in İstanbul. The reading room staff cheerfully accepted all the inconvenience connected with my commuting between Ankara and İstanbul. I will never forget the tea that Miss Filiz Karakaş used to order for me when I walked in early in the morning, somewhat the worse for wear after an eight-hour bus ride. Mr Veli Tola's and Ms Mesude Çorbacıoğlu's assistance has also been much appreciated.

A first version of the present study has benefited much from friendly criticism. Apart from the readers who commented on the manuscript prior to its acceptance by Cambridge University Press, I should like to thank Dr Michael Rogers, of the British Museum in London, and Professor André Raymond of the University of Aix-en-Provence. Their criticisms have certainly helped to make this a better book – even though of course they may still be disappointed as far as the final result is concerned. But it goes without saying that any mistakes and shortcomings are nobody's fault but my own.

Since unfortunately I know next to nothing about computers, I would have been quite unable to put together the tables upon which this study rests but for the help of Ms Elsie Pamuk and particularly of my husband Dr Rıdvan Tigrek. In addition, my thanks go to the Computer Centre at Middle East Technical University and the Office for Information Technology at Harvard University. Without the help of many people in both these institutions, the present study probably would never have come into being, for I would still be counting and recounting, or more likely would have given up in frustration. Even as things stand, I wasted much of the grant generously made available for my computer work by the Center for Middle Eastern Studies at Harvard.

A one-year appointment at the Center as an H.A.R. Gibb Fellow, under the most pleasant circumstances imaginable, substantially speeded up my work. Ms Beatrice St Laurent and Dr Nancy Pyle helped a stranger to 'Make it in Massachusetts', while the superb resources of the Widener Library made me aware of the work that has been done on the physical structure of pre-industrial cities outside of the Ottoman realm. The concern of Ms Marion Schoon made these resources more accessible. With great skill, Ms Patricia Goad and Mrs Zehra Öner Tuğlu have typed the manuscript, without even once complaining about the multitude of tables – it would be difficult to imagine an assistance more needed, and more deeply appreciated.

Suraiya Faroqhi
Ankara, November 1985

Introduction

The term 'Ottoman architecture' evokes the image of stately structures, built mainly in the fifteenth and sixteenth centuries upon the initiative of the reigning Sultans, members of their families, and high-ranking public officials. İstanbul, Bursa and Edirne contain the most monumental specimens of this type of architecture, mainly mosques, theological schools, fountains, and structures used for commercial purposes. Outside the borders of modern Turkey, the downtown area of Aleppo still bears witness to the construction activities of Ottoman provincial administrators, and Damascus or Sarajevo also feature many buildings characteristic of an Ottoman city.[1] In fact, most towns which at one point in their existence formed part of the Ottoman Empire still contain at least one mosque or public bath representing the 'classical' Ottoman style of the sixteenth century. Large blocks of stone, perfectly regular in shape, a central dome covered with lead, and elaborate stalactite arrangements, may be mentioned among the most obvious characteristics of this type of architecture.[2]

Next to these monumental buildings, the domestic architecture of Ottoman towns has always figured as a poor relation. For the period before the nineteenth century, even palace architecture is represented only by a limited number of examples: the Topkapı, Hünkâr Kasrı, and Ibrahim Paşa palaces in İstanbul, in addition to a few vestiges remaining from the Sultans' palace in Edirne.[3] With certain reservations, the architecture of the more important dervish lodges (zaviyes), such as the complex of Mevlâna Celâddin Rumî in Konya, or the hospice of Seyyid Gazi near Eskişehir, might be regarded as comparable to palace architecture; but the number of surviving major zaviye complexes is also quite limited.[4]

Nor have the dwellings inhabited by townsmen of western and central Anatolia been preserved in appreciable numbers, at least where the pre-nineteenth-century period is concerned. In many regions of Anatolia, the use of wood and sun-dried brick accounts for the relatively short life span of popular housing. Moreover, increases in the value of urban real estate during the last twenty or thirty years, as well as the construction activities of municipalities and other public institutions, have led to the rapid disap-

1

pearance of many old-style neighbourhoods in present-day Turkish cities.[5] As a result, direct documentation concerning the domestic architecture of the Ottoman sixteenth and seventeenth centuries is limited to a few more or less isolated examples.

On the other hand, the number of written documents concerning Anatolian domestic architecture is reasonably great, at least for the period after about 1600. However, this material has been utilized but very rarely. Since it is both unpublished and written in the Arabic alphabet, it is not readily accessible to architects and historians of architecture, who in consequence have limited themselves to studying the domestic architecture of Turkey as it survives today. Thus, for instance, a series of theses on old-style houses in major provincial centres of Anatolia, which was sponsored by İstanbul Technical University during the 1950s, all but ignore the existence of written documentation.[6]

However, ordinary urban housing of the sixteenth, seventeenth, or eighteenth centuries has equally been neglected by social and economic historians. This may be partly due to the fact that the immense mass of documents emanating from the Ottoman central administration, upon which the attention of most historians has understandably been con-centrated, does not deal with the problems posed by private construction. Even such scholars as Inalcık[7] and Barkan,[8] who have pioneered the study of private fortunes in the Ottoman realm, have tended to neglect the documentation on urban housing, and preferred to study such issues as money lent out at interest, household effects, and agricultural equipment. As a result, the study of sixteenth to eighteenth century urban housing in Anatolia is as yet only in its beginnings.

Research on Ottoman housing and urban society

Among the work undertaken by architectural historians on provincial Ottoman housing, Ayda Arel's book has had a considerable impact upon the design of the present study.[9] Obviously, the author's more far-reaching conclusions concerning the nomad tradition and its impact upon the Otto-man-Turkish house, and her attempt to decipher the symbolic content of certain forms, remain outside the domain of the present investigation. However, Ayda Arel's discussions of the social value placed upon the upper floor, and of the discontinuity between the ground floor and the inhabited sections of the house, have been of great help in translating the descriptions of the kadıs registers into reality. Moreover her emphasis upon changes in the manner in which a dwelling might be used, and the possible repercus-sions of these changes upon the structure of the house itself, fit in very well with a social historian's view of the problem.

With respect to Syria and Egypt, a number of recent studies have addressed themselves to the problems posed by the Ottoman house, in a manner closely parallel to the approach attempted in the present volume. In his work on Syrian cities of the Ottoman period Antoine Abdel Nour, whose untimely death in Beirut is deeply regretted, has undertaken the first systematic attempt to reconstruct the houses of an Ottoman city from data provided by the *kadı* registers.[10] Moreover his work on the dwellings and residential wards of Aleppo and Damascus allows us to place his findings concerning urban houses into the broader context of urban form. Abdel Nour's study shows up the very considerable differences between housing patterns prevalent in Central Anatolian towns and those of Aleppo. Apart from climatic factors, the most significant reason for this difference was apparently the fact that İstanbul fashions, lifestyles and decorative tastes touched Aleppo much less than Central Anatolia, but also less than for instance Damascus, even though Aleppo throughout the sixteenth and seventeenth centuries was a major centre of interregional and international trade.

A futher recent study on Aleppo has been undertaken by Abraham Marcus;[11] however, the full text of his dissertation being inaccessible to the present author, all comments made here are limited to his article on the people who held real property in eighteenth-century Aleppo. In this article, the author's main concern is with the extent to which women participated in the ownership of houses, shops, and gardens. However, he treats the question within a broader context, investigating to what extent Muslims, Christians and Jews, or else the wealthy and the poor, differed in their degree of access to residential, business, and agricultural property. On the other hand, Marcus does not, at least as far as can be judged from the published article, concern himself with the physical appearance of the buildings which were the subject of many of the real estate transactions he discusses. At the same time, his work on the social characteristics of urban house owners has produced results which are quite comparable to those which have been reached in the present study. To what extent these parallels are due to real similarities between Central Anatolian and Aleppine society, and to what extent the perspective offered by the *kadı* registers shows Ottoman society in the provinces as more uniform than it really was, is a problem which must be left for future researchers to decide. At this point, we are still trying to focus upon the functioning of different provincial societies within the confines of the Empire. The time for comparison and synthesis still lies in the hopefully not very remote future.

Abdel Nour and Marcus, like the present author, are social historians looking at houses mainly as a source for the study of Ottoman social structures as they existed during the sixteenth, seventeenth and eighteenth centuries. However, more broadly based investigations, which include architectural studies, have been undertaken for Cairo. The collective volume by Bernard Maury, André Raymond, Jacques Revault, and Mona Zakariya emphasizes architectural design and the use of building materials at least as much as the socio-economic relations which underlay residential construction in Ottoman Cairo.[12] However, the Egyptian wealthy dwelling – and as Raymond has pointed out, only the dwellings of the rich survive, thus imperceptibly distorting our vision if we concentrate exclusively upon physical evidence – had taken on its basic shape in the pre-Mamluk and Mamluk periods: İstanbul influences, which entered upon the scene at a later stage, tended to affect the decoration more than the basic design. As a result, the opportunities for comparison between Cairo and Anatolia remain somewhat limited, unless one attempts to deal with possible influences of Syrian and Egyptian building traditions upon residential construction in Central Anatolia. This however is a task which the present researcher is not qualified to undertake.

A synthesis of what is known about Arab cities during the Ottoman period has recently been undertaken by André Raymond.[13] With respect to the housing patterns of that time, Raymond emphasizes the appreciable number of people who, in large cities like Cairo or Aleppo, lived in dwellings which did not conform to the standard patterns of the one-family house. Thus Raymond discusses in considerable detail the merchants and other transients who for often lengthy periods of time resided in urban khans. In addition, the 'apartment buildings' of Cairo, and the 'ḥawš', collective dwellings around a common courtyard, which rather appear to have resembled the slum dwellings of modern Mexico City, are also brought into sharper focus. Raymond does not of course deny that the vast majority of families lived in single-family dwellings. But with his emphasis on alternative residential patterns he seems to be aiming at a less 'ideological' view of urban houses. One may deduce this frame of mind from his criticism of Abdel Nour's attempts to link the structure of the Aleppine house – closed off from the world, but open to the sky – with a metaphysical view of the world which supposedly was held by the people who had these houses built.[14] On the other hand, Raymond is much concerned with the question of a 'national style' particularly in Ottoman Egypt; that is the survival of Mamluk patterns both in publicly accessible buildings and private domestic architecture. At the risk of overstating Raymond's intentions, one might say that his concern is with the Arab city, not with the Islamic city, and the title of his book serves as a further confirmation of this point of view.

Turning from the Arab world to the Balkans, certain investigations by Nicolai Todorov are also relevant to the present undertaking. This remains true even though Todorov discusses Ottoman domestic architecture and Ottoman urban society not as aims in themselves, but rather as the means of approaching a problem which is rather remote from the present study: his basic intent is to show to the maturing of the social forces that stood behind the Bulgarian Renaissance of the nineteenth century.[15] In the course of his research into the urban population of the eighteenth-century Bulgarian vilayets, Todorov has come to the conclusion that the townsmen of the 1700s were becoming wealthier, and the sources of their wealth more diversified, than had been the case in the preceding two hundred years. While Todorov is concerned with house property only as one item among many, his work does include a brief study of residential properties as reflected in eighteenth and early nineteenth century *kadı* registers. However, since his main concern is with the composition of family fortunes, he is less interested in the physical appearance of these houses than in their monetary value and their relative importance among other items of capital investment.

From houses to people: some assumptions underlying the present study

Even though it may not sound very scholarly – at the beginning of the present study there was an 'uncomfortable feeling'. Todorov had written his book to explain the Bulgarian Renaissance, and his work served to point up a great many similarities between seventeenth-century Sofia, Vidin, or Ruschuk on the one hand, and contemporary Ankara or Kayseri on the other. A sizeable amount of interregional trade, towns which were inhabited not only by tax officials and ulama but which acted as lively centres of craft production, relatively significant opportunities for non-Muslims to pursue economic and cultural activities: in spite of war, the Kadızades,[16] and banditry, the Ottoman Empire of the seventeenth century rested upon a society with many more possibilities for 'peaceful coexistence' than were to be realized in the future. When did the different subgroups making up Ottoman society begin to grow apart? To what extent were the tensions of the nineteenth and twentieth centuries foreshadowed in the urban society of sevententh-century Ankara and Kayseri? After all, just as the conjunctural ups and downs of urban life in the Ottoman Balkans can be read off the entries in the *kadı* registers, similar data should be available concerning Anatolia. What picture do they give us concerning the everyday relations between Muslims and non-Muslims?

Obviously, this question could be investigated from many other angles than have been explored in the present study. However the urban societies of Ankara and Kayseri consisted essentially of house owners, while on the other hand, it would appear that people do make significant statements about their culture by the way in which they arrange their houses – if only we know how to decode these statements. Under the circumstances, a study of Ankara and Kayseri houses should give us certain clues concerning the development of Muslim–non-Muslim relations.

Another angle to be explored was the place of women in urban society. Recent studies have shown that for the period preceding the late nineteenth century, almost the only way to find out something about Ottoman women is to explore the *kadı* registers. Obviously the opportunity to hold property in general, and access to real property in particular, is an important feature of the 'female condition' in any culture. A previous study had already dwelt upon the relative ease of access to the court which protected women's rights to their property,[17] an observation which has been amply confirmed while preparing the present study. One only needs to remember that down into the nineteenth or even twentieth century, married women in many European countries were considered perpetual minors and could not without the permission of their guardian sue anybody, let alone their own husbands.[18] With this fact in mind, the reader will appreciate the advantages which easy access to the court gave many urban women of Anatolia.

Another preoccupation that ultimately led to the present study is the concern with change in time. Many investigators have tended to treat non-European societies, and Ottoman society in particular, as entities that scarcely changed in the course of history. Only very recently have researchers become aware of changes in social mores,[19] and thereby come to realize the importance of not assuming, without prior investigation, that an observation made in the sixteenth century is necessarily valid for the nineteenth as well. In the present study it has been assumed that patterns of family living, use of domestic space, and relations between different groups in society changed, at least in certain respects, even during the relatively short time span of ninety to a hundred years which has been investigated here. It is our job as modern researchers to determine the speed or slowness as well as the particular direction of this change. To deny the existence of change before one has even investigated the possibility seems to be little more than a form of intellectual laziness.

Last, but not least, one might mention another reason for dissatisfaction with historiography concerning the Ottoman realm as it stands today.[20] When reading through the secondary literature on the 'post-classical' period, that is the Ottoman Empire after about 1600, one is time and again confronted with the notion of a 'decline' lasting through the better part of three centuries. As a response, it seemed reasonable to try and find out how Anatolian townsmen survived 'three hundred years of crisis' or alternatively, if the crisis was really of as long duration as has sometimes been maintained. One would like to know whether there were no regions or sectors of the economy in which at least a temporary recovery could be observed. In fact a recent study has brought out that at least certain regions, such as for instance Ottoman Syria, showed a net increase in population between the sixteenth and the nineteenth centuries – contrary to what has been maintained by most authors writing on the subject.[21] A closer investigation of Anatolian developments may well bring out other positive aspects of Ottoman rule, and thereby help clear away some of the intentional and unintentional misunderstandings which have accumulated due to conflicts peculiar to the nineteenth and twentieth centuries, and which still cloud our understanding of Ottoman society.

Procedures

A study of written evidence concerning domestic architecture is possible
only for cities whose *kadı* registers (*sicil*) survive in appreciable numbers. If
one wishes to examine an early period, such as the sixteenth or seventeenth
century, the choice is therefore quite limited. As far as western and central
Anatolia are concerned, Bursa, Konya, Ankara, and Kayseri are the most
obvious choices.[22] For it seems that the *kadı*s and scribes of the larger cities
generally produced much more detailed descriptions than their colleagues in
smaller towns. Usually, the latter thought it unnecessary to list the rooms of
a given building, and considered an enumeration of the neighbours as
perfectly adequate for identifying a given piece of real estate. Moreover, the
registers of the larger towns were generally preserved with more care, and as
a result, both go back further in time and present fewer gaps. If the registers
of Ankara and Kayseri have been selected for the present undertaking, this
is mainly due to the fact that they were easily accessible to the author.[23]

To establish possible changes in houses and house ownership in the course
of the seventeenth century, two periods have been singled out for investigation. The earlier period encompasses the years around 1600; where Ankara
is concerned, the earliest documents date from Şevval 1002/June 1594 and
the latest from Receb 1010/December 1601–January 1602. Due to gaps in
the registers, it has not been possible to select exactly the corresponding
period for Kayseri. Where the latter city is concerned, the earliest document
included is dated Şevval 988/November 1580; but usable material does not
become at all frequent in the Kayseri *kadı* registers until 1013/1604–5. But
even after this period, the number of available sources is considerably
smaller than in the case of Ankara; as a result, the period under investigation
had to be extended until Ramazan 1022/October–November 1613. These
discrepancies may partly have been due to the fact that the inhabitants of
Kayseri recorded their house sales less frequently than the townsmen of
Ankara. But more importantly, the records of Kayseri present large gaps.
Thus, it is probable that certain volumes have been lost entirely, or else have
been preserved only in fragments, and that this situation accounts for the
relative paucity of documents on Kayseri shortly before and after 1600.

For the later years of the seventeenth century, the *kadı*s' record books
have survived in much better condition than for the previous period. The
years around 1690 have been selected mainly because Halil Sahillioğlu's
work on Ottoman monetary history contains information on the exchange
rates of the various monetary units which were being used in the Ottoman
Empire of that period.[24] As far as Ankara is concerned, the late seventeenth
century period under investigation begins in Safer 1099/December 1687–
January 1688, and ends in Zilkade 1103/July–August 1692. With respect to
Kayseri, the relevant dates are Safer 1100/November–December 1688 and
Rebi I 1107/October–November 1695 respectively.

Information given in the documents is of considerable variety and scope: in most cases, we learn the name and patronym of both buyer and seller, or if the document in question concerned litigation, we find the names of plaintiff and defendant. With respect to the house, we learn its price and location by town quarter; the document in many cases also gives a listing of the rooms contained in the dwelling. Moreover, we find an enumeration of the pieces of real estate which bordered the house in question. In addition, there is much incidental information; particularly in cases involving litigation, it was customary to summarize the case as it had evolved until the date on which the document recorded in the *kadı*'s register marked a new stage in the history of the dispute.

For technical reasons, the number of documents covered for each time and place is not exactly the same. Ankara in the years before and after 1600 is documented through 342 cases, many more than are available in the remaining three instances. However, since many of these documents provide only limited information, the balance between the different places and time periods has not been significantly disturbed. For Kayseri in the years shortly before and after 1600, 236 cases have been analysed, while for Ankara and Kayseri at the end of the seventeenth century, the count is 289 and 283 respectively. In order to compensate for these fluctuations, all comparisons have been based upon percentage values. At one time, it seemed advantageous to confront the information on relatively important cities, such as Ankara or Kayseri, with data from the *kadıs*' registers of smaller settlements, such as, for instance, Çorum.[25] However, this project had to be given up, since the *sicils* investigated did not provide the necessary information.

Obviously, one of the fundamental questions in a study like the present one is the extent to which the results obtained are valid for Ankara and Kayseri throughout the entire seventeenth century, or even for other Anatolian cities of the same period. To constitute a truly random sample is beyond our power, and we have to be content with whatever cases seventeenth-century townsmen happened to submit to the *kadı*. However, to avoid further distortion, a certain point in time has been selected, and from that point onward, all cases recorded in the *kadı*'s register have been included in the present investigation, except for those instances in which the data are so deficient that they were considered to not be worth analysing. Since by no means all sales ever concluded were documented in the *kadıs*' registers, it is probable that a different choice of periods investigated would have led to somewhat different results. However, if these qualifications are kept in mind, it is probable that the observations made in the present study are valid for at least the wealthier home-owners of seventeenth century Ankara and Kayseri.

That this should be so, is at least partly due to the fact that even in the largest Ottoman towns of Anatolia there was only one *kadı*, a Hanefi, and –

apart fom special purpose registers such as the collections of probate inventories – but one official collection of registers. If representatives of different schools of law (*mezhep*) had lived in Anatolian cities, this would not have been the case: Jerusalem, though quite a modest town in terms of permanent residents, had more than one *kadı*. As matters stand, the researcher dealing with Anatolian court records is spared that bane of the historian dealing with societies such as late medieval Provence. In this latter region, a number of different notaries, whose records may or may not have survived, served clientèles that often had a definable social composition. As a result, it is very easy to conclude that the preoccupations of the Provençal townsmen were changing, when in fact we are dealing only with different groups from among the urban population whose style of living actually evolved little if at all.[26] Under such circumstances, warnings against selecting limited time periods for comparative study are completely valid. But given the very different organization of the Ottoman *kadı*'s court, an approach of this type is perfectly defensible for the context of seventeenth-century Anatolia.

The sources

Kadı registers of the major Ottoman cities have been examined in various contexts, and a few samples, two of them relevant to Ankara, have been published as summaries.[27] The registers used in preparing the present study correspond very closely to the type familiar from the published materials. Documents concerning litigation are interspersed among a larger number of texts intended purely to document a transaction, such as a sale, an appointment to a guardianship, or a divorce. For the period under investigation, probate inventories are quite rare in both the Ankara and the Kayseri *sicil*s, although the later seventeenth-century registers contain more documents of this type than did their predecessors of the years around 1600. It is possible that probate inventories were entered into separate registers, as was the practice, for instance, in Bursa or Edirne, but to date, no examples of such inventory registers have been discovered. In addition, most of the registers consulted contain a section of Sultans' rescripts addressed to the *kadı*, which his scribes copied out for purposes of reference. This latter section, while of considerable interest for the history of the towns in question, does not provide much information related to houses and construction-related activities.

Among the documents more or less related to the housing issue, the vast majority concerns either a sale or a dispute. All other transactions are of minor importance; in fact, except for donations, inheritances and pious foundations they scarcely repay separate consideration. Sales records were by far the most common. The share of these documents among the totality of source materials retained for the purposes of the present study ranges from a minimum of 65 per cent (Ankara in the years around 1600) to 82 per cent (Kayseri at the end of the seventeenth century). Taken together, documents related to sales and disputes accounted for 87 per cent of all cases in Ankara around 1600, for 88 per cent of all Kayseri material of the same period, for 90 per cent of all instances connected with late seventeenth-century Ankara, and for 88 per cent of all cases retained for late seventeenth-century Kayseri. Both in Ankara and in Kayseri, the share of sales documents among the totality of usable materials tended to increase, while documents relating to litigation decreased. This fact should probably be interpreted in the sense that the number of people who when selling a house did not content themselves with the presence of eye witnesses, but sought the additional security of a court record, tended to grow in the course of the seventeenth century.

However, it must be stressed once again that the transactions recorded in the *kadıs*' registers even at the end of the seventeenth century constituted only a share of all the transactions that really took place.[28] For the *şeriat* as applied by the *kadı* considered written documentation as subsidiary to evidence provided by witnesses. Two adult male Muslims of good reputation were considered sufficient to prove the validity of a transaction, and recourse to the *kadı*'s court was in no way obligatory. These rules were applied both to Muslim and to non-Muslim inhabitants of the Ottoman Empire.[29] Only foreign merchants were exempted in many *ahidname* (capitulations), and claims against the latter could only be brought to court if the transaction from which they resulted had originally been entered into the *kadı*'s register.[30] Why late-seventeenth-century townsmen of Ankara and Kayseri should have had more frequent recourse to the court than had their ancestors ninety years earlier is difficult to determine. As is well known, the evolution of cultural attitudes has been little studied for any period before the nineteenth century.

At the same time, the amount of data contained in the individual document is considerably greater at the end of the seventeenth century than it had been some ninety years earlier. An explanation for this fact is not exactly easy to give; however, it is probably meaningful that the documents in question also tended to increase in length and in rhetorical elaboration. An ordinary sale, which at the end of the sixteenth century had often been recorded in five or six lines, might take up as much as half a page by the end of the seventeenth century. Most of this increased length was taken up by standard formulae; but apart from set phrases, there was also a tendency to report details such as the number of looms in a mohair workshop, matters which had been accorded scant attention at the beginning of the seventeenth century. Tentatively, one may assume that the scribal corps at the *kadı*'s disposal had become increasingly professionalized. That scripts used in the registers became more uniform might serve as an indicator in the same direction, or else the fact that scribes now often recorded if a certain case had

Table 1. *Transactions recorded*

Location	Sale	Dispute	Donation	Vakıf	Icare	Exchange	Rehin	Inheritance	Other	Total
Ankara, c. 1600	221 (64.6%)	77 (22.5%)	10 (2.9%)	1 (0.3%)	1 (0.3%)	0	5 (1.5%)	9 (2.6%)	18 (5.3%)	342
Kayseri, c. 1600	175 (74.2%)	32 (13.6%)	1 (0.4%)	1 (0.4%)	2 (0.8%)	4 (1.7%)	4 (1.7%)	5 (2.1%)	12 (5.1%)	236
Ankara, c. 1690	230 (79.6%)	31 (10.7%)	7 (2.4%)	1 (0.3%)	0	4 (1.4%)	1 (0.3%)	9 (3.1%)	6 (2.1%)	289
Kayseri, c. 1690	232 (82.0%)	16 (5.7%)	13 (4.6%)	1 (0.4%)	0	8 (2.8%)	0	12 (4.2%)	1 (0.4%)	283

been heard not by the *kadı* in person, but by one of his adjuncts. This state of affairs is worth noting because it runs counter to the trend that we have become accustomed to discern in Ottoman administrative history: namely, that after a high point in the middle of the sixteenth century, the bureaucratic competence of Ottoman officials steadily declined.[31] Whatever validity this assumption may have had for the central administration in İstanbul, it certainly is not appropriate where the seventeenth-century offices of the Ankara and Kayseri *kadıs* were concerned.[32]

Apart from the *kadıs'* records, the present study also uses a mid-seventeenth-century tax register, which records the taxpayers of Kayseri in the approved Ottoman style.[33] In this document, we find an enumeration of adult male taxpayers *(nefer)* and of resident households *(hane-i sükena)*; the Muslim majority and the Christian minority are recorded separately. No parallel document has been located for Ankara. However, the Kayseri count should probably be seen as part of a more ambitious undertaking, since both Tokat and Amasya taxpayers were also counted during those years.[34] Whether the surviving documents are the only counts executed, or whether others were prepared and have been lost, is impossible to say at the present state of our documentation.

In conjunction with the tax register encompassing the entire Kayseri population, the *cizye* (non-Muslims poll tax) accounts of the period can also furnish much needed evidence on population.[35] However, again it has not been possible to locate such documents for Ankara, although a respectable number of registers survives for Kayseri. It is tempting to use these documents as a basis for estimating total population. But since the available evidence shows that the share of the non-Muslims among the Kayseri taxpayers fluctuated considerably, such an extrapolation is best avoided.

Architecture and society

The present study deals among other things, with urban houses as a social phenomenon. As a result, changes in the shapes of houses have been examined because they indicate possible changes in the manner in which people used these houses while engaged in the business of living together. Certainly purely stylistic considerations, particularly the impact of İstanbul models, must also have had an impact upon the builders, especially upon the more sophisticated ones among them. Unfortunately, the sales documents contain very few data which would allow conclusions concerning architectural style. And had such evidence been available, the present author's limited knowledge in this field would probably have made its efficient use impossible. Thus, the available information concerning the physical shape of seventeenth-century houses in Ankara and Kayseri has been used purely as a starting point from which to approach such elusive problems as crowding, or the sharing of inheritances among members of a family.

While the *kadıs'* registers also record the sale of shops, this kind of material has not been incorporated into the present study. Most of these latter documents tell us little about the manner in which the shop was used, and limit themselves to the enumeration of the neighbours and the town quarter or street in which the shop was located. Since it was common practice to keep house and shop physically apart, and a good deal is already known about covered markets, shops, caravansarays and other public buildings of the city centre,[36] a study focusing upon the domestic life of Anatolian townsmen does seem to fill a certain gap. In consequence, the present undertaking is only very marginally concerned with the manner in which the inhabitants of Ankara or Kayseri made a living. What is known about the trade routes passing through the two cities in question or of the principal craft activities, is set out in the first chapter, more or less as background information. But our principal concern will be with social structure, as it is reflected in transactions which in one way or another are concerned with the houses of Ankara and Kayseri.

Throughout the present study, the reader will find a certain amount of speculation. These speculative passages generally try to explain how certain phenomena which characterize the domestic architecture and social structure of seventeenth-century Ankara or Kayseri may be connected with what has been observed in the nineteenth or even in the twentieth century. On the other hand, attempts to connect urban housing patterns with, for example, nomadic traditions, which should have been averse to elaborate and costly housing, have been avoided as far as possible. Not that such traditions never had any impact. But in the absence of written statements concerning this matter on the part of seventeenth-century townsmen, such influences are all but impossible to document. All we can say is that for most townsmen of Ankara or Kayseri in the 1600s, the nomadic past was already quite remote. Thus, it seems more profitable to concentrate upon relationships that are less elusive and easier to document. Unavoidably, this approach involves an interpretation of the domestic architecture of seventeenth-century central Anatolia as a starting point for various developments, while ignoring the fact that this architecture, in turn, had historical antecedents. But it is hoped that the advantages of such a perspective may outweigh the disadvantages.

Reconstructing the urban environment

In order to correctly view the setting in which the Anatolian townsman spent his life, the make-up of the town quarter or *mahalle* is worth examining in some detail. For the sixteenth-century the Ottoman tax registers (*tahrir*) regularly provide lists of town quarters, along with the tax-paying heads of households and as yet unmarried young men that resided in them.[37] Our information is much less ample where the seventeenth century is concerned. Regular tax registers were by this time prepared only in exceptional cases.

More frequent were listings of non-Muslim tax-payers, since the poll tax (*cizye*) continued to furnish much-needed resources to the Ottoman central treasury. These latter documents also list the townsmen by the *mahalle* in which they resided, and the same practice was current when preparing records listing the groups of taxpayers (*avarızhane*) which constituted the basic units for the collection of the tax known as *avarız*. Other more fortuitous documents, such as lists of townsmen vouching for each other's good behaviour in anticipation of a rebel attack against their town, can also be used as evidence that particular wards or town quarters were in fact inhabited at a given point in time.[38]

However, the records of house sales permit us a much closer view of what a seventeenth-century town quarter must have looked like. For the most convenient fashion of describing a given property was the enumeration of its 'neighbours'. Among the latter we might expect to encounter a public thoroughfare or semi-public right-of-way, the property of a private person, or else a public building of some kind. Public buildings usually consisted of mosques and *zaviye*s, or occasionally churches if the population of the quarter happened to be Christian. Most of these structures have today disappeared, and in many cases, it is even impossible to locate their exact sites. In sixteenth-century sources, certain mosques have been recorded because they had given their name to a town quarter. Or else, the mosques in question were included in one of the lists of pious foundations which formed part of the sixteenth-century tax registers.[39] On the other hand, the existence of buildings constructed in the seventeenth century can often only be documented because they have been mentioned as 'neighbours' to a dwelling that was sold, and the sale recorded in the *kadıs*' registers. In this fashion, the documents recording sales of private houses contribute considerably toward our knowledge of the inventory of monuments which existed in seventeenth-century Ankara and Kayseri.

Moreover, it is possible to estimate the number of public buildings relative to the houses of the town.[40] For both Ankara and Kayseri, two groups each encompassing 200–350 dwellings are documented directly as subject to sale, inheritance, or litigation, either in the years before and after 1600, or else toward the end of the seventeenth century. Assuming that each one of these houses had three neighbours apart from the public street, that gives us about 800–1200 buildings which are documented in more or less detail. Now we do not know exactly how many buildings seventeenth-century Ankara and Kayseri may have contained. But indications given by the sixteenth-century *tahrir* registers, and Evliya Çelebi's estimates from the second half of the seventeenth,[41] indicate that 800 buildings must have at the very least constituted ten per cent of all the private houses existing in either Ankara or Kayseri. This would be very good coverage if we were dealing with a random selection, but unfortunately our sample is anything but random. Even so, however, the rate of private dwellings to one mosque, public bath, or other pious foundation should provide some clue concerning the make-up of seventeenth-century town quarters.

From the public buildings of the town quarter, we pass on to the houses themselves.[42] Here, in this most private area, our information is the richest. Thus, we can easily learn how many rooms each dwelling possessed, and what most of the rooms were used for. Basic functions, such as eating or sleeping, could be carried out in any room, since table utensils and bedding were stored away after use. But a few houses possessed separate kitchens which were recorded as such in the register, the entrance hall (*sofa*) was differentiated from ordinary rooms, and the main living space described as a *tabhane* and thus set off from the ordinary rooms (*oda*). Moreover, urban dwellers of Central Anatolia possessed an extraordinarily rich terminology for porches, verandas, and other semi-open spaces. Thus, a description of the house is provided, more or less accurate according to the customs of the town and time period under consideration. Certainly, these descriptions do not provide all the information one might wish for, and references to doors, windows, lattice work or roofing are notoriously absent. But since hundreds of houses have been described, it is possible to show up certain tendencies of architectural change, and to speculate about the possible reasons for these developments.

Moreover, the uninhabited service sections of the house are equally described in some detail. These sections are of particular interest for our purposes, since they indicate that household tasks such as weaving, baking, or even the raising of animals were carried on in the house compound proper. For tasks which could not conveniently be carried out in the ordinary house, two alternatives existed. Either they might be transferred into institutions open to the public; as an example, one might cite the often very elaborate bathhouses,[43] which also provided facilities for socializing. Or else other tasks, such as the preparation of food for winter storage, might take place outside the city in the gardens and vineyards belonging to the townsmen. Under these circumstances, a detailed inventory of the service sections of a dwelling can tell us almost as much about the inhabitants' style of living as a description of the inhabited rooms.

The price of urban houses

In principle, the price of an urban house can be interpreted as an indicator of how desirable the townsmen of Ankara or Kayseri considered a given dwelling. However, in reality, the interpretation of price data is more than problematic. Quite apart from the difficulties of correctly allowing for periodical debasement and revaluation of the currency,[44] it is probable that factors not directly connected with the housing market were of considerable importance in determining the price of a house. Houses were mortgaged, and the sums mentioned as their more or less fictitious 'price' may have been considerably lower than the marketable value of the property concerned. Relatives probably allowed each other a better price than would have been demanded from an outsider, as it is likely that members of an extended family wished to live in the same neighbourhood. Some of the situations outlined above might equally occur in a modern urban setting. But their relative frequency was probably greater in the seventeenth century, indicating the fact that the ownership of houses was more widely distributed than it is today, and that the scope of the 'housing market' was as yet relatively limited.[45]

However, the availability of data concerning 200–350 houses for a given city within a given time period does allow us to compare, for instance, the distribution of house prices in Ankara around 1600 with the distribution obtaining in the same city around 1690. Of course, the same procedure can be followed for Kayseri. Moreover, the persistence of characteristic price distributions throughout the seventeenth century may indicate special characteristics of the urban population, and at the same time, increase our confidence in the value of the data studied. For if on the other hand, purely fortuitous reasons had been responsible for the fact that high-priced houses formed an unusually large or an unusually small share of the houses documented at a given time, one would have expected the relative frequency of high-priced houses to be totally different fifty or a hundred years later.

From another point of view, it is not without interest to investigate the prices paid for different types of urban dwelling. By the term 'type' in this context we mean groups of houses which showed a particular configuration of rooms, and which might or might not contain an upper floor. Such a procedure allows us to discern which kinds of houses were preferred by the wealthier inhabitants of the two towns. One might also go one step further and examine whether certain architectural features, such as the organization of a given dwelling around a double courtyard, had any noticeable impact upon its price. Or else one might try to find out whether the sturdier construction needed to support an upper floor had an effect upon the price of the dwelling. In this sense, the price paid for an urban residence may to a certain extent help us to visualize the appearance of the house in question. For while the listings of rooms do not tell us how elaborate or how shoddy the construction of a given dwelling may have been, the comparison of prices does provide indicators in this direction.

A sector of social relations for which house prices might be considered particularly illuminating is the relative material position of Muslims and non-Muslims. For as İnalcık in his work on sixteenth-century Bursa and Jennings in his studies on early-seventeenth-century Kayseri have pointed out,[46] non-Muslims did not in the Ottoman 'classical' period dominate the economic life of Anatolian towns as they were to do in the nineteenth century. One would expect, however, that by the seventeenth century the non-Muslims had begun their ascent to economic power. Certainly ostentatious acquisition of valuable house property should have occurred at a fairly late point in time, when the non-Muslims of a given town were already well established in trade. Even so, it is probable that if the non-Muslims of Ankara or Kayseri were strengthening their economic position, the fact should to some degree be reflected in the prices of their houses as recorded in the kadıs' registers.

Urban house-owners

However, for the historian dealing with an evolving Ottoman society, documents concerning urban housing are mainly of interest because of the information they provide on the urban property owners themselves. In any document concerning the sale of a house, or relating to a dispute connected with the ownership of urban real estate, both parties to the transaction are named. This permits us to discern at the very least whether the persons in question were men or women, Muslims or non-Muslims, more or less tax-exempt employees of the Ottoman central administration (askerî) or ordinary taxpayers (reaya). But in many cases, far more information concerning these property owners can be gathered from the sources. Where inheritance cases are concerned, all heirs are enumerated, and the exact functions of people serving the Ottoman administration are described as well.

To determine the degree to which the people whose personal data survive in the kadıs' registers are characteristic of the urban population as a whole, one would need to know how widespread house ownership was. Since tenancy agreements are very scarce in the registers, and to live in a rented house was rare even in nineteenth- and early twentieth-century Anatolia, it seems reasonable to assume that most seventeenth-century inhabitants of Ankara and Kayseri owned their houses. However, the concept of tenancy was not totally unknown. Merchants who planned to stay in a city for a longer period of time might prefer to rent a house in order to escape from the crowded khans where traders who came for a visit of only a few days or weeks usually resided. Pious foundations might rent out houses which had been acquired by bequests, and more particularly pieces of real estate with ruined buildings upon them, which the tenant was generally expected to repair or rebuild. Last not least, people might be living in rented houses because they were in debt; for it was quite common to secure a loan by transferring the house to the creditor. In such cases, the debtor usually continued to live in what had formerly been his house, and paid his creditor a yearly rent which constituted a kind of interest upon the money borrowed. But apart from these somewhat exceptional situations, both rich and poor usually owned their houses as freehold property.

As a result, documents dealing with the transfer of real property should give us a broadly-based overview of the condition of urban householders. Even so, it is likely that wealthy property owners are better documented than the more modest ones. For there was no legal obligation to record a sale or other property transfer in the *kadı*'s court, and many poor and illiterate people may have contented themselves with the good offices of a few neighbours serving as witnesses. This state of affairs may account for the fact that the number of one-room structures documented in the *kadıs*' registers is quite limited. But in addition, since many mudbrick houses were probably constructed with family labour from easily available raw materials, quite a few people of modest fortunes were perhaps in the position of inhabiting at least two or three rooms.

To show more clearly the implications of the data, the case of *hacıs* (pilgrims to Mecca) and of *seyyids* (descendants of the Prophet Muhammad) among the house-owners of Ankara and Kayseri merits special attention. As performance of the hajj constituted a basic duty for any Muslim who possessed the necessary means, the number of urban house-owners who had at one time in their lives undertaken the journey to Mecca might be of interest to the historian dealing with religious practice. More relevant in the present context is the question whether the *hacıs* by and large constituted a particularly wealthy section of the urban population, or whether it was common for people to mobilize their last resources in order to perform the pilgrimage. Moreover one would like to know whether in the course of the seventeenth century, there was any significant change in the percentage of people whom the documents record as *hacıs*. For the Ottoman state spent very sizeable amounts of money every year in an effort to keep the pilgrimage routes safe and open,[47] and changes in the number of Mecca pilgrims might indicate to what extent this effort was successful. Of less general importance, but still of considerable interest, is the question of the *seyyids*, who by the end of the seventeenth century constituted a sizeable proportion of Kayseri house-owners. Whether the increase of *seyyids* was mainly a local phenomenon, due to certain families establishing spurious claims to *seyyid* status, or whether migration from other localities, such as for instance Aleppo was involved, is a question which might repay further investigation.

One of the most interesting aspects of the documents contained in the *kadıs*' registers is the fact that they permit certain conclusions concerning the socio-economic relationships that existed between the contracting parties. When buyer and seller were related, the fact is usually recorded in the *kadıs*' registers. Often donations between relatives were couched in terms of a sale; the property was first 'sold' and then the donor made the beneficiary a present of the price. In many cases, the strings attached to such sales and donations within the family are not recorded in the *kadıs*' registers. However, occasionally they do become visible. Thus, people, who must have been elderly and without children to support them, occasionally sold or gave away a house under the condition that the new owners feed and clothe them for the remainder of their lifetimes.

Social and pecuniary difficulties were equally involved when the person in charge of administering a minor's property (*vasi*) sold a house inherited by the child;[48] for the *şeriat* prohibited this measure as long as other alternatives were available. Moreover, the young man or girl could contest the sale as soon as he or she came of age; the resulting insecurity concerning the legal status of the piece of real estate involved should have constituted a further deterrent against the sale of such property. If sales of this type were undertaken nonetheless, it usually meant that the child's parents had left him or her with no other means of support, or because nobody could be found who would take care of the property on the minor's behalf. Other instances of acute distress were recorded when an adult property-owner considered it necessary to declare in the sales document that he was obliged to sell in order to settle his debts.

On the other hand, it is possible to locate people who must have been in reasonably affluent circumstances, for they owned more than one house. This fact is indicated in the registers because the town quarter in which the seller resided was recorded as a matter of routine. If the residence of the seller and the location of the property sold were not the same, obviously the seller or members of his family possessed a second house. This does not necessarily indicate great wealth, particularly if the seller was a female; she might be living in her husband's home and selling some property she had inherited from her own relatives. Even so, the owners of more than one house should generally have been better off than the average townsman, and a careful interpretation of the sales records allows us to pinpoint specific examples.

As a further step, we can attempt to relate the information that we possess concerning the social characteristics of house-owners with what is known about the physical appearance of seventeenth-century houses in Ankara and Kayseri. This ties in with another question, which has in various instances been taken up by students of regional architecture: namely whether there was any significant difference in style between Muslim and non-Muslim dwellings. European travellers and Ottoman jurists sometimes refer to the rule that non-Muslims were not to paint their houses in bright colours,[49] or build them in such a way that they might overlook the roofs and courtyards of Muslim houses. Necibe Çakiroğlu in her study of domestic architecture in Kayseri has voiced the opinion that non-Muslims more frequently built houses with a façade directly facing the street than did their Muslim fellow townsmen.[50] While the data contained in the *kadıs*' registers do not allow us to judge these particular issues, they do permit us to decide whether non-Muslims preferred a different configuration of inhabitable rooms than that which was customary among the Muslim inhabitants of Ankara or Kayseri.

As has been outlined above, the *sicil* records situated every private dwelling in its particular context by mentioning the neighbours. Thus, we possess a nominal listing of a substantial number of property owners resident in seventeenth-century Ankara and Kayseri. However, the list of neighbours was often prepared with rather less care than the remainder of the document. Thus, nicknames were sometimes used in place of given names, making it impossible to distinguish between Muslims and non-Muslims. It is also probable that titles were not infrequently omitted; therefore, the distinction between *reaya* and *askerî*, already somewhat problematic where the actual house-owners are concerned, becomes completely aleatory in the case of the neighbours. Even so, however, certain rough-and-ready statements concerning a substantial number of urban property-owners alive during a given, relatively short, period of time is not without interest. Generally we can differentiate at least between men and women, between Muslims and non-Muslims, and these data are already of some value if we wish to describe the structure of seventeenth century urban property ownership.

In this context, one issue worth singling out is the existence of properties belonging to the heirs of a deceased person, which the *kadıs'* registers describe as being in the hands of the *verese-i* [so-and-so]. This designation should probably be taken to mean that the heirs had not divided up the property, but were using it as the residence of what must have been an extended family. Now it is striking to observe that properties described in this fashion were extremely rare. Certainly, one may assume that only the more careful scribes or witnesses recorded the ownership of *verese*, while the others continued to attribute the property to the deceased former owner. But if one considers that many dwellings of Ankara and Kayseri were very small, containing only one or two inhabitable rooms, it is unlikely that many houses were occupied by large families. The relatively cheap technique of mudbrick building and the availability of courtyards in most dwellings should have made it unnecessary to overcrowd the existing rooms. Where there were many residents to a house, a new room could be added with relative ease. Thus, the scarcity of houses known to have been inhabited by collaterally extended families, and the relative smallness of the houses themselves, can be taken to indicate that it was not common for extended families to live under one roof. More probably it was customary for a newly married couple to move to a separate house, preferably in the same town quarter that other members of the family already inhabited. This arrangement would also correspond to the observations that anthropologists have made concerning certain small towns in Turkey today.[51]

The fabric of urban society

An opportunity to move beyond the circumscribed issue of house sales, and into the concerns of urban society in the broader sense of the word, is provided by the data on litigation. Even though records on litigation are scanty in comparison to sales documents, they tend to give much more information concerning the social mores of Anatolian town dwellers. Thus, disputes concerning the division of inheritances inform us about the arrangements considered necessary when people belonging to the same family, but not very closely related, needed to share the same house. Agreements of this kind assumed special importance when, as sometimes happened, some of the heirs sold their respective shares to outsiders, thus obliging other members of the family to accept considerable inconvenience or else buy out the new co-owner. Other inheritance cases deal with ways of benefiting relatives whose share of a given inheritance according to the *şeriat* would have been small or non-existent. A gift *inter vivos* was the most frequently employed device in such cases. Since heirs whose interests were affected by such an arrangement were likely to contest the gift, a sufficient number of witnesses and entry into the *kadıs'* registers were particularly important in such cases.

For comparable reasons, the pious foundations established by a deceased person were likely to be challenged. In certain instances the founder appears to have anticipated such a move by contesting the foundation him or herself, and obtained a decision from the *kadı* confirming the validity of the foundation. But it also happened quite frequently that a dwelling which was meant to benefit the descendants of the founder, and a mosque or the poor after no direct descendants were left, became the subject of a court case after the death of the founder's children or grandchildren. Either the official in charge of heirless property attempted to confiscate the house on behalf of the Ottoman state, or else relatives who were not direct descendants attempted to gain control of the foundation's endowment. However the kadi generally protected the rights of the foundations, and ensured that the house was employed for the pious purpose stipulated by the founder. Under these circumstances, it does not seem fair to say, as has sometimes been done, that family *vakıfs* were never of any benefit to the community at large.

For a limited number of cases, disputes might involve the right of pre-emption (*şufa*) that co-owners and neighbours might exercise when a given piece of real property was offered for sale. However, quite a few co-owners and neighbours must have been given the opportunity to buy on an informal basis, and thus many instances of this kind of transaction probably escape us. On the other hand, seventeenth-century *kadıs* conformed to an established legal tradition by interpreting the right to pre-emption in rather a restrictive fashion.[52] People who turned to the court demanding this right could certainly not expect to benefit from any particular sympathy on the part of the *kadı*.

Conclusion

The present study constitutes an attempt to view urban social history through the medium of the domestic architecture that the townsmen produced. It is apparent that the shape of seventeenth-century Ankara and Kayseri houses was in no way immutable, but responded quite rapidly to social pressures such as crowding. Moreover, there seems to have been a tendency to build 'bigger and better' houses. At least in Kayseri these houses generally possessed better access to water than had been the case in the past. Ankara dwellings were increasingly provided with an upper floor, and in both cities, semi-open porches and verandas became popular.

While every single one of these phenomena can be interpreted in various fashions, their convergence seems to suggest that neither Ankara or Kayseri were living through a pronounced period of decadence during the seventeenth century. Doubtlessly the beginnings of the century were difficult, but it seems that both cities ultimately recovered. By the 1690s, Ankara's status as a mohair-producing centre was probably not too different from what it had been a century earlier. Gardens and vineyards around the two cities were well cultivated, with no evidence of the retreat of settlement that was observed in many parts of the open countryside. Certainly the internal strife which characterized Anatolia in the late sixteenth and early seventeenth centuries must have affected Ankara and Kayseri as well, but the effects were probably neither as prolonged nor as irrevocable as has sometimes been assumed.

In this respect, findings concerning Ankara and Kayseri tie in with the observation of the more perceptive among seventeenth-century European travellers. In Pitton de Tournefort's description,[53] Ankara appears relatively active and flourishing, and even Pococke,[54] who wrote in the first half of the eighteenth century, does not convey the impression of decay that permeates nineteenth-century descriptions. In fact, researchers who have studied Arab cities equally tend to consider that really serious economic crisis only broke out in the second half of the eighteenth century; moreover, this crisis hit all the harder because the preceding period had been reasonably prosperous.[55] Thus, the present study comes down firmly, if cautiously, in favour of a prolonged 'Indian summer' of urban life in seventeenth-century central Anatolia.

CHAPTER 1

Setting the scene: two cities of central Anatolia

Ankara in the pre-Ottoman period

After 1923, when Ankara had become the capital of the Turkish Republic, a considerable amount of archaeological research was undertaken both in the city itself and in the surrounding region.[1] Thus in spite of the scarcity of written documents, the pre-Ottoman development of the city is reasonably well-known. Ankara is located on the northern edge of the inner Anatolian steppe, in a place where small rivers and lakes provide fairly abundant water resources. As a result, the site has been occupied by settlements of varying size and importance ever since pre-Roman times. Archeological evidence and written sources show that in the third century B.C., Ankara was the centre of the Galatian tribe of the Tectosages, although it is difficult to determine to what degree this settlement possessed urban character.[2]

After incorporation into the Roman Empire, the capital of the Tectosages turned into a good-sized provincial town, of a type frequently to be found in Anatolia. Excavations have shown that Roman Ankara possessed the public buildings to be expected in a settlement of this type, including hot baths and a theatre. From the extent of the built-up area, which encompassed not only the fortified hill, but equally areas in the modern Ulus district only reincorporated into the city during the present century, it has been concluded that Roman Ankara was a city of rather more than average size. Among the public buildings of this period, the best known is the temple of Augustus and Roma, which contains an inscription relating the text of Augustus' testament. The latter has attracted the interest of researchers ever since its first modern transcription in the sixteenth century.[3]

During the later Roman Empire, the city came to possess a considerable number of churches one of which, known in the literature as St Clement, was systematically excavated in the 1920s.[4] In the history of European culture, the name of Byzantine Ankara has become attached to the text known as the Canon Episcopi, which purports to be a decision of a church council taken in Ankara in A.D. 314. Apparently, it is improbable that this document, which rejects the belief in witches flying through the air as a diabolical illusion, does in fact go back this far. But even so, the attribution documents the importance of Ankara as a centre of early Byzantine church history.[5] In the *Notitiae Episcopatum*, which record the names and titles of bishops present at Church councils, Ankara was given metropolitan rank. However, it lost its suffragan bishoprics immediately after the Seljuk conquest of Anatolia, in the last quarter of the twelfth century.[6] At the same time, the existence of a Christian community in the city does not imply that prior to the Seljuk conquest, Ankara was securely in Byzantine hands. As early as A.D. 654, the city was in fact briefly occupied by the Arabs, while in the ninth century it was conquered by the Paulicians of Tephrike (modern Divriği). Apparently the built-up area shrank during this period, until it included only the easily defended area on top of the hill, whose fortifications were renewed during this period.

In the course of the twelfth century, Ankara changed hands several times between Seljuks, Crusaders, Byzantines, and Danişmendids; but after A.D. 1143 the Seljuks established permanent control over the city. From the twelfth and thirteenth centuries date some of Ankara's more remarkable buildings. Thus, the road to Beypazarı crossed the Çubuk suyu over the bridge called Ak Köprü, which bears the date 619/1222. It is also probable that the Arslanhane mosque, founded by a locally prominent family in 689/ 1290, was meant to be the main Friday mosque of Ankara during this period. In the fourteenth century, the town paid taxes to the empire of the Mongol Ilkhans of Iran, and later to the Emir Eretna of Sivas. However, wealthy inhabitants of the city, joined together in the organization known as the *ahi*s, appear to have possessed considerable influence in local affairs. Thus, the Ottoman chronicler Neşri reports that when Ankara became an Ottoman city in 762/1361, at the beginning of the reign of Sultan Murad I, it was the *ahi*s that handed over the city to the Sultan. In fact, Murad I himself seems to have joined the association, probably to gain the support of influential *ahi*s for his expanding sultanate.[7]

In fifteenth-century Ankara, the major event is undoubtedly the battle between Bayezid I and the invading armies of Timur Lenk (Tamerlane) in 1402. During the civil wars between Bayezid's sons, the town was held by Çelebi Mehmed, who ultimately gained control of the Ottoman lands as Mehmed I. In the earlier fifteenth century, Ankara remained a stronghold of the *ahi*s, who founded several mosques that have continued to exist to the present day. However, the *ahi* organization declined and finally disappeared during the latter part of the century, although the ceremonial of *ahi* meetings was partially kept alive by the assemblies of Ottoman guildsmen.[8]

Ankara as a centre of internal trade

From the fifteenth century onwards, Ankara was one of the major cities of Ottoman Anatolia. After the conquest of Istanbul, the main route passing through the city connected the Ottoman capital and Amasya, where a number of Ottoman princes served their apprenticeships as provincial governors, and where Kanuni Sultan Suleyman resided as late as the middle of the sixteenth century.[9] Travellers leaving Ankara could initially follow this same route if their destination was Bursa; for until Eskişehir, the two were identical.[10] In addition, one might mention a road leading southeast toward Kayseri, and on a more local level, the connection to Beypazarı which had already existed during the Seljuk period. However, Ankara was quite remote from the two arteries of overland traffic crossing Anatolia, namely the İstanbul-Aleppo route, which could only be reached by travelling westward as far as Eskişehir or Seyitgazi, and the İstanbul–Erzurum road to the north. The latter led through Çağa, Bolu, and Gerede, just like the present day highway linking Ankara and İstanbul. However, once past Gerede, it continued toward the east, crossing the Kızılırmak over a monumental bridge in Osmancık. From this direction Ankara could only be reached by leaving the main route and travelling for about 140 km through hills which still carried a fairly dense cover of forests, not to mention the narrow and dangerous canyon of Azaphane Deresi.

Even so, Ankara was actively involved in interregional trade. This was mainly due to the manufacture of a unique textile, namely fine and costly fabrics made of the hair of the angora goat, today known as mohair.[11] In the sixteenth and seventeenth centuries, the mohair-producing goat was limited to the Ankara region, in the broader sense of the word, roughly from Tosya in the northeast to Eskişehir in the west. There has been considerable disagreement over the origins of the angora goat, and the reasons why this animal was bred in the region of Ankara and nowhere else.[12] It has been argued that the animal was native to Anatolia, particularly since images of the angora goat dating from the Greco-Roman period have been located. Another school of thought has maintained that the animal had originated in Central Asia, and was brought to Anatolia by immigrant Turkish tribes. More recently, the geographer Xavier de Planhol has suggested yet another explanation: namely that mutations leading to the occurrence of angora goats will occur spontaneously in any flock. But in very few environments, among which early Ottoman Ankara figured prominently, was the animal resulting from these mutations systematically bred. In de Planhol's view, it was not the existence of the mohair goat that made Ankara into a textile-producing centre. Rather, the craftsmen and merchants of Ankara, already involved in the manufacture and trade of fine fabrics, are assumed to have created the flocks of mohair goats.

Be that as it may, the mohair trade accounted for the fact that sixteenth-century Ankara was not only engaged in close commercial relations with Istanbul, but was also not infrequently visited by foreign merchants. Özer Ergenç's researches have shown the presence of Poles, Venetians, and particularly toward the end of the sixteenth century, of Englishmen.[13] Some of these merchants settled in the city for lengthy periods of time, where they sometimes rented houses, and gravestones belonging to foreign residents have been identified in Ankara cemeteries.[14] Even in the second half of the eighteenth century, there was a number of French merchants resident in Ankara, although at one point they were driven out, apparently at the instigation of their Armenian competitors.[15]

This involvement of the city in interregional and international trade is reflected in an early eighteenth-century panorama, which during the last twenty years has attracted considerable attention.[16] Art historians who have made a detailed study of the picture assume that the artist was familiar with Dutch genre painting, an art practised by several minor masters associated with the Netherlands embassy in Istanbul. Semavi Eyice has confronted the picture with an early nineteenth-century plan of Ankara, and has been able to demonstrate that the painter was reasonably familiar with the topography of the city.[17] But the most attractive feature of the painting is the account it gives of different processes forming part of the preparation of mohair yarn. Camel caravans supplying the city further emphasize its importance as a commercial centre, and document that at the beginning of the eighteenth century, Ankara could be regarded as a reasonably prosperous place.

Apart from mohair cloth, Ankara produced mainly goods for local consumption. Blacksmiths were at least occasionally engaged to repair ploughs, which proves that at least in certain land holdings near the city, the use of iron in agricultural implements was more widespread than has sometimes been supposed. Shoemaking was a craft in which considerable sums of money might be invested: the existence of what was probably a wholesale shoe dealer, with many artisans working for him, has been documented in the Ankara kadıs' registers of the late sixteenth century.[18] At the same time, certain consumer goods were brought in from towns and cities quite a distance away. Thus, dealers from Larende (Karaman) marketed simple cotton fabrics, which had been manufactured in this little town.[19] This would imply that there was more north–south traffic through the dry steppe of inner Anatolia than one might otherwise assume. It appears that the cash inflow resulting from the mohair trade served at least to some extent to animate regional trades and manufactures.

But in terms of bulk, the major commercial activity must have been the food trade. Ankara depended mainly on the surrounding steppe for its wheat supply, and bread and bulgur were basic food staples. Thus, the tax farmers in charge of collecting grain taxes in the villages of the dry lands to the west and southwest of Ankara, the crown lands of the so-called Haymana district, were in the habit of selling the grain in their storehouses to the bakers of the city.[20] Özer Ergenç has calculated that the wheat from this area, in which settled agriculture was more commonly practised than was to be the case in the eighteenth or nineteenth centuries, was sufficient to feed the seventeenth-century city for three months of the year.

In addition, wheat reached the Ankara market from villages that, unlike the Haymana district, had not been built upon crown lands, but had been distributed to the holders of tax assignments (*timar*). In exchange for military service in the Sultan's army, *timar*-holders were permitted to collect taxes from the peasantry. Part of these taxes were levied in kind, but to make sure that the *timar*-holder had an adequate supply of cash at his disposal, the peasants were required to cart the *timar*-holder's grain to the nearest market. In principle, there was a market to each administrative district, and the Ottoman administration tried to limit the time that peasants might have to spend on carting services, by prescribing that villagers drafted for this purpose needed to go no further than the nearest market. However, when a large city such as Ankara was located in the vicinity, such commands proved difficult to enforce. *Timar*-holders were attracted by the higher prices that prevailed in a city, while the local *kadı*, who might be called upon to judge disputes, often was more concerned about the city's food supply than about the time and energy wasted by the peasants' travelling to market. This, at any rate, is the impression one gains from a case involving the peasants of the district of Istanos (Zir), who were ordered by the court to frequent the Ankara market even though the market of Istanos was closer by.[21]

In addition to wheat, rice must have appeared on the tables at least of the wealthier inhabitants of Ankara. As the work undertaken by Ömer Lütfi Barkan on the accounts of public kitchens and official guesthouses (*imaret*) has amply demonstrated,[22] rice had by the later fifteenth century become a staple food, both as soup and as pilaf accompanied by meat or vegetables. However, large-scale cultivation was as yet limited, the districts of Filibe (Plovdiv), Tosya-Boyabat, and Beypazarı standing out in this respect.[23] Unlike bread grains, most rice entering the market had not been grown by independent peasants, but on state-owned enterprises which were farmed out for short periods of time, usually for three years. While the administrators of the Beypazarı rice farms were obliged to deliver specified quantities of rice to beneficiaries determined by the Ottoman government, their debt to the Treasury was basically paid in cash. As a result, the town of Beypazarı flourished, at least in part as a wholesalers' rice market. But as Ankara was a much larger town than Beypazarı, it is very probable that much of the rice sold in the latter market ultimately found its way into the kitchens of the various notables and mohair merchants of Ankara.

Merchants of Ankara

Thus, a variety of commercial activities permitted certain merchants to accumulate considerable wealth, a factor which is not without significance for the domestic architecture of seventeenth-century Ankara. Concerning the business activities and life style of these merchants, our best sources of information are the probate inventories which the officials of the *kadı*'s court sometimes prepared at the request of the heirs. Unfortunately, no such documents seem to have survived for the sixteenth and early seventeenth centuries.

On the other hand, three probate inventories dated 1096/1684–5 are quite informative in this respect.[24] Thus, a certain Hacı Yusuf b. Ibrahim, recently deceased, had owned a house in the Hacendi town quarter, which must have been comfortable and even luxurious, given its high price of 450 *esedi guruş*.[25] Moreover, Hacı Yusuf had transacted his business in a specialized khan, in which he had owned a half share, which the court estimated to be worth 530 *esedi guruş*. In addition, Hacı Yusuf was the owner of three stores. One of the latter was located in a covered street bordered by shops, known as the *arasta* (2540 *esedi guruş*), another, more modest one, in the *çarşı* of Mahmud Paşa, that is in the heart of the city's business district. Finally, Hacı Yusuf owned a third shop, probably very small, in which water jugs (*testi*) were being sold. It can be surmised that this last item had been acquired from one of his debtors. In addition, Hacı Yusuf was the proprietor of five rooms in the *arasta* worth 180 *esedi guruş* altogether, whose use is not specified. Probably they had been rented to merchants as living space or store rooms.

Hacı Yusuf, at the time of his death, seems to have been mainly involved in the textile trade, but in addition, he also dealt in chinaware. His stock of fine cotton cloths used as headgear (*tülbend*) amounted to 169 pieces and was valued at 473.5 *guruş-ı esedi*. In addition, he had a store of cotton cloths (*bogası*), some of which are described as 'Indian' (Hindi). Moreover, the type which the kadı's scribes recorded as 'Lakpuri' was also either of Indian manufacture, or else constituted an imitation of some Indian textile.[26] All in all, Hacı Yusuf owned 75 pieces of *bogası*, whose total value amounted to 241 *guruş-i esedi*. Less important was his stock of *alaca*, a textile of mixed silk and wool, which was either known by the trade name of 'Damascus', or else had actually been manufactured in Syria;[27] the value of Hacı Yusuf's *alaca* was estimated at 182 *guruş-i esedi*.

The Ankara merchant's stock of chinaware consisted almost exclusively of cups (*fincan*), a feature which demonstrates the popularity of coffee-drinking in Anatolia during the seventeenth century. Three types are distinguished in the inventory: of a kind described as 'Kabe fincani', five pieces were valued at eight *esedi guruş*, thus one item could be purchased for less than 0.2 *esedi guruş*. From the name, one would assume that these cups bore some kind of decoration associated with Mecca, or else had been brought back from the pilgrimage; it is impossible to tell where they had originally been manufactured.[28] Of approximately the same value were the porcelain cups described as *fagfuri*; 22 pieces could be had for 3.5 *esedi guruş*. However, much more expensive items were available for customers who really wished to indulge themselves; for Hacı Yusuf also possessed a single cup described as *acemi*, which by itself was evaluated at one *esedi guruş*.

In the inventory, no distinction is made between the deceased's store of trade goods, and his personal belongings; however, it is apparent that his house was fitted out in style. Eight kilims were valued at 20 *guruş-i esedi* altogether, and two prayer rugs (*seccade*) at four *esedi guruş*. Six smaller rugs and other textiles accounted for 40 *esedi guruş*, in addition there were curtains for the doors and felt rugs; the total was priced at five *esedi*. As to the kitchen, it contained an impressive array of pots and pans, worth more than 65 *guruş-i esedi*. A roasting spit and other items needed in the preparation of meat figured prominently among them. Among the merchant's personal possessions, one might mention a sword (three *esedi*), several handguns (three *esedi*), furs, 80 *esedi*'s worth of pearls, and a slave woman by the name of Esmer. Apparently the latter had not born him any children, for the price she was expected to fetch, 100 *esedi guruş*, was included in the probate inventory.[29]

As liquid capital, Hacı Yusuf kept 20 gold pieces in his cash box; nothing is said about their provenience, but they were considered equivalent to 500 *esedi guruş*.[30] It seems that Hacı Yusuf sold only against cash payment, and did not lend out money at interest; in any case, no debtors are mentioned in the inventory. However, some of the goods belonging to the merchants must still have been in other people's hands, for the not inconsiderable sum of 80 *esedi* had to be set aside for travel expenses, and it is possible that these travels were meant to recuperate items belonging to the estate. Hacı Yusuf owned 20 *esedi* to the estate of a certain Hacı Ahmed, and 90 *esedi* to his own son Ibrahim. In addition, the deceased had borrowed 58 *esedi* from a pious foundation, while his wife could claim 50 *esedi guruş* as her dowry. Compared to a fortune of 3602.5 *esedi* (or 3052 after debts and expenses had been paid), these debts were insignificant. Nor was Hacı Yusuf very deeply interested in charities. His one bequest of this type consisted of 100 *esedi*, payable to an unidentified *mescit*. 'Solid wealth without extravagance' seems to have been the motto of this substantial Ankara merchant.

On the other hand, credit-related activities are reflected in the probate inventory relating to a certain Mehmed Beşe b. Ali formerly of the Dibek quarter, who had been an armourer (*cebeci*) associated with the janissary corps. His military duties did not prevent him from owning a shop, in accordance with the custom among janissaries of the later seventeenth century.[31] While the value of his house was quite modest (50 *esedi*), Mehmed Beşe had invested a considerable amount of money in his shop, which was valued at 100 or 110 *guruş-i esedi*.[32] However, it is less clear what the deceased had been selling in this shop. The inventory names a wide variety of goods. However, all these items were present only in limited amounts or numbers, and therefore may have been household utensils as well as trade goods. As to the debts owed to the deceased, whose cash box contained only two *esedi*s worth of ready money, they were all rather small, the largest amounting to 14.5 *esedi*, and the smallest to one *esedi* and one *rub*. Whether these sums of money were outstanding payments for the delivery of goods, or outright money loans, cannot be determined from the probate inventory. But considering that Medmed Beşe owned appreciable stores of foodstuffs (oils worth 10 *esedi*, 10 keyl of wheat, and raisins worth 11.5 *guruş*), we might imagine him as a prosperous grocer, who sold on credit, and occasionally lent out money. Next to Hacı Yusuf's 3700 *esedi guruş*, Medmed Beşe's fortune of 416 *esedi* obviously looked quite paltry. But he could certainly be counted among the city's more substantial householders.

In addition, the probate inventory of an Ankara non-Muslim permits us a tantalizing glimpse of a merchant dealing at least partly in imported goods. Passing through the district of Taraklı on his way back from Istanbul, Meldun (?) veled Murad had been attacked by bandits and killed. He was probably robbed and his attackers never found; at any rate, the inventory makes no mention of the goods he had on him, and limits itself to his house and the goods found in his rooms in the Aşağı Han (Lower Khan) of Ankara.[33] Apparently, it had at first been assumed that Meldun had left no heirs, and that his property would therefore fall to the Treasury. But after the official in charge of heirless property (*beytülmal emini*) had already prepared an inventory of the deceased's possessions, heirs did in fact present themselves. Since the latter were able to prove their right to the inheritance to the satisfaction of the court, the estate, as enumerated in the list relayed in the *kadı*'s register, was handed over to them. Probably because of this complicated history, the probate inventory does not contain any money valuations, so that it is impossible to compare Meldun's wealth with that amassed by Hacı Yusuf. Even so, the list of Meldun's possessions provides some evidence on the manner in which an important non-Muslim merchant conducted business.

Meldun was much less oriented toward real property than was Hacı Yusuf. He owned a house, apparently quite elaborate with an inner and outer courtyard, but his business premises were rented. Nor does the inventory mention any credits or debts. But given the time that had probably elapsed between Meldun's death and the preparation of the inventory in the *kadı*'s register, it is possible that these matters had been wound up in the meantime. This is made even more probable by the fact that Meldun's cash holdings were not systematically recorded, either as a single sum or else grouped by the type of coin involved. Rather they appear as separate sums scattered over the inventory (total 12 gold pieces, 302 *esedi guruş*, and 200 *akçe*); these sums of money may have been paid out at different times by different people, probably while the estate was being administered by the official in charge of heirless property.

In place of real property, Meldun had acquired slaves, all non-Muslims, and jewellery. Two of the slaves were males; one of them, a certain Yovan, had been manumitted by his master. In addition, there was a slave woman by the name of Meryem. Among the valuables were recorded 61 *miskal* of gilt copper thread, 12 bunches of buttons made out of silver wire, some loose silver wire, three *miskal* of pearls, 30 pieces of coral, over 300 garnets, 42 turquoises, over 100 glass beads (*sırça taş*), a rosary handle or mouthpiece for a tobacco pipe made out of amber, some mother-of-pearl, a golden *cebe* (presumably a piece of jewellery), a belt braided out of silver wire, probably in the style which today is associated with the city of Trabzon, a second silver belt, two green stones for use in earrings, three *dirhem* of silver, a so-called Cyprus diamond, a silver ornament for a belt weighing 10 *dirhem*. Except for the golden *cebe* and possibly for the silver belts, none of these items could have been very valuable. Meldun was certainly not a jeweller by profession, but he seems to have kept an assortment of wares that one might expect to find in an antique shop of modern Ankara.

Equally intriguing are the goods that suggest Meldun's involvement with European traders, resident probably in İstanbul or else in İzmir.[34] Nine *yük* of *carçube kagıd* (possibly cartridge paper)[35] may have been imported, as well as the fourteen parcels (*deste*) of paper mentioned in another section of the inventory. A pocket knife and ten bunches of knives are described as Frankish.[36] In addition, there was a 'Frankish' pen and some candy in the Frankish manner. None of this seems of particular importance, curios rather than goods meant to appeal to a broad range of customers. A few *dirhem*s of tea must be placed in the same category, if in fact the merchant had not counted upon consuming this beverage himself, for the times in which tea was to become the national drink of Turkey were as yet a long way ahead.[37] But Meldun's warehouse also included 80 *kıyye* (102 kg) of lead and a load of iron. In the later seventeenth century, lead was very often imported,[38] and the same may have been true of the five binoculars referred to in the inventory. Moreover, Meldun apparently had close enough business deal-ings with Europeans that the only written material in his possession, apart from the Bible, were two texts which the scribe preparing the inventory described as *ahidname*s (capitulations). Possibly Meldun had even been a protégé of a European consulate in İzmir or İstanbul. Unfortunately, the probate inventory does not explain to which nation these capitulations had been issued, so that it is impossible to say anything more specific about the Ankara merchant's foreign contacts.

One could describe at length the textiles in Meldun's shop, among which we find a Kashmir shawl, the pots and pans of which he kept a sizeable store, and last but not least, different odds and ends. Even a barber's mirror, water taps for use in a barber shop, and a stove from or in the style of Diyarbakır could be purchased from this merchant. But it has already become apparent that unlike Hacı Yusuf, Meldun showed no inclination to specialize in any particular category of goods. Even so, there were limits to his activity. Meldun may have engaged in occasional wholesaleing, but the inventory bears no trace of this activity. Nor did he, in the year or so that preceded his death, have any kind of contact with the trade in mohair or mohair thread.

His rooms in the khan must have been filled to the point of overflowing. But apart from a few *kıyye* of beeswax, the inventory makes no reference at all to agricultural products, such as occurred in the estate of Cebeci Mehmed Beşe. Whatever Meldun's activities in other localities – he may well have had a store in İstanbul or İzmir – in Ankara he appeared as a general retailer, dealing mainly in textiles, shoes, jewellery, and crockery. Since the inventory contains only those goods handed over to the heirs without mentioning any liabilities, Meldun must have been reasonably successful as a businessman.

Obviously this chance selection of traders' estates does not enable us to make broad generalizations about business opportunities in Ankara. But apart from their illustrative value, the probate inventories seem to indicate that there was still room for fairly prosperous merchants in late-seventeenth-century Ankara. Even though Meldun dealt with European business partners, he does not appear simply as an outlet for European importers of cloth. In fact, the absence of textiles described as Frankish, and the weak representation of woollen cloth of any kind, is noticeable both in Hacı Yusuf's and in Meldun's estates. Thus, until further monographs allow us to be more precise, these two men may be taken to represent a type of businessman geared to the Ankara market and to Ottoman internal trade, rather than to the merchant capitalism of contemporary Europe.[39]

Population data

While the intensity of economic activity in Ankara and the surrounding area indicates a large city, direct information concerning the city's size is less readily available than on other comparable cities of Ottoman Anatolia. A tax register dealing with the district of Ankara during the fifteenth century is incomplete, and contains information on the surrounding countryside but not upon the city itself.[40] Thereby the first usable figures come from a tax register compiled during the early years of Kanunî's reign, which gives the population of Ankara as consisting of 2,317 households and 693 unmarried adult men.[41] If we assume with Ömer Lüfti Barkan that an average household consisted of five people,[42] this would result in a population of ten to twelve thousand, not counting the tax-exempt servitors of the Ottoman central administration (*askerî*). The latter must also have been represented in appreciable numbers, forming perhaps one tenth of the city population. For the second half of the sixteenth century, there is the evidence of a tax register dated 979/1571–2, which assigns the city a total of 5,344 adult male taxpayers, without distinguishing between heads of households and unmarried men.[43] If for the sake of argument we assume that the heads of households made up 77 percent of the total, just as they had done at the beginning of the century, we arrive at 4,115 householders. If we again employ a multiplier of five, the result is a population of 20,000 to 22,000, depending on whether the unmarried males are neglected as forming part of their fathers' households, or included as each constituting a household of one. In addition, allowance must be made for the tax-exempt, which would result in a total population in the range of 22,000 to 25,000. This figure corresponds reasonably well with the estimate prepared by Özer Ergenç,[44] who assumes a total population of about 25,000 for the closing years of the sixteenth century. This would mean that Ankara was about the size of sixteenth century Saragossa, Catania, or Lucca: a medium-sized city by Mediterranean standards.[45]

As to the seventeenth century, no official Ottoman figures have been located to date, even the poll tax records for Ankara's non-Muslim population have not as yet come to light. Under the circumstances, the conflicting estimates of Ottoman and European travellers must be made use of in order to at least arrive at an order of magnitude. Evliya Çelebi claims that the city consisted of 6,066 houses, which would point to a population of slightly over 30,000.[46] For the very first years of the eighteenth century, that is approximately ten years after the end of the period dealt with in the present study, Tournefort gives the figure of 45,000 inhabitants.[47] It is worth noting that this is almost one and a half times the Ottoman traveller's estimate, so that in this particular case, Evliya has certainly exaggerated less than he has been accused of doing. Writing in the first half of the eighteenth century, Pococke even records an estimate which claims a population of 100,000, of which 1,000 were supposedly janissaries.[48] Even if one views this account with a certain amount of scepticism, it can still be concluded that the city continued to grow throughout the seventeenth and eighteenth centuries; certainly there is no evidence indicating decline. However, in the absence of Ottoman official records, which alone were based upon real counts of inhabitants, however incomplete, anything that is said about the city's population development remains a more or less educated guess.

Seventeenth-century Ankara: topography

To the spatial organization of old Ankara, Eyice and Ergenç have devoted considerable attention, so that this section consists of a brief summary of the results obtained by these two researchers.[49] Eyice has analyzed the map drawn in 1838 by von Vincke, one of the officers forming part of the Prussian military mission to Mahmud II, which has been described in vivid detail by Helmut von Moltke.[50] This map shows that Ankara in the early nineteenth century was still contained in the walls which had been built at the end of the sixteenth. Apart from the new barracks built for Mahmud II's soldiers, there were only fields, vineyards and cemeteries outside the town walls.

In an age without high-rise buildings a dense network of streets will usually indicate density of habitation and/or intensity of commercial land use, and a coarse-meshed network, the opposite. According to these criteria, the most sparsely populated and extensively used tracts of land lay near the gates. In fact, von Vincke's map shows that cemeteries were partly included within the walls, and the fact that there were no town quarters *extra muros* points in the same direction. On the other hand, it would appear that one of the most densely inhabited areas of the town lay in the citadel area. However, the so-called Inner Citadel (İç kale), where today some of the last surviving houses of old Ankara are concentrated, was apparently less popular than the Outer Citadel (Dış kale). Directly under the citadel hill lay another busy and crowded area, which stretched in a band from the Bedestan and khan area in the south, immediately adjacent to the Dış kale wall, to what is today the northern city centre of Ulus.

However, the inhabitants of Ankara from the sixteenth to the twentieth century, divided the area outside of the Citadel wall into a Yukarıyüz ('Upper face') which encompassed the Bedestan and the çarşı area surrounding it, and an Aşağıyüz ('Lower face') which ran from the Hacı Bayram Mosque in the north to the Karaca Bey Imaret in the south.[51] These main sections of sixteenth-century Ankara were connected by a street known as the Uzunçarşı. Another main street, which even in the sixteenth century could be used by wheeled traffic, led from the so-called Cenabî Gate (near the Cenabi Ahmed Paşa Mosque, the only structure by Mimar Sinan which exists in Ankara) to the business section surrounding the Bedestan. In addition, the busiest area of the Aşağıyüz, called Tahte'l-kal'a (Tahtakale), was connected to one of the town gates, while a street known as Karaoğlan *çarşısı* linked the Tahte'l-kal'a area with the popular sanctuary of Hacı Bayram. A considerable number of old streets was still visible on Ankara maps drawn in the 1920s; only with the construction of the Ulus business district they have mostly been obliterated.

Geographical conditions shaped the development of old Ankara in orienting the town towards the west. As the entire area to the northeast of the Citadel hill is occupied by another even higher and rockier hill, (Hıdırlık, modern Altındağ) the course of a small river, dammed where it passed between the Hidirlik hill to the north and the Citadel hill to the south constituted the limit of urban development. Photographs of this area taken in the early years of this century still show this configuration, which seems to have characterized the entire history of Ottoman Ankara. But even the southeastern section of the town, in spite of the impressive complex of the Cenabî Ahmed Paşa Mosque, was considerably less rich in public monuments than the western sections.

The walls were pierced by a number of gates, mostly named after the cities which could be reached if one followed the road leading out of that particular gate. Thus there was a Çankırı gate to the north, İstanbul and İzmir gates to the west, a Kayseri gate in the east while surprisingly enough, the gate to the far south of the city was known not as the Konya gate but as the Erzurum gate, flanked by a *mahalle* of the same name. Since the *mahalle*

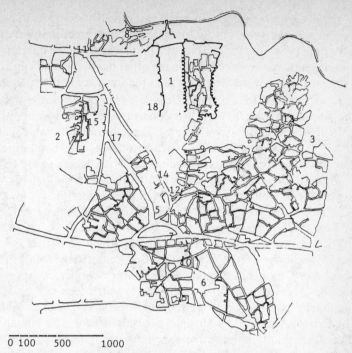

0 100   500   1000

1. Map of Ankara (drawing: Tülay Artan after Kömürcüoğlu, *Ankara Evleri*, p. 21 and Aktüre, *Anadolu Kenti*, pp. 116, 298 ff). (1) Kale (2) Itfaiye Meydanı (3) Kattanin mah. (4) Hamamönü (5) Samanpazarı (6) Erzurum mah. (7) Hacı Musa mah. (8) Debbağan mah. (9) Arab Hacı mah. (10) Imaret-i Karaca Bey mah. (11) Balaban mah. (12) Hacı Ivaz Haddad mah. (13) Avancıklar mah. (14) Koyunpazarı mah. (15) Hacı Doğan mah. (16) mah. (17) Valtarin mah. (18) Keyyalin mah.

predated the walls – it had come into existence before 1536 – it must be assumed that the gate was named after the town quarter, which may originally have been founded by settlers from Erzurum.

The citadel area constituted the political centre of Ottoman Ankara. There were no official residences for *kadı* or *sancakbeyi*, so that the top administrators of the city officiated in private accommodation. At the same time, the fortress continued to fulfil a number of official functions: it contained a garrison, was used as a storage space for money and valuables belonging to the Ottoman state, and also occasionally as a jail. However, there was no clear separation of the political centre from the rest of the town, as could often be observed in Arab towns of the Ottoman period.[52] Quite to the contrary, the citadel was filled up with private dwellings, which in the years around 1600 tended to be among the most expensive in the city. However, the descriptions of these houses do not permit us to discern whether this greater value was due to their size, their decoration, or quite

2. Map of Ankara (1838) by von Vincke, from Helmut von Moltke, *Briefe über Zystände und Begebenheiten in der Türkei*.

simply to the fact that they were the best protected. After all, before the construction of the city wall, the inhabitants of the lower-lying town quarters had more than once been obliged to seek refuge within the citadel walls.

Seventeenth-century Ankara: The urban environment

When discussing the undisputable fact that Ottoman cities were organized in town quarters (*mahalle*), and the inhabitants of any given town identified by their name, patronymic and *mahalle*, we quite unexpectedly find ourselves in the middle of a difficult problem of interpretation. In his study of Cairo and the Syrian cities during the Mamluk period, Ira Lapidus has dwelt upon the isolation of town-dwelling ethno-religious communities and social groups,[53] and has concluded that the townspeople were never in a position to act as a body *vis à vis* the Sultan and his retainers. This conclusion views the cities of thirteenth- to fifteenth-century Syria as urban entities that never gained any degree of autonomy in their relations with political rulers.

The debate concerning the validity of this description may at first glance seem somewhat remote from the realities of mid-seventeenth-century Ankara or Kayseri. However, given the fact that the Ottoman conquest did not lead to a fundamental restructuring of Damascene and Aleppine society, the researcher needs to examine whether the picture drawn for the cities of Syria during the Mamluk period applied to the early Ottoman period as well. If one goes a step further, one might also ask the question whether there existed such a thing as a specifically Ottoman city. If this question is answered in the affirmative, then the problem arises how seventeenth-century Ankara or Kayseri compared to Aleppo, Damascus or Cairo, and how these cities related to the overarching administration of the Ottoman state. Ankara and Kayseri were Muslim cities, and possessed the urban institutions characteristic of Islamic civilization, including the town quarter. Supposedly, the latter is to have focused the loyalties of the inhabitants to the point of making the city into a collection of villages.[54] Did this imply that these two cities possessed no strong urban identities, and were the local patricians unable to assert themselves *vis-à-vis* the Ottoman central administration?

A discussion of this question falls outside the scope of the present study. However, mention should be made of an important article, in which Özer Ergenç, has summarized his observations concerning the issue.[55] Ergenç has pointed out that in the later sixteenth and early seventeenth centuries, the patricians of Ankara were quite capable of making decisions affecting the whole city and getting them accepted. Such action has been documented in the *kadı*'s registers, for instance on such vital issues as the construction of a city wall. But also in more day-to-day matters, such as the employment of guardsmen in the business district, was such inter-*mahalle* and inter-community cooperation visible. Thus Ergenç has concluded that Ankara around 1600 should be classed as somewhere 'in between' autonomous and dependent status.

According to the classification system developed by T. Stoianovich, this would make Ankara a 'semi-dependent' rather than a 'dependent' city.[56] This conclusion also fits in well with Stoianovich's own opinion that Ottoman cities of the eighteenth century should be classed as 'semi-dependent' rather than as 'dependent'. The most significant result of this debate is that we find the relationship between the Ottoman state and the city evolving in time, an observation which precludes, or rather should preclude, the assumption of ahistorical typologies. Braudel's classification of cities, though less well adapted to the realities of the Ottoman case than that proposed by Stoianovich, is also usable in this context;[57] for Braudel insists on the fact that the late feudal state 'tamed' the medieval cities, robbing them of their autonomy, and making them into semi-dependent, or even dependent entities. It is difficult to imagine a more cogent argument against the practice of contrasting an 'autonomous, European' and a 'dependent, Oriental (or Islamic)' city outside of a clearly established historical context.

It is against this background that we should examine the *mahalle* structure of seventeenth-century Ankara. From Özer Ergenç's study, we learn that Ankara in the years shortly before and after 1600 consisted of 85 town quarters, 84 of which occur in the documents concerning sales and disputes which constitute the basis of the present investigation.[58] Thus, it would appear that the documents in question covered practically the entire city. Although we have no exhaustive list of Ankara town quarters for the years shortly before and after 1690, the number of *mahalle*s documented in the late-seventeenth-century *kadı*s' records is 85. Thus, it can be assumed that the number of Ankara town quarters did not significantly change in the course of the seventeenth century.

However, there was considerable change in *mahalle* names: 19 names disappeared from the records between 1600 and 1690, while 20 new ones appeared to take their place. Occasionally we can determine why and when this change came about; thus Özer Ergenç reports that in the early 1600s the town quarter of Avancıklar split up into four separate units, a process which is reflected in the *kadı*s' records of the time.[59] In other cases, the discrepancies between early and late seventeenth-century documents can be explained by the use of variant names: out of nineteen *mahalle*s which occur in the *kadı*s' records of the seventeenth century, but not in the set pertaining to the years of about 1600, eleven can also be found in the list of town quarters compiled by Ergenç for the late sixteenth and early seventeenth centuries. In spite of appearances, one can therefore assume that Ankara's *mahalle* structure remained reasonably stable throughout the seventeenth century.

When we group the available records by the religion of the seller, plaintiff, buyer or defendant and at the same time by the *mahalle* in which the house was located, we gain an idea of the manner in which the Muslim and non-Muslim population of Ankara was distributed over the city. At the end of the sixteenth and the beginning of the seventeenth century, at least twenty-three town quarters were inhabited by both Muslims and non-Muslims together, while for six others only non-Muslim sellers buyers and litigants are recorded. But given the limited number of cases documented for each town quarter, it is impossible to distinguish which of the last-named also possessed a share of Muslim inhabitants. For the later years of the seventeenth century, we find twenty-two *mahalle*s where both Muslims and non-Muslims acted as sellers, buyers and litigants in connection with real estate, while for seven others only non-Muslims are recorded. However, there is no exact correspondence between the Muslim, mixed and non-Muslim *mahalle*s of the years around 1600, and their counterparts of the period about 1690. At the same time, the Ankara tradition of living in mixed *mahalle*s seems to have been extremely stable. For the year 1830, Musa Çadırcı has established a list of fifteen town quarters in which both Muslims and non-Muslims were resident.[60] In quite a few instances, the town quarters recorded by Çadırcı had already been known as 'mixed' *mahalle*s by 1690 at the latest. This long history of 'peaceful coexistence' is particularly remarkable in an environment where it was normal for town quarters to be homogenous from the religious point of view. As long as no contradicting evidence presents itself, the popularity of the mixed *mahalle* would seem to indicate the lack of major tensions between the Muslims and non-Muslims of seventeenth- and eighteenth-century Ankara.

Another issue on which the documents concerning sales and disputes provide valuable information is the manner in which houses were aligned with respect to the various public and semi-public thoroughfares of the city. In this context, the basic category is the *tarik-i am*, by which presumably the *kadı*'s scribes meant a publicly accessible street.[61] In addition, there was the *tarik-i has*, which was probably a right-of-way not readily accessible to outsiders. However, even the *tarik-i has* was nobody's private property, or else the fact would have been mentioned in the *kadı*'s registers. Out of 276 usable descriptions related to the years around 1600, 163 (59.1%) refer to the house in question as bordered on one edge by the public way. In 70 instances (25.4%), there were even two or more sides delimited in this fashion. By comparison, the *tarik-i has* was very much a minority phenomenon, amounting to no more than 7.2 percent of all usable descriptions. Moreover, since certain pieces of urban real estate were bordered both by a public thoroughfare and by a semi-public right-of-way, the number of houses accessible only through a *tarik-i has*, or without any access to a street at all, was strictly limited.

This relative orderliness of the Ankara layout was even more apparent in 1690. For this period, out of a total of 274 usable descriptions, 192 (or 70.1%) involved pieces of urban real estate which on one side were bordered by the public way. In addition, in 60 cases (or 21.9%) were two or more sides of the house bordered by the street; the frequency of such cases makes it probable that the 'blocks' of houses and courtyards immediately adjacent to each other must have been quite small. Rights-of-way were of even less significance in 1690 than they had been in 1600 (7 out of 274, or 2.6%) in addition a very few cases in which there is no reference to any kind of street or lane. Thus emerges an overall picture that certainly had little in common with the chequerboard plans so dear to modern city planners, but in which circulation should not have been particularly difficult either.

Another feature about which the documents in the *kadı*'s register can provide some information is the frequency of public buildings in residential areas. Throughout the seventeenth century, business centres (çarşı) and residential neighbourhoods were kept separate, while most public buildings were to be found in the çarşı area. Under these circumstances, mosques, or churches in a neighbourhood inhabited by Christians, constituted the only publicly accessible buildings in residential neighbourhoods. In most cases, mosques outside the çarşı area were not fully-fledged Friday mosques, but simple oratoria intended for private prayer (mescit).[62]

For Ankara in the late sixteenth and early seventeenth centuries, 276 houses are described in such a way that we possess relatively systematic information about the neighbours. If we assume that an average house had three neighbours apart from the street, we arrive at a total of 828 pieces of urban real estate. Among the latter there were eight mosques, which amounts to one per cent of the total; the number of churches was insignificant, only two cases being mentioned in the kadı's records (0.2%). By the end of the seventeenth century, these proportions had not significantly changed. Out of an estimated 822 pieces of urban real estate, nine were recorded as mosques, which amounted to 1.1%; the number of churches was four, which corresponded to 0.5%. From this point of view, the layout of the Ankara mahalles apparently remained reasonably constant throughout the seventeenth century.[63]

Unfortunately, the kadı registers contain no systematic information on Ankara's water supply. As a result, we have to rely on occasional bits of data concerning water supplied by pious foundations. Thus we possess the response to a complaint from an Ankara müderris, dated 1047/1637-8, which refers to two water conduits named after İshak Paşa and Hasan Paşa.[64] Since both these dignitaries had built public baths in Ankara, the conduits in question must have originally brought water to the Kaledibi (İshak Paşa) and Hasan Paşa baths; however, in the seventeenth century, they mainly seem to have served the city's public fountains. Both conduits had recently been repaired by orders of Murad IV's Grand Vizier Bayram Paşa. However, certain inhabitants of the city – an investigation revealed the names of twenty-five families – had appropriated this water for their private use, channelling it to their own dwellings. Thus the street fountains ran dry, and when the matter was referred to Istanbul, the Divan ordered the previous state of affairs restored. From this document it would appear that having water piped to one's own house was a coveted privilege in seventeenth-century Ankara, while ordinary townsmen carried their water home from street fountains. But obviously this is a matter needing further study.

From official documents and private accounts, seventeenth-century Ankara appears as a city tied in with interregional and even with international trade. How deeply the trading networks of the city were affected by the Celâlî rebellions of the early seventeenth century is not easy to determine. The documents examined for the purposes of the present study do not show any evidence of far-reaching perturbation, but, given the gaps in our documentation, this fact may or may not be significant. However, it is noteworthy that European travellers of the early eighteenth century gave the city many more inhabitants than the Ottoman documents of the years around 1590, and even than Evliya Çelebi. Certainly, it is quite possible that Ankara lost population in the early years of the seventeenth century; but if it did, the city must also have witnessed quite a spectacular recovery in the years immediately before 1700.

Kayseri in the pre-Ottoman period

The present day city of Kayseri is built in the plain of the Karasu river, an affluent of the Kızılırmak, but immediately beyond the limits of the built-up area begin the slopes of the Erciyes, an extinct volcano, and the highest mountain of Anatolia (3916 m).[65] In the Roman period, Kayseri was known as Mazaca and later as Caesarea; at that time, the city was located on a site a short distance away from the present settlement, which is today known as Eski Kayseri. It is assumed that the city was moved to its present location in the early Byzantine period, but nothing is known about the reasons for this transfer. On the whole, the ruins of Eski Kayseri have yielded comparatively little historical evidence and, as a result, we do not know very much about the role or size of Kayseri in Roman times.

In the modern city of Kayseri the citadel walls constitute the only major remains that could conceivably be assigned to the Byzantine period. Moreover, even the latter have been so much changed in later years that Albert Gabriel, who studied this building in the 1920s or 1930s, was unwilling to commit himself as to the date of its construction.[66] However, Mahmut Akok, who investigated this structure in more recent times, is convinced that the core of the structure does in fact go back to the Byzantine period.[67] Given this lack of information, it is impossible to say anything about the size of the city in the eighth, ninth, or tenth centuries. Since Kayseri was for much of the time located on the eastern border of the Byzantine Empire, its population should have fluctuated greatly according to the fortunes of war.

On the other hand, during the Seljuk period, Kayseri became one of the most active centres of Anatolia, where the court frequently resided. When the fourteenth-century traveller Ibn Battuta passed through the city, he was much impressed by its activity.[68] After the collapse of the Seljuk state and the withdrawal of the Mongols from Anatolia, Kayseri was held by a number of minor dynasties in rapid succession. Throughout the fifteenth century, Ottoman political influence was strongly felt in Kayseri, but only with the elimination of the Karaman and Dulkadır principalities did Kayseri finally become an Ottoman city.[69]

Kayseri within the Anatolian communications network

After the Ottoman conquest, internal trade benefited from the *pax ottomanica*. However, compared to Tokat or Ankara, Kayseri remained a secondary centre as far as interregional trade was concerned. Neither of the two major Anatolian caravan routes led through Kayseri. Only a secondary 'feeder' route linked the city with Sıvas on the 'northern caravan route', the major thoroughfare which connected Istanbul with Erzurum and the lands beyond the Iranian frontier.[70] To reach the 'diagonal road' leading from İstanbul to Aleppo, Damascus, and ultimately to Mecca and Medina, the traveller had to journey southward through Niğde and Bor, until he came to the town of Ereğli. The road leading from Ereğli to Sıvas by way of Kayseri was quite often used by Ottoman armies campaigning on the borders of the Safavid Empire. During the sixteenth and earlier seventeenth centuries, major military traffic did not generally use the more direct route from İstanbul through Amasya and Tokat, probably because the Sultans and their responsible officials preferred to keep to the same routes and thereby minimize logistical problems.

Another route of some significance connected Kayseri with Ankara. Contacts between the two cities were frequent; this fact is documented by an appreciable number of people from Kayseri who had a transaction recorded in the *kadı*'s registers of Ankara. The Ankara–Kayseri road crossed the Kızılırmak over a bridge called Kesikköprü; in the immediate vicinity there was a village with a mosque and other pious foundations. Even so, the place had a bad reputation, for robbers could easily ambush a caravan by hiding among the boulders marking the bed of the Kızılırmak.[71] After passing through Kırşehir, the traveller might find hospitality in the *zaviye* of Haci Bektaş, which was located in a village that had taken on the name of the saint. If his destination were Mecca and Medina, the traveller who had rested in Kayseri for a few days might continue in the direction of Maraş. But this was a subsidiary route, less popular than the 'diagonal route', although Evliya Çelebi travelled this way in 1680.[72]

Among the goods travelling over long distances to and from Kayseri, two items must be singled out. Leathers, and particularly Morocco leathers (*sahtiyan*) from Kayseri were a well-known commodity in the İstanbul market.[73] As such, they were singled out for special mention in the registers recording the prices of goods and services which the Ottoman administration had established for the capital. Leather from Kayseri was equally marketed in Edirne.[74] In addition, Kayseri weavers of cotton goods received the raw materials they needed from the Adana–Tarsus area, where even in the sixteenth century the cultivation of cotton was becoming increasingly widespread.[75] On the other hand, Kayseri was located too far inland for the demands of the İstanbul grain market to make themselves felt to any notable degree, and this fact may have contributed toward the growth of the city.

However, the mountain pastures of the Erciyes area were frequently used by nomad sheep-breeders from eastern Anatolia, who allowed their animals a rest before driving them westwards toward Bursa and İstanbul.[76] While we possess no figures that might indicate the importance of these different kinds of commercial traffic, it is likely that the volume was limited, and that the Kayseri region essentially supported the city of Kayseri. In fact, this state of affairs continued even in the 1920s and 1930s, as is apparent from the account of the geographer Gerhart Bartsch, who visited the city during those years.[77]

Urban population in Kayseri

Throughout the sixteenth century, the region of Kayseri participated in the vigorous growth that characterized both urban and rural Ottoman population during that period. Tribesmen settled in the area, thus compounding the effects of natural population-growth. Where the city of Kayseri is concerned, its progress has been charted by Ronald Jennings.[78] In 905/1500, the city was inhabited by 2,287 taxpaying adult males (*nefer*); 86 per cent of these were Muslims. A number of years later, toward the beginning of Kanuni Sultan Süleyman's reign, a slight increase could be registered, and the number of *nefer* now stood at 2,367 (Muslims 81 per cent). Throughout the reign of Kanuni Süleyman's both Muslims and non-Muslims increased in the same proportion: at the end of Sultan Süleyman's reign, Kayseri numbered 3,530 taxpaying inhabitants, among which Muslims again constituted 81 per cent. According to the tax register compiled during the reign of Sultan Murad III, the number of adult male taxpayers had further increased to 8,251 (Muslims 78 per cent) by 991/1583. These figures mean that the urban population quadrupled in less than a century. With a population of about 33,000 inhabitants, exclusive of tax-exempt persons, Kayseri during these years was the largest city of Anatolia after Bursa. In sixteenth-century Europe, Amsterdam and Utrecht lay within the same order of magnitude, and the same can be said for Cordoba and Barcelona, for Ferrara, Padua or Mantua.[79] Even a century later, among the cities of France at the end of Louis XIV's reign, only seven had more than 40,000 inhabitants and culturally and economically active centres such as Strasbourg, Nantes, or Amiens held between 30,000 and 40,000 inhabitants.[80] Under these circumstances, it is obvious that late sixteenth century Kayseri was a city of respectable size, not only on an Anatolian scale, but viewed within the Mediterranean and European context of the times.

Researchers dealing with the so-called Celâlî rebellions, a series of civil wars particularly destructive during the last quarter of the sixteenth and the beginning of the seventeenth century, have stressed the negative effects of these uprisings upon rural settlement. Peasants fled to the towns, income from agricultural taxes plummeted, and in certain areas of the central Anatolian dry steppe, a long-term regression of agricultural settlement seems to have occurred.[81] In the short run, major cities absorbed most of the refugees, but after a while the interruption of inter-regional trade routes, and above all the difficulty of securing an adequate supply of food, should have had negative repercussions upon the larger cities as well.

It was with these considerations in mind that the Ottoman central administration attempted to force people who had fled their original residences to return as soon as the worst of the fighting was over. We possess some evidence concerning two more or less sustained campaigns to this effect, which were initiated in 1610 and 1635, the latter undertaken upon orders of Sultan Murad IV. From the *kadı*'s registers of this period, we learn that Kayseri during the years around 1600 had received a substantial contingent of migrants from the little town of Hacin.[82] The newcomers were permanently settled in Kayseri, after the *kadı* of Hacin had made an official statement to the effect that their return would cause insoluble problems. In the documents at our disposal, the reasons for the impossibility of carrying out the Sultan's command are not clearly stated. But it must be assumed that the lands of the migrants had passed into other hands, and that the new possessors were able and determined to hold on to the fields and gardens which they had acquired.

In addition to victims of the Celâlî rebellions, Kayseri also received a considerable number of migrants from the war-torn provinces of eastern Anatolia.[83] At the end of the sixteenth century, the 'Easterners' (Şarkiyan) had given their name to a new quarter of town. While the impact of these migrants from eastern Anatolia is less easy to observe in the seventeenth century, it is very probable that frequent warfare on the Iranian front constituted the reason for continuing immigration.

It would be of great interest to know how these migrations affected the city's population size. As is well known, the unsettled conditions of the period, and the progressive changeover from tax assignments (*timar*) to tax farming, resulted in an increasing neglect of the tax registers (*tahrir*) which had characterized Ottoman administrative practice during the sixteenth century. As a result, it becomes rather difficult to determine the population even of an important Anatolian city such as Kayseri during the seventeenth and eighteenth centuries. Evliya Çelebi, whose figures are often subject to caution, visited Kayseri around 1650. He reports that the walled-in city contained 1,000 houses, which, if we assume an average of five people per house, should have implied a population of only about 5,000 people.[84] But since we know that even in the Seljuk period many of the most prominent public buildings lay outside the city walls, this figure is not of any great significance.

Evliya's figures are, however, complemented by official data concerning the non-Muslim population of Kayseri. Revenues from the capitation tax (*cizye*) depended on the number of adult males, and this tax was levied under the direct control of the Ottoman central administration. Therefore, registers of the non-Muslim population were throughout the seventeenth century, compiled at reasonably regular intervals. Given the fact that Kayseri was one of the few Anatolian cities of the sixteenth century in which there lived a substantial non-Muslim minority (22 per cent), *cizye* data for this city are of special value. However, as the share of non-Muslims in the population of Kayseri tended to grow (from 14 per cent to 22 per cent between 1500 and 1583), we cannot use the data on the non-Muslim population to determine, by extrapolation, the total population of the city. However, even with this limitation, information concerning the growth or decline of a substantial minority of the inhabitants of Kayseri is bound to tell us something about the changing fortunes of the city.

Our first useable source is an account of the wine tax (*bedel-i hamr*), and of a surtax levied over and above the ordinary poll tax, when Sultan Mehmed III ascended the throne in 1003/1594–5.[85] This account deals only with the Christians who paid their taxes to the provincial governor of Karaman, the overarching unit of which the subprovince (*sancak*) of Kayseri formed a part. If there were other Christians present in the city, whose taxes had been assigned to some other dignitary, the number given in the account should have constituted no more than a minimal figure. However, the number of Christians referred to in the wine tax account practically corresponds to what is known from the last tax register (1,816 in 1583, 1,801 in 1594–5). Therefore, it can be assumed that the wine tax account did in fact encompass all non-Muslims resident in the city in 1594. In the wine tax account, there is no reference to the distinction between household (*hane*) and adult male taxpayer (*nefer*), so characteristic of the tax registers of the sixteenth century. But until evidence to the contrary is located, it can be assumed that the account referred to adult male taxpayers.

The second set of figures that we possess belongs to the year 1021/1612–13.[86] A brief note informs us that the number of poll-tax-paying households in the subprovince of Kayseri amounted to 2,093, but does not indicate how these households were distributed over the city itself and over the surrounding countryside. However, a second register bearing the same date contains slightly more specific information,[87] and claims that in previous years the poll tax had been collected upon the basis of a population consisting of 1,800 adult non-Muslim males. This latter figure probably referred to the entire district of Kayseri, not just to the city, because the count of 1612–13 also covered the entire subprovince, and the 1,800 taxpayers were cited to provide a standard of comparison. The introductory note to the 1612–13 register states that the new count had established an increase in the non-Muslim population. Probably the new total, which the compiler had in mind but did not specifically mention, was the figure of 2,093 that we already know from the summary statement previously referred to. The register then proceeds to give an enumeration of town quarters and villages that had a Christian population, but as the document has pages missing, the total of 752 non-Muslims for the city of Kayseri does not tell us very much. However, we are free to assume that during these difficult years, a considerable number of Kayseri's Christian inhabitants had left the city.

At the same time, the poll tax register of 1612–13 reflects not only emigration from Kayseri, but also immigration into the city. Special paragraphs in the register deal with 20 non-Muslim taxpayers from the town of Furnus, 24 from Darende, and 34 from Sis (Kozan) and the surrounding villages. These people had been living in Kayseri for 15–20 years, that is they should have arrived in the city during the very last years of the sixteenth century, when the disruption caused by the Celâlî rebellions was at its height. Under the circumstances, the tax collectors of Furnus, Darende, and Sis had not been able to levy any poll taxes on the families in question, and the migrants had paid their dues in Kayseri. However, since the new inhabitants were not legally registered in the city to which they had migrated, the tax collectors generally seized the opportunity to pocket the poll taxes which they had collected without keeping proper records. By recording the migrants as legal residents of Kayseri, the Ottoman administration attempted to prevent further losses to the Treasury. But at the same time, registration in the Kayseri poll tax records constituted a guarantee for the migrants, who were thereby protected against *timar* holders or administrators of pious foundations that might demand their return.

For the middle of the seventeenth century, we possess somewhat more information than for the preceding and the following periods. It appears that during those years, the Ottoman administration made a concerted effort to revive the sixteenth-century practice of counting all taxpayers regardless of religion. Such counts have previously been located for Amasya, Tokat, and Samsun.[88] The Kayseri document which is defined as an *avarız* register for the Muslim and as a poll-tax list for the Christian population, was compiled in or shortly before 1055/1645, and should thus be added to the series of mid-seventeenth-century registers of taxpayers. According to approved Ottoman practice, only adult males were recorded, while the heads of households were distinguished from unmarried men. In the city itself, Muslims amounted to 2,679 taxpayers, or 1,389 households. For the Christian population the relevant figures were 1,964 and 1,531 respectively. However, among the latter, 346 taxpayers were quite possibly people who did not live in Kayseri at all, but were only registered in the city. If these are subtracted, the non-Muslim population decreases to 1,618 taxpayers. Thus, the total figure of all taxpayers resident in Kayseri amounts to 4,643, or to 4,297 if the 'doubtful' cases are excluded.[89] This total of officially given taxpayers corresponded to 2,920 households, and if we assume that a household consisted of five persons, we arrive at an overall population of about 14,600. With an allowance of 10 per cent for tax-exempt persons, the city should have numbered approximately 16,000 residents.

Compared with the 1583 count of taxpayers, the population of mid-seventeenth-century Kayseri should thereby have dropped almost by half. This is a loss comparable to that which was recorded for contemporary Amasya.[90] At the same time, the Muslim population was affected more seriously than the non-Muslims, and thus the share of non-Muslims in the total population of the city increased quite appreciably; it now stood at 42.3 per cent. It is impossible to tell what processes led to this result. But in all likelihood there first occurred considerable emigration both among Muslims and among non-Muslims, with the death rate also increasing as infectious diseases took their toll. Later, a sizeable group of non-Muslims must have entered the city, possibly in part the old inhabitants returning, but, in addition, also a sizeable group of refugees from the subprovinces of Sis (Kozan) and Maraş.

Population movements of this period are equally reflected in a note later glued into the 1645 register, which deals with the units upon which *avarız* taxes were levied.[91] For the Kayseri area, the Ottoman administration decided to count 15 adult male taxpayers as one *avarızhane*, and the adoption of this relatively high figure was justified by the poverty of the inhabitants. At the same time, the document mentions that a recent count had revealed the existence of 13,000 taxpayers in the *sancak* as a whole. This figure amounted to 2,000 men over and above those that had been recorded in an older register which has not been preserved, but which evidently had been prepared at some unspecified time in the not very remote past. Thus, figures appear to indicate some slight recovery. But it is improbable that such relatively modest gains could have balanced the massive losses of the early 1600s.

Moreover, the instability of the mid seventeenth century is reflected in the fact that a separate count of non-Muslim taxpayers, executed at an unspecified date between 1051/1641–2 and 1057/1647, gives a vastly lower total, namely between 1,100 and 1,150 adult males, in place of the 1,964 men recorded in 1645.[92] This second register was in use for at least the following ten years, as an attempt was made to keep track of the increasing non-Muslim population by adding newcomers to the register. Since these later additions are only sometimes dated, and often difficult to distinguish from the main body of the text, the exact number of people included in the original document cannot be determined. Moreover, it is difficult to explain the contradictions between these two all but contemporary documents, namely the *avarız–cizye* register on the one hand, and the (unamended) poll-tax account on the other. One might imagine that the poll tax register, with its lower figures, was compiled during the summer, when some of the inhabitants had gone off to tend their fields and gardens. In the mid seventeenth century, Kayseri did in fact contain a sizeable agricultural population. Moreover, migration is documented by an entry in the *avarız* records, which mentions people leaving their houses in the town for the three summer months.[93] In addition, various irregularities not committed to writing may also have been not altogether unconnected with the contradictions between the two documents.

The last available count of the non-Muslim population of Kayseri is dated 1089/1678;[94] that is, it precedes by only about ten years the later group of housing data which has been analysed in the present study. Unfortunately, the information contained in this document is not easily comparable with the results of previous counts, since the 1678 account enumerates only households, and tells us nothing about adult males who were not heads of independent households. According to this register, the total number of non-Muslim households amounted to 1,570. If we wish to estimate the number of adult male taxpayers, we might use the data of the mid-century population count, according to which 1,531 households had corresponded to 1,964 adult males. Supposing this ratio had not changed too much, one might then assume that the non-Muslim population of Kayseri increased very slightly during the years between 1645 and 1678. Of course, the crucial problem is what happened to the Muslim majority of the Kayseri townsfolk; but concerning this matter, the poll-tax register does not contain the slightest clue.

For the closing years of the seventeenth century, we only possess some indirect evidence. Among the most valuable is a declaration of the representatives of all Muslim and non-Muslim town quarters of the city, seconded by a number of men empowered to speak for the villages of the Kayseri area. According to this document, dated Şaban 1104/April 1693,[95] the representatives of townsmen and villagers expressed their confidence in a certain Hacı Ramazan b Seydi who throughout his (unspecified) official activity, which probably was connected with the collection of taxes, had always acted as their protector. In this context, it was stated that 500 non-Muslim families had left Kayseri at some unspecified time in the past, and had settled in the towns of Tokat, Amasya, Merzifon, Adana, and Payas. However, during the last years, Hacı Ramazan's intervention had made it possible for these families to return to their homes. What the particular reasons for this migration may have been is not indicated in the document. But it is probable that both the exodus of these non-Muslim families and their eventual return were in one way or another connected with taxation. Thus, we must assume that during the last decades of the seventeenth century, the population of Kayseri must again have been subject to considerable variation. In a town which at its high point in the later sixteenth century should have contained at most 35,000 inhabitants, the departure or arrival of approximately 2,500 individuals must have made a considerable impact.

Wealth and status among the inhabitants of Kayseri

For the closing years of the seventeenth century, we possess a listing of the prominent Muslims of the city, whom contemporary documents refer to as the *ayan* and *zi-kudret* (well-known and powerful). In the year 1106/1694–5, the Ottoman administration had demanded that the Kayseri notables contribute to the war effort by equipping 70 cavalrymen; and the local patricians divided up the cost among themselves.[96] According to the registers, each notable was asked to contribute 'in accordance with his means'. This resulted in five categories of contributors: the smallest contribution lay at 7.5 *guruş*, the next higher at 12.5, 25 and 30 *guruş*, respectively. At the same time, certain notables taxed themselves 40 *guruş*, that is a sum of money equivalent to the price of a very modest house. Since we do not know what kinds of relations prevailed among the Kayseri patricians and what kinds of negotiations may have preceded the agreement, we cannot claim that the wealth of the notables is accurately reflected in this list. Even so, it does provide a guide to the hierarchy of wealth and honours prevailing in the city.

Of the four men contributing 40 *guruş* each, two were *seyyids*, that is real or supposed descendants of the Prophet Muhammad. One of the *seyyids*, and one of the other most important contributors, had moreover performed the pilgrimage to Mecca. Among the four people contributing 30 *guruş* each, there was a further *seyyid*. In addition, one man in this latter group was described as an *imam*. This appears to indicate that the function of *imam* was not always performed by people of modest wealth and status, but attracted men belonging to the well-established families in the city. Among the four contributors of 30 *guruş* each, three had performed the pilgrimage to Mecca. Thus, it appears that the title of *hacı* was valued among the wealthy men of Kayseri, who went out of their way to acquire it.

In most instances, the list does not tell us anything about the trade or profession of the contributors. However, there are some significant exceptions. One person bore the title *efendi* and probably had acquired some kind of *medrese* education. A perfumer (*attar*), a shoemaker, a blacksmith, a maker of headgear (*kavukçu*) and two *imams* were equally represented. However, it is impossible to tell whether the men designated as craftsmen were in fact exercising their craft, or had enriched themselves and turned into merchants. One suspects some such development in the case of men who bore the indication of a trade or profession as a patronymic, while the document does not mention how they themselves earned a living. Thus we encounter descendants of a market gardener (*bostancızade*), of a tinsmith (*kalaycızade*), and of a dealer in leather (*göncüoğlu*), while the patronymic of two other men appears to refer to the pressing of oil from linseed (*bezircilioğlu*). Very few Kayseri patricians showed a connection with the military in their names and titles, for we encounter only one *beğ* and one *beşe*. On the other hand, the frequency of *seyyid* and *hacı* titles is remarkable. Out of 37 men mentioned by name, 17, or almost one-half, bore the title of *seyyid*; 15 had performed the pilgrimage to Mecca. Thus, we get the impression of an urban elite of markedly civilian status, in which religious distinction and involvement constituted a common denominator.

The family relationships which must have existed between the wealthy and prestigious inhabitants of Kayseri are only partially reflected in the contributors' list. Two men are explicitly described as uncle and nephew; no patronymics are given. Instead, the uncle is in turn identified as being the nephew of a certain Hacı Ibrahim, who must have been a prominent man to completely eclipse the father of his younger relatives as a point of reference. Most probably this Hacı Ibrahim is identical with a person of this name equally mentioned in the list. In addition, the document mentions three pairs of relatives, one pair explicitly characterized as brothers who paid their contribution together. Where the other cases are concerned, the family relationship is apparent through a common patronymic which may or may not by this time have developed into a surname. It is probable that in an urban elite of this type, family relationships were more common than is discernible from this brief list. We probably should imagine the prominent and well-connected inhabitants of Kayseri as divided into several coteries of cousins.

The urban way of life: some Kayseri examples

Concerning the material wealth of the inhabitants of Kayseri, the best source would be the probate inventories which in sixteenth- and seventeenth-century Bursa or Edirne filled entire registers.[97] However, for seventeenth-century Kayseri, as for Ankara, such inventories are quite rare. Therefore in the present context, we will limit ourselves to a few examples, and make no attempt at quantification. Even so, the inventories at our disposal are quite instructive, for they allow us a glimpse into the houses which form the subject of this study, at a time when they were inhabited. Thus we can at least begin to imagine the daily lives of seventeenth-century Anatolian townsmen, and after all, the investigation of domestic architecture is meant to lead us to an understanding of urban society.

The first example concerns a certain Mehmed Dede b. Hacı Isa and his son Abdürrahim, residents of Hasbey *mahalle*. Mehmed Dede's probate inventory is dated Safer 1100/November 1688. He was survived by his wife and four adult children, three of them sons. No other heirs are mentioned. Unfortunately, the value assigned to Mehmed Dede's house can only be estimated because the relevant figure is quite illegible; but it cannot have been worth more than 75 *guruş*. It appears that Mehmed Dede's main source of income was agriculture. In this respect he was not atypical; even in the first half of the twentieth century, Bartsch commented on the large number of townsmen that made a living by tilling the land.[98] Apart from the indispensable donkey, Mehmed Dede owned three cows with their calves (value 17.5 *guruş*) and four oxen (value 16 guruş). In his storehouse were found 10 *keyl* of barley, 55 *keyl* of rye, 10 *keyl* of wheat, 5.5 *keyl* of bulgur and small quantities of lentils and vetches. Household goods consisted of some pots and pans, a small tray, a pail, two water jugs, and a coffee pot. In addition, the household possessed about a dozen rugs and kilims, most of them old, and the indispensable bedding. However, the head of the household kept a sword stored away, and must occasionally have ridden a horse. At any rate, stirrups were found among his possessions.

Mehmed Dede left no ready cash, or at least the probate inventory does not mention its existence. Nor was there any evidence of people owing him money. However, the family was just about breaking even, because the only creditor in evidence was the deceased's widow, who received her dowry (*mihr-i müsbet*) of 80 *guruş*. This amounted to almost half the estate, so that only 95 *guruş* remained to be distributed. The sons were assigned a little over 23 *guruş* each; the widow and her daughter were both given shares of 11 *guruş*. We do not know which of the heirs received which goods, but given the importance of the dowry, it is quite probable that the house remained in the widow's possession.

Within a short time after Mehmed Dede's death, his son Abdürrahim also died.[99] The latter was already married and had two children, as yet under age. His wife was from a *seyyid* family, and the title was inherited by her children; apparently the *seyyid*s of Kayseri did not insist upon endogamy. Since Mehmed Dede's estate had not yet been distributed at the time of Abdürrahim's death, the estate inventory assigned the latter a claim of slightly over 23 *guruş*, against his father's estate. But then comes the big surprise: this young man, who must have been living in his father's house because he owned no household goods (and for that matter, barely two sets of clothes) left a library of 76 volumes. The more costly books in Abdürrahim's collection were estimated at 4–7 *guruş* each, that is, they were comparable in value to Mehmed Dede's oxen. Since the probate inventories give Abdürrahim no title, he had probably not yet attained any kind of office; one may imagine him as an assistant tutor in one of the local *medrese*s. Interestingly enough, Abdürrahim's interests were by no means exclusively religious and legal, as might be expected of a future member of the Kayseri ulama. It is difficult to be very specific, given the rather less than satisfactory description which the court scribes made of Abdürrahim's library – often enough they capitulated and settled for a catchall such as *risail-i müteferrika* ('various tracts') or *turki manzume* ('poetry in Turkish'). But Abdürrahim apparently owned a commentary on the poetry of Hafiz by Surûrî,[100] a book ascribed to the astronomer Ali Kuşçu, a commentary to Sa'dî's Gulistân, a Persian volume on the rules of poetry, and last but not least, what may have been a volume by Mevlâna Celâleddîn Rûmî – the scribe, at the end of his tether, simply put down the word 'Celâleddîn'. Taken together, this library was worth over 70 *guruş*; that is, Abdürrahim could probably have bought a house if he had been willing to sell his beloved books. Obviously both Mehmed Dede and Şerife Meryem, Abdürrahim's wife, must have shown considerable sympathy and toleration for their eccentric scholarly relative.

A wealthier and more conventional environment is reflected in the probate inventory of Hacı Mehmed, son of Hacı Ahmed, of late residing in the *mahalle* of Bozatlı. Hacı Mehmed, whose estate was recorded in Rebi I 1101/December 1689, left possessions valued at slightly over 292.5 *guruş*. He had been married to two wives, from whom he had two sons and four daughters. His house was valued at 70 *guruş*; in addition, he owned two gardens and/or vineyards, valued at 50 *guruş* each. As a result, his storehouse contained not only small amounts of raisins and vinegar, but 31 *batman* of yellowberries used in dyeing, valued at the not inconsiderable sum of 23 *guruş*. Otherwise there is no evidence of how Hacı Mehmed earned his living, possibly he supported his family on the income derived from his rather valuable vineyards. However, unlike Mehmed Dede, Hacı Mehmed apparently did not engage in field agriculture; there were no oxen among his possessions and no grain in his storehouse.[101]

A solid property owner with a sizeable family needed a well-stocked kitchen. In fact, the scribes did not bother to enumerate individual pots and pans, but simply recorded a *batman*'s weight of copper (value: 50 *guruş*). Moreover, rugs and kilims were mostly of relatively high value; the best piece was valued at three *guruş*. Among Hacı Mehmed's personal effects, the most remarkable was a full array of weaponry: apart from a sword, the deceased had acquire two flintlock guns and another gun described as 'long'. Even so, the sword remained the most costly of Hacı Mehmed's weapons. It is probable that the deceased had used to hunt, and felt the need for protection when working in his vineyards outside the city. However, the presence of firearms in the estate of an ordinary townsman also indicates that the Ottoman administration was not very successful in preventing the spread of firearms among the inhabitants of the Empire.[102]

Another inhabitant of Kayseri who combined residence in the city with agricultural occupations was Yusuf b. Osman.[103] He owned half a field, valued at the low price of six *guruş*. This field must have been freehold property (*mülk*), for even though the right to cultivate state-owned land was inheritable, it was not customary to include these rights in probate inventories. According to the Ottoman land system as applied during the fifteenth and sixteenth centuries, the cultivator could not hold fields in freehold property, even though extensive rights of ownership were upon occasion granted to prominent commanders on the Balkan frontier.[104] However, by the late seventeenth century, the custom of owning fields as freehold property constituted a well-established peculiarity of the Kayseri district.[105] Thus, Yusuf b. Osman's case once again proves that the *kadis* did not seriously challenge this practice, but to the contrary, sanctioned it by treating the fields in question just like any other personal property. In addition, Yusuf owned half a vineyard in the well-known vineyard district of Belbaşı, which had been assigned the value of six *guruş*. Moreover, the fruits of this land, recently harvested and stored away in a wooden storehouse, were valued at one *guruş*.

Yusuf b. Osman had been married twice; his eldest son was not the child of the woman mentioned as his widow. However, the fact that only one widow is mentioned among the heirs, although the mother of his eldest son was still alive, indicates that this was a case of divorce and remarriage, rather than of polygamy. Or else Yusuf's first companion had been a slave woman, later emancipated, as her patronymic 'b. Abdülmennan' appears to indicate. However, if this had been the case, she should have appeared among the heirs of her former master, and therefore a marriage and subsequent divorce seems more likely. Yusuf's second wife had borne him a son, and was pregnant at the time of his death; a son's share was therefore set aside for the unborn child. Thus, the heirs consisted of the deceased's wife, his three children including the one yet unborn, and his mother. However, since Yusuf's young son by his first wife died shortly after his father, the child's share was divided among his siblings and his mother. In this roundabout fashion, the deceased's former wife thus participated in her divorced husband's inheritance.

Among Yusuf's household effects, one might mention a large curtain from Mardin, probably made out of cotton, for the town had been famous for this industry even in the sixteenth century.[106] It is well-known that in sixteenth- and seventeenth-century Anatolia, clothing tended to be expensive when compared with land. But even so, it is noteworthy that the curtain, priced at five guruş, was worth almost as much as Yusuf's field or vineyard. From the kitchen utensils, it appears that Yusuf's household quite frequently consumed coffee, for we find a large coffee can, a small coffee can, and a small plate which was also used in serving or preparing this beverage.

From all this, it is obvious that Yusuf and his family were not rich; although their house was comparatively valuable (150 guruş), the total inheritance only amounted to something over 220 guruş. However, certain modest luxuries were obviously indulged in: Yusuf owned a coat of green woollen cloth, lined with marten fur and valued at eight guruş. He combed his beard with a special comb, which had its own receptacle, and a cap embroidered in silver thread was counted among his effects. Obviously this standard of living could not have been supported by the tiny bits of field and vineyard owned by the deceased. But as usual, the inventory does not list any ready money, and there is no mention of a shop or workshop. The most likely solution is that Yusuf was employed in the shop of a relative, who was probably not his father because the latter's name does not appear among the heirs, but possibly an uncle or cousin. It is not very probable that the deceased had kept up his standard of living by borrowing; at any rate, no creditors had presented themselves prior to the division of the inheritance.

The last family to be introduced in the present context was also the poorest.[107] When Veli, formerly of the town quarter of Tus, died at some time before Cem I 1103/January 1692, the value of his total estate was only 145 guruş, of which the house accounted for 80 guruş. Veli must have been a man of at least middle age; from his son Süleyman he had two grandchildren, the latter as yet minors. Süleyman died shortly after his father, and the inheritance was much diminished by the fact that both Veli's and Süleyman's widows each had a claim of 25 *guruş* upon the estates of their deceased husbands. In both cases, these claims constituted the dowries which had been settled upon the women when they were married; otherwise, no creditors had presented themselves before the division of the inheritance.

Veli and Süleyman must also have been employed in somebody else's business, for no shop, workshop or tools indicate that they earned a living as shopkeepers or craftsmen. Nor did they own any real property apart from their house, and in a city like Kayseri, where gardens and vineyards were very much part of town life, this in itself indicates straitened circumstances. Even so, Veli and Süleyman were not totally divorced from agricultural pursuits, for they owned a stock of linseed worth ten *guruş*, which appears too valuable to have simply been stored away as part of the family's food supply. One might imagine the two men at least occasionally manufactured oil for sale. Equally, a store of 40 *batman* of wool was probably not used for domestic consumption alone.[108] Possibly the women of the family spun or wove, as relatively independent domestic workers, since the raw material belonged to the head of the family himself, rather than to a merchant. Even so the frequency of household goods described as 'old' or 'used' documents the family's modest standard of living, although minor luxuries such as coffee or baklava were occasionally consumed even on this level.

These five families constitute nothing more than individual cases, yet they do allow us to make a few observations with somewhat broader implications. Given the frequency of multiple deaths within the same family, one suspects that there was an epidemic going on in Kayseri at the time, although the records do not indicate the nature of the sickness. A study of the *kadıs'* registers over long periods would probably yield some data concerning food shortages and contagious diseases. Seen from a different angle, the records show that quite a few of the townsmen were not craftsmen or merchants at all, but made their living by cultivating gardens, vineyards, and even fields. Gardens and vineyards tended to be more profitable in the vicinity of a town, so it is not surprising that many of the families cultivating them should have lived in Kayseri. As far as field agriculture is concerned, the unsettled state of the countryside must have encouraged certain peasants to settle permanently in Kayseri. During the busy summer months, some of these agriculturalists probably lived out in the fields, just as their descendants did during the late nineteenth and early twentieth centuries. Thus the rural features of Kayseri are apparent even at a casual glance.

Other observations concern patterns of family life. It is noteworthy that in all the instances documented, the deceased husband was survived by his wife. This pattern, if in fact it applied to Kayseri society as a whole, should have resulted in a considerable number of widows. Whether these women generally remarried, returned to their families, or acted as the heads of their households until their sons had reached adulthood, is of course not indicated in the probate inventories. However, it is worth noting that only three of the seven widows mentioned were credited with the dowry that the *şeriat* accorded a woman whose husband died or divorced her.[109] What had happened in the other four cases is unknown. One might imagine that the husband in certain cases had set aside a sum of money for his wife's dowry, which then was not recorded in the inventory, just as some people seem to have made arrangements for their funeral expenses. Or else the woman may have renounced her rights. Moreover, the three women whose claim to a dowry was documented in the probate inventories were in one case of peasant background, while the other two probably contributed to the family income by spinning or weaving. It is not clear whether these economic factors had any bearing upon the payment or non-payment of a dowry.

Seventeenth-century Kayseri: topography

Information on Ottoman Kayseri's topography is less detailed than that concerning Ankara. For one, the oldest map, prepared by Albert Gabriel in the 1920s,[110] is almost a century later than that draw by von Vincke, and thus incorporates changes in the urban tissue which may be nineteenth-century innovations. Nor do we possess any detailed information concerning the topography of the city as reflected in the *kadı* registers. However, due to Gabriel's and later Akok's attempts at reconstructing the 'medieval' town, a certain amount of topographical information has come to light,[111] even though it apparently relates more to the Seljuk than to the Ottoman town. In the present sketch, information presented by Gabriel and Akok has been combined with a few scraps of information from a sixteenth-century register of pious foundations. However, this document is unfortunately much less informative than similar registers relating to many other Anatolian cities.[112]

Kayseri possessed a double ring of walls: the İçkale still survives, while gates, towers and the course of a modern boulevard indicate the location of the Dışkale fortifications. However, even in the Seljuk or Mongol periods, the city did not end at the walls. To the contrary, some of Kayseri's major buidings, such as the Hvand Hatun Mosque and Medrese, the Lala Mosque, and the Sahibiye Medrese were all located outside of the city walls, even though in each case, the distance was only a few steps. Moreover, the Külük Mosque, which probably existed by about 1600 since at that time we find a *mahalle* known by the same name, was located at a much greater distance. It would seem that after the completion of the walls, the city expanded toward the southeast (Külük Camii) and to the west under the protection of the bastion that probably completed the walls in the area of the modern Vilayet Konaği (Kurşunlu Cami, Çifte Medrese, Mosque of Hacı İkiz, Afgunu Medrese). However, none of these structures came to form the nucleus of a *mahalle*, unless the name Sultan Camii Mahallesi refers to the Kurşunlu Mosque, which had been erected by Mimar Sinan and as such differed from the architecture of the older buildings by its large lead-covered domes in the classical Ottoman ('sultanic') style. In the northeast, Kayseri appears to have possessed a veritable 'street' lined with funerary monuments; as late as the 1920s, there existed no urban development in a large sector to the north of this line. In addition, it is worth noting that to the southeast of the old urban centre, Gabriel's map shows a broad band of 'traditional' urban tissue. This area does not seem to have contained any noteworthy public buildings. But seventeenth-century Kayseri possessed a sizeable number of *mahalle*s which did not apparently take their name from any known mosque or *mescit* (Tepecik, Kuşakçılar Hamamı, Sultanhamam, Tavşancı Hamamı, Taşguncuk etc.) and one may assume that some of them were located in the 'monumentless' belt to the southeast. In any case it is difficult to imagine how the over sixty *mahalle*s of seventeenth-century Kayseri could all have fitted into the walled perimeter and its immediate vicinity, particularly if one keeps in mind that the Kayseri of the sixteenth-century tax registers was noted for the large size of its *mahalle*s. In fact, we know that by the sixteenth century not only private houses but also shops were located outside of the city gates.

While Ankara's commercial centre was located outside of the Dışkale walls, the two *bedestan*s of Kayseri formed part of the walled town. Evliya's remark on the existence of two such structures is borne out by a register of pious foundations dated 992/1584, which refers to a *bezazistan-ı atik* apart from a '*bezazistan-ı Kaysariye*'.[113] According to this latter document, a *kervansaray* was associated with the *vakıf* of Pir Mehmed Paşa; in addition the *vakıf* register also mentions a '*kaysariye*', which in this case may have meant an *arasta* of some kind, possibly located within the present Kapalı Çarşı. Gabriel's map records a Pamuk Hanı and Vezir Hanı as the last survivors among Kayseri's khans; whether they can in any way be related to the khans mentioned in the *vakıf* register remains obscure. Kayseri was remarkable for the monumental street which led from the İçkale and the adjacent *bedestan* to the Boyacılar Kapusu: past the Pamuk Hanı and the Vezir Hanı to the medrese of Melik Gazi and the Kadı Hamamı. Then, after a bend in the street, came the Mosque of Hoca Bey, and the visitor found himself face to face with the massive city walls and the 'Gate of the Dyers'. Unfortunately it has not been possible to locate the structure where the dyers of Kayseri exercised their craft. This may well have been a substantial building, since it is mentioned time and again in the Ottoman records of the sixteenth and seventeenth centuries; originally state property, in the seventeenth century it was transformed into a pious foundation.[114]

Even though Kayseri was only a simple *sancak* centre, whose administrative rank was not in any way higher than that of Ankara, the town boasted an official residence for the provincial governor (Paşa Sarayı). Gabriel suggests

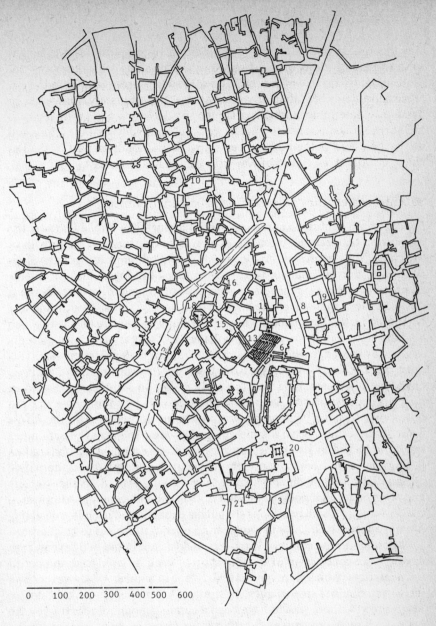

8. Map of Kayseri (drawing: Tülay Artan after Çakıroğlu, *Kayseri Evleri*, p. 16
and Gabriel, *Monuments turcs* pp. 9 and 17). (1) Kale (2) Gübgüboğulları mansion
(3) Zennecioğulları mansion (4) Mollaoğulları mansion (5) Aslandağ house (6)
Business district (7) Unnamed small house (8) Hacı İkiz mosque (9) Afğunu
Medrese (10) Külük mosque (11) Pamuk hanı (cotton khan) (12) Bedesten
(covered market) (13) Vezir Hanı (Vizier's Khan) (14) Ulu Cami (Great Mosque)
(15) Melik Gazi Medrese (16) Kadı hamamı (17) Hatuniye Medrese (18) Hoca
Bey mosque (19) Hatıroğlu mosque (20) Hvand Medrese (21) Siraceddin Medrese
(22) Lala Paşa mosque.

that this building was located in the bastion which protected the north-western part of the town, and was torn down, along with the walls that protected it, to make way for the Vilayet Konağı. Other *paşa*s in and out of office had equally built themselves residences. Unfortunately it has not been possible to determine in which part of the city these structures were located. If Gabriel's assumptions are correct, we should probably view the İçkale and the bastion area as the political centre, while the southern part of the Dış kale constituted the centre of Kayseri's commercial activities.

Seventeenth-century Kayseri: the urban environment

For sixteenth-century Kayseri, Ronald Jennings has already shown the connection between the founding of new town quarters and the growth of the city.[115] In the present investigation, we will attempt to trace developments for the one hundred years that followed. From the documents recorded in the *kadı*s' registers, it is possible to compile a list of the Kayseri town quarters that were inhabited at the end of the sixteenth and the beginning of the seventeenth century. When we compare this list, which contains sixty-four town quarters, with the list of seventy-two town quarters as given by the tax register of 1583, we find that eight items are missing. This must not necessarily mean that the town quarters in question had been abandoned between 1583 and the early 1600s. In some cases, the town quarters in question may have been inhabited only by poor people who did not bother to have their property transactions documented in the *kadı*'s court. In other instances, the missing town quarters may have been rather small, and accordingly, few or no property transactions were undertaken during the period under consideration. But in spite of these alternative explanations, one might still assume as a working hypothesis that the city had reached its high point at the end of the sixteenth century. Afterwards, the crisis of the Celâlî rebellions should have manifested itself in a declining urban population and also in a smaller number of inhabited town quarters.

According to the count of taxpayers undertaken in the mid seventeenth century, the contraction of the city showed itself in a reduced number of town quarters, which were now only sixty-one in number.[116] However, if an increasing number of *mahalle*s constitutes, by and large, an indicator of urban growth, there should have been a certain amount of recovery by the later years of the seventeenth century, for from the *kadı*s' records of the 1690s, we can compile a list of sixty-seven town quarters. Moreover, since the number of non-Muslim inhabitants does not seem to have changed substantially between the middle and the end of the seventeenth century, the hypothetical increase in the number of Kayseri inhabitants must have concerned the Muslim population.

When we compare the list of town quarters documented in the *kadı*s' records of the years around 1600 with its counterpart from the 1690s, the amount of turnover is quite remarkable. Out of the sixty-four names mentioned in the sale documents of the late sixteenth and early seventeenth centuries, twenty-eight could no longer be located in the documents issued ninety years later. On the other hand, thirty-one names occurred in the later documents which had been unknown to the texts dating from the beginning of the seventeenth century. Some of this turnover is certainly fortuitous. Thus, the town quarters of Rumiyan and Sayeci had existed in the later sixteenth century, and probably continued to exist throughout the seventeenth century, even if they are not mentioned in the transactions of the period before and after 1600.[117] In addition, certain *mahalle*s might be known by more than one name over long periods of time, a fact which renders the interpretation of name changes somewhat hazardous. Even so, one gains the impression that the names of town quarters were less stable in Kayseri than in Ankara. This in turn may have been connected with an unusually large number of people migrating into and out of Kayseri.

In addition, the documents contained in the *kadı*s' registers provide some information concerning the distribution of Muslims and non-Muslims over the *mahalle*s of Kayseri. According to the register of 1583, there were fifty Muslim, thirteen Christian and nine mixed *mahalle*s in the city. When we break down the transactions concerning urban real estate of the years around 1600 both by the religion of the seller, buyer, or litigant and also by the town quarter in which the relevant house was located, the number of mixed town quarters turns out to be even higher. In fact, twenty-six *mahalle*s out of a total of sixty-four contained a population of both Muslims and non-Muslims. In five town quarters, only Christian sellers, buyers and litigants were recorded, while in the remaining *mahalle*s only Muslims were in evidence. Thus it would seem that mixed *mahalle*s were more common at the beginning of the seventeenth century than they had been twenty years earlier.

From the tax register compiled in the middle of the seventeenth century, the changing religious composition of the city can be read off without too much difficulty. The number of all-Muslim *mahalle*s had declined to thirty-five, the number of Christian quarters stood at fourteen, while twelve town quarters contained a mixed population. Just as Jennings has observed for the sixteenth century, these 'mixed' *mahalle*s generally contained a solid majority belonging to one community, with a few members of the other group interspersed.[118] However, towards the end of the seventeenth century, the *kadı*'s records show rather a different kind of distribution. In four *mahalle*s, namely Sultanhamamı, Kiçi, Karakeçili, and Sayeci, only non-Muslim litigants, buyers or sellers were recorded. Twenty-five *mahalle*s should have been 'mixed' in religious composition, while in the remaining *mahalle*s there were only Muslim buyers, sellers or litigants. However, given the fact that Kayseri non-Muslims during this late period sold only a few houses (while buying many more), this distribution may to some extent have been accidental. Even so, it is safe to say that 'mixed' *mahalles* constituted a permanent feature of the Kayseri townscape; this may indicate that just as in seventeenth-century Ankara, inter-confessional strife was not very common. For the beginning of the seventeenth century, this situation has already been commented upon by Jennings.[119] Apparently, the relations between the Muslims and non-Muslims of Kayseri were reasonably relaxed even in the 1690s.

Descending from the *mahalle* level to the smaller units of streets and individual buildings, the documents recorded in the *kadıs'* registers allow us to establish how the houses of Kayseri were located with respect to more or less public places. Just as in Ankara, two different types of thoroughfare are indicated: the public road (*tarik-ı âm*) and other more private lanes, which the documents call *tarik-i has*. However, in many of the texts relating to Kayseri, this differentiation is given up in favour of a more general term, denoting 'right of way' (*tarik*) without further specification. Among the houses of the late sixteenth and early seventeenth centuries, 204 are described in such a way as to provide usable information concerning the adjacent pieces of real estate. In 138 (67.6 per cent) instances, some kind of a *tarik* is mentioned; in most cases (76 out of 204, or 37.3 per cent) this was a right-of-way whose degree of privacy cannot be determined. Moreover, thirty-four houses had two sides which touched upon this kind of an undefined public or semi-public space (16.7 per cent). Only in twenty-eight cases (13.7 per cent) is the description more specific: sixteen cases involved houses adjacent to the public street (*tarik-i âm*), a further six residences had two sides limited by a publicly accessible thoroughfare, while the remaining six houses were bordered only by private or semi-private lanes. Thus, it would appear that houses with no direct access to the street did occasionally occur. It is probable that some of these latter dwellings were entered through private arrangements among neighbours, of the type which were sometimes recorded when a house was divided among heirs. In other cases, the lanes connecting these houses with the public street may have been semi-public, but the *kadı* registers do not contain any information on this matter.

Surprisingly enough, at the end of the seventeenth century Kayseri presented a much more regular picture. Out of 278 case records providing usable information concerning the pieces of land adjacent to a property bought, sold, or disputed, 168 pieces of real estate (60.4 per cent) had access to the public street (*tarik-i âm*). Another fifty-one cases (18.3 per cent) referred to houses which possessed access to a private or semi-private lane, while in thirty-two instances (11.5 per cent) the property in question was bordered by the public street on two sides. Properties bordered on two sides by a private or semi-private lane constituted an unimportant exception (3 cases, 1.1 per cent). At the same time, the desire for more accuracy had led to the total disappearance of the term 'right-of-way with no further qualification' (*tarik*). Certainly, we must make allowance for the fact that a few houses possessed access both to the public thoroughfare and to a semi-private lane, so that the number of houses which were not bordered by a public or semi-public area cannot be neatly determined. Even so, it is obvious that the number of houses bordered solely by other people's properties cannot have been very great, and at any rate much smaller than had been the case at the end of the sixteenth and the beginning of the seventeenth century. It is probable that the population turnover of the seventeenth century had led to a reorganization of the settlement pattern. When a group of newcomers established itself in a half-abandoned town quarter, house lots were probably rearranged so as to make every house accessible without passing over other people's property. Thus, the great upheaval of the early and middle seventeenth century may well have resulted in a more orderly city.

Concerning the distribution of publicly accessible buildings in residential areas, Kayseri did not present a very different picture from Ankara. It has already been observed that in the late sixteenth and early seventeenth centuries, 204 Kayseri houses were described in such a way as to provide usable information concerning the adjacent pieces of land. If we assume that every one of these houses had three neighbours apart from a public or semi-public right-of-way, we arrive at 612 built-up pieces of land. Thus the twelve mosques recorded in the documents under investigation amounted to two per cent of the total, while the four Christian churches corresponded to 0.7 per cent. In other words, in every fifty buildings in the Kayseri residential quarters of the late sixteenth and early seventeenth centuries should have been a mosque, while one out of every 143 buildings should have been a Christian church.

In themselves, these figures are not very meaningful, but they do allow us to compare the city as it presented itself in the years around 1600 with its appearance about ninety years later. For the 1690s, we possess 278 usable cases, therefore the number of 'adjacent structures' that we assume to have existed amounts to 834. Under these circumstances, the ten mosques that have been located amount to only 1.2 per cent of the total, while the four churches of 1690s Kayseri correspond to 0.5 per cent of all recorded buildings.

Given the limited number of cases involved, it is obviously not recommendable to draw very far-reaching conclusions from these figures. But it does appear probable that Kayseri in the 1690s possessed fewer small mosques and churches than had been the case some ninety years earlier. Given the fact that both Muslims and non-Muslims had entered and left the city in appreciable numbers, and that the newcomers had often established themselves in half-deserted town quarters, this state of affairs is readily understandable. Mosques and churches without a congregation would have decayed, and some of them may even have been torn down. In certain cases, the decay may well have been temporary, and places of worship were probably restored once the town quarter had reconstituted itself. But this was a time-consuming process, and the set of buildings studied here probably belongs to a period when the city was still in the process of stabilization.

Concerning Kayseri's water supply, we again possess only occasional data, but these are not without interest. In 1056/1646–7, that is during the years in which population was at its nadir, the Divan in İstanbul responded to a petition from the administrator of the Hacı Ahmed Paşa foundation in Kayseri and Üsküdar.[120] This latter dignitary had built a mosque and a double *hamam* in Kayseri; unfortunately nothing is known about their size or location, since both structures had disappeared by the time Gabriel made his survey. Hacı Ahmed Paşa had died before he could make proper provision for the water supply of his foundation. For a while, his administrator tried a temporary solution: he promised to pay all the expenses needed for repairs to certain water conduits which already served public fountains in Kayseri, and in return, was allowed to make use of the water they brought into the city. But this arrangement worked only for a few years, and now the foundation administrator had another solution to offer: he had found an abandoned water conduit, which had not been in use 'for fifty years', that is since the climactic years of the Celâlî rebellions at the end of the sixteenth century. This he offered to repair, and optimistically assured that not only would there be enough water available to satisfy the needs of mosque and *hamam*, but that there would be sufficient water left over to supply a number of street fountains. This correspondence shows that depopulated as mid-century Kayseri may have been, a certain recovery was underway. For if the town had been totally abandoned without hope of eventual recuperation, the foundation administrator would scarcely have pursued his project with so much energy; nor would he have tried to gain official support by promising to help supply Kayseri's water fountains.

Conclusion

From the present analysis, it is apparent that Ankara and Kayseri had many features in common. Both cities would have been classified as 'medium-sized' by contemporary Mediterranean standards. Both Ankara and Kayseri were situated in the midst of a vast steppe hinterland of limited agricultural possibilities, but the townsmen made use of localized water resources to practise partly irrigated garden cultures.[121] Last but not least, both cities were accessible from İstanbul only by caravan. Therefore, the resources of the Ankara and Kayseri hinterlands were available for local consumption, for the high cost of transport forbade the mobilization of grain produced in these areas for the benefit of the Ottoman capital. It is probable that this state of affairs contributed toward the growth of both cities in the course of the sixteenth century. Moreover, the commercial role of both

Ankara and Kayseri was enhanced by specialized crafts. In the case of Ankara, the manufacture of mohair cloths was directed both toward the export market and toward wealthy consumers in the Ottoman capital. Leather from Kayseri was not quite as prominent an item in interregional trade. But even so, it was well established in the market of İstanbul and was occasionally transported to towns of the Balkans as well.

At the same time, the differences between the two towns were not negligible either. Ankara was frequently visited by foreign merchants throughout the sixteenth and seventeenth centuries, some of whom resided there for lengthy periods of time. On the other hand, Kayseri and its hinterland were so little known in Europe that when Paul Lucas first published his account of the Göreme valley, its caves and rock formations, his veracity was doubted by many people.[122] By conventional criteria, one would thus expect Ankara to have been a much larger city than Kayseri. However, this was only true of certain time spans in the two cities' existence. During the earliest period for which comparisons are possible, namely the beginning years of Kanuni Süleyman's reign (1520 to about 1535) Ankara was in fact appreciably larger than Kayseri. But in the course of the later sixteenth century, Kayseri overtook Ankara. By the 1580s or 1590s, Kayseri contained about 3,000 adult male taxpayers more than Ankara, which should have resulted in a size difference of about 10,000 people. Thus, it seems that plentiful agricultural resources, and active local commerce, could support a larger settlement than a far-flung trade in luxury products.

For the seventeenth century, we do not possess figures that are strictly comparable, but it does appear that the pendulum swung back in favour of Ankara. Kayseri had lost about half of its 1583 population by the middle of the seventeenth century, and even though the losses were in part made up in the years between 1650 and 1700, it is impossible to determine when – and whether – the city again approached the high-water mark of the late sixteenth century. On the other hand, the figures given by European travellers of the early eighteenth century, even though often of doubtful reliability, all concur in describing a city substantially larger than the 22,000–25,000 inhabitants which Ankara apparently contained at the end of the sixteenth century.

How long Ankara was able to keep its leading position is difficult to tell. But it is probable that the decline of the mohair trade in the early nineteenth century resulted in Ankara's losing population not only absolutely, but also relatively to Kayseri. Writing at the very end of the nineteenth century, Vital Cuinet considered Kayseri a much more prosperous place than Ankara.[123] Even though in the second half of the nineteenth century Ankara had been accorded a higher rank in the administrative hierarchy than Kayseri, and had moreover been connected to İstanbul by a newly inaugurated railway, these advantages were not sufficient to compensate for the decay of the mohair trade. Only in the twentieth century, when it was made the capital of the Republic of Turkey, was Ankara given an impulse which permitted it to overtake not only Kayseri, but all other provincial towns of Anatolia as well.

From these observations, one can conclude that Ankara, with its deeper involvement in international trade, lived according to a quite different rhythm than the overgrown market-town as Kayseri may be described during much of its history. At first glance, one might think that Ankara was more vulnerable, since it had to respond to conjunctures which lay quite outside the area which its merchants and tax farmers could hope to control. Yet on the other side, there are Kayseri's difficulties of the mid seventeenth century to be considered. This latter crisis may well have been more severe than that which Ankara was going through at the time, precisely because gains from the mohair industry could serve to cushion the negative impact of rural unrest. But these matters can only be touched upon in the present context, and fuller treatment is only possible against the backdrop of a general economic history of Ottoman Anatolia during the seventeenth and eighteenth centuries.[124]

CHAPTER 2

The physical shape of urban houses

Terminology

In sixteenth and seventeenth century Ankara or Kayseri, a house was usually known as *menzil*, or more simply as *ev*. More ambiguous was the term *mülk* ('freehold property'). For when referring to the properties bordering a given house, the documents commonly call the former '*mülk* of N.N.'. Given the fact that in a residential neighbourhood most pieces of land not explicitly described as serving a different purpose must have been occupied by houses, one might assume that the word *mülk* was in this context used for purposes of clarification. Thus a '*mülk menzil*', a term which frequently recurs in the documents, means a 'house held as freehold property'. Therefore, it appears more appropriate to translate the term *mülk* as 'property'.

A *mülk menzil* regularly consisted not only of a building but of a courtyard as well, while it was quite rare to find a garden (*bahçe*) attached to the house. For the courtyard, different terms were in current use. In late sixteenth and early seventeenth Kayseri, the most frequently used expression was *muhavvata* ('enclosed') or else a term which appears to be '*havlu*' and should correspond to the modern Turkish *avlu*. On the other hand, Ankara documents of the 1590s and early 1600s frequently refer to a *hayat*. Now in modern Turkish parlance, a *hayat* is not a courtyard but a veranda.[1] One might thereby conclude that Ankara houses usually possessed no courtyard, if it were not for the fact that occasionally trees are mentioned as growing in the *hayat*. Now one may discount the unlikely possibility that somebody had been raising a potted pear tree on his veranda, and that the fact somehow got included into the description of the house. For in texts of the later seventeenth century the term *muhavvata* can be found in relation to Ankara as well, and houses that had a *muhavvata* did not possess a *hayat*. If further confirmation were needed, one might refer to the fact that the documents recorded in the *kadı* registers often contain the note *bir mıkdar hayat* ('a certain quantity of courtyard'). Now such an expression cannot be used of rooms and other built-up areas, but only of an open and relatively undefined space such as a garden or a courtyard. Under these circumstances, the interpretation of the term *hayat* for late sixteenth- and early seventeenth-century Ankara seems to rest on fairly firm grounds.[2]

Within the actual structure, one of the most notable features was the *tabhane*. At present, this term is no longer employed in describing the traditional Turkish house. However, popular parlance in Kayseri employs the term *togana*, which refers to a kitchen. Moreover, dervish hospices and other pious foundations sometimes possessed a *tabhane* or guest room.[3] Given the small size of many of the houses studied, it seems probable that the *tabhane* was the principal room of the house, sometimes called *başoda* in modern terminology, and probably the only one to possess a hearth.[4] Visitors were certainly received there, but the room was also used as living space by the family inhabiting the house, particularly in winter. Thus one might, with some reservations, regard the *tabhane* as a 'living room'. At night, bedding was spread out and certain members of the family presumably slept in the *tabhane*.

Another distinctive part of the house was the *sofa*. Studies of eighteenth- to twentieth-century vernacular housing in Anatolia show the *sofa* as a partially open or completely enclosed room providing access to other rooms in the house. As the documents studied do not contain any evidence to the contrary, 'hall' seems to be a reasonably appropriate translation.[5] In a few exceptional instances, seventeenth-century Anatolian townsmen might use the term *örtme sofa* to describe what was probably the *dış sofa* (porch also serving as hallway) of modern architectural parlance.[6] But in most cases this distinction, unfortunately for the modern researcher, was apparently considered unnecessary. Rooms without any special characteristics were called *oda* as they are today. Only in certain very sketchy descriptions are the words *oda, sofa, tabhane*, replaced by the general term *buyut-i müteaddide* ('a number of structures'). For the purposes of the present investigation, *tabhane, sofa*, and *oda* have been grouped together as 'inhabitable spaces'.

Given the protracted cold of the winter in central Anatolia, porches and verandas can be fully used for only about six months of the year. Even so, sixteenth and seventeenth-century houses contained quite a large number of semi-open spaces. Most frequently, the latter were known as *örtme* and *çardak*. Twentieth-century inhabitants of Kayseri use the term *örtme* for a roofed-over veranda. Since the term *çardak* today refers to a trellis for vines, it has been assumed that the *örtme* had a solid roof, like a modern porch, while the *çardak* was covered with either some kind of fabric or else a trellis.[7] Both types of temporary covering can still be observed in the bazaar areas of Turkish cities today. However, the distinction between *çardak* and *örtme* remains somewhat conjectural. Even less clear is the meaning of *sayegah*, or *sayeban*, which literally means 'a shady place' and thus should equally refer to some kind of light and open structure.[8] Certain descriptions specify that the *sayegah* might be situated on top of another room, such as for instance an *örtme*. Among semi-open spaces one might also name the *köşk*, which seems to have been popular, particularly in nineteenth-century Kayseri. In modern parlance, a *köşk* is a kind of garden house. As the term has not been clarified in the documents studied, it can only be assumed that the word was used in a sense not too far removed from the modern one. Rarely we also encounter the term *şahnişin*, which if modern parlance is any guide, should also have been a veranda-like structure usually offering a pleasant view.[9]

Among 'special purpose' rooms one might mention the *matbah* or kitchen, the bathroom (*hamam*),[10] and in Ankara workshops in which mohair was treated (*sof karhanesi*). In a considerable number of cases, these shops contained looms. Therefore, it can be assumed that the workshops in question were not simply places where raw mohair was dried and cleaned, but constituted actual weavers' workshops. Non-Muslim homes, particularly in Kayseri, sometimes possessed a *şırahane*, or room in which grape juice was allowed to ferment until it had turned into wine. Moreover, on many properties some accommodation was provided for animals (*ahır*), often accompanied by a small barn in which to store fodder (*samanlık*). It was a peculiarity of some Kayseri house owners to have special camel stables built on their properties (*develik*). Not that camel caravans were absent from Ankara, but it appears that property owners in that city kept their animals in the surrounding villages, or else stabled them in caravansarays; at any rate, the *develik* as a specialized structure is conspicuously absent from the Ankara records.

The house and its rooms: surviving examples in Ankara

But before embarking on an analysis of the dwellings described in the *kadı* registers it has seemed advisable to interpolate a short discussion of the features which characterize so-called 'traditional' houses as they exist in Ankara and Kayseri today. Certainly from the point of a researcher wishing to study seventeenth-century housing, these buildings present a considerable drawback: namely that, in spite of certain notable exceptions, they are usually difficult to date. Moreover, few of them are older than about a hundred or a hundred and fifty years. Very roughly speaking, we must assume that most of the 'traditional' houses which exist today represent styles of living popular during the late eighteenth, nineteenth, and early twentieth century. This means that we should consider the surviving 'traditional' houses of Ankara and Kayseri as the final results of the developments whose beginnings form the subject of the present study.

Now there is a certain disadvantage in using features of 'traditional' houses to interpret the written sources at hand; we run the risk of glossing over differences from one century to the next, thereby returning to the notion of a more or less immutable 'vernacular architecture' which the present study is particularly trying to demolish. On the other hand, the written sources of the seventeenth century, unsupported by any visual

1. Street scene in the Citadel area of Ankara, the fortification walls in the background. Note the height of the buildings, the corbelling which supports the overhanging second floor, and the prevalence of tiled roofs (Author's photograph).

2. The Citadel area of Ankara. In the foreground a nineteenth-century structure, obviously built for a well-to-do family; recognizable by its balcony, the 'classicist' mouldings over the windows and the generous use of decorative iron grilles (Author's photograph).

evidence, scarcely allow us to visualize the houses in question. To mention just some of the more obvious questions left unanswered: what was the average size of the different rooms making up a dwelling? How were they arranged with respect to each other and to the courtyard? Were all parts of a dwelling generally located under the same roof, or was it customary to construct a number of separate buildings? Under these circumstances, it has seemed indispensable to present the solutions favoured by Ankara's and Kayseri's 'traditional' architecture, so as to allow the reader to at least in part visualize the state of affairs prevailing in Ottoman towns of central Anatolia. But as modern restoration principles with respect to historical buildings require that sections added by the restorer be clearly distinguishable as such, the present section on surviving vernacular architecture has been kept firmly separate from the analysis of the seventeenth-century material.

For Ankara, the study by Eyüp Kömürcüoğlu constitutes a convenient starting point, as this researcher[11] saw old Ankara as it was forty years ago, and was able to study buildings which have since been altered or torn down. In Kömürcüoğlu's view Ankara houses were generally simple in plan, belonging to Types B and C of the typology which Sedad Hakkı Eldem has established for Turkish houses in general.[12] More complicated types, which were popular for instance among the wealthier house-owners of eighteenth- and nineteenth-century İstanbul, could not be found in the provincial environment of Ankara.

3. A half-ruined house in the Ankara Citadel area; note the framework construction, the small top windows, the wooden beams of the ceiling, the overhanging eaves and the use of 'traditional' roof tiles (Author's photograph).

4. A half-ruined house in the Ankara Citadel area: lower walls of rubble supported by beams, upper floor with decorative brickwork (Author's photograph).

5. A modernized house (Ankara, Citadel), the upper windows, have been drastically altered. Note beams supporting the first floor, and the abundance of decorative brickwork (Author's photograph).

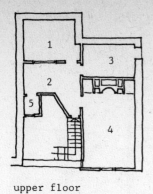
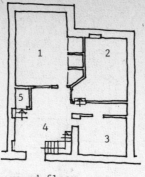

upper floor   ground floor

                               scale: 1:200

3. House in Hamamönü, Ankara, Koyungöz Sok 25 (drawing: Tülay Artan after Kömürcüoğlu, *Ankara Evleri*, p. 35). Ground floor: (1) room (2) room (3) room (4) courtyard (5) toilet. Upper floor: (1) room (2) *sofa* (3) kitchen (4) room (5) toilet.

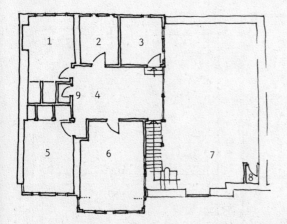

upper floor

scale: 1:200

4. House of Sallantoğlu family, Ankara, Yenice Sok 50 (drawing: Tülay Artan after Kömürcüoğlu, *Ankara Evleri*, p. 37). (1) kitchen (2) room (3) room (4) *sofa* (5) room (6) room (7) courtyard (8) toilet (9) ablutions room.

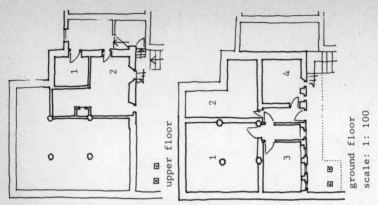

5. House in Erzurum Mahallesi, Ankara, Erzurum Sok 60 (drawing: Tülay Artan after Kömürcüoğlu, *Ankara Evleri*, p. 39). Ground floor (1) stable or cowshed (2) *samanlık* (storage space for fodder) (3) stable or cowshed (4) servant's room. Mezzanine (upper floor) (1) storage room (2) room.

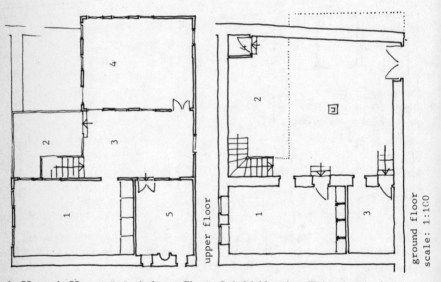

6. House in Hamamönü, Ankara, Cingöz Sok 26 (drawing: Tülay Artan after Kömürcüoğlu, *Ankara Evleri*, p. 48). Ground floor (1) room (2) courtyard (3) room (4) toilet. Upper floor (1) room (2) terrace (2) *sofa* (4) *divan* room.

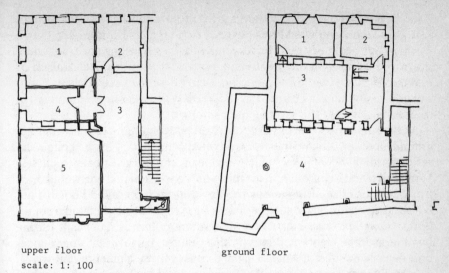

upper floor   ground floor
scale: 1: 100

7. Mansion of Kadınkızızade Müftü Abdülhalim Efendi, Hamamönü, Kadınkızı
Cd., Ankara (drawing: Tülay Artan after Kömürcüoğlu, *Ankara Evleri*, p. 49).
Ground floor (1) *samanlık* storage space for fodder (2) kitchen (3) stable or
cowshed (4) courtyard. Upper floor (1) room (2) kitchen (3) *sofa* (4) room (5)
reception room.

According to Eldem's typology, type B consists of buildings in which all
rooms open onto a hallway or *sofa*, which runs lengthwise along the outer
edge of the house. The rooms may be arranged in a straight line or else in the
shape of an L or a U. In Type C on the other hand, the *sofa* runs through the
middle of the house, receiving its light from windows at one or both ends. At
one end of the *sofa*, near the main window, both Types B and C often
featured a seat, to be reached by a few steps, which in 1940s Ankara was
known as *tahtseki* or *köşk*. This would imply that in the context discussed
here, the *köşk* was not necessarily a freestanding structure, but part of the
main building proper. Kömürcüoğlu describes the typical Ankara house as
consisting of a ground floor and a single upper floor; at least among the
houses examined by him, dwellings with two upper stories seem to have
been somewhat exceptional. In the same way, basements were not a regular
feature of the houses studied by this historian of Ankara's vernacular
architecture; although basements did occur in a number of instances.

Most of Kömürcüoğlu's plans show the existence of separate kitchens on
the ground floor. However, this was by no means an invariable rule: thus the
house in Cingöz Sok 26 (Ankara, Hamamönü) and the more important
residence which at one time had belonged to the Müftü Kadınkızızade
Abdülhalim Efendi (Ankara, Hamamönü, Kadınkızı Cd.)[13] both show a
kitchen (locally called *mutbak*) on the upper floor, complete with built-in
hearth. In the Müftü's residence, there was a second kitchen on the ground

floor, next to the stable or cowshed and the room in which fodder was stored. In this location one would have expected a servant's room rather than a kitchen, but obviously the Müfti's family used its dwelling space in a non-standard manner. On the other hand, none of the residences examined by Kömürcüoğlu was without a room specifically described as a kitchen. This is worth stressing since its equivalent, the *matbah*, was so rarely mentioned in the *kadı* registers of the seventeenth century.

At the same time, the examples studied by Kömürcüoğlu show that the ground floor of Ankara houses was often inhabited – even though the residents might be servants – and by no means entirely given over to stables, barns and storage spaces. At least this is the conclusion that one would draw from the existence of numerous rooms (*oda*) on the ground floors of the houses in question, since storage spaces were generally designated by other terms (*samanlık, kiler* etc.). This observation in turn is significant for the hypothesis to be elaborated later in this chapter, namely that upper floors only became popular in Ankara in the course of the seventeenth century. If, as is sometimes claimed, the inhabitants of 'traditional' Ankara houses had really considered the ground floor as more or less unfit for human habitation, the hypothesis suggested here would appear rather weak. For in such a case, we would need to explain how people in the short span of a century or two, were able to forget that they had ever lived in houses consisting of only a single floor, and it would be much more reasonable to assume that two-storey residences had been popular from time immemorial. But as it stands, no such explanations are needed, and it is easy enough to understand why people, once they had begun to construct upper floors, should have preferred the latter as living spaces.

Unfortunately Kömürcüoğlu's plans contain no information about drains, although many Ankara houses did, at least in the nineteenth century, possess conduits for the evacuation of used water. Neither did the dwellings examined by Kömürcüoğlu possess any visible arrangement for the provision of fresh water, for neither fountain nor well is visible on his plans. Thus if Kömürcüoğlu's plans are complete, one must assume that these houses received all their water by having it carried to the front door, and housewives or else servants must have brought containers of water to the bathrooms (*gusulhane*) which are found in many houses. Given the lack of piped water, it was customary to locate toilet facilities in a separate structure, often at some distance from the main buildings.

The houses analysed by Kömürcüoğlu all show slightly sloping roofs, covered with tiles, although in the dry Ankara climate flat roofs would not have caused any serious problems. As a result, the practice of 'traditional' households of the eighteenth or nineteenth century cannot serve as a guide with respect to the use of roof space in sixteenth century Ankara, where, if Dernschwam's description is at all reliable, such roof space should not have been at all unusual.[14]

Many houses documented in Kömürcüoğlu's book were of substantial size. To cite an example, the house in Göztepe Sok. 27 (Hamamönü, Ankara) consisted of two rooms on the ground floor, two rooms in the mezzanine (one of them explicitly described as a servant's room), and three further rooms on the upper floor. In addition the house possessed a *sofa*, a storage room, a kitchen, a courtyard, two stables or cowsheds, closets in some of the rooms, a bathroom on the first floor with a toilet underneath, and a basement under one wing of the U-shaped building. Rooms were generally about 5–6 metres long, 3–4 metres wide and about 3 metres high. Even larger houses could be found, such as the residence in Erzurum Mahallesi, which had four rooms on the first floor ('*l'étage noble*' with its spacious reception chamber or *divanhane*), apart from the mezzanine and the servant's room on the ground floor. However, it must be kept in mind that large and wealthy houses possessed a better chance of survival than the flimsier structures inhabited by the poor. Moreover, for an architectural historian, these larger and more elaborate dwellings present many more features of interest, so that it would not be reasonable to draw conclusions from Kömürcüoğlu's sample with respect to the size of eighteenth- or nineteenth-century Ankara houses in general.

The house and its rooms: surviving examples in Kayseri

For Kayseri, discussion of surviving 'traditional' houses is based upon the monograph by Necibe Çakıroğlu, who completed her research in 1951–2.[15] Here we are fortunate in possessing several houses that can be dated with more precision than the 'traditional' houses of Ankara: in the *sofa* of the residence built for the Zennecioğulları family, N. Çakıroğlu found an inscription bearing the date 1001/1593.[16] The Mollaoğulları family's dwelling also features an inscription, which establishes that the main section of this dwelling was built in 1198/1784.[17] Only the most famous of Kayseri's wealthy residences, the Gübgüboğulları mansion, possesses no inscription and must be dated by stylistic criteria alone. Necibe Çakıroğlu assumes that the oldest parts were constructed between 1419 and 1497.[18] However, both the Gübgüboğulları and the Zennecioğulları residences were much altered in the eighteenth century, so much so that certain authors have regarded these structures as eighteenth-century buildings. In addition, N. Çakıroğlu's study also includes some smaller, anonymous houses. But as even these more modest structures feature an upper floor and a considerable number of decorative elements, they must have belonged to families of at least moderate wealth.[19]

In their present shape the wealthy residences of Kayseri show a much clearer division into *harem* (family dwelling) and *selamlık* (room for male visitors) than could be observed in Ankara.[20] From the Ankara plans it is often not clearly apparent which of the larger rooms was used as the *selamlık*, since the upper storey was usually accessible only by a single staircase. This was true even of a wealthy residence such as the Kadınkızızade house previously mentioned. On the other hand, wealthy families in Kayseri preferred to construct two totally separate buildings. These might communicate by means of a hall, such as was the case in the Zennecioğulları residence, or else might be accessible only by passing through a courtyard. Moreover, the arrangement of the *sofa* differed from the setup encountered in Ankara. The *sofa* was centrally located, as would be expected in a 'Type C' plan, but instead of cutting all the way through the dwelling, it extended only to about half the width of the house, so that the rooms were arranged around this relatively short rectangle in the shape of a U. Eldem considers this arrangement as a subtype of Type B, since the *sofa* does not touch both the front and back walls of the building.[21] A similar arrangement could be observed not only in the mansions, but also in the smaller Kayseri houses. Thus, if Necibe Çakıroğlu's sample is reasonably characteristic in this respect, this subtype of Type B ('outside *sofa* surrounded by rooms on three sides') would seem to have been a favourite arrangement among Kayseri builders throughout the ages.

In the mansions of the wealthy families of Kayseri, the *köşk* constituted a separate structure, not just a raised seat near a window as seems to have been usual in 'traditional' houses of Ankara. In the Gübgüboğulları residence, the *köşk* takes the shape of an open veranda facing the courtyard, while it is bordered on one side by the wall surrounding the entire property and on the other by the *harem*, with which it communicates. In the Zennecioğulları mansion, the *köşk* again faces the courtyard, but one side is adjacent to the *selamlık*; however, the *köşk* is not accessible from the latter, but has to be entered from the hall which in this case connects the *harem* and *selamlık* divisions. In the Mollaoğulları house, the arrangement resembles that which has been observed in the Gübgüboğulları mansion. However, in the dwelling described only as 'the house of Nihat Aslandağ', of uncertain age but considerable architectural elaboration, the *köşk* constitutes an integral part of the *selamlık* and is accessible only once one has entered the latter building. Even the courtyard which it faces is separated by a wall from the larger courtyard associated with the *harem*. In the smaller houses published by N. Çakıroğlu, a *köşk* was usually lacking. In the one instance where it was present, it served as a hallway providing access to rooms and a staircase, thereby resembling to a degree the 'raised seat' *köşk* which was found in the *sofa*s of certain Ankara houses.[22]

Just as in Ankara, basements were by no means universal, and even in those dwellings in which they were present, only one wing might be constructed over a basement. On the other hand, the Kayseri residences differed from their Ankara counterparts by the prominent place accorded the kitchen or *togana*. While in Ankara it was usual to tuck the kitchen away in a more or less unobtrusive corner, in the Gübgüboğulları *harem* building

6. Kayseri: General view (Deliklitaş Mahalle). Note the prevalence of flat roofs, houses consisting of either one or two floors (Photograph: Latife Bayraktar).

7. In the old non-Muslim quarter of Tavukçu (Kayseri): niches serving both for storage and as a decoration in the reception room or *başoda* (Photograph: Latife Bayraktar).

8. Corbelling supports an upper floor in the so-called 'Goldsmith's house'
(*Kuyumcunun evi*) (Photograph: Latife Bayraktar).

9. Carefully cut stone gives this house in Tavukçu quarter its decorative quality.
The ironwork is a nineteenth-century feature (Photograph: Latife Bayraktar).

10. A view of the Gübgüboğulları residence. While its core goes back to the fifteenth and sixteenth centuries, the building has been many times altered and repaired (Photograph: Latife Bayraktar).

the *togana* along with the *sofa*, constitutes the largest room of the building. In the Zennecioğulları residence as well, the *togana* was assigned a good-sized room. One feels reminded of the monumental emphasis placed upon the kitchen in the Sultan's Palace, or in certain major *zaviye*s like Seyyid Gazi (near Eskişehir) or Hacı Bektaş (between Ankara and Kayseri). Possibly the kitchen – and the food prepared in it – were viewed as symbols of hospitality, which the more important Kayseri families felt bound to exhibit as a symbol of grandeur; *noblesse oblige*. But that still does not explain why, in Ankara similar notions of hospitality do not seem to have resulted in equally prominent kitchens.

Among the small houses published by Necibe Çakiroğlu, two are particularly remarkable, for they assign the upper floor to the *selamlık*, the lower floor to the *harem*, thereby showing again that in central Anatolia the ground floor was often inhabited, not only by servants, but even by members of the family. In this case, the *harem* section was pared down to the bare essentials: apart from the courtyard, it consisted of a *sofa*, a kitchen, possibly a hallway, storage spaces and a detached toilet in the yard. The more 'residential' part of the house was thus entirely located in the *selamlık*.[23] It would be interesting to know whether this arrangement was a common one among Kayseri houses in general. Unfortunately N. Çakiroğlu's publication provides no clue in this respect.

As to matters related to the water supply, N. Çakıroğlu's study is somewhat more informative than Kömürcüoğlu's.[24] Kayseri residents received their water from two sources. Water conduits, the oldest of which dated from the Seljuk period, brought drinking water to the public fountains of the city: in addition, most houses possessed their own wells, which might supply drinking water if dug deeply enough; otherwise well water was used only for cleaning. Moreover given the vicinity of the Erciyes dağı, many households kept themselves supplied with snow brought down from the mountain, while others stored the winter snow which fell into their courtyard in special icehouses for use during the summer. In the vineyard areas, it was customary to build water reservoirs which supplied residents with water when they spent the hot season in summer houses outside of the city. Disposal of waste water – and sewage from the detached toilets usually located in backyards – was a more serious problem, since the perfectly flat land on which Kayseri was built made the construction of a proper canalization system difficult. Foreign observers in the nineteenth and early twentieth centuries occasionally commented upon the dirtiness of the streets.[25] Even so, however, Kayseri was considered a healthy place, probably because prolonged winter cold and the dispersal of many townsmen during the summer months limited the spread of epidemic diseases.

The houses published by N. Çakıroğlu all had flat roofs covered with a layer of earth;[26] as A. Gabriel has already remarked,[27] Evliya's claim that Kayseri houses were covered with tiled roofs should be regarded wth a good bit of scepticism. From the very few lines that N. Çakıroğlu devotes to the roofs it is not possible to guess what the rooftops were used for, if indeed they were used for anything. But it is probable that the author would have mentioned any specific functions the rooftop terraces may have had in the lives of Kayseri families during the 1940s, and in the absence of any such information, we may assume that their functions were not very vital. Whether the situation was any different in the seventeenth century is of course impossible to determine.

Several of the Kayseri residences analysed in N. Çakıroğlu's study are expressly described as 'large-scale houses'; if anything they are even less typical of the ordinary family dwelling than their Ankara counterparts. Unfortunately most of the house plans given do not contain any indications as to scale. However, it would appear that the *sofa* of the Gübgüboğulları, famous for its sumptuous decoration, was a large-scale structure, about 12 metres long, 7 metres wide and 8.6 metres high – and the other major rooms of this residence were of a size to match. Even the Nihat Aslandağ house, which was a much less monumental structure, contained a room for male visitors (*şelamlık*) which was 8.8 metres long and 5 metres wide. When discussing urban houses in general, N. Çakıroğlu describes a *sofa* of 7–7.5 metres length and 4–5 metres width as normal.[28] In the smaller houses published by her we do in fact find *sofa*s of the size indicated. But it must be kept in mind that these 'small houses' were small only if compared to

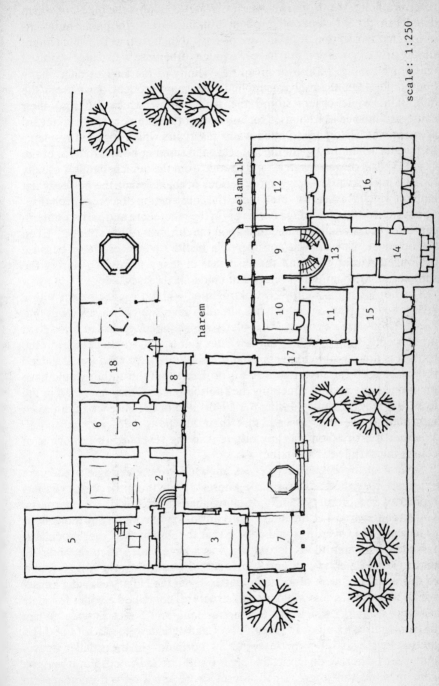

9. Mollaoğulları mansion (drawing: Tülay Artan after Çakıroğlu, *Kayseri Evleri*, p. 34–35). (1) *sofa* (2) *harem* room (3) room (4) *toğana* (kitchen) (5) store room (6) store room (7) *köşk* (8) toilet (9) *selamlık* (entrance hall) (10) *selamlık* room (11) *hamam* (12) reception room (13) service hall (14) room for the preparation of coffee (15) stable or cowshed (16) stable or cowshed (17) passage (18) *köşk*.

scale: 1:250

selamlık

harem

84

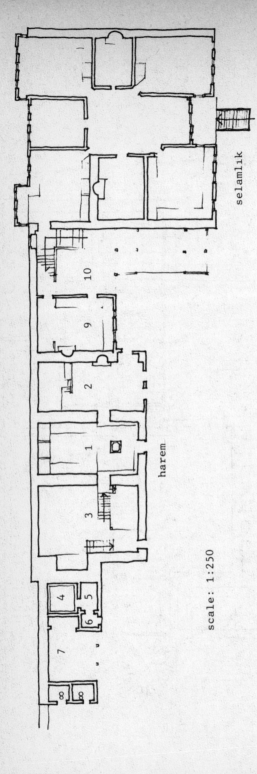

10. Zennecioğulları mansion (drawing: Tülay Artan after Çakıroğlu, *Kayseri Evleri*, p. 30). (1) *sofa* (2) *harem* room (3) *togana* (kitchen) (4) *hamam* (5) vestibule of *hamam* (6) anteroom (7) summer kitchen (8) toilet (9) guest room (10) hall leading to staircase (11) *köşk*.

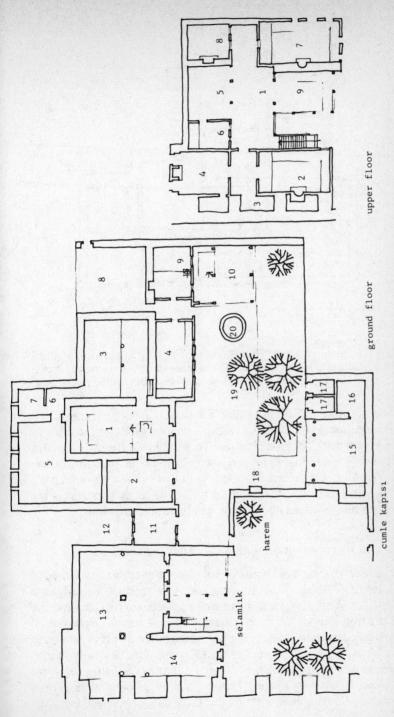

ground floor

upper floor

cumle kapısı

harem

selamlik

11. Gübgüboğulları mansion, ground floor (drawing: Tülay Artan after Çakıroğlu, *Kayseri Evleri*, p. 25). (1) *sofa* (2) *harem* room (3) *togana* (kitchen) (4) guest room (5) storeroom (6) passageway (7) servant's room (8) courtyard (9) room for the preparation of coffee (10) *köşk* (11) *hamam* room (12) *hamam* room (13) stable or cowshed (14) *samanlık* (storage space for fodder) (15) summer kitchen (16) woodshed (17) toilet (18) fountain (19) fountain (20) decorative pond.

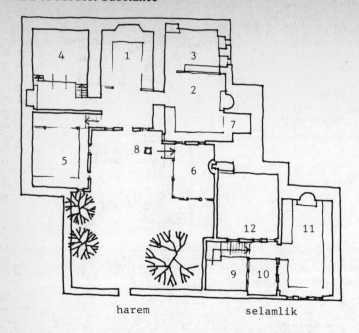

scale: 1:250

12. Gübüboğulları mansion, upper floor (drawing: Tülay Artan after Čakıroğlu, *Kayseri Evleri*, p. 25). (1) hall (2) *salamlik* (3) ablution room (4) *togana* (kitchen) (5) service hall (6) servant's room (7) reception room (8) room for the preparation of coffee (9) *köşk*.

structures the size of the Gübgüboğulları mansion. Under what conditions the really poor people may have lived cannot be understood from an analysis of published 'traditional' Kayseri houses. To paraphrase Brecht's remark, at present we know nothing about the homes of the construction workers who built the Gübgüboğulları mansion.[29] But we ought to search all available historical records – *kadı* registers included – so that one day in the not too remote future we may be able to supply this information.

The house and its rooms according to the *kadı* registers

In order to assess what kinds of houses were most frequently represented in sevententh-century Ankara and Kayseri, we now turn to the evidence provided by the *kadı* registers. It seems practical to first review the frequency distributions of the more current types of rooms. Now not all documents studied contain a full description of the house involved, although fortunately for us, most of them do. Moreover, some of the descriptions may be incomplete. When only a share of a given house was being sold, this incompleteness is easy to detect. However, it is possible that certain descriptions were incomplete without the facts being apparent from the

Table 1. *Distribution of* tabhane[1]

(1)	(2)	(3)	(4)	(5)	(6)	(7)
		Houses with		Number of *tabhanes* recorded		
	None	1 or more				
Location	(unknown)	*tabhanes*	Total	1	2	3
Ankara, c. 1600	122 (35.7%)	220 (64.3%)	342	192 (87.3%)	24 (10.9%)	4 (1.8%)
Kayseri, c. 1600	57 (24.2%)	179 (75.8%)	236	159 (88.8%)	19 (10.6%)	1 (0.6%)
Ankara, c. 1690	64 (22.1%)	226 (78.2%)	289	179 (79.2%)	44 (19.5%)	3 (1.3%)
Kayseri, c. 1690	39 (13.8%)	244 (86.2%)	283	210 (86.1%)	32 (13.1%)	2 (0.8%)

[1] In the last three columns (Number of *tabhanes* recorded) percentages are based upon the figure given in column no 3 (Houses with 1 or more *tabhanes*).

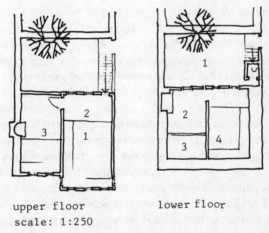

upper floor
scale: 1:250

lower floor

13. Aslandağ house (drawing: Tülay Artan after Çakıroğlu, *Kayseri Evleri*, p. 37). (1) *sofa* (2) *harem* room (3) storage room (4) *togana* (kitchen) (5) room (6) *köşk* (7) *hamam* (8) storage space for snow (9) *selamlık* courtyard (10) *köşk*)11) *selamlık* room (12) *togana* (kitchen).

documents available for our inspection. While this state of affairs may have been the source of a few errors, it appears probable that the vast majority of all descriptions was in fact complete, and the margin of error thus introduced should not be of very great importance.

As Table 1 shows, both in Ankara and in Kayseri the number of *tabhane* was definitely increasing throughout the seventeenth century. In part, this may be due to the fact that descriptions were generally made with more care

Table 2. *Distribution of* sofa[1]

(1)	(2)	(3)	(4)	(5)	(6)	(7)
	None	Houses with 1 or more		Number of *sofa*s recorded		
Location	(unknown)	*sofa*s	Total	1	2	3
Ankara, c. 1600	190 (55.6%)	152 (44.4%)	342	147 (96.7%)	4 (2.6%)	1 (0.7%)
Kayseri, c. 1600	75 (31.8%)	161 (68.2%)	236	158 (98.1%)	3 (1.9%)	0
Ankara, c. 1690	193 (66.8%)	96 (33.2%)	289	94 (97.9%)	1 (1.0%)	1 (1.0%)
Kayseri, c. 1690	74 (26.1%)	209 (73.9%)	283	202 (96.7%)	7 (3.3%)	0

[1] In the last three columns (Number of *sofa*s recorded) percentages are based upon the figure given in column no 3 (Houses with 1 or more *sofa*s).

at the end of seventeenth century than had been the case a hundred years earlier. However, this state of affairs can probably account for only a small part of the increase. For while the number of houses with one or two *tabhane* grew, there was no significant change where the largest houses (with 3 *tabhane*s) were concerned. If the entire increase were due to a declining number of incomplete descriptions, one would have expected all categories to grow, apart of course from the category labelled 'none/unknown'.[30] Moreover, Ankara and Kayseri showed a consistently different pattern: both at the beginning of the seventeenth century and at its end, the percentage of houses without a *tabhane* was much lower in Ankara than in Kayseri. This consistency also indicates that the differences between the two cities were real, and not simply due to more or less accurate recording. The distribution of *tabhane*s thus observed makes it quite clear that this latter type of room was an essential part of both Ankara and Kayseri houses. Particularly toward the end of the seventeenth century, the dwelling that did not possess a *tabhane* was definitely an anomalous case.

*Sofa*s differed from *tabhane*s in that throughout the seventeenth century, the *sofa* was always much less popular than the *tabhane*.[31] In Ankara at the end of the sixteenth and at the beginning of the seventeenth century, not even one-half of all houses was reported to possess this type of room. Moreover, in this instance, faulty recording cannot explain the relative rarity of *sofa*s. For in absolute terms, the number of houses without *sofa*s remained remarkably constant throughout the seventeenth century, both in Ankara and in Kayseri. In the case of Ankara this fact resulted in a percentual increase of *sofa*-less houses, while in Kayseri houses without any *sofa*s at all became relatively rare. Since *tabhane*s and *sofa*s thus evolved in a somewhat different fashion, the reliability of our figures receives a most welcome confirmation. Because if the distortion due to incomplete descriptions had been very great, the number of both *tabhane*s and *sofa*s should have tended to increase throughout the period under study, not only in Kayseri but also in Ankara.

As to the ordinary room without any special properties, Table 3 shows that it was a more frequent phenomenon in Ankara than in Kayseri. While one-half of Ankara's houses at the beginning of the seventeenth century possessed one or more rooms described as *oda*, only slightly over a quarter of all Kayseri houses were in this position. Moreover, even after the share of houses with at least one *oda* had appreciably increased in the course of the seventeenth century, only forty per cent of all Kayseri houses had come to possess an *oda* around 1690. It is possible that the greater frequency of *tabhane* and *sofa* in Kayseri is connected with the rarity of *oda*. If differences in locally used terminology are not leading us astray, the inhabitants of Ankara should have favoured a set-up in which the *tabhane* was supplemented by an ordinary *oda*, while in Kayseri, the *sofa* was the preferred living space.

When analysing the figures contained in Table 4 concerning the number of inhabitable spaces, the first category (none/unknown) must obviously be left out of consideration, since houses without inhabitable space were either houses that had not been described at all, or else dwellings whose description was incomplete. Therefore, in this particular case, percentage values have been computed not on the basis of all recorded cases, but upon the total of houses containing at least one room that could be inhabited year-round. A glance at Table 4 and the accompanying diagram shows that throughout the seventeenth century, houses with two permanently lived-in rooms were by far the most popular type. One-room houses were much less frequently represented. But it must be kept in mind that the owners of the smallest houses were also the people who were least likely to go to the *kadı*'s office to have their sale and inheritance transactions recorded. Thus it is probable that in a real-life neighbourhood of seventeenth-century Ankara or Kayseri, the share of one-room dwellings was higher than it appears from Table 4. We gain the impression that the share of one-room houses was consistently somewhat lower in Ankara than in Kayseri. But at the present state of our knowledge, it is not easy to propose a convincing explanation for this phenomenon.

At the same time, it appears that dwellings containing three to five rooms which could be inhabited year-round became more popular in the course of the century. This applies to both Ankara and Kayseri, although local peculiarities can also be observed: in late sixteenth- and early seventeenth-century Ankara, three-room dwellings had already become quite common, more widespread than in Kayseri during the same period. While the share of two-room dwellings declined in Ankara, that of four-room dwellings

Table 3. *Distribution of oda*[1]

(1)	(2)	(3)	(4)	(5)	(6)	(7)	(8)	(9)	(10)	(11)	(12)
Location	None (unknown)	Houses with 1 or more *odas*	Total	1	2	3	4	5	6	7	At least 12
Ankara, c. 1600	172 (50.3%)	170 (49.7%)	342	119 (70%)	37 (21.8%)	6 (3.5%)	5 (2.9%)	0	2 (1.2%)	1 (0.6%)	0
Kayseri, c. 1600	173 (73.3%)	63 (26.7%)	236	50 (79.3%)	10 (15.9%)	2 (3.2%)	1 (1.6%)	0	0	0	0
Ankara, c. 1690	80 (27.7%)	209 (72.3%)	289	97 (46.4%)	68 (32.5%)	30 (14.4%)	7 (3.3%)	3 (1.4%)	4 (1.9%)	0	0
Kayseri, c. 1690	169 (59.7%)	114 (40.3%)	283	97 (85.1%)	13 (11.4%)	2 (1.8%)	1 (0.9%)	0	0	0	1 (0.9%)

[1] In the last eight columns (Number of *odas* recorded) percentages are based upon the figure given in column no (3) (Houses with 1 or more *odas*).

Table 4. *Distribution of inhabitable spaces (tabhane, sofa, oda, divanhane, selamlık, harem)*[1]

(1)	(2)	(3)	(4)	(5)	(6)	(7)	(8)	(9)	(10)	(11)	(12)	(13)	(14)
		Number of inhabitable spaces recorded											
	None (unknown)	1	2	3	4	5	6	7	8	9	At least 15	Total usable descriptions	Grand total
Location													
Ankara, c. 1600	100	34 (14.0%)	101 (41.7%)	66 (27.3%)	25 (10.3%)	7 (2.9%)	4 (1.7%)	1 (0.4%)	2 (0.8%)	2 (0.8%)	0	242	342
Kayseri, c. 1600	44	33 (7.2%)	102 (53.1%)	38 (19.8%)	14 (7.3%)	2 (1.0%)	3 (1.6%)	0	0	0	0	192	236
Ankara, c. 1690	32	29 (11.3%)	87 (33.8%)	71 (27.6%)	36 (14.0%)	17 (6.6%)	10 (3.9%)	4 (1.6%)	0	3 (1.2%)	0	257	289
Kayseri, c. 1690	24	42 (16.2%)	110 (42.5%)	73 (28.2%)	23 (8.9%)	9 (3.5%)	1 (0.4%)	0	0	0	1 (0.4%)	259	283

[1] In this table, percentages have been based not upon the Grand total, but upon the Total of usable descriptions.

91

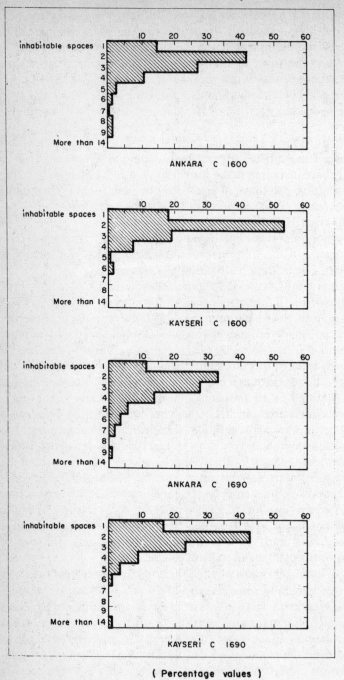

(Percentage values)

1. Frequency distribution of inhabitable spaces

increased, resulting in a frequency histogram of fairly 'squat' appearance. Three-room dwellings, and to a lesser degree, houses containing four rooms, also grew more frequent in seventeenth century Kayseri. However, Kayseri remained the town of the two-room house *par excellence*, and therefore all that one can say is that the diagram became less 'needle-like' in shape as time passed by. Smaller houses, containing only *tabhane* and *sofa*, seem to have been characteristic of the Kayseri townscape of the seventeenth century.

Houses of five and more rooms that could be lived in throughout the year appear to have been rather a luxury. More common in Ankara than in Kayseri, their share increased in the former town, so that by the end of the seventeenth century, dwellings of five or more permanently inhabitable rooms had reached the quite respectable level of 13.3 per cent.

Remarkably enough, however, the one and only dwelling which reached palatial proportions stood not in Ankara but in Kayseri.[32] This impressive *konak* was located in the Lala *mahalle*, and belonged to the family of Mehmed Bey b. Hasan Paşa b. Ibrahim Ağa. Hasan Paşa had moved to İstanbul, and the family possessed another house in the Ottoman capital. The total value of the Kayseri residence is not known, but since a share amounting to only about 17.1 per cent was sold for the rather impressive sum of 632.5 *guruş*, one might estimate that the house would have sold for more than 3,000 *guruş* if it had come up for sale in its entirety. In the interior courtyard stood, among other structures, a main hall (*kebir sofa*) and a hall which could also be regarded as a porch. There was no *tabhane* in the inner courtyard – although in all probability one of the rooms in the outer courtyard may be regarded as such. On the other hand, the main living space of the inner courtyard was apparently a room known as the *harem odası*. The existence of such a room should probably be regarded as a sign of luxury and Istanbul fashion, for the term is otherwise rare in the Kayseri records of the seventeenth century, and totally absent in Ankara.[33] In the outer courtyard, there were 12 rooms on the first floor, 4 janitors' rooms which may or may not have been used as dwelling places for servants, apart from 5 *oda* whose exact location could not be established. Even by the most conservative estimate, this *konak* must have contained 15 permanently inhabitable rooms, and upwards of 20 seems to be even more probable.[34]

It would be of interest to know whether the houses of seventeenth-century central Anatolia generally consisted of only a ground floor, or whether Ankara and Kayseri in the 1600s possessed a significant number of buildings several stories high. For in the nineteenth and early twentieth centuries, the vernacular architecture of these two cities was characterized by buildings of several stories, with the ground floor if at all possible, used mainly for non-residential purposes.[35] To answer this question, our only evidence consists of the fact that the documents occasionally refer to such and such a room as being located on top of another (*fevkanî*). In general, no explicit reference is made to houses of three floors and more, although it is of course possible that the very vague term *fevkanî* was used to cover these higher buildings as well. In Ankara, upper floors of all kinds were much more popular than in Kayseri: in the early 1600s 36 dwellings (or 10.5 per cent of all houses referred to in the documents) possessed at least one room that was situated on an upper floor. Towards the end of the seventeenth century, this figure had jumped to 152 (52.6 per cent of all recorded dwellings). On the other hand, structures with an upper floor seem to have been almost non-existent in Kayseri during the early 1600s; no more than 4 cases are recorded (1.7 per cent). In the course of the seventeenth century, dwellings with at least one room described as *fevkanî* increased in Kayseri as well, and in the 1690s, slightly over 10 per cent of all houses fell into this category. But even so, no more than 30 Kayseri dwellings definitely possessed an upper floor. Rooms described as *fevkanî* were only in rare instances *tabhane* or *sofa*; more commonly, an *oda* or a semi-open structure of some sort (*örtme*, etc.) was located on the upper level. In some cases, the space below the *örtme* was described as a stable or cowshed;[36] perhaps this state of affairs indicates a stage in the process by which the upper floor was turned into the main living space.

It is of course somewhat risky to sketch the development of Anatolian domestic architecture on the basis of the ambiguous evidence outlined above. But it does appear probable that buildings of more than one floor grew to be more common as the seventeenth century wore on. Even so, it is unlikely that, at least in ordinary houses of Ankara and Kayseri during this period, the main residential area was already located on the first floor, as was to be the case in later periods. More probably, the latter was used as a semi-open space inhabited only during the summer months. If this assumption is at all valid, the type of house which still survives in places like the citadel (*kale*) area of old Ankara must have become dominant not too long ago, most probably in the eighteenth century. It is possible that the trend towards houses with more living space led to an increasing popularity of dwellings with upper floors. According to a picture showing Ankara in the years around 1700, all houses were contained in the walled-up area, and thus the space available for residential expansion was probably limited.[37] One might also consider the influence of İstanbul or Bursa houses, for Ankara constituted a trading centre of some importance. Thus it is probable that well-to-do merchants imitated the houses which they saw in the Ottomon capital. But those Ankara dwellings which may contain seventeenth century elements have been so much changed in later periods as to be virtually unrecognizable, and therefore nothing definite can be said in this respect.

Semi-open spaces

Verandas and other porch-like spaces seem to have been so popular among the inhabitants of seventeenth century Ankara and Kayseri that they deserve a separate study. The *örtme* was apparently the most frequently represented type. In the closing years of the sixteenth and the beginning years of the seventeenth century, 14.6 per cent of all Ankara dwellings covered by the documentation at hand possessed one or two *örtme*s; by the end of the century, this figure had increased to 24.1 per cent. Much more dramatic was the increase in Kayseri, where the percentage of houses with *örtme*s increased from 17.8 to 56.6 per cent. At the same time, there was an appreciable increase in the number of *sayegah*s: from 12.8 per cent, the Ankara figure jumped to 37.2 per cent. In Kayseri, *sayegah*s were apparently less popular, but even so, they increased from 4.2 to 13.5 per cent. Only the *çardak* stagnated in Kayseri and declined in Ankara, but in fact, this may have been part of the general trend toward larger and more elaborate houses, if it is true that the *çardak* is the most temporary and least elaborate of all the semi-open spaces documented.[38] At the same time, the decline of the *çardak* in Ankara again confirms the at least relative reliability of our documentation; if all the increases observed had simply been due to improved recording techniques, the number of *çardak* should have grown along with the rest (compare Table 5).

Thus, it appears that the trend towards a larger number of permanently inhabitable rooms was accompanied by an increase in the number of seasonably usable spaces. Altogether, this indicates more elaborate and comfortable houses, and it might be suspected that more time and effort was spent upon internal decoration as well. However, the latter aspect of domestic architecture has unfortunately been totally neglected by the *kadı*s and their scribes, so that nothing is known about lattice work on windows and porches, decorated doorways, and the various other features that so enhance the decorative qualities of traditional Turkish houses.

Rooms serving special purposes

While it is well known that in the traditional Anatolian house eating and sleeping were not assigned to any specific rooms, many of the more elaborate dwellings of seventeenth-century Ankara and Kayseri contained one or two rooms particularly set aside for special purposes, such as the storage of foodstuffs, and occasionally for cooking or washing. It is rather surprising that the *kadı* registers contain so few references to kitchens; the only place where they were at all common was late-seventeenth-century Ankara. One may of course assume that the existence of a kitchen was automatically assumed, and therefore often omitted from the scribes' descriptions. At the same time, this explanation is not very satisfying, since at least the houses of Kayseri featured kitchens that were large and located in places where they were immediately visible, and it is hard to believe that such a prominent part of the house was easily ignored. Or should one assume that cooking was done in the *tabhane*? But while a combination of cooking and living facilities was frequent enough in northwestern Europe, the houses

Table 5. Distribution of semi-open spaces

(1)	(2)	(3)	(4)	(5)	(6)	(7)	(8)	(9)	(10)	(11)	(12)
	Number of semi-open spaces recorded										Total of all houses documented
	Örtme			Çardak		Şahnişin		Sayegah			
Location	1	2	3	1	2	1	2	1	2	3	
Ankara, c. 1600	48 (14.0%)	2 (0.6%)	0	28 (8.2%)	0	0	1 (0.3%)	37 (10.8%)	7 (2.0%)	0	342
Kayseri, c. 1600	36 (15.3%)	6 (2.5%)	0	11 (4.7%)	1 (0.4%)	1 (0.4%)	0	9 (3.8%)	1 (0.4%)	0	236
Ankara, c. 1690	65 (22.5%)	4 (1.4%)	0	0	0	6 (2.1%)	0	97 (33.6%)	11 (3.8%)	3 (1.0%)	289
Kayseri, c. 1690	142 (50.2%)	18 (6.4%)	1 (0.4%)	11 (3.9%)	1 (0.4%)	0	0	37 (13.1%)	1 (0.4%)	0	283

of central Anatolia as they survive today generally show a kitchen that is separate from the main 'living and reception room'. Thus it is unclear how the lack of reference to kitchen facilities in the *kadı* registers should be interpreted. But if it is necessary to choose between two evils, the assumption that the *kadı*'s scribes frequently omitted kitchens from their enumerations does seem to create fewer problems than a hypothetical combination of kitchen and reception room in seventeenth century dwellings. Perhaps future researchers will be able to clear up the mystery . . .

Such as they are, the data concerning kitchens (see Table 6) allow us to clarify certain observations made by Necibe Çakıroğlu in her monograph on old Kayseri houses. The author commented upon the existence, in some of the buildings studied by her, of separate kitchens for summer and winter use.[39] She also remarks that at the time of observation, the 'summer kitchens' were falling into disuse because families preferred to spend the summer in their gardens and vineyards. From this evidence, N. Çakıroğlu arrives at the conclusion that semi-open air kitchens for summer use must have become popular at a time when chronic insecurity made prolonged visits to the open countryside inadvisable.

In fact, the rise and decline of the 'summer kitchen' can probably be dated somewhat more precisely than N. Çakıroğlu was able to do, for apart from oral information she had to rely almost exclusively upon the evidence provided by the buildings themselves. However, from written sources we know that even in the second half of the sixteenth century, the inhabitants of certain towns in the eastern part of central Anatolia used to spend their summers in gardens and vineyards some distance away from their winter habitations.[40] Obviously, the possibility of attack by roving Celâlî bands must only have deterred the townsmen during certain especially difficult years. With respect to the Kayseri area, seventeenth-century records show that quite a few gardens and vineyards contained a more or less solidly constructed building (*bağ evi*), so that the tradition of *villegiatura* in this particular part of the country can be traced back at least to the seventeenth and probably even to the sixteenth century.

Even so, N. Çakıroğlu's argument remains valid, provided the case is not overstated. We may assume that from the second half of the nineteenth century onwards, the countryside was calm enough that many families began to spend the summer out-of-town, and that therefore the construction of summer kitchens was given up. On the other hand, separate kitchens of any kind were rarely referred to in Kayseri court registers of the 1690s, and one would assume that double kitchens would have been too notable a feature to escape the attention of the *kadı*'s scribes. If these assumptions are at all realistic, one could risk the conclusion that the 'summer kitchen' must have become fashionable during the hundred-and-fifty years between 1700 and 1850.

More common were records showing a storage room for foodstuffs (*kiler*).

Table 6. *Distribution of kitchens (matbah), pantries (kiler), ovens (fırın), and wells (kuyu)*

(1)	(2)	(3)	(4)	(5)	(6)	(7)	(8)	(9)	(10)
	Number of kitchens, pantries, ovens, wells recorded								Total of all houses documented
	Kitchens	Pantries			Ovens		Wells		
Location	1	1	2	3	1	2	1	2	
Ankara, c. 1600	2 (0.6%)	26 (7.6%)	0	0	18 (5.3%)	1 (0.3%)	10 (2.9%)	2 (0.6%)	342
Kayseri, c. 1600	0	16 (6.8%)	1 (0.4%)	1 (0.4%)	0	0	31 (13.1%)	1 (0.4%)	236
Ankara, c. 1690	10 (3.5%)	57 (19.7%)	0	0	5 (1.7%)	2 (0.7%)	21 (7.3%)	1 (0.3%)	289
Kayseri, c. 1690	5 (1.8%)	37 (13.1%)	2 (0.7%)	0	0	0	105 (37.1%)	2 (0.7%)	283

This is easily explained if we remember that many townsmen had access to a garden or vineyard, and thus stored raisins, grape syrup, and other food-stuffs for winter consumption. Here again, Ankara led the way: while in the years around 1600, 7.6 per cent of all documented dwellings were provided with a storage room, by the end of the century the relevant percentage had risen to 19.7 per cent. In Kayseri the rise was less dramatic, and the number of dwellings provided with a separate *kiler* increased from 7.6 to only 13.1 per cent. But even in this latter town, the number of homes with a *kiler* almost doubled (see Table 6).

Difficult to explain is the fact that baking ovens, a notable feature of Ankara houses, lost popularity in the course of the seventeenth century (from 5.5 to 2.4 per cent of all dwellings investigated). Two alternatives present themselves: perhaps the inhabitants of Ankara followed the exam-ple of the countrymen who baked their bread in the ashes of an open fire. One must assume that this was the normal practice in Kayseri, for there baking ovens in private houses were not observed throughout the seven-teenth century. But it is also possible that commercial baking of bread in baker's ovens,[41] which is well attested for the second half of the sixteenth century, expanded to a degree that households which had previously prepared their bread at home now increasingly had recourse to the com-mercial baker.

The greater frequency of wells in private households of Kayseri has mainly to do with the configuration of the terrain. No water can be found on Ankara's citadel hill, and well into the twentieth century, the inhabitants of the upper town quarters had their water carried up on the backs of donkeys. Thus, the increase of private wells in the city of Ankara presumably reflects a growing popularity of the lower-lying town quarters. Since at least part of this area was included in the city walls of the early seventeenth century, there is nothing inherently implausible about such a development. At the same time, the extension of private wells in seventeenth-century Kayseri constitutes a truly remarkable phenomenon. Almost 40 per cent of all houses documented in the 1690s possessed a private water supply, and it may be assumed that this fact contributed to the city's reputation of being a healthy place to live in.[42]

Since donkeys, horses and other animals were indispensable for seven-teenth-century transportation, it is not surprising that many houses should have possessed accommodation for them. Unfortunately, the term *ahır* is very broad in scope and permits no conclusions concerning the kinds of animals that were being kept. In this sector, Kayseri had a clear lead over Ankara, which it did not lose throughout the seventeenth century. By the late 1690s, more than half of all dwellings documented in the Kayseri *kadı* registers possessed at least one *ahır*. One might feel tempted to speculate that Kayseri was somewhat more of a local marketing centre than Ankara with its strong interregional and even international trade. In this case, the

Table 7. *Distribution of stables, cowsheds* (ahır), *and barns* (samanlık)[1]

(1)	(2)	(3)	(4)	(5)	(6)	(7)	(8)	(9)
	Ahır[2]			Total of houses	Samanlık[3]		Total of houses with	Total number of houses
Location	1	2	3	with ahır	1	2	samanlık	documented
Ankara, c. 1600	92 (92.9%)	6 (6.1%)	1 (1.0%)	99	3 (100%)	0	3	342
Kayseri, c. 1600	85 (96.6%)	3 (3.4%)	0	88	7 (100%)	0	7	236
Ankara, c. 1690	101 (99.0%)	1 (1.0%)	0	102	17 (100%)	0	17	289
Kayseri, c. 1690	140 (90.3%)	13 (8.3%)	2 (1.3%)	155	38 (97.4%)	1 (2.5%)	39	283

[1] Percentages have been calculated: for columns 2, 3, 4 (*ahır*) on the basis of column 5 (Total of houses with *ahır*); for columns 6, 7 (*samanlık*) on the basis of column 8 (Total of houses with *samanlık*).
[2] Camel stables not included.
[3] In the sense of 'a storage shed for fodder'.

greater number of *ahır* would reflect a deeper involvement in rural affairs. What is more one might even try to connect the increase of dwellings with *ahır* with a possible 'ruralization' of the larger Anatolian towns, populated by recent refugees who had fled villages sacked by the Celâlîs or ravaged during the ever-recurrent campaigns in Iran. But in the absence of corroborating evidence, such assumptions remain pure speculation.

Courtyards, gardens, and open spaces

In seventeenth century Anatolia, the courtyard constituted an integral part of the dwelling. This can be read off from the fact that at least 62.9 per cent, and up to 87.2 per cent, of all Ankara and Kayseri houses documented were known to possess at least one courtyard. This courtyard, though occasionally planted with a few trees, should not be considered a garden. For gardens the documents employed a distinct term (*bahçe*), and houses with gardens seem to have been quite rare. In Ankara around 1600, only two per cent of all houses documented appear to have possessed a garden, and the situation did not change significantly in the course of the century that followed. In Kayseri, the increase in houses supplied with a garden was slightly more notable, from 2.1 to 4.6 per cent in the course of almost a century. But since only a small number of cases was involved, the percentual increase is not of any great significance. It appears that the gardens and vineyards outside the limits of the Anatolian towns were used as green spaces by the townsmen, according to a custom which was already quite ancient by the seventeenth century.[43] Thus, the courtyard appears to have been something rather like an extra room to the house. It was the space onto which porches might open; if the house possessed a well of its own, it would be located in the yard. Moreover, the yard provided access to stables and storage sheds; in brief, it constituted an integral part of the family dwelling.

Since the courtyard was of such importance in the domestic life of an Anatolian urban family, it is not surprising that certain wealthier households should have owned not one but two courtyards. As Table 8 shows, dwellings with two courtyards constituted a small minority in both Ankara and Kayseri around 1600. While, however, the number of houses with a double courtyard dwindled to near insignificance in Ankara, the exact opposite happened in Kayseri. Why the share of houses with two courtyards should have declined in Ankara and increased in Kayseri is difficult to explain. One might suggest that space was more limited in Ankara, which after all had surrounded itself by a city wall to keep away Celâlî rebels that might attempt to surprise the town. However, this explanation is based upon the assumption that the population of the city was increasing, or else relocating itself in a more concentrated form of habitat. While these assumptions are not in themselves implausible, they are impossible to prove or disprove because of the scarcity of population data for seventeenth-century Ankara.

It would be of interest to know whether there was any functional differentiation between outer and inner courtyard. Moreover, if such a differentiation existed, the criteria applied would be of some interest. Even a casual reading of descriptions concerning the Topkapı Palace in İstanbul indicates a definite hierarchy: the outer courtyard was more or less public, the janissaries had been installed in the former church of Hagia Eirene, and

Table 8. *Distribution of courtyards*[1]

(1)	(2)	(3)	(4)	(5)	(6)	(7)
		Houses with	Total number	Number of courtyards recorded		
	(None)	1 or more	of houses			
Location	(unknown)	courtyards	documented	1	2	3
Ankara, c. 1600	127 (37.1%)	215 (62.9%)	342	191 (88.8%)	24 (11.2%)	0
Kayseri, c. 1600	62 (26.3%)	174 (73.7%)	236	169 (97.1%)	5 (2.9%)	0
Ankara, c. 1690	82 (28.4%)	207 (71.6%)	289	195 (94.2%)	11 (5.3%)	1 (0.4%)
Kayseri, c. 1690	36 (12.7%)	247 (87.2%)	283	207 (83.8%)	40 (16.2%)	0

[1] In the last three columns (Number of courtyards recorded), percentages are based upon the figure given in column no 3 (Houses with 1 or more courtyards).

high-ranking Ottoman dignitaries might even enter this courtyard on horse-back.[44] On the other hand, even the Grand Vizier was expected to dismount at Orta Kapı, the viziers met in a structure that opened into this second courtyard, and at the far end of the court, the Sultan received viziers and foreign envoys in public audience. The third courtyard with the garden, *köşk*s and terraces beyond it, constituted the Palace proper, while the women of the Imperial Harem occupied a structure situated somewhat apart.

A comparable hierarchy may be observed in the *zaviye* of Hacıbektaş, as it is known from drawings and descriptions of the nineteenth and early twentieth centuries:[45] an outer courtyard with stables and other service buildings, a second courtyard into which opened the assembly hall (*meydanevi*), guest rooms and the kitchen. Mosque, graves, and mausolea were located in a separate garden or courtyard, which might with some audacity be interpreted as the Palace grounds belonging to the saint. Obviously one would not expect so elaborate a hierarchy in a private house, and in fact dwellings with three courtyards were all but absent from seventeenth-century Ankara and Kayseri. But even so, a hypothesis involving some kind of functional differentiation appears to be worth testing.

For this purpose, the data concerning late seventeenth-century Kayseri have been investigated, both because they are relatively abundant and because the scribes of this later period were generally more careful about recording whether a structure was located in the outer or in the inner courtyard. The results are conclusive: the inner court was definitely the preferred living space. In 28 out of 29 cases, the *tabhane* or *tabhane*s were located in the inner courtyard.[46] There was only one exception: the *konak* belonging to the family of Mehmed Bey b. Hasan Paşa, and even this exception is doubtful because the word *tabhane* in the relevant document could not be read with any degree of certainty. On the other hand, there were seven cases in which the dwelling possessed two *tabhane*s; in every single case, both *tabhane*s were located in the interior courtyard. In the case of the *sofa*, we encounter the same picture: in all 29 cases the *sofa* was located in the interior courtyard, and the owners of the two dwellings with two *sofa*s each do not seem to have considered it necessary to erect a building with *sofa* in the outer courtyard. Under these circumstances, it is not surprising that the five documents referring to a *harem odası* also record that structure as being located in the interior courtyard. It might also be worth recording that the *harem odası*, a unique feature of late-seventeenth-century Kayseri, was considerably more frequent in houses with two courtyards than in less elaborate dwellings: 17 per cent of all residences with two courtyards possessed such a room (5 out of 29), while the rate drops to 6 per cent if the totality of late seventeenth century Kayseri dwellings is taken into consideration (16 out of 283).

On the other hand, the *oda* or *oda*s were preferably placed not in the inner courtyard, but were entered from the outer yard. In only four instances do we learn that an *oda* formed part of the interior courtyard, while there were 23 cases in which the *oda* or *oda*s were counted as a part of the *hariciye* (outer) compound. In the vast majority of cases, there was only one *oda*, 4 houses out of 29 were credited with 2 each, and then of course there was the *konak* of Mehmed Bey b. Hasan Paşa with its 12 or possibly 21 rooms. Remarkably enough, of the vast number of rooms in this *konak*, not a single one was definitely located in the inner compound.

As to the architectural shape of the dwellings concerned, two possibilities must be taken into account. Either the *oda* in the outer courtyard formed an entirely separate structure, detached from the main building which contained *tabhane* and *sofa*. Or else the house itself divided the outer courtyard from its counterpart; in this case, the *oda* may have formed part of the main building, but was entered from the exterior courtyard while the *tabhane* and *sofa* opened into the back yard. In those cases in which the dwelling possessed a garden, the latter was also considered part of the interior courtyard. Moreover, the well, which was a common feature in Kayseri homes, was normally located in the inner court as well. Only in two instances do we learn that the well was located in the outer part of the yard. This arrangement enabled the women of the household to go about their tasks without concerning themselves about possible male visitors, who would probably have transacted their business in the outer courtyard.

On the other hand, a well situated in the inner courtyard must have obliged whoever was responsible for the household's animals to make frequent trips between the two courtyards, for stables, cowsheds and other accommodations for animals were generally located in the outer part of the compound. Not that such structures were never found in the interior courtyard; in 7 out of 29 instances, or almost a quarter of all cases, a stable or cowshed was found in the *dahiliye* (inner) part of the compound. But it was far more frequent to place these structures in the outer courtyard, and this custom is recorded for 23 out of 29 cases.[47] Sheds for the storage of straw and fodder must generally have been built right next to the stables and cowsheds. On the other hand, families had not yet developed a clear-cut preference with respect to the kitchen, or rather, the modern researcher gets this impression because the number of kitchens documented in the *kadı* registers is very small. Normally, one would expect the kitchen to have been located in the inner court. But in the *konak* of Mehmed Bey b. Hasan Paşa, the cooking was probably largely done by servants, so that this residence possessed two kitchens in the outer courtyard and two others next to the family living quarters. But of the other two double-courtyard houses for which a separate kitchen is recorded, one had it in the outer and the other in the inner part of the dwelling compound. Obviously, these data do not allow us to recognize any particular pattern.

Thus, in late-seventeenth-century Kayseri, the inner courtyard must have constituted the family residence. Service functions, such as cooking, the heaving of water, or the feeding of animals, were not entirely relegated to the outer courtyard. But in the wealthier residences examined here, the preference was obviously towards keeping the animals a good distance away from the main living spaces. It is less clear what the *oda*s in the outer compound were used for. They may have been unpretentious structures, which housed servants and were used as storage space when needed. On the other hand, one could also imagine these *oda*s as rather ornate and elaborate rooms for the reception of male visitors. In this case, they would have taken the place of the *selamlık* or *divanhane*, which are almost never recorded for seventeenth century households in either Ankara or Kayseri. Unfortunately, the surviving documents contain no data which would permit us to resolve this problem.

Workshops within the house

Throughout the seventeenth century, both Ankara and Kayseri craftsmen generally seem to have kept their houses and their workshops separate. Among the 573 houses investigated for the closing years of the seventeenth century, no instance has been found of a house being contiguous to a shop, although it is of course possible that some of the 'properties' mentioned were in reality not houses but shops. On the other hand, the fact that many craftsmen rented their shops from a pious foundation must have contributed toward a general separation of shops and dwelling places. For while occasionally an unmarried master or journeyman may have slept in his own or his master's shop, shops constructed on behalf of pious foundations contained no 'back room' which could have provided shelter for a family. This also explains why the documents investigated here do not contain much information on the shops and workshops in which craftsmen went about their work.

However, there is one major exception, namely the workshops used for the manufacture of cloth from the hair of the angora goat (*sof*). Down into the early nineteenth century, this branch of activity was Ankara's mainstay as a commercial centre. For as the seventeenth-century traveller Evliya Çelebi noted with satisfaction, all attempts on the part on the unbelievers to acclimatize the angora goat in territories under their control had ended in failure.[48] As a result, Ankara producers enjoyed something like a monopoly position, until the angora goat was successfully introduced into South Africa. Down into the early eighteenth century, fabrics made of *sof* were sold to European traders in limited quantities. But it was mainly the yarn that was exported to France and England, where it was used in the manufacture of buttons. However, mohair yarn from the English point of view at best played second fiddle to Iranian raw silk. Moreover, when metal buttons progressively replaced buttons worked out of angora yarn, the

Levant Company rapidly lost interest in this article.[49] On the other hand, the French market continued to buy ready-made mohair fabrics until well into the eighteenth century,[50] for local manufacturers were quite slow in offering replacements for this product.

As a result of the demand originating from exporting merchants, local craftsmen were often hard put to find the raw material which they needed for their work. In fact it would appear that occasionally even ordinary goats'-hair was in demand as an export article, for in 1678–9 we find the Konya felt makers clamouring for an export prohibition to protect their supplies of raw material.[51] However, the mohair weavers of Ankara in their attempts to protect their sources of supply, were more fortunate than many other craftsmen in a similar position. For the craftsmen's demands were supported by the tax farmers in charge of collecting taxes from dyers' workshops and presses (*cendere*).[52] Since these presses were used at the end of the manufacturing process, to give the finished product its silk-like lustre, the tax farmers' interests tended to coincide with those of the craftsmen, namely both groups benefited from the marketing of a finished product. As a result, from at least the mid seventeenth century onward, the exportation of the best quality yarn was prohibited.[53] This prohibition was still in force when Richard Pococke visited Ankara in the eighteenth century,[54] and Ottoman documents mention it as still existing in the early years of the nineteenth century. Obviously, it is difficult to judge how seriously the prohibition was being enforced, but the very fact that the demand for mohair yarn was limited must have made enforcement easier, and helped to protect the Ankara weavers' sources of raw material supply.

To a certain degree, the presence or absence of mohair workshops may indicate the prosperity or crisis of the Ankara textile industry. From this point of view, the seventeenth-century evidence sounds reassuring. Out of the 342 houses documented toward the end of the sixteenth and the beginning of the seventeenth century, 28, or 8.2 per cent, possessed a mohair workshop. Approximately ninety years later, 29 out of 289 buildings were put on record as containing a workshop suitable for mohair weaving (10 per cent). Not too much should be made out of the slight increase, since the available sample is anything but perfect. However, it is probable that the number of house owners who thought it worthwhile to install a mohair workshop on their premises remained more or less stable.

On the other hand, it would be necessary to know what these workshops were being used for, for the actual weaving process or simply for cleaning and drying the mohair prior to spinning. Part of the manufacturing process was actually carried out in the villages. In the middle of the sixteenth century, the Habsburgs' ambassador Busbecq observed peasant women spinning yarn for delivery to Ankara merchants.[55] Towards the end of the sixteenth century, certain villages near Ankara claimed to derive their livelihood not from agriculture, but from the manufacture of mohair yarn or cloth.[56] In addition, not all the preliminary processes were necessarily carried out in a workshop. Thus, Busbecq's travelling companion Hans Dernschwam observed specialized washermen washing angora wool in the small rivers near the town.[57] Moreover, women used to spin wherever they went, and needed no workshop for this kind of work. Under these circumstances, it seems reasonable to view the workshops in Ankara houses mainly as weavers' sheds.

In fact, for 8 out of the 30 workshops documented for the years around 1600, the number of looms installed in each shed is given, generally about 2–3 looms per shed. For the later seventeenth century, data are slightly more abundant, and we possess evidence concerning the number of looms installed in 16 out of 28 cases. As to the average number of looms per shed, there seems to have been a slight increase, but with the limited number of cases at our disposal, the change is probably not significant. Thus, it seems that in the worst of cases, we may have overestimated the number of looms active in Ankara around 1600, and relatively speaking, we may have underestimated the manufacturing activity around 1690. If that is in fact the case, the number of looms active in Ankara may even have increased somewhat in the course of the seventeenth century.

That the *sof* industry of Ankara did in fact move towards recovery after a crisis at the beginning of the seventeenth century appears rather likely when one takes note of a Sultan's rescript preserved in the Mühimme registers and dated 1018/1609–10. According to this text, insecurity of the roads, and other disturbances resulting from the Celâlî rebellion had for a while interrupted deliveries of *sof* to İstanbul. Recently, however, Muslim and non-Muslim merchants had again taken up the trade, but were being hampered by over-zealous administrators who claimed that the merchants were taking foreign silver coins (*guruş*) out of İstanbul, and that this drain of coin from the capital was forbidden. Now the merchants requested and received a rescript which assured them that their commerce was perfectly legitimate, and that they could transport whatever coin was needed for their trade. Obviously, the merchants' wish to get business back on its feet again does not necessarily imply that they were able to realize it. But on the other hand, for private persons to secure a rescript of this kind could be a complicated matter, and it is unlikely that the Ankara merchants would have invested the time and money required if they had not had reasonable expectations of better times.[58]

Given the fact that the mohair-weaving industry was the key industry of Ottoman Ankara, its probable recovery is obviously of some importance in explaining the development of local domestic architecture. For in the second half of the nineteenth century, when the *sof* industry had been eliminated by competing European products, outside observers were unanimous in describing the town as run-down and the buildings as in a poor state of repair.[59]

For Kayseri, the documents investigated unfortunately do not provide any evidence on the town's economic activity, for the only business premises habitually mentioned are the *şırahane*, or wine cellars, which presumably were to be found in the houses of non-Muslim families only. As the vineyards around Kayseri were and are reasonably productive, wine manufacture may in fact have been of some economic importance; but the data are too scanty too make analysis worthwhile.

Towards a typology of urban houses

After this discussion of enclosed, semi-enclosed, and open spaces to be found in Ankara and Kayseri houses of the seventeenth century, the next step is to group these buildings into several distinct types. Unfortunately, the types developed by historians of architecture are not usable for our purposes, for they assume that the plan of the building is known, and the documents recorded in the *kadıs*' registers do not contain any evidence that would permit reconstruction of the plan. As a result, the only way to group the houses is by taking as a criterion the different categories of rooms which they do or do not contain. Even though this kind of classification is less desirable than a classification based upon knowledge of the plan, it is not without interest, particularly when at a later stage in our investigation the different categories of houses can be related to different types of house owners and different levels of price.

For the purpose of analysis, the houses documented in the *kadıs*' registers have been divided into six categories. The first category constitutes the most complete type of house, consisting of at least one *tabhane*, one *sofa*, one *oda*, and a courtyard. Since the courtyard appears to have been such a basic component of an urban house, categories 2–5 all contain a courtyard, but otherwise one or more elements are lacking: in category 2 there is no *oda*, in category 3 there is neither an *oda* nor a *sofa*, and in category 4 it is the *sofa* alone which is missing. Category 5 is marked by the fact that the houses in question lacked a *tabhane*, while the sixth and last group contains dwellings which possessed a *tabhane* but no courtyard. Though it is possible that a few incomplete descriptions have slipped in, it is probable that the vast majority of these annoying intrusions have in fact been relegated into category 'zero'.

When reading the lines of Table 9 horizontally, it immediately becomes apparent that different types of houses were favoured in different towns at different times. In late-sixteenth- and early-seventeenth-century Ankara, the most popular type of house seems to have been the most complete setup, with a full array of *tabhane, sofa, oda*, and courtyard (Type 1). However, in the 1690s, this type had largely been abandoned in favour of Type 4, reflecting the fact that houses without a *sofa* were gaining in popularity. However, it was not just that the most complete type of house was being less frequently constructed than previously. House owners were also giving up the simpler form described here as Type 2, consisting only of *tabhane, sofa*

Table 9. Dwellings grouped according to type

(1)	(2)	(3)	(4)	(5)	(6)	(7)	(8)	(9)	(10)
	0			Types of Houses					
				1	2	3	4	5	6
Location	Description not usable	Total usable descriptions	Total documented dwellings	Tabhane sofa oda avlu	Tabhane sofa avlu	Tabhane avlu	Tabhane oda avlu	Avlu, no tabhane	Tabhane, no avlu
Ankara, c. 1600	91 (26.6%)	251 (73.4%)	342	79 (31.5%)	52 (20.7%)	14 (5.6%)	44 (17.5%)	27 (10.8%)	35 (13.9%)
Kayseri, c. 1600	48 (20.3%)	188 (79.7%)	236	45 (23.9%)	95 (50.5%)	17 (9.0%)	2 (1.1%)	9 (4.8%)	20 (10.6%)
Ankara, c. 1690	42 (14.5%)	247 (85.4%)	289	52 (21.1%)	17 (6.9%)	15 (6.1%)	96 (38.9%)	23 (9.3%)	45 (18.2%)
Kayseri, c. 1690	19 (6.7%)	264 (93.3%)	283	82 (31.1%)	102 (38.6%)	24 (9.1%)	10 (3.8%)	24 (9.1%)	22 (8.3%)

[1] In columns no 5 to 10, percentages have been calculated upon the figures in column no 3 (Total Usable Descriptions).

and courtyard. One wonders what this change may have implied from an architectural point of view. Were some of these *sofa*s that were being abandoned in fact open galleries, something like the *örtme sofa* the documents occasionally record, or certain varieties of *dış sofa* as the term is used in modern architectural terminology?[60] Were people converting these hallways into separate rooms? Questions of this type cannot be answered for the time being. On the other hand, it is worth noting that in spite of all these changes, the typical dwelling of seventeenth century Ankara and Kayseri retained its *tabhane*. Even though in Kayseri a slight tendency towards dwellings without a *tabhane* seems to have asserted itself, the *tabhane* remained the central room of the urban house.

Kayseri domestic architecture during the seventeenth century appears to have evolved rather differently from that of Ankara. At the end of the sixteenth and at the beginning of the seventeenth century, by far the most popular type of house was that which contained a *tabhane* and a *sofa* apart from its courtyard (Type 2). In fact, this type seems to have dominated the Kayseri townscape as no single type ever did in Ankara (40.3 per cent of all houses documented and more than half of all usable descriptions). In addition, the complete dwelling (Type 1) was also quite frequently encountered; taken together, these two categories encompassed about 60 per cent of all houses documented in Kayseri around 1600, and almost three quarters of all usable descriptions. By the later years of the seventeenth century, houses consisting of *tabhane, sofa, oda,* and *avlu* (Type 1) had become more fashionable, while the former favourite showed noticeable decline. But throughout the seventeenth century the two most favoured types of house between themselves dominated the Kayseri scene (74.4 per cent around 1600, 69.7 per cent around 1690). In comparison, all other types of house must be considered of relatively limited significance.

In order to refine the categorization introduced, it appears useful to separately analyse a few groups of buildings which stand out for their special characteristics. Thus, one might wish to find out whether a particular type of house was preferred for buildings which possessed an upper floor. Moreover, one would expect smaller houses, with only two permanently inhabitable rooms, to belong to a different type than larger and presumably more opulent dwellings. Conversely, one might examine houses with two courtyards, which at least in late-seventeenth-century Kayseri seem to have been popular mainly among the well-to-do, and find out whether a particular type was dominant in this category. Tables 10–12 provide the bases from which these questions can be answered.

In the closing years of the sixteenth century and the beginning of the seventeenth, about 40 per cent of all Ankara buildings with more than one floor belonged to Type 1, that is they contained all the basic units of *tabhane, oda,* and *sofa*. Reflecting the general trend away from the *sofa* (compare Table 9), quite a few owners of two-storied buildings in the course of the

Table 10. *Dwellings with an upper floor, grouped according to types*

Location	0 Description not usable	1 Tabhane sofa oda avlu	2 Tabhane sofa avlu	3 Tabhane avlu	4 Tabhane oda avlu	5 Avlu no tabhane	6 Tabhane no avlu	Total dwellings, more than one floor
Ankara, c. 1600	4 (11.1%)	15 (41.7%)	2 (5.6%)	3 (8.3%)	3 (8.3%)	3 (8.3%)	6 (16.7%)	36
Kayseri, c. 1600	1 (33.3%)	2 (66.7%)	0	0	0	0	0	3
Ankara, c. 1690	8 (5.3%)	37 (24.3%)	0	0	71 (46.7%)	15 (9.9%)	21 (13.8%)	152
Kayseri, c. 1690	2 (6.7%)	17 (56.7%)	7 (23.3%)	0	1 (3.3%)	3 (10.0%)	0	30

Table 11. *Distribution of different house types among dwellings with two permanently inhabitable rooms*

Location	0 Description not usable	2 Tabhane sofa avlu	3 Tabhane avlu	4 Tabhane avlu oda	5 Avlu no tabhane	6 Tabhane no avlu	Total dwellings with two rooms
Ankara, c. 1600	1 (1.0%)	45 (44.6%)	5 (5.0%)	34 (33.7%)	4 (4.0%)	12 (11.9%)	101
Kayseri, c. 1600	2 (2.0%)	84 (82.4%)	0	2 (2.0%)	2 (2.0%)	12 (11.8%)	102
Ankara, c. 1690	4 (4.6%)	15 (17.2%)	3 (3.4%)	38 (43.7%)	9 (10.3%)	18 (20.7%)	87
Kayseri, c. 1690	1 (0.9%)	80 (72.7%)	3 (2.7%)	10 (9.1%)	4 (3.6%)	12 (10.9%)	110

seventeenth century switched to the type which contained only a *tabhane* and an *oda* (Type 4). However, the trend was much more pronounced among two-storied dwellings than among the general run of buildings. This may well be linked to the very nature of the *sofa*, one of whose main functions was to provide access to other rooms. If a single room was placed on the upper floor, obviously this could never have been a *sofa*, and given the rarity of *tabhanes* located on second floors, in most cases the room on the first floor should have been an *oda*. If in the process a ground-floor room needed to be sacrificed, in most cases this should have been a *sofa*. Thus, we may assume that the two phenomena were in fact connected: at least to a certain extent, *sofas* disappeared because people were adding rooms on to what had previously been the roofs of their houses.

Table 12. *Distribution of types among houses with more than one courtyard*

Location	0 Description not usable	1 Tabhane sofa oda avlu	2 Tabhane sofa avlu	3 Tabhane avlu	4 Tabhane oda avlu	5 Avlu no tabhane	Total dwellings with more than one courtyard
Ankara, c. 1600	0	17 (70.8%)	3 (12.5%)	1 (4.2%)	2 (8.3%)	1 (4.2%)	24
Kayseri, c. 1600	0	4 (80.0%)	1 (20.0%)	0	0	0	5
Ankara, c. 1690	0	6 (54.5%)	0	1 (9.1%)	3 (27.3%)	1 (9.1%)	11
Kayseri, c. 1690	3 (7.5%)	26 (65.0%)	11 (27.5%)	0	0	0	40

Concerning Kayseri, much less can be said because dwellings built on more than one level were all but unknown in the years shortly before and after 1600. But during the 1690s, the fully developed dwelling, containing *tabhane, sofa,* and *oda* (Type 1), came to be the type of house most favoured by owners of two-storey buildings. Only an examination of eighteenth-century records would allow us to judge whether developments in Kayseri parallelled those in Ankara except for a certain time-lag, or whether two-storied buildings in this latter city evolved among totally different lines.

In the years around 1600, the small dwellings of Ankara were mostly of two types: either they consisted of a *tabhane* and a *sofa* apart from their courtyard (Type 2), or else the *sofa* was replaced by an *oda*. In the closing years of the seventeenth century, however, emphasis had shifted. Not only was there a trend away from the *sofa* among the builders of small houses. Such a development is only to be expected, since it characterized seventeenth-century Ankara dwellings in general. But at the same time, there was a notable increase in the number of dwellings without any courtyard at all. While this shift was noticeable among the general run of Ankara houses as well, the share of houses without courtyard (Type 6) increasing from 10.2 to 15.5 per cent of all documented dwellings (or from 13.9 to 18.2 per cent if only usable descriptions are taken into account), the change was much more clearly visible among the smaller dwelling places. For among the latter, the relevant rates jumped from 11.9 to 20.7 per cent. These data confirm the impression that building space in Ankara was getting scarce, and as might be expected, the inhabitants of the smaller houses were particularly affected. Moreover, the data showing a decline in available yard-space are of particular significance, since the information on late-seventeenth-century houses is generally much more complete than it had been for the decades shortly before and after 1600. Thus it is possible that in actual fact, the loss of courtyard-space was even more serious than might be assumed at first glance.

In seventeenth-century Kayseri, on the other hand, the housing situation seems to have been much more stable. Among small houses around 1600, by far the most popular type was the dwelling whose permanently inhabitable rooms consisted of a *tabhane* and a *sofa* (82.4 per cent). In the early 1600s, this type was also most widely represented among Kayseri dwellings in general, but since almost one-half of all Kayseri houses documented at this time consisted of houses with only two rooms, nothing else could have been expected. By the last years of the seventeenth century, some owners of small houses in Kayseri had also switched to a house without a *sofa*. But the change was much less dramatic than in Ankara, and the dwelling consisting of a *tabhane, sofa*, and courtyard (Type 2) remained by far the dominant type. Moreover, the percentage of small houses without a courtyard remained quite stable. Throughout, it appears that the pressures charac-terizing the Ankara housing situation were largely absent from Kayseri.

Among the houses possessing more than one courtyard (see Table 12) the preferred type in the years around 1600 was obviously the 'complete dwelling', consisting of *tabhane, sofa, oda*, and *avlu* (Type 1). In the course of the century, this preference became somewhat less exclusive. In Ankara the arrangement consisting of *tabhane, oda*, and courtyard seems to have gained favour; but since the overall numbers involved are very small, it is impossible to draw any hard and fast conclusions. Among the two-courtyard dwellings of late-seventeenth-century Kayseri, there was remarkable uniformity, with only two types (Types 1 and 2) represented at all. It is noteworthy that in these dwellings, where space was presumably not a major consideration, the *sofa* continued to form an essential element of the house.

Conclusion

Until now, it has been our aim to describe the patterns of housing in seventeenth-century Ankara and Kayseri, and as far as possible to pinpoint changes that may have taken place in the course of the period under investigation. The first important conclusion is that central Anatolian domestic architecture did in fact evolve in the course of the seventeenth century. In fact, it probably developed at quite a rapid pace, since so many tendencies of change can be shown up within what was, after all, only the span of three or four generations, or a period of 90 to 100 years. That change did occur is not in itself very surprising. Even so, the fact is worth stressing. for the emphasis that modern students of domestic architecture place upon surviving examples of older styles of building, while perfectly reasonable from a certain point of view, does tend to obscure the fact that this architecture had a history of its own.

Our appreciation of this history is limited by the fact that at least before the age of photography, but even beyond, many aspects of style are lost forever, once the buildings that represented a certain stylistic tendency have been destroyed. The documents investigated here tell us nothing about construction materials, façades, or architectural decor. However, they do reflect significant changes in the distribution and configuration of the rooms that made up a seventeenth-century Anatolian house. Thereby, this historical material can serve as a useful corrective against the tendency to regard the domestic architecture of the late eighteenth or early nineteenth century as 'the' Ottoman Turkish house.

Among the changes to be pinpointed, one might mention the increase in houses provided with a *tabhane* and an *oda*, both in Ankara and in Kayseri. At the same time, the *sofa* lost in popularity among Ankara home-owners, while it made some modest gains in Kayseri. These changes were accompanied by a slight tendency toward houses with more living spaces, an inclination somewhat more visible in Ankara than in Kayseri. In the latter city, the two-room house continued to be by far the most favoured dwelling place. Moreover, the need for more rooms was partly satisfied by adding semi-open spaces. Both in Ankara and in Kayseri, the number of houses that boasted either an *örtme*, a *sayegah*, or even both these structures increased significantly, and the decline of the probably less elaborate *çardak* was not important enough to cancel out this gain.

At least in Ankara, a tendency towards more elaborate houses seems to have come up against limitations of space. Thus, we may explain why the house owners of Ankara were not able to construct more dwellings with two courtyards, and why a sizeable number of small dwellings lost all access to a yard. On the other hand, in Kayseri the double courtyard notably increased in popularity in the course of the seventeenth century, a tendency that might form part of the trend, previously commented upon, toward more elaborate dwellings. At the same time, two-storey buildings were much slower in gaining popularity among Kayseri home owners than was the case in Ankara. Thus it may be assumed that space-constraint was not nearly as noticeable in the former city as it was in the latter.

Hence, Ankara home owners began to distribute their rooms over several floors. In this context, it is possible that in the eyes of many families needing additional living space, the *oda* became more desirable than the *sofa*. The *oda* permitted more privacy than the hall, whose main function it was to provide access to the remaining rooms of the dwelling. Under these circumstances, one might interpret the declining popularity of the *sofa* in Ankara as yet another manifestation of space-constraint.

It would be tempting to view the interest in porches and other semi-enclosed spaces as a further expression of the need for additional rooms. However, this interpretation would not be logical, because we observe the same phenomenon both in Ankara and in Kayseri, although we possess no significant evidence for crowding where the latter city was concerned. It is more consistent to see the increase in porches, verandas, and the like as an indicator of the trend toward increasingly elaborate dwellings, which seems to have manifested itself both in Ankara and in Kayseri.

At the same time one might speculate as to whether the Ankara tendency toward houses without a *sofa* was reversible or not. In this connection, one might point to a feature that is not recorded in the seventeenth-century documents, but characterized Ankara domestic architecture of the nineteenth and early twentieth centuries. Researchers have frequently pointed out how during this later period, the upper floors were reserved for family living,[61] while the ground floor as far as possible was used for servicing purposes. If this custom did not exist at the beginning of the seventeenth century, and was only beginning to evolve at the century's end, then it must have taken shape mainly after 1700. Wholesale transference of the family residence to an upper floor should have helped to resolve the space problem. Moreover, even though buildings of more than one storey were more costly to erect than dwellings limited to the ground floor, upper floors must generally have been more pleasant to live in, better protected from the mud and noise of the streets and often permitting the inhabitants a pleasant view. Once the family residence had been transferred to the first floor, the *sofa* may even have reappeared. Obviously, these hypotheses have not been tested to date, and only after eighteenth-, and nineteenth-, and early-twentieth-century records have been studied will it become possible to determine what relationship, if any, these assumptions have with reality. Possibly the present study overreacts against the assumption of more or less immobile vernacular building, and therefore tends to assume too rapid a change in pace. These matters will have to be taken up in further investigations.

Possibly somewhat more certain is the information which the available documents provide concerning the question of the 'two courtyards'. Again the first observation that needs to be made is that 'double-courtyard compounds' are a historical phenomenon that became a regular feature of domestic architecture in the course of a definite period. Where Kayseri was concerned, this period appears to have been the seventeenth century. These courtyards were not built to enable two families to share the same compound. Rather, the existence of an outer courtyard permitted certain service functions, such as the stabling of animals, to be removed from the vicinity of permanently inhabited rooms. It is probable, but not certain, that male visitors were received in the *oda* which so frequently formed part of the outer courtyard. On a more modest scale, these wealthier houses of late-seventeenth century Kayseri thus reproduced the functional divisions which characterized Ottoman palaces and *zaviye*s.

Obviously changes in the number and function of rooms must have resulted from the changing needs of families inhabiting these houses. In the present chapter, recorded physical characteristics of seventeenth-century houses have been used as indicators, from which such social features as crowding, or the desire for a larger and more elaborate dwelling, have been deduced. The same problem, namely how the townsmen of seventeenth-century central Anatolia viewed their habitat, can be analysed from a different angle, this time using the information available on the prices of urban houses as a starting point. Crowding should have expressed itself in rising prices for urban real estate, and certain essential building materials. Given the fact that the great majority of townsmen had to construct their houses on a limited budget, the price of urban dwellings must have had certain repercussions upon the shape given these buildings. To this issue, the following chapter will address itself.

CHAPTER 3

The cost of buying a house

In seventeenth-century Ankara and Kayseri, it was not totally unknown for people to live in rented houses.[1] However, the case was exceptional, and the majority of people appear to have owned their dwellings. Yet that does not mean that every family purchased a house built by a professional craftsman. Evidence for the organization of the building crafts is not very plentiful in the *kadıs'* registers, and thus we know very little about how ordinary town dwellers built their houses. However, this very fact makes it appear probable that many people, particularly if they were poor, constructed their own houses, perhaps with the help of a few neighbours or relatives. If these assumptions are at all realistic, houses of the period with which we are dealing should be considered a 'marketable commodity' only in a limited sense.

Monetary units

On the other hand, the buying and selling of houses occurred frequently enough that we can make more or less coherent statements about the price of urban dwellings. However, as a preliminary, a few remarks about the monetary units used in seventeenth-century Anatolia are indispensable. Least complicated, at least at first glance, is the case of late-sixteenth- and early-seventeenth-century Ankara. For in this town the standard Ottoman monetary unit of the times, the *akçe*, was employed in almost all cases in which the relevant monetary unit has been clearly stated by the *kadıs'* scribes. There were a few rare instances in which house prices were expressed in gold coins (*altın*), by which term the scribes probably designated the standard Ottoman gold coin of the times, the *sikke-i hasene* (cf. Table 1). But basically, Ankara during the last years of the sixteenth and at the beginning of the seventeenth century seems to have clung to the monetary system of the 'classical' period of Sultan Süleyman the Lawgiver and his predecessors.

However, even in Ankara the situation was less straightforward than it might appear at first glance, for in the last quarter of the sixteenth century, the *akçe* was repeatedly devalued. This was one of the causes leading to an

Table 1. *Monetary units used in sales of Ankara and Kayseri houses*

Location	Akçe	Guruş	Guruş-ı kebir	Guruş-ı esedi	Altın	Ak altın	Unknown	Total
Ankara, c. 1600	241 (70.5%)	0	0	0	7 (2.0%)	0	94 (27.4%)	342
Kayseri, c. 1600	39 (16.5%)	118 (50.0%)	13 (5.5%)	1 (0.4%)	7 (3.0%)	6 (2.5%)	52 (22.0%)	236
Ankara, c. 1690	5 (1.7%)	145 (50.2%)	0	90 (31.1%)	0	0	49 (17.0%)	289
Kayseri, c. 1690	2 (0.7%)	122 (43.1%)	1 (0.4%)	126 (44.5%)	0	0	32 (11.3%)	283

increase in prices that has been described as nothing short of revolutionary, and as extremely disruptive of the Ottoman order of state and society.[2] Moreover, devaluation was followed by revaluation, even though the *akçe* never regained the value it had possessed before the crisis. The effects of this monetary instability have been studied mainly in the wholesale food markets of İstanbul and Edirne; as yet not much is known about the manner in which the housing market of these two cities may have been affected by the inflationary movement of the times.

Concerning the value of the *akçe* in relation to other coins in circulation, Özer Ergenç's investigations have established a somewhat surprising fact: throughout the years before and after 1600, Ankara certainly maintained reasonably close commercial relations with the Ottoman capital. However, successive devaluations and revaluations often affected the Ankara rates of exchange (*akçe* against Ottoman gold coin, or else *akçe* against *guruş*) only after several years had elapsed.[3] It must be assumed that people continued to employ old coins in their transactions, and that local authorities tolerated the practice, possibly because the supply of coin was smaller than the volume of transactions would have rendered desirable. But under these circumstances, it is not possible to link changes in house prices very closely to currency mutations. Such a relationship undoubtedly existed, but it was less direct than it must have been, for instance, in the Ottoman capital.

Where late-sixteenth- and early-seventeenth-century Kayseri is concerned, matters are complicated by a bewildering array of monetary units circulating among house proprietors, and thus, presumably, in the urban market in general.[4] Less than 17 per cent of all buyers and sellers of houses made use of the *akçe*. Gold coins were slightly more popular than in Ankara; however, some prices were expressed in *ak altın* ('white gold'), a coin whose exact identity has not been established. More than half of all houses were paid for in foreign silver coins of one sort or another. However, very rarely do the sale documents refer to the exact type of coin used: in one single case, the price was expressed in what was probably a Dutch coin, called *esedi* because of the image of a lion on one of its faces. In thirteen instances, payment was made in *guruş-ı kebir*, probably Spanish silver. Given the vagueness of the data, it is impossible to convert the *guruş* into *akçe* with any degree of accuracy. However, since such a conversion is necessary if even very broad comparisons are to be attempted, a rough-and-ready equivalent has been assumed (one *guruş* equivalent to 120 *akçe*).[5] But it must be kept in mind that this estimate permits us to discern overall trends at most, and any attempt at sophisticated calculations is inappropriate.

By the end of the seventeenth century, the Ottoman monetary situation was somewhat less complex than it had been ninety years earlier. While the *akçe* was still used in everyday transactions, it was by now so far devalued that it had been virtually abandoned for payments in which major sums of money were concerned. Moreover, the documents contain no further references to Ottoman or foreign gold coins. Thus the *guruş* in its different varieties had become virtually the only means of payment where the purchase of houses was concerned, a situation which can further be explained by the fact that the Ottoman Sultans during the period under investigation had very few silver coins minted in the provinces. Both in Ankara and in Kayseri, practically the only two units referred to are the *guruş* and the *guruş-ı esedi*.

Equally, very little documentation has been found concerning the rates of exchange which prevailed in Ankara and Kayseri at the end of the seventeenth century. Therefore, in one case the exchange rate adopted is based upon figures published by Sahillioğlu, which refer to the rates applied by the Ottoman Treasury during those years (1 *esedi guruş* = 140 *akçe*).[6] Where the ordinary *guruş* is concerned, we have adopted a rate of exchange occasionally mentioned in the *kadıs'* registers of the time, namely 1 *guruş* = 200 *akçe*. However, in spite of all attempts on the part of the Ottoman central administration to ensure uniformity, rates of exchange might vary from one city to another, or even within different areas of what is today Greater İstanbul.[7] Under these circumstances, the procedures adopted here doubtlessly introduce a certain margin of error. On the other hand, one may reasonably hope that the error in question is more or less the same for late seventeenth-century Ankara and Kayseri, and therefore cancelled out by the process of comparing. Even so, all the comparisons attempted in the present chapter should be taken with rather more than the customary grain of salt.

At the same time, an attempt to avoid all conversions from *guruş* into *akçe* would have denied us even a casual glimpse of the structure of house prices in seventeenth-century Ankara and Kayseri. Given the existence of what is, when all is said and done, a surprisingly rich collection of price data, it seemed indefensible to pass by the information which these figures contain. Doubtless further investigations will be undertaken in the future, and these will allow researchers to confirm or disprove the assertions which have been made in the present chapter.

Determining the price of a house

In the absence of any documents which explain in some detail why townsmen of central Anatolia considered certain houses more desirable than others, we have to start with what we know, or hope we know, about the layout of the Ottoman town in general. In addition, some common sense assumptions must be included in the analysis. To begin with, one would assume that, other things being equal, a larger and more elaborate house should have been more expensive than a small and primitive one. Equally, the amount of open space (courtyards, garden, etc.) or even a pleasant view should have had some influence upon the market value of the building, and the availability of water at a convenient distance must have been a consideration as well. Moreover, the physical condition of the house was certainly taken into account; occasionally the sales records mention the fact that a dwelling was totally or partially in ruins. In fact, some descriptions include the expression '*bir sofa yeri*' or '*bir oda yeri*' ('the space in which to erect a *sofa* or *oda*').[8] Obviously, such more or less ruinous structures, or even empty building lots, should have fetched a lower price than a comparable house in good condition.

At least as important as physical factors were social considerations, and in this respect common sense is much less helpful. It is generally accepted that in Ottoman towns, there was no clear-cut differentiation between 'wealthy' and 'poor' sections, and people from different income groups might reside in the same *mahalle*. However, given the concentration of public buildings – and thereby of amenities like mosques, libraries, and water fountains in the centre of an Ottoman town – one might assume that the wealthy preferred to build their houses in the *mahalle*s close to these foundations.[9] Moreover, there was the effect of the city walls to consider. It seems that seventeenth-century Ankara confined itself to the walled-up area, and crowding should have tended to increase the price of building land. Where security was better assured, as appears to have been the case in Edirne, during approximately the same period, the Muslim population had moved out into the spacious quarter around the Selimiye mosque, leaving the cramped and walled-in old town to the non-Muslims.[10] Tendencies of this kind should have had repercussions upon prices, even if these effects were often not very easy to trace.

Moreover, certain town quarters (*mahalle*s) might possess special advantages from the taxpayers' point of view. Thus, the inhabitants of the *mahalle* surrounding the dervish hospice of Mevlâna Celâleddin Rumî in Konya were exempted from the payment of *avarız* taxes, in return for the services which they were expected to render the dervishes. As a result, the Türbe-i Celâliye quarter was by far the most popular section of the city.[11] No such exemptions seem to have existed in Ankara and Kayseri, but certain *mahalle*s might possess substantial endowments to help the inhabitants pay their *avarız* taxes. These endowments might fall to the lot of a given *mahalle* rather than to its neighbours, for the fortuitous reason that this particular quarter happened to possess wealthy inhabitants that had chosen to establish charities of this kind. Such endowments may have attracted residents, and it is possible that when the attraction was sufficiently strong, the price of building land went up as a result. However, since we do not possess systematic data on pious foundations instituted after 1590, this hypothesis cannot at present be tested.

At first glance, the existence of separate non-Muslim *mahalle*s might also have led to crowding and high real estate values if the non-Muslim population of the town in question happened to increase. However, upon closer consideration, this does not seem likely. For non-Muslim *mahalle*s in Ottoman Anatolian towns differed from ghettos in medieval and early modern Europe, in that segregation was in no way rigid.[12] Houses in Muslim *mahalle*s could be sold to non-Muslims and vice versa, and it was not uncommon to have *mahalle*s change their religious composition in the course of time. Thus 'ghetto effects' should have rarely if ever become visible, particularly since both Muslims and non-Muslims generally owned their houses, thus eliminating speculation on the part of landlords.

The only situation in which the existence of separate Muslim and non-Muslim *mahalle*s should have had an effect upon the price of houses was when the Ottoman government ordered a Muslim *mahalle* which had been settled by non-Muslims to be returned to its former state. In such cases, the value of houses should have dropped, because the inhabitants moving out probably needed to sell in a hurry to raise money to build a house somewhere else. But such evacuation orders, which can occasionally be found in sixteenth- and seventeenth-century *Mühimme* registers,[13] have not been located for either Ankara or Kayseri during the period under investigation.

Under these circumstances, it seems reasonable to relate our information concerning Ankara and Kayseri house prices first to what is known about the physical shape of the houses concerned. Moreover, it might be useful to compare the values of urban residential properties owned by Muslims and non-Muslims, and to treat in the same fashion the prices of houses owned by *askerî* and by ordinary townsmen. But before investigating these matters, we must first take a brief look at the overall distribution of property values in seventeenth-century Ankara and Kayseri.

Price categories and average prices

Tables 2 and 3 reflect the distribution of cheap and valuable houses, for the end of the sixteenth and the beginning of the seventeenth century (Table 2), as well as for the years immediately before and after 1690 (Table 3). A glance at the prices documented for Ankara about the year 1600 indicates

Table 2. *House prices in Ankara and Kayseri around 1600 (expressed in akçe)*

Location	Usable data	1–2,500 akçe	2,501–5,000 akçe	5,001–7,500 akçe	7,501–10,000 akçe	10,001–12,500 akçe	12,501–15,000 akçe	Over 15,001 akçe
Ankara, c. 1600	207	47 (22.7%)	52 (25.1%)	41 (19.8%)	31 (15.0%)	10 (4.8%)	6 (2.9%)	20 (9.7%)
Kayseri, c. 1600	151	49 (32.5%)	31 (20.5%)	23 (15.2%)	8 (5.3%)	10 (6.6%)	7 (4.6%)	23 (15.2%)

[1] Percentages based upon the total of usable cases. Sales of shares have been excluded.

Table 3. *House prices in Ankara and Kayseri around 1690[1] (expressed in akçe)*

Location	Usable data	1–5,000 akçe	5,001–10,000 akçe	10,001–15,000 akçe	15,001–20,000 akçe	20,001–25,000 akçe	25,001–30,000 akçe	30,001–35,000 akçe	35,001–40,000 akçe	Over 40,000 akçe
Ankara, c. 1690	221	51 (23.1%)	57 (25.8%)	36 (16.3%)	15 (6.8%)	15 (6.8%)	13 (5.9%)	6 (2.7%)	5 (2.3%)	23 (10.4%)
Kayseri, c. 1690	237	33 (13.9%)	79 (33.3%)	38 (16.0%)	24 (10.1%)	6 (2.5%)	19 (8.0%)	10 (4.2%)	7 (3.0%)	21 (8.9%)

[1] Percentages based upon the total of usable cases. Sales of shares have been excluded.

that the vast majority of all houses was worth 10,000 *akçe* or less. One hundred and seventy-one houses (50 per cent of all cases documented, or 82.6 per cent of the 207 cases for which usable data are available) fell into this particular category. Moreover, as is apparent from Graph 2, the lower part of the pyramid is not particularly steep; in fact, the second category (2,501–5,000 *akçe*) is even slightly larger than the lowest category. However, beyond 10,000 *akçe*, the pyramid comes to resemble a needle: a number of size categories, each containing but a very few cases, is piled one on top of the other. In fact, the appearance of the last category (15,001 *akçe* and over) is in a sense deceptive, for even within this particular group, the range of documented prices was extremely broad: two of the most valuable dwellings were valued at 60,000 *akçe* each, one house was priced 62,000 and another 63,000 *akçe*. Thus, one feels tempted to claim that two separate groups of houses existed in late-sixteenth- and early-seventeenth-century Ankara. On one side there was the 'ordinary' dwelling, which was represented by the mean and median values which characterize this particular group of data. The mean lay at 8,475 *akçe*, while the median was no higher than 5,303 *akçe*, the discrepancy between these two values reflecting the distorting impact of the most expensive residences. On the other hand, there was a handful of really valuable homes, worth twenty, thirty, or even fifty thousand *akçe*, which must have constituted an attractive background for the lives of the wealthier families of the city.

Where the late sixteenth and the early seventeenth centuries are concerned, the distribution of prices in Kayseri resembles that recorded for Ankara in its basic features, while differing considerably with respect to the details. In both instances, usable price data were encountered in 60–70 per cent of all recorded cases. As in Ankara, the number of houses worth 15,001 *akçe* and more was higher than the number of dwellings in the 10,001–15,000 range, thus creating on the graph an effect rather like that of an overhanging rock. However, had all size categories that were represented in the distribution been shown individually on the graph, the overall effect would have been more like a needle. In this respect as well, the situation in Kayseri was parallel to that observed in Ankara. In fact, the range over which house prices recorded in late-sixteenth- and early-seventeenth-century Kayseri might vary, is even broader than the range encountered in the case of contemporary Ankara, for in one instance, a price of 120,000 *akçe* was recorded.

Moreover, the share of houses valued at over 15,000 *akçe* was greater in Kayseri than in Ankara: 15.2 per cent of all houses documented fell into this highest category of our frequency distribution. However, the number of extremely expensive homes (40,000 *akçe* and over) was smaller in Kayseri than in Ankara. Only two houses lay in the 50,000–60,000 range, while most of the residences belonging to the wealthiest families of the city were priced at 20,000–30,000 *akçe*.

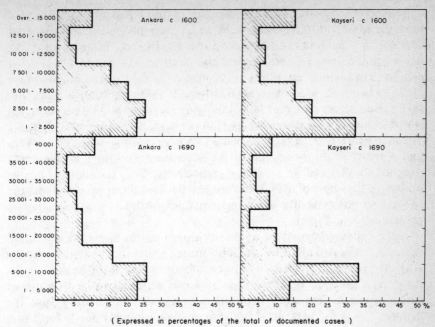

(Expressed in percentages of the total of documented cases)

2. House prices

Mean and median prices as computed for Kayseri are broadly comparable to their Ankara counterparts. The mean amounted to 8,995 *akçe*; to a large degree the difference between Ankara and Kayseri means was due to the one 'freak' case mentioned above, and is therefore of no great importance. At the same time, the median for Kayseri stood at 4,560 *akçe* and thereby was lower than the comparable figure for Ankara (5,303 *akçe*). This difference can be explained by the fact that Ankara was more involved in interregional trade than Kayseri, therefore it is possible that the overall level of prices, homes included, was slightly higher than in the more isolated town of Kayseri.[14]

Table 3 reflects the prices of houses paid by the inhabitants of Ankara and Kayseri in the 1690s, converted into *akçe* in order to facilitate comparison. In both instances, but particularly in the case of Kayseri, the share of unusable data is much smaller than it had been ninety years earlier, reflecting the greater professionalism of late-seventeenth-century scribes. By this period, houses valued at 5,000 *akçe* or less had dwindled from 47.8 per cent to 23.1 per cent in the case of Ankara, and from 53.0 per cent to 13.9 per cent in the case of Kayseri. The impact of the price revolution and of subsequent devaluations is clearly visible; unfortunately Barkan's price index does not extend into the 1690s, so that it is not possible to compare the development of food and housing prices.

Between the 1600s and the 1690s the share of Ankara houses priced between 5,001 and 10,000 *akçe* decreased appreciably, falling from 34.8 per cent to 25.8 per cent. In Kayseri on the other hand, the more dramatic decline in the share of lowest-priced houses (from 53.0 per cent to 13.9 per cent) was to some extent offset by an increase in the share of houses which changed hands at a price between 5,001 and 10,000 *akçe*: from 20.5 per cent in the years before and after 1600, this figure increased to 33.3 per cent, that is to one third of all Kayseri dwellings. As a result, houses priced 10,000 *akçe* and less, which had made up 82.6 and 73.5 per cent of all houses in Ankara and Kayseri at the beginning of the seventeenth century, by the 1690s declined to 48.5 and 47.2 per cent respectively. Thus the share of houses accessible to people of modest income had become about equal for both the two cities; but what the social repercussions of this fact were cannot at present be determined.

In the upper reaches of the frequency histogram, the distribution of house prices in 1690s Ankara is considerably more regular than that observed for Kayseri (compare Graph 2). The price categories into which Ankara houses have been grouped decrease in size as one proceeds toward the upper categories of the frequency distribution. In Kayseri, on the other hand, the category '20,001–25,000 *akçe*' is all but missing, probably due to fortuitous causes, while the next higher category (25,001–30,000 *akçe*) is much more frequently represented in Kayseri than in Ankara. Thus the share of dwellings priced between 20,001 and 30,000 *akçe* is again more or less similar (12.7 per cent in Ankara, 10.5 per cent in Kayseri). This state of affairs would lead one to assume that there was also considerable similarity between the upper income levels of the two cities. Given our knowledge about Ankara and Kayseri, this does not appear surprising; and even Ankara's slight edge over Kayseri is well in keeping with what must have been the former town's greater commercial opportunities during those years.

As is apparent from Graph 2, the 'overhanging rock' effect in the highest price category (40,001 *akçe* and beyond) can once more be observed in the case of both Ankara and Kayseri during the 1690s. Again this peculiarity of the frequency distribution of prices is due to the fact that the sums of money paid for the most expensive residences were spread over a very broad range. For Ankara, the most valuable dwelling on record fetched a price which, expressed in *guruş* was equivalent to 180,000 *akçe*, while for Kayseri, the highest price documented was 173,600 *akçe*. In both cities, the share of houses priced over 40,000 *akçe* was in the same order of magnitude (8–10 per cent of all dwellings documented).

In addition, the means and medians of the prices paid for dwellings in both cities are virtually identical for the closing years of the seventeenth century. In both cases, the median lay at 11,000 *akçe*, while the Ankara mean amounted to 18,655, and Kayseri mean to 18,453 *akçe*. This remarkable parallelism indicates that the differences between the two price distributions tended to cancel each other out, and probably reflects basic similarities where the housing standards of the two cities were concerned.

At the same time, one may speculate about the meaning of the fact that Ankara houses were no longer more expensive than the dwellings of Kayseri. From certain pieces of indirect evidence, such as the stable number of mohair looms in the city and the population estimates relayed by European travellers of the eighteenth century, we had concluded that Ankara recovered reasonably well after the prolonged crisis of the late sixteenth and early seventeenth century. Moreover, in various contexts we have observed features that might be interpreted as evidence of crowding. Under these circumstances, one would have expected Ankara dwellings to have been more expensive, on the average, than those of Kayseri. But since the social and economic history of seventeenth- and eighteenth-century Anatolia is as yet known only in its barest outlines, all explanations of necessity remain somewhat speculative. One might assume that in Kayseri during the 1690s, the return of former inhabitants gave rise to a housing shortage, and that for a limited amount of time, as long as the boom lasted – the level of Kayseri house prices equalled that which prevailed in Ankara in a more sustained fashion. But this explanation is no more than a simple hypothesis, to be confirmed or proven wrong as our knowledge of the period advances.

Types of houses, levels of prices

As a next step, we will investigate whether the different configurations of rooms that have been studied in a previous chapter were situated at different price levels (Tables 4–7 and Graphs 3–6). Table 4 shows that in Ankara during the later sixteenth and early seventeenth centuries, Type 1 was the most popular type among the owners of high-priced houses. Out of a total of 51 cases, fifteen concerned houses priced higher than 10,000, and ten even involved residences worth more than 15,000 *akçe*. By contrast, all other types were represented at most three times in the medium and upper price categories (over 10,000 *akçe*). At the same time, it is obvious that wealthier owners avoided dwellings which possessed either no *tabhane* or else no courtyard. (Types 5 and 6.) While these two more modest types of houses were reasonably well represented, each encompassing slightly over one-tenth of the total, they were to be found almost exclusively in the two lowest price categories, that is, among the houses priced 5,000 *akçe* or less. All this is not particularly surprising, since one would expect that, by and large, the wealthy lived in more elaborate houses than the poor. Thus, the distribution is remarkable mainly for the negative conclusions that it allows us to formulate. For instance, the *sofa*, that characteristic feature of traditional Turkish houses, did not serve as a status symbol, to be found only in higher priced dwellings. Quite to the contrary, Type 2, which encompassed a *sofa*

Table 4. *The price of different types of houses, Ankara c. 1600*

Type of House	1–2,500 akçe	2,501–5,000 akçe	5,001–7,500 akçe	7,501–10,000 akçe	10,001–12,500 akçe	12,501–15,000 akçe	15,001–17,500 akçe	17,501–20,000 akçe	20,001–22,500 akçe	22,501–25,000 akçe	25,001– akçe	Total
Type 1 (*tabhane, sofa, oda, avlu*)	1	10	17	8	3	2	1	1	0	3	5	51 (30.7%)
Type 2 (*tabhane, sofa, avlu*)	9	10	9	8	1	1	0	0	0	0	1	39 (23.5%)
Type 3 (*tabhane, avlu*)	5	1	2	0	0	0	0	0	0	1	0	9 (5.4%)
Type 4 (*tabhane, oda, avlu*)	5	13	6	5	1	0	0	1	0	0	1	32 (19.3%)
Type 5 (*avlu, no tabhane*)	6	8	1	1	1	0	0	0	0	0	0	17 (10.2%)
Type 6 (*tabhane, no avlu*)	8	5	2	0	2	0	0	0	0	0	1	18 (10.8%)
Totals	34 (20.5%)	47 (28.3%)	37 (22.3%)	22 (13.3%)	8 (4.8%)	3 (1.8%)	1 (0.6%)	2 (1.2%)	0	4 (2.4%)	8 (4.8%)	166

Percentages based upon 166, that is, the total of cases usable in the present context.

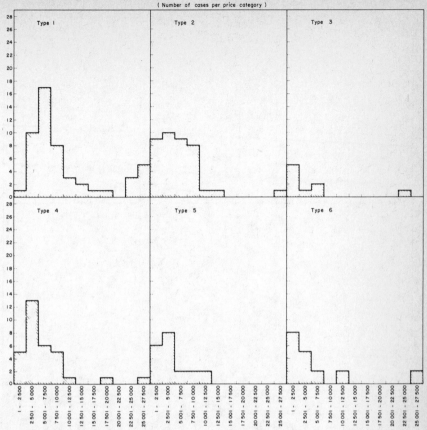

3. The prices of different types of houses, Ankara c 1600

but no *oda*, was almost exclusively to be found among modest dwellings, valued at 10,000 *akçe* or less.

Compared to their Ankara counterparts, the owners of the more highly priced houses of Kayseri showed a somewhat less marked preference for the 'completely developed' type of dwelling represented by Type 1. Out of 27 houses classed as Type 1, 11 dwellings (40.7 per cent) had been assigned a price of over 10,000 *akçe*; while seven were valued at more than 17,501 *akçe*. However, at the same time, 21 dwellings sold at a price of over 10,000 *akçe* belonged to Type 2, that is they contained *tabhane* and *sofa* but lacked the probably secondary feature of an *oda*. This fact must be viewed in context, as Type 2 was the characteristic configuration of rooms preferred in late sixteenth and early seventeenth century Kayseri. Thus, it would seem that the wealthier inhabitants of this latter city departed from local custom only to a limited extent, although they had begun to show an inclination toward dwellings which contained a full array of rooms (Type 1). By contrast,

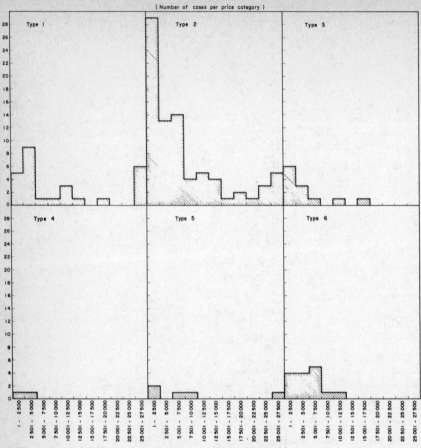

4. The prices of different types of houses, Kayseri c 1600

better-off house-owners were not attracted by Types 3, 4, 5, and 6; among houses valued at over 10,000 akçe, only a few dwellings fell into all four of these types taken together. But then Types 3, 4, 5, and 6 were not much favoured among the inhabitants of late sixteenth- and early seventeenth-century Kayseri in general. In this particular instance, the wealthier house owners again appear to have simply followed local custom.

By the end of the seventeenth century, the preferences of the men owning Ankara's most valuable residential property had changed quite appreciably (see Table 6). In consideration of the devaluation of the akçe, and the attendant increase in prices, we will for the time being consider a price of 30,000 akçe as the lower limit for really valuable residential property. In that case, we find that in ten instances the wealthy inhabitants of Ankara still remained attached to Type 1. However, Types 4, 5, and 6 were noticeably gaining ground. Type 4, consisting of a *tabhane*, an *oda* and a courtyard, was

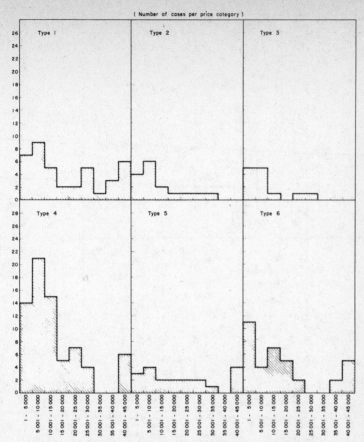

5. The prices of different types of houses, Ankara 1690

represented by six dwellings priced at more than 40,000 *akçe*. For Type 5 (a dwelling with a courtyard, but lacking a *tabhane*) five dwellings valued at over 30,000 *akçe* are on record; among these, four were even priced more than 40,000 *akçe*. Even more remarkably, some of the more valuable residences of late-seventeenth-century Ankara no longer included a courtyard (Type 6). This becomes apparent from the fact that out of thirty-six residences belonging to Type 6, seven were priced at over 30,000, and five were valued at more than 40,000 *akçe*. Nonetheless, the less elaborate Types 5 and 6 were mainly to be found among the more modest residences, a state of affairs which conforms to common sense expectations. It has previously been suggested that in late seventeenth-century Ankara land for building was becoming scarce. Now, we might amplify this hypothesis in the sense that even the wealthier inhabitants of the city were beginning to feel the strain. As a result, some of them began to economize on land by building houses without a courtyard, possibly compensating for the discomforts of a

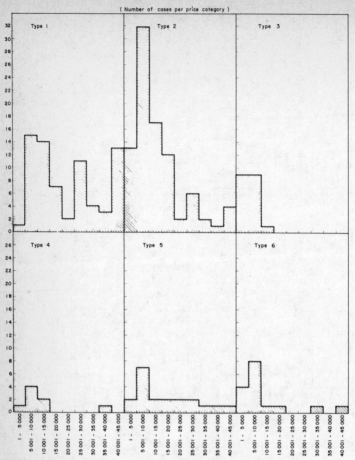

6. The prices of different types of houses, Kayseri c 1690

more crowded environment by spending more on materials and decoration.[15] Or looking at the same facts from a slightly different perspective, we might say that the price of houses increased to a point that even certain residences without a *tabhane* or courtyard might be considered very valuable.

Seventeenth-century Kayseri, on the other hand, differed from Ankara in that the wealthier inhabitants of the town showed an increasing interest in houses of Type 1, which had only been very moderately favoured during the years before and after 1600 (Tables 4 and 6). Out of the 70 dwellings belonging to Type 1, 20 residences were worth more than 30,000 *akçe*; this meant that the share of these valuable houses amounted to almost one-third. At the same time, Type 2 dwellings had become less common among high-priced houses: only 7 out of 89 houses belonging to Type 2 were considered

Table 5. *The price of different types of houses, Kayseri c. 1600*

Type of House	1–2,500 akçe	2,501–5,000 akçe	5,001–7,500 akçe	7,501–10,000 akçe	10,001–12,500 akçe	12,501–15,000 akçe	15,001–17,500 akçe	17,501–20,000 akçe	20,001–22,500 akçe	22,501–25,000 akçe	25,001– akçe	Total
Type 1 (*tabhane, sofa, oda, avlu*)	5	9	1	1	3	1	0	1	0	0	6	27 (19.0%)
Type 2 (*tabhane, sofa, avlu*)	29	13	14	4	5	4	1	2	1	3	5	81 (57.0%)
Type 3 (*tabhane, avlu*)	6	3	1	0	1	0	1	0	0	0	0	12 (8.5%)
Type 4 (*tabhane, oda, avlu*)	1	1	0	0	0	0	0	0	0	0	0	2 (1.4%)
Type 5 (*avlu,* no *tabhane*)	2	0	1	1	0	0	0	0	0	0	1	5 (3.5%)
Type 6 (*tabhane,* no *avlu*)	4	4	5	1	1	0	0	0	0	0	0	15 (10.6%)
Totals	47 (33.1%)	30 (21.1%)	22 (15.5%)	7 (4.9%)	10 (7.0%)	5 (3.5%)	2 (1.4%)	3 (2.1%)	1 (0.7%)	3 (2.1%)	12 (8.5%)	142

Percentages based upon 142, that is, the total of cases usable in the present context.

Table 6. *The price of different types of houses, Ankara c. 1690*

Type of House	1–5,000 akçe	5,001–10,000 akçe	10,001–15,000 akçe	15,001–20,000 akçe	20,001–25,000 akçe	25,001–30,000 akçe	30,001–35,000 akçe	35,001–40,000 akçe	40,001– akçe	Total
Type 1 (tabhane, sofa, avlu, oda)	7	9	5	2	2	5	1	3	6	40 (20.3%)
Type 2 (tabhane, sofa, avlu)	4	6	2	1	1	1	1	0	0	16 (8.1%)
Type 3 (tabhane, avlu)	5	5	1	0	1	1	0	0	0	13 (6.6%)
Type 4 (tabhane, oda, avlu)	14	21	15	5	7	4	0	0	6	72 (36.5%)
Type 5 (avlu, no tabhane)	3	4	2	2	2	2	1	0	4	20 (10.2%)
Type 6 (tabhane, no avlu)	11	4	7	5	2	0	0	2	5	36 (18.2%)
Totals	44 (22.3%)	49 (24.9%)	32 (16.2%)	15 (7.6%)	15 (7.6%)	13 (6.6%)	3 (1.5%)	5 (2.5%)	21 (10.7%)	197

Percentages based upon 197, that is, the total of cases usable in the present context.

Table 7. *The price of different types of houses, Kayseri c. 1690*

Type of House	1–5,000 akçe	5,001–10,000 akçe	10,001–15,000 akçe	15,001–20,000 akçe	20,001–25,000 akçe	25,001–30,000 akçe	30,001–35,000 akçe	35,001–40,000 akçe	40,001– akçe	Total
Type 1 (*tabhane, sofa, oda, avlu*)	1	15	14	7	2	11	4	3	13	70 (31.5%)
Type 2 (*tabhane, sofa, avlu*)	13	32	17	12	2	6	2	1	4	89 (40.1%)
Type 3 (*tabhane, avlu*)	9	9	1	0	0	0	0	0	0	19 (8.6%)
Type 4 (*tabhane, oda, avlu*)	1	4	2	0	0	0	0	1	0	8 (3.6%)
Type 5 (*tabhane,* no *avlu*)	2	7	2	2	2	2	1	1	1	20 (9.0%)
Type 6 (*avlu,* no *tabhane*)	4	8	1	1	0	0	1	0	1	16 (7.2%)
Totals	30 (13.5%)	75 (33.8%)	37 (16.7%)	22 (10.0%)	6 (2.7%)	19 (8.6%)	8 (3.6%)	6 (2.7%)	19 (8.6%)	222

Percentages based upon 222, that is, the total of cases usable in the present context.

133

Table 8. *The price of houses sold by Muslims and non-Muslims, Ankara c. 1600*

	1–2,500 akçe	2,501–5,000 akçe	5,001–7,500 akçe	7,501–10,000 akçe	10,001–12,500 akçe	12,501–15,000 akçe	Over 15,000 akçe	Data not usable	Total
Data not usable								173	173 (50.6%)
Seller(s) Muslim	30 (83.3%)	31 (73.8%)	25 (71.4%)	17 (68.0%)	6 (85.7%)	4 (80.0%)	14 (73.7%)		127 (37.1%)
Seller(s) non-Muslim	6 (16.6%)	11 (26.2%)	10 (28.6%)	8 (32.0%)	1 (14.3%)	1 (20.0%)	5 (26.3%)		42 (12.3%)
Total	36	42	35	25	7	5	19	173	342

Percentages based upon the total of each column.

Table 9. *The price of houses sold by Muslims and non-Muslims, Kayseri c. 1600*

	1–2,500 akçe	2,501–5,000 akçe	5,001–7,500 akçe	7,501–10,000 akçe	10,001–12,500 akçe	12,501–15,000 akçe	Over 15,000 akçe	Data not usable	Total
Data not usable								95	95
Seller(s) Muslim	38 (90.5%)	25 (83.3%)	13 (56.5%)	5 (71.4%)	6 (60.0%)	3 (42.9%)	12 (54.5%)		102
Seller(s) non-Muslim	4 (9.5%)	5 (16.7%)	10 (43.5%)	2 (28.6%)	4 (40.0%)	4 (57.1%)	10 (45.5%)		39
Total	42	30	23	7	10	7	22	95	236

Percentages based upon the total of each column.

to be worth more than 30,000 *akçe*. At the same time, Type 2 continued to be popular among people whose houses were moderately priced. Thus 45 houses, or 20.3 per cent of all residences on which we possess usable data, belonged both to Type 2 and were priced at 10,000 *akçe* or less. Certainly the shift toward Type 1 houses was apparent among less expensive dwellings as well: 16 out of 70 Type 1 houses were priced at 10,000 *akçe* or less. But nothing prevents us from assuming that it was the wealthy owners who had started the trend, whose example was later imitated by their less prosperous fellow citizens. At the same time, the wealthy inhabitants of Kayseri continued to avoid houses of Types 3, 4, 5, and 6, thus continuing the trend which had already been visible during the years shortly before and after 1600. However, among the more modest houses, priced 10,000 *akçe* or less, particularly Types 3 and 6 enjoyed some popularity, prolonging a tendency which had already been noticeable in the early years of the seventeenth century.

Muslims and non-Muslims

In previous chapters of the present study, it has been established that the non-Muslim community was playing an important role in the economic life of Ankara and Kayseri, and constituted a growing share at least of the Kayseri population. Therefore, it is of particular interest to find out whether this economic role was reflected in the prices of the houses which Muslims and non-Muslims inhabited. Tables 8 and 9 reflect the distribution of houses over different price categories which could be observed for the end of the sixteenth and for the beginning of the seventeenth century.

In Ankara, the share of non-Muslims selling houses was lowest for the cheapest categories (1–2,500 *akçe*), and for one of the upper medium levels (10,001–12,500 *akçe*, see Graph 7). However, we must take into account that the number of cases in the upper categories tends to be rather small, and as a result, the percentage values are less meaningful than for the lower categories. In the ranges of 2,501–10,000 *akçe*, the share of non-Muslims selling houses grew progressively from one category to the next. Non-Muslims were most frequently represented in the category ranging from 7,501–10,000 *akçe*. To a lesser degree, they could moreover be found among the sellers of houses priced 2,501–5,000 *akçe*, and also in the highest level of the frequency distribution. Thus as a result of some significance, we should retain the fact that during the years shortly before and after 1600, non-Muslims were little represented among the owners of the most modest houses. If the value of the dwellings sold is any guide to the place of the sellers in the hierarchy of wealth, the non-Muslims of Ankara should have been most frequently found among people of middle income. Many of them must have been craftsmen manufacturing mohair cloth, a characteristic feature of Ankara's industrial scene. At the same time, there were certain wealthy non-Muslims, who in all likelihood had acquired their wealth as merchants and tax farmers.

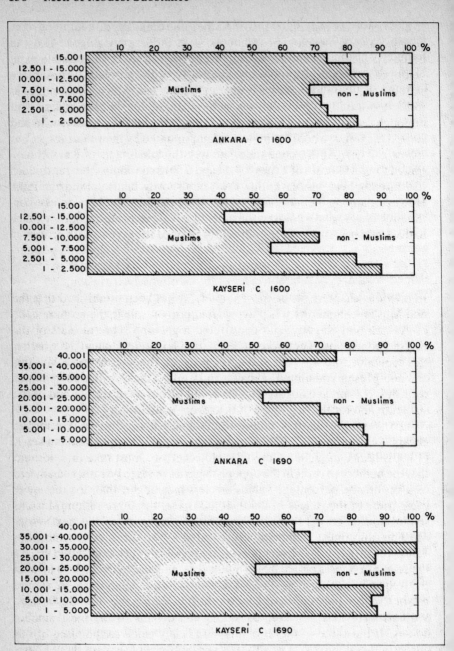

7. Prices of Muslim and non-Muslim houses

Much more regular is the distribution for late sixteenth and early seventeenth century Kayseri. As we move into the upper categories of the frequency histogram and look at houses priced 7500 *akçe* and more (Graph 7), the share of non-Muslims grows more or less regularly with each increase in value of the houses sold. However, the highest category (over 15,000 *akçe*) does not fit into this pattern, as the share of non-Muslim sellers to be found in it amounts to 45.5 per cent, as opposed to 57.1 per cent in the preceding category. Again assuming that the relative wealth of urban houseowners was more or less accurately reflected in the value of their dwellings, the non-Muslim owners of Kayseri belonged mostly to the middle income and to the wealthier inhabitants of the city. They had even managed to penetrate into the wealthiest group, although here the Muslim element maintained itself better than elsewhere.

Surprisingly enough, by the end of the seventeenth century the situation was more or less reversed (cf. Graph 7). As is apparent from Tables 10 and 11, now the situation in Ankara was represented by a regular pyramid-shaped frequency histogram, while the distribution of Muslim and non-Muslim owners over the different price categories appeared much more irregular in Kayseri. In the latter city, the price category in which non-Muslim sellers were most frequently represented ranged from 20,001 to 25,000 *akçe*. Up to that point, the share of non-Muslims tended to increase as one moved upward from one price-level to the next, even though the pattern involved was somewhat irregular. Beyond the 25,000 *akçe* level, the sequence of price categories does not seem to follow any definite pattern. Probably the reason is that Kayseri non-Muslims of the late seventeenth century bought many houses and sold but a few; therefore in the rarified upper regions of the frequency distribution, the number of recorded cases is so limited that a definite trend does not emerge. However, we can once again observe that if high prices received for houses generally indicated wealth, the non-Muslims of the late-seventeenth-century Ankara and Kayseri were rarely to be found among the poorest townsmen (cf. Graph 7). It appears that the majority of non-Muslim inhabitants owned houses situated comfortably in the upper middle reaches of the relevant frequency histogram. An appreciable number of non-Muslims are also on record as having sold very expensive houses; however, in this price range, the share of Muslims tended to be more prominent.

When we compare the means and medians of the prices which Muslim and non-Muslims received for the houses which they sold, we arrive at similar conclusions (Table 12). In every single case, both where means and where medians were involved, non-Muslims received higher prices for their houses than Muslims. Remarkable was the difference in prices recorded for 1690s Kayseri where the average (mean) price paid to non-Muslims amounted to 156 per cent of the average price paid to Muslims. Even more extreme was the situation in Ankara at the end of the seventeenth century, as in this city

Table 10. The price of houses sold by Muslims and non-Muslims, Ankara c. 1690

	1–5,000 akçe	5,001–10,000 akçe	10,001–15,000 akçe	15,001–20,000 akçe	20,001–25,000 akçe	25,001–30,000 akçe	30,001–35,000 akçe	35,001–40,000 akçe	40,000– akçe	Data not usable	Total
Data not usable										92	92 (31.8%)
Seller(s) Muslim	40 (85.1%)	44 (84.6%)	20 (76.9%)	10 (71.4%)	8 (53.3%)	8 (61.5%)	1 (25.0%)	3 (60.0%)	17 (81.0%)		151 (52.2%)
Seller(s) non-Muslim	7 (14.9%)	8 (15.4%)	6 (23.1%)	4 (28.6%)	7 (46.7%)	5 (38.5%)	3 (75.0%)	2 (40.0%)	4 (19.0%)		46 (15.9%)
Total	47	52	26	14	15	13	4	5	21	92	289

Percentages based upon the total of each column.

Table 11. The price of houses sold by Muslims and non-Muslims, Kayseri c. 1690

	1–5,000 akçe	5,001–10,000 akçe	10,001–15,000 akçe	15,001–20,000 akçe	20,001–25,000 akçe	25,001–30,000 akçe	30,001–35,000 akçe	35,001–40,000 akçe	40,000– akçe	Data not usable	Total
Data not usable										76	76 (26.9%)
Seller(s) Muslim	27 (87.1%)	58 (85.3%)	34 (89.5%)	14 (70.0%)	2 (50.0%)	14 (87.5%)	8 (100.0%)	4 (66.7%)	10 (62.5%)		171 (60.4%)
Seller(s) non-Muslim	4 (12.9%)	10 (14.7%)	4 (10.5%)	6 (30.0%)	2 (50.0%)	2 (12.5%)	0	2 (33.3%)	6 (37.5%)		36 (12.7%)
Total	31	68	38	20	4	16	8	6	16	76	283

Table 12. *Mean and median house-prices received by Muslim and non-Muslim sellers (expressed in* akçe)

Seller	Ankara c. 1600	Kayseri c. 1600	Ankara c. 1690	Kayseri c. 1690
Muslims, mean	8,555	8,247	18,285	15,623
Muslims, median	5,300	3,600	9,000	10,080
non-Muslims, mean	10,576	12,204	20,938	24,398
non-Muslims, median	6,050	8,280	17,600	14,100

the median price paid to non-Muslims was almost double that which Muslim sellers received. (However, the difference in mean prices was much less notable.) Even if one assumes that this difference in price level was partly caused by extra-economic factors, it does appear likely that, at least in part, the cause was a disparity in financial resources.

Reaya and askerî

As the next step, we will examine the prices paid to servitors of the Ottoman administration (*askerî*) who sold houses in Ankara during the late sixteenth and early seventeenth centuries (compare Table 13 and Graph 8).[16] In the lower reaches of the frequency histogram, the number of *askerî* is quite limited. Only from 7,501 akçe onward does the share of *askerî* house proprietors increase notably; they were most numerous in the ranges of 7,501–10,000 and 12,501–15,000 akçe. Given the small number of cases involved, far-reaching conclusions should not be drawn from this state of affairs; in fact a slight modification in the definition of *askerî* group membership will result in quite a different distribution. But it is worth noting that even in the topmost price category, most of the houses were owned not by *askerî*, but by ordinary townsmen.

But even if, in the Ankara of the early 1600s, there lived a few *askerî* who were by no means wealthy, and a few *reaya* who could afford expensive dwellings, on the average there was a clear difference between the price paid to a 'typical' *askeri* house owner and that paid to his *reaya* counterpart. Table 14 shows that the mean value of the houses sold by *askerî* house-owners in late-sixteenth- or early-seventeenth-century Ankara was 169 per cent of the price paid to an average *reaya* owner. Moreover, *askerî*, who were almost exclusively Muslims, probably constituted a wealthier group than the local non-Muslim inhabitants. *Askerî* house-owners received an average price of 14,187 akçe for their dwellings, while the non-Muslims of

Table 13. *The price of houses sold by* askerî *and* reaya, *Ankara c. 1600*

	1–2,500 akçe	2,501–5,000 akçe	5,001–7,500 akçe	7,501–10,000 akçe	10,001–12,500 akçe	12,501–15,000 akçe	15,001– akçe	Data not usable	Total
Data not usable								166	166 (48.5%)
Seller(s) askerî	3 (7.7%)	4 (8.5%)	2 (5.9%)	8 (33.3%)	0	2 (40%)	6 (30%)		25 (7.3%)
Seller(s) reaya	36 (92.3%)	43 (91.5%)	32 (94.1%)	16 (66.7%)	7 (100%)	3 (60%)	14 (70%)		151 (44.1%)
Total	39	47	34	24	7	5	20	166	342

Table 14. *Average (mean) house-prices received by* askerî *and* reaya *sellers (expressed in* akçe*)*

Seller	Ankara c. 1600	Kayseri c. 1600	Ankara c. 1690	Kayseri c. 1690
Askerî mean	14,187	15,341	23,416	15,164
Reaya mean	8,387	8,213	17,887	17,817

Ankara could count on an average of 10,576 *akçe*. On the other hand, the average price paid to *reaya* proprietors was 8,387 *akçe*, but since this figure involves both Muslims and non-Muslims, the average sum of money received by Muslim *reaya* selling their houses must have been even lower. Thus for late-sixteenth- and early-seventeenth-century Ankara, we might postulate the following hierarchy of wealth: first the *askerî*, then the local non-Muslims, and finally the majority of Muslim inhabitants.

Table 15 reflects the frequency distribution of house prices in late-sixteenth- and early-seventeenth-century Kayseri. Here the prices paid to *askerî* sellers are very irregularly distributed. Most houses sold by local *askerî* fetched prices between 1 and 7,500 *akçe*, but no very far-reaching conclusions should be drawn from what was, after all, a fairly limited number of cases. On the other hand, the *reaya* of Kayseri were quite clearly dominant in the upper reaches of the frequency histogram (cf. Graph 8).

In the case of late-sixteenth- and early-seventeenth-century Kayseri, the distribution of wealth among the local *askerî*, the Muslim *reaya*, and their non-Muslim counterparts shows some surprising features. When the average prices received from the sale of urban dwellings are compared, the pattern is parallel to that of Ankara: *askerî* sellers received on an average 15,341 *akçe* for their houses, non-Muslim *reaya* 12,204 *akçe*, while the mean for all *reaya*, Muslims and non-Muslims taken together, was 8,213 *akçe*. Thus again, the mean for Muslim *reaya* should have been below this figure. However, the high average for *askerî* is due to the inclusion of one single very high price; if that is eliminated, the *askerî* mean drops to 9,527 *akçe*, and thus on the average the houses of Kayseri non-Muslims should have been more valuable even than those of the local *askerî*. This would seem to indicate that the non-Muslims of Kayseri were turning into the wealthiest group in town, and moreover, that they had no particular qualms about showing the fact. It is probable that the difference in pattern between Ankara and Kayseri had something to do with the fact that Ankara, with its greater involvement in interregional trade, was dominated by a relatively well-to-do group of *askerî*. In Kayseri, on the other hand, many of the local *askerî* were simply descendants of the Prophet Muhammad, who apart from their exemption from certain taxes, were not easily distinguished from the

Table 15. *The price of houses sold by askerî and reaya, Kayseri c. 1600*

	1–2,500 akçe	2,501–5,000 akçe	5,001–7,500 akçe	7,501–10,000 akçe	10,001–12,500 akçe	12,501–15,000 akçe	15,000– akçe	Data not usable	Total
Data not usable								94	94 (39.8%)
Seller(s) askerî	3 (7.0%)	7 (23.3%)	3 (13.0%)	1 (14.3%)	0	0	5 (22.7%)		19 (8.1%)
Seller(s) reaya	40 (93.0%)	23 (76.7%)	20 (87.0%)	6 (85.7%)	10 (100.0%)	7 (100.0%)	17 (77.3%)		123 (52.1%)
Total	43	30	23	7	10	7	22	94	236

Percentages based upon the total of each column.

Table 16. *The price of houses sold by askerî and reaya, Ankara c. 1690*

	1–5,000 akçe	5,001–10,000 akçe	10,001–15,000 akçe	15,001–20,000 akçe	20,001–25,000 akçe	25,001–30,000 akçe	30,001–35,000 akçe	35,001–40,000 akçe	Over 40,000 akçe	Total
Data not usable									96	96 (33.2%)
Seller(s) askerî	7 (14.9%)	7 (14.0%)	9 (34.6%)	3 (21.4%)	1 (6.7%)	2 (18.2%)	0	1 (20.0%)	6 (28.6%)	36 (12.5%)
Seller(s) reaya	40 (85.1%)	43 (86.0%)	17 (65.4%)	11 (78.6%)	14 (93.3%)	9 (81.8%)	4 (100.0%)	4 (80.0%)	15 (71.4%)	157 (54.3%)
Total	47	50	26	14	15	11	4	5	21	289

Percentages based upon the total of each column.

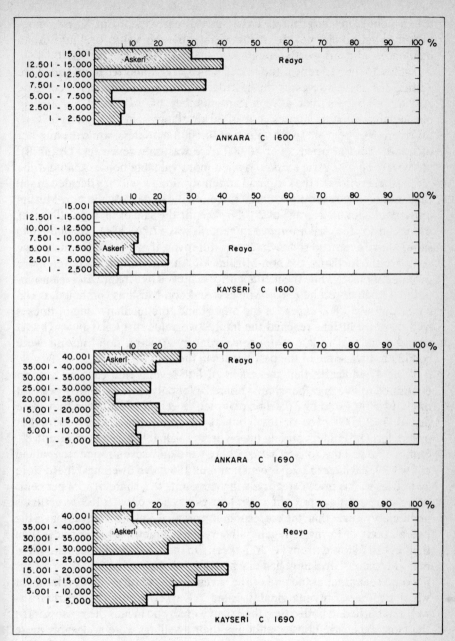

8. Prices of houses sold by *askerî* and *reaya*

urban population in general. Even so, this early record of Kayseri non-Muslims and their wealth, made visible by the value of their urban residences, appears worth retaining.

Tables 16 and 17 reflect the prices which *askerî* and *reaya* owners were getting for their houses in the last decades of the seventeenth century. Again, it appears that a significant number of *askerî* did not live in particularly valuable houses: out of 36 dwellings sold by Ankara *askerî*, fourteen (38.9 per cent) were valued at 10,000 *akçe* or less, while the number of houses sold at prices over 30,000 *akçe* was only seven (cf. Graph 8). However, on an average *askerî* owned more valuable houses than did the *reaya*; for servitors of the Ottoman administration, when they decided to sell their houses, received an average price of 23,416 *akçe*, while non-Muslim *reaya* could get an average of 20,938 *akçe* for the sale of their dwelling. As the mean for the Ankara *reaya* in general was 17,887 *akçe*, Muslim *reaya* should have averaged somewhat less. Moreover, if instead of the means we compare the medians, the non-Muslims of Ankara occupied an even more prominent place: while the median price achieved by Ankara *askerî* amounted to 13,340 *akçe*, the *reaya*, Muslims and non-Muslims combined, could count on only 9,800 *akçe*. On the other hand, the median value of houses sold by non-Muslims reached the impressive value of 17,600 *akçe*. Thus it would seem that in late seventeenth century Ankara, non-Muslims were coming to own some of the best houses in the city.

Table 17 indicates that the *askerî* of late-seventeenth-century Kayseri continued to live in rather simple houses. Not only must over forty per cent of all dwellings sold by *askerî* be regarded as very modest, since they were priced at 10,000 *akçe* or less, but at the same time, *askerî* were not particularly prominent among the owners of valuable houses (cf. Graph 8). Out of 53 dwellings sold by *askerî*, there were only seven residences valued at over 30,000 *akçe* (13.2 per cent); among 156 *reaya* dwellings, there were 24 houses in this price category, which amounts to a share of 15.4 per cent. Moreover, the mean price of *askerî* houses was now only 15,165 *akçe*, that is appreciably lower than the corresponding price in Ankara. *Reaya*, that is the overall body of townsmen, generally even got somewhat better prices than their *askerî* fellow citizens (17,817 *akçe*). On the other hand, the mean value of non-Muslims' dwellings had reached the high point of 24,398 *akçe*.[17] Thus it would seem that at the end of the seventeenth century, the development which had been only marginally visible in Kayseri ninety years earlier was well established in both cities: the *askerî* were by no means the possessors of the most expensive houses, although their dwellings were noticeably more valuable than those of the ordinary inhabitants. But as a group, they lived in houses whose market value was far less than those inhabited by the local non-Muslims.

Table 17. *The price of houses sold by* askeri *and* reaya, *Kayseri c. 1690*

	1–5,000 akçe	5,001– 10,000 akçe	10,001– 15,000 akçe	15,001– 20,000 akçe	20,001– 25,000 akçe	25,001– 30,000 akçe	30,001– 35,000 akçe	35,001– 40,000 akçe	40,001– akçe	Data not usable	Total
Data not usable											74 (26.1%)
Seller(s) askeri	5 (16.7%)	18 (25.0%)	12 (31.6%)	7 (41.2%)	0	4 (23.5%)	3 (33.3%)	2 (33.3%)	2 (12.5%)		53 (18.7%)
Seller(s) reaya	25 (83.3%)	54 (75.0%)	26 (68.4%)	19 (58.8%)	4 (100.0%)	13 (76.5%)	6 (66.7%)	4 (66.7%)	14 (87.5%)		165 (55.1%)
Total	30	72	38	17	4	17	9	6	16	74	283

Percentages based upon the total of each column.

Rich and poor

It has sometimes been claimed that in medieval cities of the Islamic world there was no segregation by income, and that even in the smallest unit, the town quarter or *mahalle*, rich and poor lived side by side. Recently this view has been questioned, and with particular reference to Cairo scholars have pointed to the concentration of palaces and mansions on the one hand, and to the existence of what amounted to squatters' settlements on the other.[18] Closer to home, in seventeenth- and eighteenth-century İstanbul, wealthy residential quarters outside of the old city limits developed on the shore of the Bosphorus.[19] Under these circumstances, one would like to know whether there was any segregation by income in larger provincial towns, such as Ankara or Kayseri; and if one assumes that to a certain extent the price of a house reflected the financial situation of the family that owned it, our data on house prices should provide something of a clue.

However, the main difficulty lies in the fact that usually but a small number of cases is known for every single *mahalle*. Certainly, if we knew in some detail where all *mahalle*s were located, we could combine them into larger units, as is in fact the custom of city administrations in modern Turkey. But since particularly for Kayseri, the location of quite a few *mahalle*s is not known, this solution is not feasible in most instances. Only for the rather large area encompassed in the Ankara Citadel (not town) walls, the so-called Kale district, do the data allow us to cover a good-sized area. Otherwise we have to rely on single *mahalle*s which are particularly well-documented. Table 18 reflects all *mahalle*s for which the *kadı* registers document a minimum of ten cases, although in most instances, actually usable price data as mentioned both in sales documents and in entries concerning the solution of disputes fall far below that desideratum.

Even so, however, a number of conclusions can be drawn. For any given *mahalle*, the range of prices was extremely broad, thus the most valuable house might be about twenty to thirty times as expensive as the cheapest one. This would imply that a single *mahalle* did in fact often contain rich and poor families. However, if we look at the mean and median prices for certain *mahalle*s and compare them with the same values computed for Ankara and Kayseri as a whole, it does in fact appear that certain quarters were noticeably better off or poorer than the average. Thus in early 1600s Ankara, the well documented Imaret *mahalle* seems to have contained a large number of poor families. While the median for the city as a whole was 5,300 *akçe*, it was only 1,900 for the Imaret quarter, which due to its marginal location near the city gates was probably favoured by recent migrants from the countryside. By the same token, the Hacı Musa quarter and the Kale district should have had a large admixture of wealthy residents, even though the means for these two areas are still below the means for Ankara as a whole.

For Kayseri during the closing years of the sixteenth and the beginning of

Table 18. *House prices in selected* mahalles *(all prices are expressed in* akçe*)*

Mahalle	Median	Mean	Range	Number of usable cases
Ankara 1600				
Avancıklar	4,500	4,917	1,500–10,000	6
Hacı Musa	8,000	7,014	1,500–10,010	7
Imaret	1,900	3,078	500–7,200	16
Kale	8,000	7,617	1,200–15,000	6
Kayseri 1600				
Debbağlar	2,760	3,780	1,200–9,360	6
Eslempaşa	6,120	16,440	2,400–51,600	6
Külük	2,400	11,808	1,200–48,000	5
Gürcü	12,000	10,956	2,520–22,560	7
Ankara c. 1690				
Hacı Murad	30,000	30,757	3,500–80,000	7
Kale	18,000	26,060	3,800–100,000	13
Kayseri c. 1690				
Hisanili (?)	13,000	29,364	7,000–140,000	9
Hasbey	12,000	15,071	3,600–40,000	9
Deliklitaş	8,250	10,438	5,000–29,400	8
Selaldı	4,830	5,040	2,800–8,400	6
Tavukçu	15,050	15,880	4,200–31,000	8

the seventeenth century, the tanners' quarter was apparently the poorest; and if the tanneries were actually still located in this area, it is not surprising that no wealthy people lived there. In the largely non-Muslim quarter of Eslempaşa, and the overwhelmingly Muslim quarter of Külük, the range between the most valuable and the cheapest houses was extremely broad; this again indicates that many wealthy families did in fact live in 'mixed' *mahalle*s. Where late-seventeenth-century Ankara is concerned, Hacı Murad *mahalle* would seem to have been more 'posh' than the Citadel area. Both means and medians of house prices in these two areas of Ankara lay well above the corresponding values for the city as a whole.

For late-seventeenth-century Kayseri, we can pinpoint what must have been a poor quarter in the *mahalle* of Selaldı (the name, which means 'the flood took [it]', points to its vulnerability to flash floods). Both median and mean for the seven houses documented in this quarter were less than half the corresponding value for the total city. Noteworthy is the situation in the largely non-Muslim quarter of Tavukçu. As one would expect, the median lay well above the city-wide value, but the mean (average) was less than the corresponding value for the entire city. This would seem to be due to the fact that even the best houses documented for this quarter were comfortable middle-class homes and not of the mansion type which was, for instance, represented in Hisanili (?) *mahalle*.

Conclusion

Taking into account the weaknesses of our data base, the present investigation has largely concentrated upon those areas in which the margin of error is not too broad. We have mainly compared the prices received by different sub-groups in the same city and at the same time period. Under these circumstances, it is not particularly important whether a given average amounts to ten thousand or else to fifteen thousand *akçe*. What counts is the relative weight of Muslims and non-Muslims, of *askerî* and *reaya*, and the distribution of wealthy and poor houses over the city. Luckily these results are probably affected only to a moderate degree by the uncertainties of the conversion rate between *guruş* and *akçe*.

Given these conditions, we can retain the following observations as significant: At the end of the sixteenth and the beginning of the seventeenth centuries, the persons whom our documents allow us to identify as *askerî* tended to own the most valuable houses in their respective cities. This state of affairs allows us to class them among the wealthier inhabitants, even if we need to make allowance for the fact that social customs may have made it necessary for *askerî* to spend more on their residences, and on their appearance in general, than run-of-the-mill townsmen. At the same time, however, the Kayseri *askerî* were in a weaker position than their Ankara counterparts. This makes good sense in view of Ankara's position in interregional trade, for it can be assumed that by and large the *askerî* resident in a given city derived their income from local sources, and were dependent, in this particular instance, upon the cash that flowed into Ankara due to the sale of mohair cloth.

But in the course of the seventeenth century it would appear that both in Ankara and in Kayseri, non-Muslim *reaya* grew increasingly wealthy, or at any rate social customs that required non-Muslims to refrain from displaying their wealth in public tended to break down. As a result, non-Muslims not only received higher prices for their houses than did Muslim inhabitants, but even surpassed the local *askerî*. One might object that given a considerable amount of immigration on the part of non-Muslims, the town quarters which they inhabited were becoming increasingly overcrowded, and that the prices paid for houses rose mainly in response to this factor. This objection may not be totally invalid. But it must be kept in mind that both Muslims and non-Muslims could acquire houses in town quarters not inhabited by their coreligionists, and 'ghetto effects' upon property values thus remained limited. When crowding pushed up real estate prices, the entire city was probably affected, not just the town quarters inhabited by non-Muslims. As a result it would appear that the higher prices paid to non-Muslim owners parting with their property reflected, to a considerable extent, a real advance in the economic position of the non-Muslim communities. This assumption is strengthened by the observation that, exceptions to the contrary notwithstanding, non-Muslims tended to trade real property mainly with their own coreligionists, and the high prices paid to the sellers also demonstrate the monetary resources of the buyers. Moreover, given the leading role of non-Muslims in the economic life of Ankara and Kayseri during the nineteenth century, it is not surprising that certain indicators of this future role were visible even two centuries earlier.

With respect to the question whether Anatolian towns were divided into wealthy and poorer town quarters, it would seem that we can answer with a qualified 'yes'. Certainly it is true that in many *mahalle*s, rich and poor lived side by side. But at the same time, the average level of house prices in a given town quarter might be considerably higher or lower than the urban average. At least in Ankara it would seem that the old centre of the city, that is the Citadel, was among the more desirable residential neighbourhoods, a status which it was able to maintain throughout the nineteenth century, as is apparent even today from the handsome structures whch still survive in that area. On the other hand, a 'marginal' *mahalle*, located near the city walls, was inhabited by poorer people, although they were probably not the poorest of the poor, who probably did not bother to register their property transfers. In this sense, the geographical distribution of wealth and poverty in Ankara and Kayseri confirms Traian Stoianovich's vision of the Ottoman city of the Balkans.[20] Further investigations will show how far this was a general rule, and what factors might intervene to modify it.

CHAPTER 4

Urban property-owners

In the course of the present investigation, we have gradually moved from a description of the built-up environment towards investigating the social characteristics of urban house-owners. A discussion of prices commonly paid for dwellings has provided some data which can be used in identifying the rich and the poor. Both the description of the urban environment and the discussion of prices were intended as a means towards understanding the social structure of a large Anatolian town, and to find out how this structure evolved in the course of the seventeenth century. At the same time, we also possess some data which directly inform us whether a given urban house-owner was a male or a female, a Muslim or a non-Muslim, an official associated with the Ottoman central administration (*askerî*) or an ordinary taxpayer (*reaya*). In the present chapter, we will concentrate upon the analysis of these personal data concerning house owners of seventeenth-century Ankara and Kayseri.

Since the main sources of information on these matters are the names of the people involved, a few remarks concerning naming practices are necessary. As is well known, only wealthy and influential families possessed what might be regarded as a surname. In certain instances, the family's name might attach itself to the building inhabited by its members. Thus, the remains of an elaborate Kayseri dwelling, whose core may go back to the fifteenth century, are still known today as the *konak* of the Gübgüb oğulları.[1]

However, in the vast majority of cases, both Muslims and non-Muslims were identified by their given names and by their fathers' names.[2] With respect to women, the same rules were observed. As a result, we often cannot tell whether a woman mentioned as buying or selling a given piece of property was married, or else widowed or divorced. Normally, Muslims and non-Muslims were clearly distinguishable by their given names; moreover, one can easily identify an 'Anastas' as Greek or a 'Bagdasar' as Armenian. However, certain names were used in common, of which 'Murad' is perhaps one of the better known. Moreover, in the Karamanlı community of Kayseri, people consistently bore Turkish names. Some of the latter, such as

'Körpe' for men or 'Turfanda' for women, were more or less limited to this particular group, but others, such as, for instance, Arslan, might be found among the members of other communities as well. In the major cities of the Empire, such as Bursa or İstanbul, one might in addition encounter more complex situations, such as *zimmi*s known by Muslim names, either because their given names were difficult to pronounce or for other reasons. However, this kind of complication is not often documented in the *kadı*s' records of seventeenth-century Ankara or Kayseri.[3]

Differentiation between Muslims and non-Muslims was furthermore made easy by the custom of recording a Muslim as Ahmed b. Mehmed and a non-Muslim as Murad v(eled-i) Arslan. This distinction, however, was limited to the *kadı*'s records; in the tax registers of the sixteenth century, *veled* had been used to express filiation among Muslims and non-Muslims alike. As a result, there are only a few cases in which a person's religious affiliation is really doubtful, provided the registers contain the full name. However, when given names, or else nicknames, are used in isolation, we often encounter cases that cannot be readily classified.

Much more problematic is the identification of people affiliated with the Ottoman central administration (*askerî*). Janissaries, *sipahi*s, and higher ranking provincial administrators are usually recorded as such, and moreover bear the title *bey*. Since this title is not otherwise very common, it has been assumed that all the men bearing the title *bey* were *askerî* of one sort or another. Moreover, teachers in theological schools (*müderris*), descendants of the Prophet Muhammad (*seyyid*), as well as present and former *kadı*s have all been regarded as *askerî*.[4] However, the title *efendi*, which in those years described a man of some scholarly attainment, has not in itself been considered sufficient to classify a man as *askerî*. Given the nature of the source material, a certain amount of inaccuracy has inevitably crept in; but even a rough and ready classification can help us identify certain peculiarities of social structure in seventeenth-century Anatolian towns.

The problem of joint ownership

But before proceeding to analyse the data concerning the sex and religious affiliation of urban property owners, we need to look at the manner in which real property circulated among seventeenth-century urban town dwellers. A clue is provided by the number of houses sold not in their entirety, but as shares (*hisse*). Or else one might also examine the data on houses which, although sold in their entirety, are on record as having been owned by a group of people, probably but not necessarily in indivision.[5]

In Ankara at the end of the sixteenth and the beginning of the seventeenth century, 35 out of 342 cases (10.2 per cent) involved the sale of shares in a house, or else litigation concerning such shares. In Kayseri during the same period, the same applied to 29 instances, or 12.3 per cent of all cases documented. For the later seventeenth century, the relevant figures were 21 (7.3 per cent) and 16 (5.7 per cent) respectively. Thus, the number of references concerning isolated shares in a dwelling decreased both in Ankara and in Kayseri, although this tendency was much more pronounced in the latter than in the former. At the present stage, it is difficult to give a satisfactory reason why the sale of shares in a house, or litigation concerning such shares, tended to become less frequent. It is possible that such sales were in many cases signs of acute distress, given the inconveniences they caused to buyers and sellers alike. If that should have been the case, it appears reasonable that the sale of shares should have declined once the worst convulsions of the Celâlî rebellions had subsided.

Tables 1 and 2 present evidence concerning the houses sold by more than one owner, a situation constituting an additional manifestation of joint ownership. It immediately becomes apparent that joint ownership was much more common among sellers than among buyers. In fact, among buyers it was altogether exceptional for more than two people to pool resources. In Ankara during the years around 1600, we but once find four people purchasing a dwelling together; nothing is known about the relationship between the men involved, but it is probable that they were either brothers or cousins.[6] Moreover, in one instance three Jews bought a compound containing three separate dwellings. From their names it is apparent that they were not brothers, but again, they could have been more remotely connected.[7]

In the later seventeenth century, the situation had not significantly changed. At one point, three Kayseri *seyyid*s pooled resources to buy a modest dwelling, again a family relationship cannot be proven, but is nonetheless probable.[8] In another instance of the same type, the three purchasers in question were definitely brothers.[9] For late-seventeenth-century Ankara, we also know of an instance in which three non-Muslim brothers purchased a house together.[10] In a further case involving three relatives, the association was purely involuntary, since all three happened to be heirs to the property of a deceased person. Moreover, in this case the 'purchase' of the house was simply a cover for a loan, and the house was transferred to the three creditors in order to provide security.[11] It is unlikely that the creditors ever lived in it. In fact, even though the document tells us nothing about the matter, it is very possible that the old owners continued to inhabit the property, paying rent in guise of interest. Moreover, it is worth noting that even purchase by two people was not very common. Particularly husband and wife occur as joint purchasers much less frequently than might be expected. Thus, among the five instances of two people purchasing a house in Ankara during the years around 1600, only one case involved a husband and wife.[12] In all other instances, the men and women referred to were brothers and sisters.

Thus we may assume that when a house was purchased in seventeenth-

Table 1. *Number of people involved in the sale of urban real-estate*[1]

Location	Usable data	Number of sellers								
		1	2	3	4	5	6	7	8	9	Total
Ankara, c. 1600	217	184 (84.8%)	14 (6.5%)	9 (4.1%)	6 (2.8%)	1 (0.5%)	1 (0.5%)	1 (0.5%)	1 (0.5%)	0	342
Kayseri, c. 1600	175	140 (80%)	17 (9.7%)	9 (5.1%)	8 (4.6%)	0	1 (0.6%)	0	0	0	236
Ankara, c. 1690	229	177 (77.3%)	32 (14.0%)	12 (5.2%)	2 (0.9%)	4 (1.7%)	2 (0.9%)	0	0	0	289
Kayseri, c. 1690	225	167 (74.2%)	24 (10.7%)	15 (6.7%)	8 (3.6%)	7 (3.1%)	0	1 (0.4%)	2 (0.8%)	1 (0.4%)	283

[1] Percentages are based upon the number of usable data.

Table 2. *Number of people involved in the purchase of urban real-estate*[1]

Location	Usable data	Number of buyers				Total
		1	2	3	4	
Ankara, c. 1600	216	209 (96.8%)	5 (2.3%)	1 (0.5%)	1 (0.5%)	342
Kayseri, c. 1600	174	171 (98.2%)	3 (1.8%)	0	0	236
Ankara, c. 1690	228	220 (96.5%)	6 (2.7%)	2 (0.9%)	0	289
Kayseri, c. 1690	225	210 (93.3%)	13 (5.8%)	2 (0.9%)	0	283

[1] Percentages are based upon the number of usable data.

century Ankara, the purchaser was normally a single individual. Fragmented ownership was mainly the result of partible inheritance. On the other hand, it was not an uncommon occurrence for heirs to sell the property which had devolved upon them, and to share out the price according to the rules of inheritance codified in Muslim canon law (*şeriat*). Certainly, it should not be assumed that all houses inherited by a large group of heirs were sold in this manner, since those houses that heirs continued to possess in indivision do not show up in the *kadıs*' registers. However, we can safely conclude that brothers rarely bought a house with a view to inhabiting it as an extended family, nor was it common to purchase certain shares in a house while the owner retained the remainder. On the other hand, it is probable that quite a few men purchased dwellings because they wished to set up a separate household. Where two or more related nuclear families inhabited one and the same dwelling, the arrangement was in most cases due to the fact that they were living on inherited property.

Muslims and non-Muslims

There was no obligation for the non-Muslims of the Ottoman Empire to bring their affairs before the *kadı*. But when they did, the rules of the *şeriat* concerning inheritance and similar matters were applied to non-Muslims as well.[13] At the same time, the frequency of non-Muslim names recorded in the *kadı* registers shows that non-Muslims turned to the court very readily.[14] Most probably, the possibility of obtaining unassailable proof that a given transaction had actually been concluded must have attracted non-Muslims to the *kadı*'s court. This state of affairs in the long run tended to obscure the differences between Muslim and non-Muslim patterns of real estate ownership – if indeed such differences ever existed – and thus should have contributed toward the cultural assimilation of the non-Muslims.

Table 3. *The religion of people selling houses*[1]

Location	Info. not usable	Sellers all Muslim	Sellers all non-Muslim	Mixed	Total usable descrip.	Grand total
Ankara, c. 1600	124	169 (77.5%)	47 (21.6%)	2 (0.9%)	218	342
Kayseri, c. 1600	61	127 (72.6%)	48 (27.4%)	0	175	236
Ankara, c. 1690	60	176 (76.9%)	53 (23.1%)	0	229	289
Kayseri, c. 1690	58	181 (80.4%)	42 (18.7%)	2 (0.9%)	225	283

[1] In this table, percentages are based not upon the grand total but upon the total of usable descriptions.

Table 4. *The religion of people buying houses*[1]

Location	Info. not usable	Buyers all Muslim	Buyers all non-Muslim	Mixed	Total usable descrip.	Grand total
Ankara, c. 1600	124	165 (75.7%)	51 (23.4%)	2 (0.9%)	218	342
Kayseri, c. 1600	61	125 (71.4%)	49 (28.0%)	1 (0.6%)	175	236
Ankara, c. 1690	61[2]	161 (70.6%)	67 (29.4%)	0	228	289
Kayseri, c. 1690	59[2]	142 (63.4%)	82 (36.6%)	0	224	283

[1] In this table, percentages are based not upon the grand total but upon the total of usable descriptions.
[2] The divergencies between Table 3 and 4 result from the fact that in a few cases, information may be available on the buyer but not on the seller. Cases with incomplete information on both buyer and seller show up in the 'information not usable' category.

The religious allegiance of buyers and sellers is of particular interest when compared to the total population of the cities in question. For Ankara in the years shortly before and after 1600, such comparison is not feasible, because no data exist that allow us to estimate the town's religious composition. Where Kayseri is concerned, Ronald Jennings has established a population 78 per cent Muslim and 22 per cent Christian for the year 1583;[15] thus the share of non-Muslims in the housing market was somewhat higher than their share of the total population. For Ankara during the 1690s, official Ottoman data are even less available than for the beginning of the seventeenth century. Thus, we have no option but to fall back upon the estimates of European travellers, even though the latter are known to be far from reliable. Writing in the early 1700s, Pococke claims that the city contained 100,000 inhabitants, of which 10 per cent supposedly were non-Muslims.[16] If this percentage value is even approximately correct, Ankara non-Muslims should have bought and sold many more houses than was warranted by their share in the total population.

Where the city of Kayseri during the years around 1690 is concerned, we only possess a listing of non-Muslim inhabitants and can therefore say nothing about the ratio between Muslims and non-Muslims.[17] According to the tax register of 1055/1645–6, non-Muslims made up 37.7 per cent of the local population. But since the city experienced considerable ups and downs in population, no far-reaching conclusions can be drawn from this state of affairs. It appears that in Kayseri the percentage of non-Muslims was increasing in the earlier years of the seventeenth century, then difficulties with local administrators brought about fairly widespread emigration. However, by 1104/1692–3 most of the *émigrés* had returned, and this stabilization of the local non-Muslim community is reflected in increasing activity as buyers and sellers of houses.[18]

If it can be assumed that participation in the local real estate market constituted a rough measure for the relative strength of the non-Muslims in both cities, then it would appear that the non-Muslims of Ankara were increasing in number. While in the years around 1600 they made up 21.6 per cent of all sellers and 23.4 per cent of all buyers, towards the end of the century 23.1 per cent of all sellers and 29.4 per cent of all buyers were non-Muslims. In Kayseri, the situation was a little more complicated: between the beginning and the end of the seventeenth century, the proportion of non-Muslim sellers decreased from 27.4 per cent to 18.7 per cent. But on the other hand, the share of the non-Muslims among purchasers of houses increased dramatically, namely from 28 per cent to 36.6 per cent. Since houses were not generally acquired in order to be rented out, it must be assumed that buyers of houses were people who intended to reside in the city. On the other hand, no comparable statement is possible with respect to the sellers, for we do not know whether they left the city, or else simply moved to another part of town. Thus, the increasing share of non-Muslims who bought houses in Kayseri seems more significant than their declining share among sellers, and one can assume that the non-Muslim population of Kayseri was at the very least remaining stable.

Seen from another point of view, the relationship between buyers and sellers allows certain conclusions concerning the rising or declining importance of Muslims and non-Muslims as owners of houses. At the beginning of the seventeenth century, buyers and sellers were more or less in equilibrium, both in Ankara and in Kayseri, although Ankara non-Muslim buyers seem to have had a slight edge over sellers even at this early date. On the other hand, by the closing years of the seventeenth century, non-Muslim buyers of houses by far outnumbered sellers both in Ankara and in Kayseri. In Ankara, the relevant percentages stood at 29.4 and 23.1 per cent respectively. Where Kayseri was concerned, the difference was even more pronounced: non-Muslims constituted 18.7 per cent of all sellers of houses but 36.6 per cent of all buyers. This means that non-Muslims in late-seventeenth-century Kayseri acted as buyers of urban real estate about twice as frequently as they acted as sellers. Probably part of this imbalance was due to the fact that the returning *émigrés* were recovering their place in urban society. However, even so, it is very likely that the Christian community of Kayseri was well on the way towards controlling a considerable share of local real estate.

Muslims and non-Muslims in individual mahalles

After this global view, we will compare the respective shares of Muslims and non-Muslims buying selling or disputing house property in a number of Ankara and Kayseri *mahalle*s about which we happen to have a reasonable amount of information. This is quite a different matter than to determine which *mahalle*s were officially considered Muslim or non-Muslim; for about this matter, which could be rather a thorny one in İstanbul and other cities of the Ottoman Empire,[19] no information has been located in the Ankara and Kayseri registers. Only those *mahalle*s for which at least five sales or disputes could be located have been taken into consideration; *mahalle*s for which we can document ten or more cases being very rare indeed.

As one would expect, the breakdown of cases by *mahalle* reveals the existence of certain solidly Muslim town quarters. Thus in Ankara during the years before and after 1600, urban dwellings in town quarters such as Avancıklar, Belkıs, Hacı Murad, Hacı Musa and Hacı Arab were sold, bought and disputed only by Muslims. Moreover, at least in the cases of Hacı Musa, Hacı Murad, and Hacı Arab *mahalle*s, the same situation still obtained at the end of the seventeenth century. By this time Avancıklar had been dissolved and Belkıs was too poorly documented for any conclusion to be possible. On the other hand, exclusively non-Muslim *mahalle*s must have been fairly rare. Makramacı may have been such a place at the end of the sixteenth and the beginning of the seventeenth century; but we know nothing about its further fate, because the name does not occur in the records of the 1690s. On the other hand, even though in the years before and after 1600 Keyyalin, Vattarin, or even Kepkebir zimmi must have contained mainly non-Muslim inhabitants, they were still mixed *mahalle*s. However, by the later seventeenth century, the non-Muslim character of Kebkebir zimmi and Keyyalin had become more pronounced. But at the same time, Valtarin maintained its character as a *mahalle* shared by Muslims and non-Muslims.

If we concentrate on those quarters which were particularly well documented in 1690s Ankara, the picture is not essentially different. The spotlight of the available documentation falls upon different *mahalle*s, such as the exclusively Muslim Hacı Bayram quarter (which however had contained at least one non-Muslim family in the years around 1600). On the other hand, Hacı Doğan showed up as a mixed *mahalle*, while the Citadel district, now one of the best-documented parts of town, seems to have been an area in which Muslims and non-Muslims nearly balanced one other (11 Muslim and 9 non-Muslim sellers or plaintiffs against 8 Muslim and 12 non-Muslim buyers or defendants in 1690). Thus as far as we can judge from the admittedly scanty documentation, there was no clearly visible trend towards religious segregation or its opposite. While a sizeable number of *mahalle*s maintained themselves as solidly Muslim units of settlement, in others there was a constant flux and reflux, which seems to have continued well into the nineteenth century.[20]

Among the *mahalle*s of Kayseri which were reasonably well-documented at the end of the sixteenth and the beginning of the seventeenth century, comparatively few were solidly Muslim: the poor quarter of the tanneries, Eski Bezazistan, Lala (?), Kürdler, Tepecik and Yenice. By the closing years of the seventeenth century, the tanneries quarter and Tepecik were no longer documented. On the other hand, Lala, Eski Bezazistan, Kürdler, Yenice and Hisanili, for which latter *mahalle* we happen to have a fair amount of cases, were still solidly Muslim. At the same time, the number of *mahalle*s in which both Muslims and non-Muslims bought or disputed urban real estate was much reduced, and the number of predominantly or totally Muslim *mahalle*s had grown: however, we rarely find heavy concentrations of non-Muslims in any one *mahalle*. Even in the quarter named Rumiyan, there were 5 Muslim and 4 non-Muslim sellers or plaintiffs recorded in the 1690s register and 7 non-Muslims acted as buyers or defendants. Probably Eslempaşa, Tavukçu and Şarkiyan came closest to being solidly non-Muslim, while Harbit, Sultan and the poor quarter of Selaldı were more or less mixed.

Why a tendency towards confessional segregation should have been apparent in Kayseri but not in Ankara cannot at present be satisfactorily explained. One might guess that Ankara's greater involvement in inter-regional trade led to a greater fluidity in settlement patterns. But not too much emphasis should be placed upon these results, as the number of cases documented for each *mahalle* is so very limited. If by chance we had selected our documents by slightly different criteria, it is quite possible that the results would have turned out rather differently. Only an extension of the present investigation into the eighteenth and even nineteenth centuries will tell us whether the tendencies dimly discerned here were significant in the long run.

Men Women and Property[21]

As a glance at Tables 5 and 6 will show, male buyers and sellers clearly outnumbered their female counterparts. Moreover, females were more frequently represented among sellers than among buyers, and we must assume that most women acquired real property by inheritance rather than by purchase. However, in the course of the seventeenth century, the proportion of women purchasing urban real estate, either alone or in conjunction with a male relative, increased appreciably. As this trend can be observed both for Ankara and for Kayseri, there is some reason to assume

Table 5. *Male and female sellers of houses*[1]

Location	Info. not usable	Sellers all male	Sellers all female	Mixed	Total usable descrip.	Grand total
Ankara, 1600	124	139 (63.8%)	56 (25.7%)	23 (10.6%)	218	342
Kayseri, 1600	61	122 (69.7%)	31 (17.7%)	22 (12.6%)	175	236
Ankara, 1690	60	135 (59.0%)	68 (29.7%)	26 (11.4%)	229	289
Kayseri, 1690	58	138 (61.3%)	53 (23.6%)	34 (15.1%)	225	283

Table 6. *Male and female buyers of houses*[1]

Location	Info. not usable	Buyers all male	Buyers all female	Mixed	Total usable descrip.	Grand total
Ankara, 1600	124	192 (88.1%)	23 (10.6%)	3 (1.4%)	218	342
Kayseri, 1600	61	156 (89.1%)	16 (9.1%)	3 (1.7%)	175	236
Ankara, 1690	61	197 (86.4%)	30 (13.2%)	1 (0.4%)	228	289
Kayseri, 1690	58[2]	180 (80.0%)	38 (16.9%)	7 (3.1%)	225	283

[1] In Tables 5 and 6, percentages have been based not upon the grand total, but upon the total of usable descriptions.

[2] Divergencies between Tables 3 and 4 on the one hand, and Tables 5 and 6 on the other, are due to the fact that in a few cases, information may be lacking, for instance, on the sex but not on the religion of the buyer. Cases with ambiguous information show up in the 'information not usable' category.

that it was real, and not just due to the fortuitous composition of one of the samples analysed.[22]

On the other hand, it is not easy to explain why female house-owners should have become more frequent in seventeenth-century Ankara and Kayseri. Since almost nothing is known about marriage and migration patterns, it is impossible to speculate upon the reasons that might conceivably have resulted in a larger proportion of widows and/or divorcees; for women in such a position must have been more likely to acquire a house in their own name than those living within an intact nuclear family. But seen from a commonsense point of view, a tendency toward increasing female house-ownership does not point to a grave economic crisis in the two cities investigated. Female ownership of real property, in the Ottoman Empire as elsewhere, tends to occur more frequently among the wealthier sectors of society. This state of affairs would confirm the impression, which has already been voiced in a different context, that the economic decline of the two towns, so often commented upon by nineteenth-century European observers, had not yet begun in the seventeenth century.

Servitors of the Ottoman central administration

Urban dwellers of wealth and social position were often counted among the *askerî*, largely exempted from taxation in return for services rendered to the Ottoman central administration. Whether the wealth of the *askerî* residing in Ankara and Kayseri had been gained in trade, or was in itself a reward of office-holding, cannot be decided with the data at our disposal. However, for instance in fifteenth- and early-sixteenth-century Bursa, the wealth of public officials tended to surpass by far that of the leading merchants.[23] Thus, it can be accepted as a working hypothesis that in Ankara and Kayseri as well, office-holding constituted a major avenue toward wealth.

To determine whether locally resident *askerî* were gaining control over urban real estate, it is of interest to compare the balance of buyers and sellers as indicated in Tables 7 and 8. In Ankara at the end of the sixteenth and the beginning of the seventeenth century, *askerî* buyers and *askerî* sellers of houses tended to cancel each other out. As a result the *askerî* share of urban real estate should have remained about constant. Moreover, if Özer Ergenç has correctly estimated Ankara *askerî* as constituting about 10 per cent of the urban population,[24] the share of these men in the local housing market of the years around 1600 corresponded pretty well to their share of the total population. However, the share of *askerî* in the house-owning population of Ankara seems to have increased in the course of the seventeenth century. In the 1690s, approximately 15 per cent of both buyers and sellers or urban real estate can be identified as *askerî*: a new state of equilibrium had been reached, though the process by which it had been achieved remains unknown to us.

One might surmise that the growing share of Ankara *askerî* had something

Table 7. *Servitors of the Ottoman central administration as sellers of urban houses*[1]

Location	Number sellers unknown	1	2	3	4	5	Total sellers	Total cases
Ankara, c. 1600	1	30	1	2	0	0	39 (at least)	34 (9.9% of 342)
Kayseri, c. 1600	0	25	0	1	0	0	28	26 (11% of 236)
Ankara, c. 1690	0	42	3	0	0	0	48	45 (15.6% of 289)
Kayseri, c. 1690	0	54	4	3	1	1	80	63 (22.3% of 283)

Table 8. *Servitors of the Ottoman central administration as buyers of urban houses*[1]

Location	Number buyers unknown	1	2	Total buyers	Total cases
Ankara, c. 1600	4	34	0	38 (at least)	38 (11.1% of 342)
Kayseri, c. 1600	1	41	0	42 (at least)	42 (17.7%) of 236)
Ankara, c. 1690	0	42	1	44	43 (14.9% of 289)
Kayseri, c. 1690	0	39	2	43	41 (14.5% of 283)

[1] There is a discrepancy between these two tables and Ch. 3, Table 13, due to the fact that the latter table was reproduced by hand and certain variations have crept in.

to do with locally stationed janissaries becoming the partners of artisans, and with artisans claiming affiliation with the janissary corps.[25] Or else one might recall Mustafa Akdağ's remarks about officials sent out by the Ottoman central administration and making their fortunes in the provinces.[26] Equally pertinent are Ömer Lütfi Barkan's references to increasing employment provided by pious foundations.[27] Last but not least, the servitors of the provincial governor (*sancakbeyi*), who had become more and more essential for the advancement of their employers, should have been in a position where they could grow wealthy, and buy themselves a house if they were stationed in Ankara for any length of time.[28]

Quite different was the situation in Kayseri, where *askerî* house-owners were more numerous than in Ankara. Moreover, at the end of the sixteenth and the beginning of the seventeenth century, the number of *askerî* that purchased houses by far surpassed the number of *askerî* selling residential property. However, by the 1690s, the situation was exactly reversed. Only in 14.5 per cent of all cases investigated could the purchasers of houses in Kayseri now be identified as *askerî*. At the same time, in 22.3 per cent of all recorded cases, the person selling his house was known to be in the service of the Ottoman central administration. Thus, one must assume that towards the end of the seventeenth century, Kayseri was losing some of its *askerî*

Table 9. Seyyids and şerifs in the urban real-estate market of late-seventeenth-century Kayseri

No seyyid or şerif involved	Buyer seyyid or şerif	Seller seyyid or şerif	Both buyer & seller seyyid or şerif	Total
220 (77.7%)	24 (8.5%)	33 (11.7%)	6 (2.1%)	283

inhabitants. From Vital Cuinet's account, we know that by the late nineteenth century Kayseri, though a reasonably prosperous town, had ceased to function as the centre of a sub-province (sancak)[29] and only ranked as the centre of a district (kaza). Given these circumstances, one might almost wonder whether the process which was to lead to Kayseri's demotion as an administrative centre had not already begun in the closing years of the seventeenth century.

The decrease in Kayseri's askerî population would have been even more noticeable if in the course of the seventeenth century, a sizeable community of real or supposed descendants of the prophet Muhammad (seyyid, şerif) had not established itself in the city. While seyyids and şerifs were not totally unknown in Kayseri at the end of the sixteenth and the beginning of the seventeenth century, their dramatic increase in the years that followed must have been due to immigration or else to usurpation of privileges.[30] If these seyyids and şerifs had not swelled the ranks of the tax exempt, the number of askerî active in the Kayseri real estate market would have been even lower. Only in 30 cases (10.6 per cent) was an askerî not descended from the Prophet acting as a seller of real estate during the closing years of the seventeenth century. Among buyers, participation was even lower, for only 17 instances (6.0 per cent) involved an askerî buyer who was not a seyyid or a şerif. Moreover, even the şerifs of Kayseri were apparently not very firmly established; for during the 1690s, the descendants of the Prophets were also selling more houses than they were buying. If this process did in fact continue for any length of time, it should have resulted in the disappearance of the askerî from the real estate market of Kayseri. But since so little is known about the history of Anatolian urban population during the seventeenth century, the data at our disposal should be interpreted with a great deal of prudence.

Pilgrims to Mecca as urban property-owners

Since people who had completed the pilgrimage to Mecca were given the honorific title of hacı for the remainder of their lives, it is possible to single out these men and women among the crowd of urban house-owners. Table 10 reflects the frequency of former pilgrims to Mecca among the buyers and sellers of urban dwellings. Contrary to what might have been expected, the number of house sales in which a hacı was involved did not increase in the

Table 10. Hacıs *as urban house-owners*

(Percentage values based upon 'grand total' in the last column)

Location	Buyer *hacı*	Seller *hacı*	Both buyer and seller *hacı*	Total cases involving *hacıs*	Grand total
Ankara, c. 1600	20 (5.8%)	10 (2.9%)	2 (0.6%)	32 (9.3%)	342
Kayseri, c. 1600	16 (6.8%)	9 (3.8%)	0	25 (10.6%)	236
Ankara, c. 1690	16 (5.5%)	4 (1.4%)	1 (0.3%)	21 (7.3%)	289
Kayseri, c. 1690	18 (6.4%)	10 (3.5%)	1 (0.4%)	29 (10.2%)	283

course of the seventeenth century.[31] In Kayseri, the share of cases involving at least one *hacı* remained virtually constant, amounting to about 10 per cent. On the other hand, in Ankara the share of transactions involving at least one *hacı* even declined, from 9.3 per cent to 7.3 per cent of all buyers and sellers of urban real estate.

At the same time, the share of *hacıs* among the houseowners of both Ankara and Kayseri was not negligible, particularly if one takes the large number of non-Muslims into account. Thus, in Ankara during the late sixteenth and early seventeenth centuries, 51 cases involved a non-Muslim buyer (compare Table 4). If these are disregarded, the cases involving the 22 *hacıs* that bought houses according to Table 10 amount to 7.6 per cent of the total. For Kayseri in the years before and after 1600, the relevant figure is 16 out of 187, or 8.6 per cent. The change is even more visible when the data concerning the latre seventeenth century are treated in the same fashion; for if non-Muslim buyers of urban real estate in Ankara are eliminated, the total of pertinent cases drops to 223, and the share of *hacıs* correspondingly reaches 7.6 per cent. In late-seventeenth-century Kayseri, 82 cases involved non-Muslim buyers of houses. Thus, only in 201 instances was the buyer a Muslim, while the share of *hacıs* among Muslim purchasers of houses reaches 9.5 per cent.

Given these circumstances, it is probable that in Kayseri, the real proportion of *hacıs* among the wealthier houseowners tended to slightly increase, and was maintained at the same level only because the proportion of non-Muslim houseowners equally tended to grow. On the other hand, the proportion of *hacıs* in Ankara remained constant. Given the limited number of cases involved, no great importance should probably be attached to these slight differences.

Both in Ankara and in Kayseri, *hacıs* as purchasers of houses always outweighed sellers. This is not surprising, since pilgrimage to Mecca was an

Table 11. *Types of houses sold by Muslims*[1]

Location	(1) Tabhane sofa, oda avlu	(2) Tabhane sofa avlu	(3) Tabhane avlu	(4) Tabhane oda avlu	(5) Avlu, no tabhane	(6) Tabhane no avlu	Total of usable cases
Ankara, c. 1600	50 (36.2%)	27 (19.6%)	7 (5.1%)	25 (18.1%)	13 (9.4%)	16 (11.6%)	138 (40.4% of 342)
Kayseri, c. 1600	25 (22.3%)	57 (50.9%)	12 (10.7%)	1 (0.4%)	6 (5.4%)	11 (9.8%)	112 (47.5% of 236)
Ankara, c. 1690	37 (23.4%)	8 (5.1%)	9 (5.7%)	59 (37.4%)	16 (10.1%)	29 (18.3%)	158 (54.6% of 289)
Kayseri, c. 1690	53 (30.8%)	67 (39.0%)	16 (9.3%)	6 (3.5%)	17 (9.9%)	13 (7.6%)	172 (60.8% of 283)

[1] Except for the last column, all percentages are based upon the total of usable cases.

Table 12. *Types of houses sold by non-Muslims*[1]

Location	(1) Tabhane sofa, oda avlu	(2) Tabhane sofa avlu	(3) Tabhane avlu	(4) Tabhane oda avlu	(5) Avlu no tabhane	(6) Tabhane no avlu	Total of usable cases
Ankara, c. 1600	10 (26.3%)	8 (21.1%)	3 (7.9%)	8 (21.1%)	4 (10.5%)	5 (13.2%)	38 (11.1% of 342)
Kayseri, c. 1600	9 (20.0%)	29 (64.4%)	1 (2.2%)	1 (2.2%)	1 (2.2%)	4 (8.9%)	45 (19.1% of 236)
Ankara, c. 1690	8 (16.3%)	8 (16.3%)	4 (8.2%)	16 (32.7%)	4 (8.2%)	9 (18.3%)	49 (17.0% of 289)
Kayseri, c. 1690	11 (26.8%)	17 (41.5%)	4 (9.7%)	2 (4.9%)	3 (7.3%)	4 (9.8%)	41 (14.5% of 283)

[1] Except for the last column, all percentages are based upon the total of usable cases.

obligation only to those people who possessed sufficient means. We may even imagine that a *hacı*, shortly after his return from the pilgrimage, might feel inclined to purchase a large house to document his increased status in the community. It was apparently not expected that a pilgrim use up his last resources in an attempt to visit Mecca. People who ran out of money on the road were a common enough phenomenon, and special charities existed to provide for their needs. But for the wealthier townsmen, performance of the pilgrimage was part of upward and not of downward mobility.

Differential housing patterns among Muslims and non-Muslims?

European observers of Ottoman society tended to have more contact with non-Muslims than with Muslims, and often enough their accounts reflect tensions between the different non-Muslim minorities and the Muslim majority. On the other hand, non-Muslims adopted many features of the dominant culture surrounding them. Where houses were concerned, it appears that in certain contexts, such as, for instance, Kayseri during the nineteenth and early twentieth centuries, non-Muslim dwellings were easily recognized by the casual observer.[32] It is probable, however, that the differences became more pronounced in relatively recent periods, when non-Muslims were more inclined to imitate European patterns than were their Muslim fellow townsmen. In this context, it is noteworthy that Nurhan Atasoy's analysis of the eighteenth-century dwelling of the Armenian Kavafyan family in Bebek has shown the house to represent a well-established type of Ottoman house.[33]

Given our ignorance of house plans and decoration, we were obliged to concentrate upon the different configurations of rooms, which in a previous chapter have been described as 'types'. Table 11 shows the type of houses sold by Muslim owners, while Table 12 gives the relevant information for non-Muslims. Obviously, there is no way of guaranteeing that a house sold by a non-Muslim had not previously belonged to a Muslim and *vice versa*. In fact, certain dwellings may well have changed hands several times. But in most cases, the house sold by a non-Muslim, particularly if it was located in a non-Muslim quarter of town, would also have been constructed by and for a non-Muslim. Thus, the data presented here should at least indicate certain overall trends.

When we look at the distribution of different house types among the Muslim and non-Muslim inhabitants of late-sixteenth- and early-seventeenth-century Ankara, we find that the differences between Muslim majority and non-Muslim minority were relatively slight. Only where Type 1, consisting of a full array of inhabitable rooms is concerned, is the difference at all notable: this type was sold by 36.2 per cent of all Muslims but only by 26.3 per cent of all non-Muslims. If this difference reflects the real situation, the most elaborate type of house should have been somewhat more widespread among Muslims than among non-Muslims. On the other hand, in Ankara in the 1690s, it was mainly Type 2, consisting of *tabhane, sofa*, and a courtyard but lacking an *oda*, which very much fell from favour among Muslims, but maintained its popularity among non-Muslims. At the same time, the shift to Type 4 consisting of *tabhane* and *oda* apart from the courtyard, was a preference shared by Muslims and by non-Muslims in seventeenth-century Ankara.

In Kayseri during the years before and after 1600, Muslims and non-Muslims alike favoured Type 2 (*tabhane, sofa*, courtyard) which constituted by far the most popular combination of rooms. However, this tendency was far more remarkable among non-Muslims than among Muslims; 64.4 per cent of all non-Muslims are on record as having sold this kind of house, while the relevant share of Muslims amounted to only 50.9 per cent. During the same period, the usually small dwellings of Type 3, consisting of only a courtyard and a *tabhane*, were somewhat more widespread among Muslims than among non-Muslims (10.7 per cent against 2.2 per cent). However, not too much should be made out of this difference, since the absolute figures involved are quite small. By the 1690s, the residents of Kayseri, whether Muslim or non-Muslim, seem to have favoured very much the same types of houses. In this respect, differences between the two communities were so small that they are best neglected.

As a glance at the graphs will show, the respective local patterns of Ankara and Kayseri are much more significant than the differences between Muslim and non-Muslim houseowners in either city. One might say that an overall pattern characterizing a given city evolved, and that both Muslims and non-Muslims followed the trend, with certain variations peculiar to either one of the two communities. But, given the fact that Muslims constituted the majority and the culturally dominant group within the Ottoman Empire, it can be assumed that the latter set the tone, and that the non-Muslims followed their lead. Moreover, sales between members of different religions must have contributed towards ironing out any differences that might remain.

At the same time, certain types of rooms or courtyards were often favoured by Muslims more than by non-Muslims, or else the opposite might be true. In a previous chapter, we have discussed the case of the Ankara mohair workshops. In Kayseri domestic architecture, one of the more remarkable features was the house containing a double courtyard. Table 13 shows that this was essentially a characteristic of Muslim houses. This fact, in turn, might be taken to indicate that the outer courtyard was designed, at least in part, to receive male visitors, and not just as a convenient place where stables and other service functions could be located at a distance from the dwelling. Be that as it may, the double courtyard as a peculiarly Muslim feature is all the more noteworthy as in late-seventeenth-century Kayseri, Muslims and non-Muslims favoured the same combinations of inhabitable

Table 13. *Sellers of houses with a double courtyard*[1]

Location	Data usable	Seller Muslim	Seller non-Muslim			Total cases documented
Ankara, c. 1600	124	139 (63.8%)	56 (25.7%)	23 (10.6%)	218	342
Kayseri, c. 1600	61	122 (69.7%)	31 (17.7%)	22 (12.6%)	175	236
Ankara, c. 1690	60	135 (59.0%)	68 (29.7%)	26 (11.4%)	229	289
Kayseri, c. 1690	58	138	53 (93.3%)	34 (6.7%)	225	283

[1] Percentages based on the total of usable data.

Table 14. *Houses with more than three permanently inhabitable rooms, as sold by Muslims and non-Muslims*

Location	Data usable	Seller Muslim	Seller non-Muslim	Buyer Muslim	Buyer non-Muslim	Total
Ankara, c. 1600	33	31 (93.9%)	2 (6.1%)	30 (90.9%)	3 (9.1%)	41 (12.0% of 342)
Kayseri, c. 1600	15	12 (80.0%)	3 (20.0%)	14 (93.3%)	1 (6.7%)	19 (8.1% of 236)
Ankara, c. 1690	55	43 (78.2%)	12 (21.8%)	38 (69.1%)	17 (30.9%)	70 (24.2% of 289)
Kayseri, c. 1690	27	21 (77.8%)	6 (22.2%)	18 (66.7%)	9 (33.3%)	34 (12.0% of 283)

(Percentages, except in the last column, are based upon the number of usable cases.)

rooms. This fits in nicely with the assumption that the spatial arrangement of these rooms, and possibly their decoration, was what distinguished Muslim from non-Muslim houses, while the combination of basic rooms was more or less the same.

Apart from the configuration of rooms, one might reasonably expect that differences in size existed between Muslim and non-Muslim dwellings. Table 14 summarizes the information concerning people who sold and bought houses of more than three rooms inhabitable the year round. Given the average size of the seventeenth-century dwelling, these were the larger and in most cases the wealthier houses in town. Moreover, except where Ankara of the 1690s is concerned, the share of these dwellings in the totality of documented cases did not amount to more than 12 per cent. In Ankara at the end of the sixteenth and the beginning of the seventeenth century,

Muslims accounted for the vast majority of larger dwellings, while the role of non-Muslims both as buyers and as sellers of these houses was negligible. But, by the 1690s, the situation had changed quite appreciably. Now non-Muslims sold good-sized houses in 21.8 per cent of all cases, while their share of large houses purchased was even more important, namely 30.9 per cent. Obviously certain Ankara non-Muslims had not only become quite wealthy (such people could be found even during the early 1600s), but the social climate had changed in a fashion that permitted non-Muslims the acquisition of relatively elaborate homes.

In Kayseri during the late sixteenth and early seventeenth centuries, the situation was not significantly different from what could be observed in contemporary Ankara. There were few non-Muslim sellers or buyers of good-sized houses, and the relatively high percentage values simply reflect the fact that the overall number of dwellings with more than three permanently inhabitable rooms was quite small. By the closing years of the seventeenth century, a somewhat larger number of Kayseri non-Muslims had begun to acquire more spacious dwellings, however, the number of Muslims owning good-sized residences had equally increased. Thus it would appear that in Kayseri as well as in Ankara, certain members of the non-Muslim community had acquired considerable wealth and were beginning to imitate the style of living which characterized their well-to-do Muslim fellow townsmen.

To test the validity of this conclusion, we have equally analysed the data concerning the buyers and sellers of houses containing just two permanently inhabitable rooms. Dwellings of this type must generally have been rather modest. Morever, throughout the seventeenth century, houses of this size were the most widespread kind of dwelling both in Ankara and Kayseri. In the course of the seventeenth century, the share of Ankara Muslims selling a house of this size remained more or less stable. Where Kayseri is concerned, the situation appears somewhat different. Relatively speaking, more Muslims sold two-room houses in the 1690s than at the end of the sixteenth or the beginning of the seventeenth century. But contrary to what happened in Ankara, the corresponding share of non-Muslims decreased quite noticeably, namely from 34.4 to 20.2 per cent. During the same time period, the share of Muslims buying two-room houses declined, while the number of non-Muslims engaging in the same activity showed a corresponding increase. It must be remembered that there probably was a massive influx of non-Muslims into Kayseri during the last quarter of the seventeenth century, partly former inhabitants returning but some at least newcomers as well.[34] If in fact something of the sort occurred, it might explain the figures in Tables 15 and 16. We might then assume that immigrating non-Muslims of a certain wealth, who bought houses of four and more inhabitable rooms, were accompanied by a sizeable number of families whose station in life was more modest. Due to this influx of non-Muslim buyers, the share of Muslim

Table 15. *Sellers of small houses (2 rooms inhabitable the year round)*[1]

Location	Data usable	Seller(s) Muslim	Seller(s) non-Muslim	Sellers mixed		
Ankara, c. 1600	124	192 (88.1%)	23 (10.6%)	3 (1.4%)	218	342
Kayseri, c. 1600	61	156 (89.1%)	16 (9.1%)	3 (1.7%)	175	236
Ankara, c. 1690	61	197 (86.4%)	30 (13.2%)	1 (0.4%)	228	289
Kayseri, c. 1690	58[2]	180 (78.7%)	38 (20.2%)	7	225	283 (1.1%)

[1] Percentages based upon the total of usable cases.

Table 16. *Buyers of small houses (2 rooms inhabitable the year round)*

Location	Data usable	Buyer(s) Muslim	Buyer(s) non-Muslim	
Ankara, c. 1600	18	15 (83.3%)	3 (16.7%)	24
Kayseri, c. 1600	3	3 (100%)	0	5
Ankara, c. 1690	11	11 (100.0%)	0	11
Kayseri, c. 1690	30	28 (57.4%)	2 (42.6%)	40

sellers increased and that of Muslim buyers declined. On the other hand, the non-Muslim population of Ankara also grew; but at least during the years investigated, the process was more gradual and did not show the violent ups and downs that could be observed in Kayseri.

For the conclusions concerning the architectural preferences of Muslims and non-Muslims to be totally valid, one would have to assume a society in which Muslims sold their houses only to Muslims, while non-Muslims equally bought and sold only from and to their coreligionists. What is known about relations between Muslims and non-Muslims in the Ottoman Empire makes it clear that this was not the case.[35] But we need to find out how frequently Muslims and non-Muslims confronted each other in the real estate market. Tables 17 and 18 reflect the particular conditions of Ankara and Kayseri. In general, Muslims and non-Muslims certainly preferred to sell to other members of the same religious community. But at the same time, the strength of this preference varied considerably according to time and place. In the course of the seventeenth century, the proportion of

Table 17. *Buyers of houses sold by a Muslim*

Location	Data usable	Buyer Muslim	Buyer non-Muslim	Buyers mixed
Ankara, c. 1600	170	154 (90.6%)	15 (8.8%)	1 (0.6%)
Kayseri, c. 1600	127	109 (85.8%)	17 (13.4%)	1 (0.8%)
Ankara, c. 1690	175	151 (86.3%)	24 (13.7%)	0
Kayseri, c. 1690	179	136 (76.0%)	43 (24.0%)	0

Table 18. *Buyers of houses sold by a non-Muslim*

Location	Buyer Muslim	Buyer non-Muslim	Buyer(s) mixed	Total
Ankara, c. 1600	10 (21.3%)	36 (76.6%)	1 (2.1%)	47
Kayseri, c. 1600	16 (33.3%)	32 (66.7%)	0	48
Ankara, c. 1690	10 (18.9%)	43 (81.1%)	0	53
Kayseri, c. 1690	5 (11.9%)	37 (88.1%)	0	42

Muslims selling to non-Muslims tended to increase, while that of Muslims selling to Muslims declined in pro rata. At the same time, the inverse tended to happen where non-Muslims were concerned, especially in Kayseri. In the latter town, the percentage of non-Muslims selling to Muslims dropped from 33.3 per cent to 11.9 per cent; in Ankara the change went in the same direction, but was less marked in intensity.

Thus, it would appear that the non-Muslim communities of Ankara and Kayseri, as they gathered in strength, also tended to close in upon themselves. As more and more non-Muslims sold their houses only to their co-religionists, previously existing spheres of interaction were being narrowed down. This in turn, one might assume, could in the long run have contributed toward transforming the reasonably relaxed relations that existed between the two communities during the late sixteenth or even during the seventeenth century. With the limited amount of material at our disposal, we cannot tell whether this tendency of the non-Muslim community to close in upon itself was an outcome of preferences that had existed previously, but could only be realized once the community had reached a certain size. It is also possible that new cultural trends were involved, which in the more expansive environment of the sixteenth century had been pushed into the background, but came out into the open during the less buoyant years that were to follow.[36]

At the same time, the cultural climate of the 1600s did not prevent those non-Muslims of Ankara and Kayseri who possessed the necessary capital from building themselves good-sized houses. Thus, it would appear that the sumptuary laws which forbade non-Muslims to ride horses, wear luxurious clothing, and live in decorated houses, were not enforced with undue severity.[37] In commercial centres such as Ankara or Kayseri, which seem to have survived the prolonged crisis of the Celâlî rebellions reasonably well, economic factors probably affected the size of dwellings more directly than administrative intervention. As a result, the growing economic stature of the non-Muslims was reflected in the increasing size of the houses which they inhabited.

Why a house was sold

In the typical document recording the sale of a house, the seller did not dwell upon the reasons which caused him to alienate his dwelling. Nor do most texts tell us very much about the specific relationships which may have existed between buyers and sellers. However, the exceptions to this rule are numerous enough to warrant separate analysis. Even so, it must be kept in mind that the validity of the transaction was not affected by the presence or absence of these supplementary data. Whether they were included or not seems to have been mainly a matter of scribal elaboration; therefore, the more professionally executed documents of the later seventeenth century contain more such supplementary information than their predecessors. In consequence, the figures contained in Table 19 are simply intended to represent orders of magnitude.

If we assume that a sale to pay debts or to secure the upbringing of an

Table 19. *Specified reasons for the sale of a house*

Location	Sale for debts	Sale to support a child	Sale of house rented to seller	Sale by auction[1]	Total
Ankara, c. 1600	13 (3.8%)	8 (2.3%)	12 (3.5%)	10 (2.9%)	342
Kayseri, c. 1600	21 (8.9%)	7 (3.0%)	1 (0.4%)	6 (2.5%)	236
Ankara, c. 1690	39 (13.5%)	4 (1.4%)	2 (0.7%)	2 (0.7%)	289
Kayseri, c. 1690	18 (16.4%)	4 (1.4%)	0	0	283

[1] No further information.

orphan child generally reflected social distress, it must be assumed that between 6 per cent and 18 per cent of all sales must have been made out of dire necessity. Sales caused by indebtedness are frequently documented, because debts needed to be paid before an inheritance could be divided among the heirs. When the procedure was carried out in a formal manner, creditors would first present themselves in the *kadıs'* office with the appropriate number of witnesses, and officially register the fact that a certain person, now deceased, owed them a given sum of money. Armed with a certificate to that effect, they would then present themselves before the executors and demand payment.[38] However, the *kadıs'* registers do not contain very many documents of this type. Therefore it appears likely that many debts were settled upon the testimony of witnesses alone. Or else, the heirs might themselves be sufficiently aware of their deceased relative's situation to recognize certain claims as valid without further formality.

It is not clear what prompted certain debtors who were still alive to declare in court that they were selling due to debts. In a society in which houses were frequently the subject of a mortgage, such a step should have made them less credit-worthy in the future. Possibly these declarations should be understood as a way of demonstrating good intentions where the payment of debts was concerned, for such a step should have assured the creditors that the debtor was in fact capitalizing his assets in order to settle his liabilities. Moreover, elderly people may sometimes have made such a declaration in order to make it less likely that their heirs contest the sale. Be that as it may, it is very probable that the number of house-owners who sold their dwellings due to debts was in fact much greater than it appears from the *kadı's* registers.

Where the property belonging to an orphan child was concerned, it was wise to be as explicit as possible, for after having attained legal majority, the young man or girl could contest a sale made on his or her behalf. Two reasons might legally be adduced for selling a minor's property.[39] In case the boy or girl had no other means of support, the *kadı* permitted a sale. The same thing applied when the property was falling in ruins because there was nobody available who would take care of it. Apart from children, the mentally ill (*mecnun*) might require a guardian to administer their property; in these cases the rules applied were apparently the same as those regarding children.

An interesting group of documents deals with the temporary 'sales', which were really a cover for a loan at interest. These cases were akin to, but legally distinct from, the pledging of property to guarantee a loan (*rehin*). In these temporary sales, the borrower turned over his house to the lender, and sometimes even claimed to have evacuated the property. After that, he 'rented' the house from the man to whom he had just sold it; after the loan had been repaid, the process was reversed. In what way the 'sale' price was related to the marketable value of the house is not known; but it definitely represented the amount of money borrowed. Quite frequently, this latter point is proven by the fact that the 'rent' was clearly related to the 'sale price', and amounted to 10 to 15 per cent of the capital invested.[40] This rate, as is well known from a large number of documents, was also the commonly accepted rate of interest, which even pious foundations did not hesitate to collect.[41]

Sale by auction was a measure commonly resorted to when the seller not only wanted to get the best possible price for the house that he was selling, but also wanted an official record to be made of the fact. Thus this procedure, which the *kadıs*' records describe in certain set formulae,[42] was used particularly where the interests of minors were involved. Probably for this reason, when records concerning property belonging to minors became infrequent in the later seventeenth century, references to sales at auction all but disappeared from the *kadıs*' registers.

Islamic law granted neighbours the right of first refusal when a property came up for sale (*şufa*). This right occasionally gave rise to disputes,[43] but in most cases neighbours might informally agree to buy and sell pieces of real estate from one another, without ever referring to the formal rights that the law gave them. Thus, the best way of identifying such cases is by finding out whether the buyer was also named as the owner of one of the properties adjacent to the house being sold. Table 20 does in fact indicate that certain families, presumably from among the wealthier members of the community, quite frequently purchased a house adjacent to their own property. Since it was not common for individuals, as opposed to pious foundations, to invest in houses as a source of rental income, we may assume that quite a few buyers of such properties wished to acquire a dwelling for a son or cousin about to be married. Or else the buyers may have intended to join two houses and provide room for a larger family. Others may have wished to institute a pious foundation, for it was common to assign a house in perpetuity to a local mosque, to house the prayer leader (*imam*) or simply to provide the institution with a reasonably secure source of income.[44]

Table 20. *Relations between buyers and sellers of houses*

Location	Buyer a neighbour of seller	Buyer a relative of seller	Total
Ankara, c. 1600	19 (5.6%)	16 (4.7%)	342
Kayseri, c. 1600	23 (9.7%)	5 (2.1%)	236
Ankara, c. 1690	35 (12.1%)	26 (9.0%)	289
Kayseri, c. 1690	21 (7.4%)	18 (6.4%)	283

Even more obvious are the reasons why real estate deals between relatives should have been a common occurrence. In many instances, one shareholder bought out the shares of co-owners to secure the dwelling for himself alone.[45] In other cases, sales of this kind were probably devices for raising money without seeking a loan; particularly husbands and wives selling urban real estate to their partners probably acted from motives of this type.[46] Moreover, it is probable that relatives preferred to stay close together, and often the property may have changed hands within the immediate family without ever being offered to outsiders. Taken together, these different motives, and others that are more difficult to guess, seem to have accounted for a share that ranged between two and nine per cent of all sales of urban real estate. But given the limited number of cases involved, not too much importance should be placed upon the differences between Ankara and Kayseri on one hand, or between the early 1600s and the 1690s on the other.

Heads of households buying up their neighbours' properties should generally have been better off than the average townsman. Within certain limitations, the same should have applied to people who owned a house in a town quarter other than the one in which they ordinarily resided. Late-sixteenth- and early-seventeenth-century documents do not dwell upon this matter very frequently. But the more professionally kept records of the later seventeenth century permit us to single out the owners of multiple dwellings if they sold off one of their houses. In Ankara, 31 out of 289 cases (10.7 per cent) fell into this category; in Kayseri, 82 instances were recorded, which amounts to 29 per cent. Given the scarcity of criteria by which to establish socio-economic stratification, one might hazard a guess and assume that at the end of the seventeenth century, between 10 and 30 per cent of all owners selling their houses were more or less comfortably off. On the other end of the socio-economic scale, we have the townsmen that sold a house to pay off debts or to support an orphan child and thus were probably in financial difficulties: these instances amounted to between fifteen and eighteen per cent of all recorded cases.

Urban property-owners: a control group

The present investigation deals with house owners in a special situation, namely those who had just sold or else acquired a house. Obviously people in this situation can only in a limited sense be taken to represent urban property owners in general. It would be highly desirable to compare buyers and sellers of urban real estate with a more stable group of their contemporaries, that is, with people who are known to have owned dwellings in Ankara and Kayseri at the time the transactions recorded in the *kadıs'* register were being undertaken.[47] Such a control group is in fact available, for in Ottoman practice it was customary to delimit a property by naming the neighbours. From these names we can draw certain conclusions with respect

Table 21. *Religion of house-owners recorded as 'neighbours'*[1] *compared with their house-selling counterparts*

Location	Muslim neighbours	Non-Muslim neighbours	Total neighbours	Muslim sellers	Muslim buyers
Ankara, c. 1600	468 (83.3%)	94 (16.7%)	562	169 (77.5%)	165 (75.7%)
Kayseri, c. 1600	336 (77.6%)	97 (22.4%)	433	127 (72.6%)	125 (71.4%)
Ankara, c. 1690	487 (74.0%)	171 (26.0%)	658	176 (76.9%)	161 (70.6%)
Kayseri, c. 1690	520 (71.1%)	211 (28.9%)	731	181 (80.4%)	142 (63.4%)

[1] Cases in which the neighbours' religion is unknown have been disregarded.

to the religion, sex and socio-political status of the people involved. In turn, these data can then be compared with what has been established in the present chapter concerning the buyers and sellers of seventeenth-century houses in Ankara and Kayseri.

As a first step, we will compare the religious affiliations of the people recorded as 'neighbours' with those of their counterparts engaged in the buying and selling of houses (Tables 3, 4, and 21). In Ankara at the end of the sixteenth and the beginning of the seventeenth century, Muslims predominated by a wider margin among the 'established' house-owners listed as 'neighbours', than among the buyers and sellers of urban real estate. However, in the later seventeenth century, this discrepancy had largely disappeared. In Kayseri during the years shortly before and after 1600, Muslims were also more numerous among the 'neighbours' than among the buyers and sellers of urban real estate. On the other hand, during the closing years of the seventeenth century, the share of Muslims among the 'neighbours' was lower than among the sellers of urban real estate, but higher than among the buyers. In this respect, the patterns prevailing in Ankara and Kayseri thus appear to have been remarkably similar.

However, these patterns are more easily described than explained. One might feel tempted to claim that there was an 'irruption' of non-Muslims into the housing market during the unsettled times of the Celâlî rebellions, while something more like an equilibrium prevailed during the 1690s. However, this interpretation would contradict what has previously been deduced from the widening gap between non-Muslim 'buyers' and 'sellers'; for this phenomenon had appeared to indicate that the end of the seventeenth century was the time in which non-Muslim house-owners were gaining ground, particularly in Kayseri. Given these circumstances, it seems more reasonable to assume that in the years before and after 1600, non-

Muslim buyers and sellers of houses showed a particular inclination to have their transactions documented in the *kadıs*' court. This would explain why non-Muslims were more frequent among the buyers and sellers of urban real estate than their share among house-owners warranted. On the other hand, the real 'growth spurt' in non-Muslim house ownership could still have taken place in the closing years of the seventeenth century. This interpretation is retained because it seems unreasonable to assume that there should have been two separate periods of non-Muslim expansion, manifesting themselves in different ways, and both conveniently coinciding with the time span investigated in the present study. But obviously future research may modify our conclusions in this respect. At the same time, it is comforting to observe that the respective proportions of Muslims and non-Muslims among the 'neighbours' are situated within the same order of magnitude as those previously established for the buyers and sellers of houses in Ankara and Kayseri. Even though the data used are full of gaps, the conclusions that have been drawn from them thus appear to be reasonably reliable.

Problems of a different order are encountered when we compare the sex distribution of urban house-owners recorded as 'neighbours' with that which prevailed among the buyers and sellers of dwellings, as described in Tables 5 and 6. As Table 22 demonstrates, house-ownership as acknowledged by the inhabitants of seventeenth-century Ankara and Kayseri was definitely a man's world; slightly less so at the end of the seventeenth century than at the beginning. Apparently, a woman stood a slightly better chance of getting herself recognized as a house-owner in Ankara than in Kayseri; but particularly in the 1690s, the difference was marginal.

The low level of female house-ownership, particularly noticeable because women were reasonably active as buyers and sellers of houses, can be explained by two complementary lines of argument. First of all, women were consistently buying houses much less frequently than they sold them. If in the long run, there were any female owners of houses left at all, this was due to the fact that women could also acquire houses by inheritance. In fact, acquisition from deceased relatives was probably more common than acquisition by purchase. Moreover, it can also be assumed that in reality there existed more women owners than were named in the records. Given the fact that they were less well known in the community than their menfolk, it would not be surprising if neighbours continued to refer to Ahmed's or Mehmed's house, long after the dwelling had in fact been inherited by the deceased owners' daughters. But even when allowance has been made for this factor, it does seem likely that women were owners of houses much less frequently than their relatively high degree of participation in the real estate market would lead one to expect.

In the context of seventeenth-century Anatolia, names are reasonably reliable as indicators of religious affiliations and sex, but tell us little about the holder's socio-political status. The latter could be read off only from

Table 22. *Male and female house-owners recorded as 'neighbours'*[1]

Location	Male	Female	Total
Ankara, c. 1600	615 (96.7%)	21 (3.3%)	636
Kayseri, c. 1600	495 (98.2%)	9 (1.8%)	504
Ankara, c. 1690	633 (94.8%)	35 (5.2%)	668
Kayseri, c. 1690	698 (95.5%)	33 (4.5%)	731

[1] Cases in which the neighbours' sex is unknown have been excluded.

Table 23. *Political status of house-owners recorded as 'neighbours'*[1]

Location	*Reaya*	*Askerî*	*Seyyid, şerif*	Total
Ankara, c. 1600	599 (93.6%)	41 (6.4%)	–	640
Kayseri, c. 1600	441 (87.7%)	62 (12.3%)	–	503
Ankara, c. 1690	583 (87.9%)	80 (12.1%)	–	663
Kayseri, c. 1690	609 (84.0%)	65 (9.0%)	51 (7.0%)	725

[1] Doubtful cases, including all women, have been considered *reaya*. Only for Kayseri around 1690 have *seyyid*s and *şerif*s been counted as a separate category.

titles, such as *müderris* or *kadı*. However, such titles were probably quite often omitted in the rapid enumerations of the 'neighbours'. Thus, in Table 23 the share of *askerî* in the property-owning population of Ankara and Kayseri has, if anything, been underestimated. Given these circumstances, we can only make a very rough comparison between the contents of Tables 7–9 and that of Table 23.

Askerî tended to be less numerous in Ankara than in Kayseri, a state of affairs which is documented for the buyers and sellers of urban property, and for the 'neighbours' as well.[48] Where Ankara was concerned, members of the Ottoman administration tended to increase their share among urban house owners (from 9.9 to 15.6 per cent among sellers, from 11.1 to 14.9 per cent among buyers, from 6.4 to 12.1 per cent among 'neighbours'). In this respect as well, Table 23 confirms what has already been established with respect to the buyers and sellers of urban dwellings. Moreover, it is worth retaining that many of the 'neighbours' classed as *askerî* are recognizable as such because they bear the 'military' title of *bey*, which in this provincial environment, often denoted a janissary. As has already been explained in a different context, it was probably the proliferation of military units that accounted for the increase in *askerî*.

At the same time, the situation in Kayseri appears to have been more complex. Contrary to what can be observed among the buyers of urban houses, the overall share of *askerî* among the 'neighbours' of Kayseri increased between the early 1600s and the 1690s. At the end of the sixteenth and the beginning of the seventeenth century, the share of *askerî* among the 'neighbours' more or less corresponded to the share of *askerî* among the sellers of urban houses (12.3 and 11.0 per cent respectively). On the other hand, *askerî* were more strongly represented among the buyers of urban houses than among the 'neighbours' (17.7 per cent as opposed to 12.3 per cent). Towards the end of the seventeenth century, however, the situation was reversed: the share of *askerî* among the 'neighbours', including *seyyid*s), was now closer to that of the buyers of urban houses than to that of the sellers. (At this time, 16 per cent of all 'neighbours' ranking as *askerî*, the percentages among buyers and sellers lay at 14.5 and 22.3 respectively.) This would lead us to assume that the 'neighbours' did in fact reflect the status quo as it existed at a given point in time. When *askerî* were gaining ground among urban houseowners, the 'neighbours' contained a smaller share of *askerî* than the buyers. When *askerî* came to be a declining force, the share of *askerî* among the 'neighbours' was higher than the relative position that they held among the buyers of urban real estate.

Apart from functioning as a control group, data on house-owners known only as 'neighbours' are also useful in their own right. One of the features characterizing a given structure of real-estate ownership in any society is the degree of fragmentation. Under certain conditions, people may transfer the bulk of their property intact to one of their children, thereby forcing the others to seek alternative sources of livelihood. Or else, inheritances may be divided up among a large number of heirs, leading in time to rather fragmented patterns of real estate ownership. As a compromise solution, a considerable number of families may decide to hold real property in indivision, sharing out only the income produced by the land or houses in question.[49] These matters are only very imperfectly reflected in the data concerning buyers and sellers of urban real-estate; for when a group of relatives sold a house that they had owned in indivision, the sales records tell us nothing about the families who retained their patrimony intact. On the other hand, when the neighbours of a house to be sold were enumerated, we often learn whether a group of heirs (*verese*) or else an individual person was the owner of the property in question. Certainly, there appear to have been instances in which family ownership of a given house is obscured by the way in which the owners are enumerated: a property belonging to 'Ahmed, Mehmed, and Yusuf' may be held in indivision, or else have been divided into three separate and distinct parts. However, this ambiguity does not exist where the term '*verese*' is employed, and therefore the frequency of this latter expression has been counted.[50]

Properties held by groups of *verese* were quite rare throughout the seventeenth century, both in Ankara and in Kayseri. In Ankara at the end of the sixteenth and the beginning of the seventeenth century, 19 pieces of real estate were owned by *verese* or otherwise clearly designated as family property. Since information is available on 669 pieces of real estate owned as private property (apart from publicly accessible buildings), the share of such properties lay at less than 3 per cent. In Kayseri during those same years, the term '*verese*' was practically unknown. As to the later years of the seventeenth century, the relevant figures amounted to 8 and 25 pieces of real estate respectively, this again constituted but a minuscule share of all privately owned properties. Thus, even allowing for possible ambiguities of terminology and for faulty recording, it seems reasonable to say that houses in seventeenth-century Ankara or Kayseri were normally personal property. The concept of collectively-owned family property was not unknown, but seems to have involved only a small minority of cases. Correspondingly, houses were thrown onto the market with considerable frequency. Thus, people newly established in the city, provided they possessed the necessary means, should not have found it too difficult to find a suitable house in the town quarter of their choice.

Conclusion

From the data analysed above emerges the image of an urban society that corresponds well enough to what has been established for certain other Ottoman cities, such as fifteenth- to sixteenth-century Bursa,[51] or else eighteenth-century Aleppo.[52] There was no rigid compartmentalization between Muslims and non-Muslims, no equivalent of the ghettos of early modern Europe. Probably, at least in part, as a result of frequent real-estate transactions between Muslims and non-Muslims, members of the different communities generally preferred the same configurations of rooms. With one exception: houses with double courtyards, so popular among the wealthy Muslim townsmen of late-seventeenth-century Kayseri, did not appear very attractive to their non-Muslim counterparts.

At the same time, however, there existed indications that this relative freedom of interaction, which seems to have characterized the 'classical' Ottoman state of the fifteenth and sixteenth centuries, was being increasingly restricted. If the data presented here have been correctly interpreted, it would seem that this change was initiated by the non-Muslims rather than by the Muslims. As the non-Muslim community increased in size, and probably in wealth as well, its members seem to have increasingly viewed their groups as a self-sufficient entity. At least where Ankara and Kayseri are concerned, this process can now apparently be dated.[53] It began, or at any rate was considerably intensified, in the course of the seventeenth century.

Students of nineteenth-century Ottoman social history, as well as European observers who visited the Empire during this latter period, have frequently commented upon the economic preponderance of non-Muslims in trade and related activities.[54] More recently, it has been established that no non-Muslim commercial monopoly existed during the fifteenth and sixteenth centuries,[55] a period during which many towns of western and central Anatolia in fact possessed only a very small number of non-Muslim inhabitants. As a result, the increase of the non-Muslim population in commercial centres such as Ankara or Kayseri, both in terms of numbers and in terms of wealth, documents the sequence of changes that finally led to the state of affairs observed in the nineteenth century.

Apparently, during the still fairly prosperous conditions of the later seventeenth century, the number of non-Muslims in both Ankara and Kayseri increased substantially. Difficulties with local administrators might cause certain members of the non-Muslim communities to leave the city for longer or shorter periods of time. But these emigrations were temporary, and did not in the long run interrupt the growth of the non-Muslim community. Moreover, the non-Muslims of Ankara and Kayseri apparently established themselves in these two cities with the intention of living there for a reasonably long period of time. If they had been temporary immigrants only, for instance refugees from the Ottoman–Iranian borderlands intending to return to their home towns at the earliest possible opportunity,[56] they would probably have been less inclined to buy houses in their new places of residence.

Given revived interest in the status of women, the data concerning male and female ownership can also be interpreted in the light of broader trends. Recently published studies about women in Kayseri or Bursa have shown that female inhabitants of the city quite frequently possessed property in their own right, which was protected by the possibility of recourse to the kadıs' court.[57] In many cases, the kadıs' tribunal, which was easily accessible to the townswomen, actively intervened to protect the latter's rights as enunciated in the şeriat. From the data analysed here, it appears that female wealth was much more often held in money than in real property. Women participated actively in the real estate market, both as sellers and as buyers. But women sold many more houses than they bought, and without the effects of inheritance, there would soon have been no female house-owners left. As it stood, a limited number of women was mentioned as property-owners by their neighbours. Moreover, female house-owners were probably somewhat more numerous than the documents record. In addition, it is worth noting that the share of female houseowners increased slightly in the course of the seventeenth century, a fact which can probably be interpreted as a sign of moderate economic prosperity.

Servitors of the Ottoman central administration (*askerî*) constituted a significant share of Anatolian townsmen, apparently never less than ten per cent of all urban house owners. Given the political influence of certain *askerî*, their control, or lack of control, over the urban real estate market and urban wealth in general, is an issue of some importance for Ottoman history. In this respect, the available data have turned out to be somewhat contradictory. In Ankara, the shares of buyers, sellers, and 'neighbours' described as *askerî* tended to increase throughout the seventeenth century. This observation fits in very well with the growth of military units throughout the Ottoman Empire, and thus conforms to an expected pattern. On the other hand, the situation in Kayseri was much more ambiguous; but it does appear that *askerî* were withdrawing from the urban real-estate market and probably from the city in general. In all likelihood, this trend was connected with Kayseri's relatively eccentric position. While both Ankara and Kayseri were centres of sub-provinces (*sancak*s), Ankara was not only closer to İstanbul, but also more important as a manufacturing city. In such a place, one might expect that the Ottoman central administration attempted to maintain closer control than in a city of more localized economic importance.

Thus, it appears that patterns of house-ownership in seventeenth-century Ankara and Kayseri were anything but immobile. One should not imagine these cities as 'traditional' in the sense that the same patterns were constantly being reproduced. Quite to the contrary, considerable change was possible within the Ottoman framework, even in a period such as the seventeenth century, generally considered 'difficult' and 'post-classical'. The time has come to re-examine well established notions with respect to the inflexibility and stagnation of Ottoman society before the mid nineteenth century, and to try to discern the long-term rhythms by which this society moved.

CHAPTER 5

The difficulties of an urban property-owner

Property-owners of seventeenth century Ankara and Kayseri applied to the *kadı*'s court mainly to record transfers of real property. On the other hand, contested cases involving ownership or possession of a house were relatively few. But at the same time, records concerning contested cases usually contain much more incidental information than the entries dealing with ordinary sales. Thus these documents oppose a stubborn resistance to all attempts on the part of the researcher to reduce their contents to a standardized format, while at the same time allowing us to view aspects of Ankara and Kayseri society which the sales documents do not reveal.

All disputed cases discussed in the present chapter concern in one way or another the ownership or possession of houses. These matters were decided by the *kadı* according to the *şeriat*, for houses, unlike agricultural lands, were held as freehold property. As a result, the Sultans had promulgated no body of rules and regulations dealing with the ownership of houses and gardens, while they had done so in the case of fields and meadows.[1] In principle, the latter were regarded as state property, in respect to which the cultivator could only claim an hereditary right of usufruct. On the other hand, *ad hoc* interventions on the part of the Ottoman central government were not excluded, even where freehold property was involved. But direct interventions were unusual, dictated by exceptional conditions such as rebellions and civil war. Under more normal circumstances, disputes concerning the ownership of houses were generally left to the local *kadı* to decide.[2]

Unfortunately, we do not in all cases know the verdict which he arrived at. Particularly for the years around 1600, when entries were often quite sketchy, we often only know the statements of the two parties, and must use our own knowledge of court procedure to guess the results.[3] At the end of the seventeenth century, however, most of the documents contained some indications concerning the verdict. If the plaintiff's claim was rejected, the record was concluded with a statement to the effect that he had been forbidden to raise any further objections,[4] while a decision in his favour was recorded in less standardized language. Moreover, in a certain number of cases, the dispute was concluded with an agreement among the two parties. If the standard formula in such cases has any concrete meaning, such an agreement was always proposed to the parties by third persons, who are, however, never mentioned by name.[5] A *fetva* might be presented by one of the contestant parties, but most cases seem to have been fairly standard, and could be decided without elaborate legal preparation.[6]

Most contested cases are found in the Ankara records of the late sixteenth and early seventeenth centuries (77 out of 342, or 22.5 per cent). By the later seventeenth century, however, the custom of recording ordinary sales had gained in popularity, and as a result, the share of contested cases declined to 11.4 per cent. In Kayseri, the share of contested cases had been quite low even at the end of the sixteenth and the beginning of the seventeenth centuries; by the 1690s, it had dropped to the low level of 5.7 per cent. In all probability, the discrepancy between the two cities should not be taken to mean that the inhabitants of Kayseri got along better with their relatives and neighbours than their opposite numbers in Ankara. Rather, the decisive feature was probably that the inhabitants of Kayseri were more inclined to have ordinary sales recorded in the *kadıs'* registers than the townsmen of Ankara. One can only speculate why that should have been so. But it appears quite likely that the uncommonly large number of non-Muslims in Kayseri caused the custom to establish itself; for by turning to the *kadı's* court and registering a sale to which they were a party, non-Muslims avoided the difficulties which might arise from the fact that the *şeriat* did not permit them to testify against Muslims.[7]

Religious affiliations of plaintiffs and defendants

From the evidence at hand, it appears that the non-Muslims of Ankara and Kayseri also trusted the court when they were party to a dispute. In Ankara during the difficult years before and after 1600, 64 cases involved Muslims and thirteen cases involved non-Muslims who turned to the court as plaintiffs (see Table 1). It appears unlikely that during those years, the non-Muslim population of Ankara amounted to more than ten per cent. Thus the share of non-Muslim plaintiffs probably surpassed, or was at the very least equal to, the non-Muslim share among the total urban population. During the closing years of the seventeenth century, the situation had not appreciably changed; for even if we assume that the non-Muslims living in Ankara had increased both relatively and absolutely, it is all but impossible that they should have made up one third of the Ankara population. In Kayseri, the share of cases involving non-Muslim plaintiffs amounted to 21.9 per cent in the last years of the sixteenth and the beginning years of the seventeenth century, and to 25 per cent in the 1690s.

Where the earlier period is concerned, non-Muslims thus seem to have acted as plaintiffs in numbers roughly corresponding to their share of the

Table 1. *Plaintiffs*[1]

Location	Muslim	Non-Muslim	Male	Female	*Askerî*	*Reaya*	Total
Ankara, c. 1600	64 (83.1%)	13 (16.9%)	56 (72.7%)	19 (24.7%)	7 (9.1%)	68 (88.3%)	77
Kayseri, c. 1600	25 (78.1%)	7 (21.9%)	17 (53.1%)	15 (46.9%)	2 (6.3%)	29 (90.6%)	32
Ankara, c. 1690	22 (66.7%)	11 (33.7%)	22 (66.7%)	8 (24.2%)	7 (21.2%)	26 (78.8%)	33
Kayseri, c. 1690	12 (75.0%)	4 (25.0%)	9 (56.3%)	4 (25.0%)	1 (6.3%)	14 (87.5%)	16

[1] Minor discrepancies are due to lack of data, or to the occurrence of 'mixed' groups, consisting of both males and females etc. Percentages based upon the total in the last column.

Table 2. *Defendants*[1]

Location	Muslim	non-Muslim	Male	Female	*Askerî*	*Reaya*	Total
Ankara, c. 1600	58 (75.3%)	16 (20.8%)	64 (83.1%)	12 (15.6%)	7 (9.1%)	69 (89.6%)	77
Kayseri, c. 1600	25 (78.1%)	7 (21.9%)	23 (71.9%)	8 (25.0%)	4 (12.5%)	28 (87.5%)	32
Ankara, c. 1690	23 (69.7%)	10 (30.3%)	18 (54.5%)	13 (39.4%)	4 (12.1%)	29 (87.9%)	33
Kayseri, c. 1690	12 (75.0%)	4 (25.0%)	7 (43.8%)	9 (56.3%)	3 (18.8%)	13 (81.3%)	16

[1] Minor discrepancies are due to the lack of data, or to the occurrence of 'mixed' groups, consisting of both males and females etc. Percentages based upon the total given in the last column.

urban population as a whole. As to the closing years of the seventeenth century, our lack of information does not permit us to formulate a clear judgment. If the respective shares of Muslims and non-Muslims in the urban population were still the same as they had been in the mid-seventeenth century (that is 57.7 and 49.3 per cent), 1690s Kayseri should have constituted an exception to the general rule.[8] Only in this instance non-Muslims may well have been less strongly represented among the plaintiffs than their numbers among the total population warranted. However, since the number both of Muslim and of non-Muslim plaintiffs in late-seventeenth-century Kayseri was exceptionally low, no far-reaching conclusions can be drawn from this state of affairs.

If we wish to get a better picture concerning the relations between Muslims and non-Muslims, it is also worth looking at the balance between plaintiffs and defendants, both on the Muslim and non-Muslim side (see Table 2). A certain degree of balance would indicate fairly normal relations, while a marked concentration of defendants on one side or the other should probably be interpreted as indicative of tension. Apart from Ankara during the late sixteenth and early seventeenth centuries (cases involving Muslim plaintiffs : 64 out of 77, or 83.1 per cent, cases involving Muslim defendants : 58 out of 77, or 75.3 per cent)[9] the balance is almost perfect. Even in this latter case, the difference is probably not large enough to be significant. Certainly, we must allow for the fact that a fair number of the cases studied concerned inheritance cases, in which members of one and the same family took each other to court, and these people would normally be of the same religion. But even so, these observations also contribute to the impression which has already been formulated in a different context,[10] namely that relations between Muslims and non-Muslims in seventeenth-century Ankara and Kayseri were not particularly tense.

Men and women pleading in court

Since the *kadıs*' registers generally allow us to determine not only the religion but also the sex of plaintiffs and defendants, the data analysed here allow us to add a few observations concerning the role of women in Ottoman society during the seventeenth century.[11] Throughout this period, both Ankara and Kayseri women seem to have had no hesitations about bringing their problems to the *kadı*'s court. In Ankara during the late sixteenth and early seventeenth centuries, 19 out of 77 cases involved a female plaintiff (24.7 per cent). In addition we find a number of women among the two groups of plaintiffs who addressed themselves to the court. In Kayseri during the early 1600s, the balance was even more impressive from the women's point of view: for among 32 cases, there were 17 involving male and 15 involving female plaintiffs, so that the share of women amounted to almost one half. In Ankara toward the end of the seventeenth century, 22 cases involved male and 7 cases female plaintiffs (24.2 per cent); in addition, we again find two groups of plaintiffs in which women were represented. As to Kayseri during the same period, the share of cases involving female plaintiffs amounted to 25 per cent; but due to the small number of actual cases involved, this figure should be treated with circumspection. Under the circumstances, it seems fair to say that well over a quarter of all court cases involved female plaintiffs, and Jennings' remarks about the accessibility of the courts to women appear to be valid not only for the early 1600s, but for the seventeenth century in general.[12]

Females did not only attend the court to sue, they also appeared as defendants. Out of the 77 cases on record for late-sixteenth and early-seventeenth-century Ankara, the sex of the defendant is known in 76 instances; out of these, 12 were females (15.6 per cent). For Kayseri during the same period, the share of female defendants amounted to 25.0 per cent, while in Ankara during the later seventeenth century, 13 out of 33 defendants were women (39.4 per cent; one of the remaining cases involved a group of defendants consisting mainly of females). In 1690s Kayseri, women even outnumbered men as defendants. Looking at the available data as a whole, women were the defendants in 42 out of 158 cases (26.6 per cent), which corresponds very well to their share of all plaintiffs (46 cases, or 29.1 per cent). These figures are worth retaining, particularly if we compare them with what has previously been found about female participation in the housing market. Women sold urban real-estate much more frequently than they bought it and typically their savings were held in the shape of money. On the other hand, informal mechanisms of depriving women of their share in the inheritance must, to a considerable extent, have been frustrated by the easy accessibility of the court.[13]

At the same time, one might assume that the growing habit of seventeenth-century townsmen to have ordinary uncontested transfers of property registered in the *kadıs*' court contributed towards making the court more accessible to women who needed to plead a case. However, this does not seem to have occurred. In Ankara, the share of female plaintiffs remained more or less constant, while in Kayseri, if the very few contested cases recorded for the later seventeenth century do not deceive us, there may even have been a decline in the number of women plaintiffs. Certainly at the same time, the share of female defendants increased quite dramatically, but this fact cannot be interpreted as a sign of growing female initiative in court. Given our as yet rudimentary knowledge of the history of women in pre-nineteenth-century Anatolia, it is not easy to interpret the divergence between a stable or declining trend among female plaintiffs, and a growing share of female defendants. Was the notion that women could own real property, which had always been upheld by the Ottoman courts, increasingly being challenged by urban males? At the present stage of our investigations, it is impossible to tell, but the problem might repay investigation in a broader context.

Servitors of the Ottoman administration and their role in contested cases

Another aspect of urban life was the relatively high concentration of people exempted from taxes because they served the Ottoman central administration, or else because of their descent from the Prophet Muhammad. Tax exemption did not mean that the person in question could not be sued in the *kadı*'s court, although in criminal cases, janissaries could be punished only upon the order of their commander.[14] As a result we encounter soldiers, *medrese* teachers, and descendants of the Prophet both among the plaintiffs and among the defendants in the courts of Ankara and Kayseri. Moreover, we quite frequently find 'mixed groups' of plaintiffs or defendants, certain members of which appear to have been tax-exempt while others were ordinary subjects of the Ottoman Empire. This may well be due to the fact that the brother of a *medrese* teacher might easily be associated with the latter in a court case, but would enjoy no special status if he was not himself a member of the ulama. In addition, janissaries and others who had entered the service of the Ottoman administration by way of the 'levy of boys' or *devşirme*,[15] usually maintained some contact with their non-Muslim relatives in the provinces. Occasionally a janissary, adorned with the honorific title of *bey*, might thus appear in a court case along with his brothers or cousins among the townspeople.

In Ankara during the late sixteenth and early seventeenth centuries, seven cases out of seventy-seven (9.1 per cent) involved a probable *askerî* as plaintiff, while in addition, two groups of people turning to the court comprised at least one *askerî* among their number.[16] In Kayseri, the involvement of *askerî* was significantly less (2 *askerî* plaintiffs, in addition to a 'mixed' group among a total of 32 cases, or 6.3 per cent). It is likely that the higher percentage of Ankara *askerî* who expected redress from the *kadı*'s court was a consequence of the greater wealth and prestige of the urban 'upper middle class' in this active commercial centre. When we look at the figures for the 1690s, we encounter the same disparity. In seven cases out of a total of thirty-three which came before the court of Ankara, (21.2 per cent) the plaintiff was a member of the *askerî*. At the same time, court participation on the part of the *askerî* of Kayseri was minimal: out of sixteen contested cases studied here, only one involved an *askerî* plaintiff (6.3 per cent).

One might assume that members of a group anxious to uphold its position of pre-eminence would sue whenever their real or imagined rights and privileges had been infringed, while more modest members of the community might refrain from suing their 'betters'. Obviously, the limited number of contested cases involving *askerî* in whatever capacity makes general conclusions somewhat hazardous. However, *askerî* plaintiffs were more or less balanced by *askerî* defendants both in Ankara around 1600 and in Kayseri throughout the seventeenth century. Only in 1690s Ankara do we find seven *askerî* plaintiffs against only four defendants associated in one way or another with the Ottoman central administration. These observations tend to confirm the impression that the *askerî* of seventeenth-century central Anatolia were not, as a group, in a position to overwhelm their fellow townsmen either by their wealth or by their social privileges. They were probably, at the beginning of the seventeenth century, wealthier than the average inhabitant of Ankara or Kayseri, although as the century wore on, their position was increasingly challenged by the rise to wealth of certain non-Muslim families. There is, however, little evidence to the fact that the *askerî* were actively using the courts to defend their accustomed positions.

The garment and the lining

In Turkish, the notion 'it wasn't worth the effort' is traditionally expressed by the saying 'the lining came to be more expensive than the garment'.[17] In the present section, we will examine whether Ankara townsmen who brought their disputes involving the ownership of residential property to the *kadı*'s court were concerned about unusually valuable property, thus making the expenses incurred appear worthwhile. Or as an alternative, one might assume that the distribution was purely random, only reflecting the breakdown of traditional arbitration procedures. In such a case, there would be no clear relationship between the price of the 'garment' (i.e. the house) and the 'lining' (i.e. the expenses, both financial and social, which may have been involved in going to court). Moreover, if people frequently went to court over houses which were in themselves of small value, it is permissible to conclude that in spite of frequent complaints about exorbitant registration fees in inheritance cases, the expenses involved in initiating a court case were not usually very high.[18]

compare the prices of disputed properties with the mean and median prices of houses bought and sold in the ordinary fashion (see Chapter 3). Particularly, we must make allowance for the fact that house prices mentioned in contested cases did not necessarily refer to a recent sale of the property involved. Quite to the contrary, in many cases the last sale or valuation might have occurred many years earlier. As the later sixteenth century was a period of galloping inflation, this state of affairs should mean that the prices mentioned in contested cases show a downward bias; they would have been higher if the properties involved had all been sold in the years around 1600. This situation probably accounts for the fact that at the end of the sixteenth and the beginning of the seventeenth century, both the mean and the median prices which had been paid for disputed houses were lower than those demanded for dwellings which were actually changing hands at the time. At the end of the seventeenth century, inflation and debasement of the coinage were certainly no unknown phenomena.[19] But their impact upon the level of real-estate prices seems to have been much less marked. In 1690s Ankara, the median prices of houses disputed and of houses sold were substantially the same, while with regard to the mean (average), the houses disputed were more valuable than the houses transferred by ordinary sales. In late-seventeenth-century Kayseri, the difference in price-levels was even more pronounced: the median price for houses bought and sold was 11,000 *akçe*, while the median value in disputed cases amounted to 18,000 *akçe*. While not equally pronounced, the difference between mean (average) prices was also substantial.

Given the fact that overall conditions in Ankara and Kayseri during the closing years of the seventeenth century differed in certain respects, one may speculate whether the financial and social costs of conducting litigation

Table 3. *The value of disputed houses*

Location	Number of contested houses, with price known	Mean price	Median price	Conversion rate	Mean price, all houses	Median price, all houses
Ankara, c. 1600	30	5,243	4,100	–	8,475	5,303
Kayseri, c. 1600	9	5,160	2,160	1 *guruş* = 120 *akçe*	8,995	4,560
Ankara, c. 1690	16	20,225	11,600	1 *guruş* = 200 *akçe* 1 *esedi* = 140 *akçe*	18,655	11,000
Kayseri, c. 1690	7	22,857	18,000	1 *guruş* = 200 *akçe* 1 *esedi* = 140 *akçe*	18,453	11,000

All prices have been expressed in *akçe*.

were higher in Kayseri than in Ankara, so that people turned to the court only when the 'garment' was definitely more valuable than the 'lining'. On the other hand, it would appear that at least in Ankara, people brought their complaints to court very readily, even if only a very ordinary dwelling was involved. Or were informal mechanisms of conflict settlement less effective in Ankara than they were in Kayseri? At the present level of information, we can only raise the question.

Families and inheritances

After analysing the personal data concerning plaintiffs and defendants, additional information concerning the social structure of Anatolian towns can be gained by studying the issues that might divide the inhabitants. The largest body of data relates to inheritance cases.[20] Muslim religious law demands that an inheritance be divided among what might amount to a large number of heirs: children and spouses figure most prominently, but other relatives may also appear among the heirs. In addition, many inheritances could only be divided after the widow had received the money due to her as a 'dowry' or nuptial gift (*mihr-i müeccel*).[21] Ottoman Sultans of the sixteenth century had frequently ordered that inheritances might be divided without recourse to the court if none of the heirs was absent or a minor,[22] and many families must have availed themselves of this possibility. A fee, calculated on a pro rata basis, was to be paid if the inheritance was divided by the court, and in the confused years before and after 1600, *kadıs* were frequently accused of fraudulently raising their fees.

When applied to a dwelling, these practices meant that court officials might be sent to view a house to be divided among several heirs, and to prepare a record of their findings (*keşif*). Thus in Cemaziülevvel 1101/ February–March 1690 a scribe of the Ankara court and a member of the Sultan's corps of architects (*hassa mimarı*)[23] were sent to a house in the Sed quarter of Ankara to resolve a dispute among the members of a large non-Muslim family.[24] Its head, recently deceased, must have been engaged in the manufacture of mohair cloth, for the house contained a workshop necessary for the exercise of this trade. Individual rooms were assigned to the various heirs, while the courtyard was divided among them. To forestall future disputes, a record of the award was made in the court registers.

In certain cases the heirs might use the room or rooms which had been assigned to them as their share of the inheritance, as the core of a new residence. In this context, a dispute recorded in the Kayseri registers in 1107/ 1695–6 informs us of the arrangements made by the heirs of a certain Mustafa of the Deliklitaş town quarter.[25] One of Mustafa's sons, who according to his title of *beşe* must have been a military man, had received the principal room of the house (*tabhane*) along with part of the courtyard. The *sofa* and the remainder of the courtyard were assigned to the deceased's second son and to his widow, who then proceeded to enlarge their dwelling by adding an upper storey with a room, a veranda, a larder, and a stable or cowshed on the ground floor. Thus the dwelling conformed to what in the present study we have been calling Type 6 (compare Chapter 2), and had become more comfortable to live in, even if the heating must still have presented a problem, since the newly built dwelling did not contain a *tabhane*.

In other cases, shares of an inherited house were not inhabited by the owners, but changed hands by means of a sale. Through an Ankara court case recorded in 1099/1687–8,[26] we hear of a widow and her two daughters inheriting shares in a house worth 60 *guruş*. According to the testimony of the husband of one of the daughters, which was backed up by witnesses and therefore accepted by the court, the women had sold their shares to him. As a result, the demands of the other daughter, who had sent her own husband to court to plead her case, were summarily rejected.

When a house was sold, so that an often sizeable number of heirs might receive the value of their respective shares in money, it was in the buyer's interest to keep a proper record of the transaction. Apparently it could easily happen that one of the sellers involved, or even the latter's sons and daughters, later went to court and, in good faith or otherwise, laid claim to the shares they had originally been assigned. Thus in the late-seventeenth-century Kayseri, Kirkor veled Habil, along with his sisters Beşe Sultan and Kadem, took the heirs of Ömer b. Hacı Veli to court, claiming that their mother Çınar had sold the family's property to the deceased, and demanding their share of the sale price.[27] Fortunately for the young children of Ömer, the administrator of their property was able to produce witnesses that Çınar had sold the house in its entirety, not just her own share, and that her children had approved of the sale. Less lucky was Rabia b Mustafa, of the Bektaş *mahalle* in Kayseri,[28] who was confronted with the *zimmi* Ayan's claim that she had usurped his share in a house.[29] This building must originally have been owned by a non-Muslim family, for it contained a wine cellar (*şırahane*). Rabia admitted that a share of the house had originally belonged to Ayan, but claimed that he had had it sold to her husband, now deceased, from whom, in turn, she had inherited the dwelling. However, Rabia was unable to prove her case, and the court ordered her to hand over her share of the house to Ayan.

Additional complications often arose when one of the people owning shares in a given house claimed to have been a minor at the time of sale. In certain instances, the dispute hinged upon the problem whether this was in fact true, or whether the plaintiff had not, even at the time of sale, been a young adult capable of giving his consent.[30] This type of dispute would seem to imply that the sale had not, at the time of its conclusion, been recorded in the *kadı*'s registers, for when a very young person was involved, the court scribes generally took the precaution of recording that the boy or girl in question had declared him- or herself to have entered puberty.[31] When matters were particularly difficult to sort out, it was of course preferable to reach an amicable settlement, and this is what happened in the court case which Mehmed Çelebi initiated against the purchaser of his father's property, the 'highly respected' (fahrülekran) Abdi Ağa b. Mehmed. Mehmed Çelebi himself must have come from a wealthy family, judging from the purchase price of the house which had been the cause of the dispute. Accordingly, the former minor was offered, and accepted, a compensation in harmony with his lifestyle. There was a horse worth 30 guruş; in the towns and villages of seventeenth-century Anatolia, horses were generally a privilege of the wealthier members of society. In addition, there were 30 guruş in cash, and a piece of mohair cloth worth 15 guruş – one hundred and fifty years earlier, Kanuni Süleyman himself had usually worn garments of this material.[32] For the monetary value of these items, Mehmed Çelebi could have bought himself a modest house, and in exchange for this compensation, he abandoned all claims against Abdi Ağa.

Another manner in which a young man or woman, after coming of age, could challenge a sale made during his or her childhood was by claiming that the house in question had by right belonged to his deceased parents, and that whoever had sold it had no right to do so.[33] Thus we find Ibrahim b. Mustafa claiming that a house now in the possession of a certain Ahmed b. Hasan belonged by right of inheritance to himself and to his mother. On the other hand, the defendant proclaimed that he had bought the house in good faith, and paid 36 gold pieces for it, knowing nothing about any rights of either Ibrahim or his mother. However, as witnesses confirmed Ibrahim's claim, it is probable that he ultimately obtained the return of his father's house.

Less common were court cases arising from the şeriat rule that Muslims could not inherit from non-Muslims and vice versa.[34] This might result in complications if one of the members of a family had converted to Islam, or else if a Muslim husband had married a non-Muslim wife. One rather picturesque example of the latter case occurred in late-seventeenth-century Kayseri, and was reflected in the local court records on Şevval 1103/June–July 1692.[35] Mustafa beşe, a military man, had died in foreign parts, leaving a son, and a widow who was a Christian. The son went to court and claimed that due to the difference in religion, the widow could not inherit from her deceased spouse, demanding that the kadı put him in possession of the house and its furnishings. In court the widow declared that the house was hers by right, for her husband during his lifetime had sold some of her rugs and personal possessions to buy and repair the house, and had subsequently donated it to her. Probably Mustafa beşe had had a fairly clear idea of his son's character, for he had provided his wife with an ample number of witnesses to the fact that he had given her the house before he began his last journey. As a result, the court decided that the son had no right to the house or to any part of it. One might even imagine that Mustafa beşe's son had made himself a bad reputation as the local ne'er-do-well, and that his fellow townsmen eagerly seized the opportunity of removing him from the neighbourhood.

An inheritance case complicated by the rule that a Muslim could not inherit from his non-Muslim relatives was decided by the Kayseri court in 1019/1610–1.[36] Abdi bey b. Abdullah, member of the military corps known as the *ebnai sipahiyan*, demanded that the non-Muslim Erdoğdu veled Nikol and his sisters turn over to him a house which he claimed to have inherited from his father. In reply, Erdoğdu and his sisters stated that their father had bought the house from Abdi bey's father thirty to forty years ago, and that according to established Ottoman judicial practice, cases older than fifteen years were not to be heard in court. Moreover, Abdi bey's father had been a non-Muslim and Abdi bey thus could not inherit from him. This state of affairs was in fact indicated by Abdi bey's patronymic 'b. Abdullah', for while 'Abdullah' might occur as a given name, many people bearing this patronymic in the Ottoman context of the sixteenth or seventeenth centuries were in fact converts to Islam.[37] The court accepted the arguments brought forth by Erdoğdu and his sisters, and decided that too much time had elapsed for Abdi bey to have any rights in the matter. For this reason, the enterprising military man was ordered to leave the defendants in undisturbed possession of their property.

As the case of Mustafa beşe's son versus his mother or stepmother has already shown, Ankara and Kayseri townsmen occasionally sold or else donated all or part of their dwelling to their wives. Sometimes this gesture was intended as a compensation for the nuptial gift or 'dowry' (*mihr-i müeccel*) which the wife might have foregone in her husband's favour. Or else, a husband might be worried that the relatively small share of his inheritance which the *şeriat* allotted to a surviving wife[38] might not be sufficient to assure the widow of a decent livelihood. For reasonably harmonious families, such sales or donations would be tacitly recognized by the surviving children, and thus never be mentioned in the court record. But not all sons and daughters could be trusted to behave in this manner. Thus in Şaban 1019/October–November 1610 we find a certain Mehmed b. Yakub in court, contesting the right of his mother Yasemin b. Abdullah, possibly a former slave woman, to the *tabhane* which she occupied in her deceased husband's home.[39] Yasemin could prove, by the testimony of two witnesses, that she had purchased the *tabhane* from her husband for 3,000 *akçe*, and in consequence, the court confirmed her as the owner.

Less clear is the case that Umm Gülsüm b. Ahmed opened against Gülbeşe b. Halil.[40] The plaintiff claimed to have inherited a share in the house of her deceased husband, and she accused Gülbeşe of having illegally appropriated it. On her side, Gülbeşe claimed that her own husband, 'the aforementioned Muzaffer' had donated the entire dwelling to herself. As she could produce two witnesses, the court accepted her claim.

Unfortunately Umm Gülsüm did not mention her deceased husband by name. But since both women were obviously referring to the same house, and there is no mention of two separate male owners, the most probable solution is that Umm Gülsüm and Gülbeşe had been married to the same man. Muzaffer had either preferred Gülbeşe, or else provided for Umm Gülsüm in other ways. Be that as it may, he had used the institution of the donation *inter vivos* to assure the future of one of his wives.

In other instances the donation *inter vivos* might be used to make sure that a member of the family who could not inherit from his relatives due to the difference in religion,[41] was not deprived of his share. Thus in Ramazan 1009/March–April 1601, Mustafa b. Abdullah took his niece, the non-Muslim Hatunbola b. Emre, to court.[42] At stake was a house in the Hendek quarter of Ankara, reasonably well appointed because it contained a baking oven. Mustafa b. Abdullah claimed that this house had been donated to him by his non-Muslim mother Hundi. For some time, however, this niece had been denying that such a donation had ever taken place, thereby contesting his right to the house, which the plaintiff had possessed for nine years. It is probable that Hatunbola laid claim to the house by right of inheritance, since Mustafa was excluded from the succession of his mother. But since the latter was able to produce two competent witnesses in his favour, the court ordered Hatunbola to stop interfering with her uncle's property.

Disputes arising from a sale

The sale of urban property frequently gave rise to court cases, because the majority of all transactions were probably not entered in the *kadı*'s register at all, but simply concluded in front of two witnesses. It is well known that a sale concluded in this fashion was considered perfectly legal; in fact, the *şeriat* regarded the testimony of witnesses as the principal evidence in a case, written testimony being only subsidiary.[43] Even so, however, due to the statute of limitations mentioned above, it was not generally possible to contest sales which had been concluded in the distant past. However, certain townsmen apparently had no very clear idea concerning the limits of their rights in these matters.

One reason for disputes was the fact that a house might be sold while one of the co-owners was absent, who could then object to the sale upon his return.[44] Or else one of the partners to the sale might change his or her mind about the transaction. Thus Seydi b. Iskender had sold his house under the condition that he be allowed to live in it until his death. However, the buyer did not abide by this agreement and denied Seydi, who was probably an old man, access to the house. Thereupon the latter obtained a *fetva* to the effect that if Amr drove Zeyd out of the house after a sale had been concluded under the condition outlined above, the sale itself became invalid.[45] Acordingly the court ordered the purchaser to return the dwelling, and Seydi was enjoined to pay back the purchase price.

Other disputes might result from the fact that many people buying houses could not pay the purchase price as a lump sum, but took possession of the house after they had only paid for part of it. Thus in Şevval 1007/April–May 1599 Şaban b. Mustafa began a court case against Piyale b. Abdullah, who had bought Şaban's house, but still owed him about half the price. Piyale reported that he had been granted a delay of sixty days in which to pay. When Şaban denied this, Piyale produced two witnesses, one of them a member of the ulama, to support his claim, and it must be assumed that he won his case.[46] Rather similar were the problems of Mustafa b. Sinan, of Kâfirköy in Ankara, who had sold his house to a certain Iskender v. Arslan for 3100 akçe. At a later date, he took Iskender to court, claiming that the latter still owed him money on account of this transaction.[47] In other instances, the case might be complicated by the fact that the buying and selling of a house was only part of the ongoing business relations between buyer and seller. As a result, debts arising from this particular transaction might be difficult to sort out, and at least in one instance, the two parties were so unsure of their respective cases that they preferred to settle out of court.[48]

Other disputes might arise from the fact that a given sale had been concluded not in the town where the house in question was situated, but in some other locality. If at the same time, the number of people owning shares in the house was sufficiently large, and communication between them difficult, the house might occasionally even be sold to two different purchasers. Moreover, one of the owners might not be in good faith, and attempt to gain a personal advantage from a confused situation. Something of the sort had probably happened in the case involving a house in the Ankara town quarter of Ahi Hacı Murad, which had been sold once in Ankara and once in Bursa, with the two buyers obliged to sort out the situation in court.[49] The plaintiff was induced to conclude an amicable settlement; his legal position must have been quite strong, for when he renounced his claim, he was awarded an indemnity of over half the purchase price of the house. Even though the document recorded in the kadı's registers tells us nothing about the matter, it is likely that the original sellers were made to contribute to the indemnity.

Pious foundations

An appreciable number of court cases involved the institution and operation of pious foundations. Both cash vakıfs and the more traditional foundations based upon urban real estate quite often included houses;[50] in the former instance a house might constitute the security for a loan, in the latter case, it provided the income which the institution required for its functioning.

In the early stages of instituting a foundation, the founder would sometimes initiate a fictitious 'contested case'. In this instance, the plaintiff did not aim at achieving the result he stated in his plea, namely the abolition

of the foundation. Rather, he was aiming at the very opposite, a verdict
rejecting his demand, in which the *kadı* would state *expressis verbis* that the
foundation had been legally constituted and could not be dissolved. In this
fashion, the *vakıf* would then be protected by a formal statement on the part
of the court.[51] It is quite possible that this was what Canfeda Hatun b.
Abdullah had in mind, when in Cemaziülahır 1101/March–April 1690 she
demanded the retrocession of a house that she had made into an *avarız*
foundation for the town quarter in which she lived.[52]

Moreover, when a *vakıf* was instituted after the death of the donor and
according to his will, a court case might also often be necessary before the
foundation could begin operations. At least this happened in Ankara in the
year 1002/1593–4 when Kaya Balı b. Mehmed, administrator of the foundation to aid the taxpayers of Leblebici town quarter in paying their taxes
(*avarız akçesi*), initiated proceedings against Şaban b. Nesimi, the official in
charge of confiscating heirless property.[53] A woman by the name of Kamer
b. Abdullah, without known heirs, had made over her little house, consisting of a *tabhane*, an *oda* and a courtyard, to various foundations of the
quarter. Half of the proceeds were to be spent on prayers to be recited for
the repose of her soul, while the other half was to help the inhabitants of
Leblebici town quarter defray their *avarız* taxes. However, the official in
charge of heirless property – these people had a bad reputation on account of
their rapacity, not only among the inhabitants at large, but with the Ottoman
central administration as well[54] – had seized the house of Kamer after her
death. Unfortunately, the *kadı*'s registers do not record whether the
foundation administrator was able to regain control of the property.

Court cases of this type were even more probable if a *vakıf* had been
instituted in such a fashion that it benefited the general public only after the
donor had no more direct descendants living. In Şevval 1007/April–May
1599, such a case was heard by the *kadı* of Ankara.[55] A woman by the name
of Raziye b. Ibrahim had made her house in the Börekçiler quarter into a
foundation in favour of her homonymous granddaughter Raziye b. Hüseyin.
As long as there were direct descendants of Raziye b. Hüseyin living, the
foundation was intended for their sole benefit. But after the direct line was
extinguished, the house was to be sold – an interesting example of a founder
having a choice between a traditional foundation and a cash *vakıf*, and
deliberately opting for the latter.[56] The proceeds were to be lent out at 15
per cent interest, and the resulting income was to be divided in two halves.
One went to the *imam* of the local mosque, who in return was expected to
say prayers for the soul of the deceased, and of all Muslims in general. Out of
the other half, the inhabitants of the town quarter were to be given help in
paying their *avarız* taxes. After some time had elapsed, Raziye b. Hüseyin
died without surviving issue. Thereupon the administrator of the Börekçiler
mosque's foundation money demanded that the house be turned over to
him. However, he was confronted by the rival claims of two people. Raziye
b. Hüseyin had an heir, a woman whose relationship to the deceased is not

known, but who could lay claim only to a share of the inheritance, the official in charge of heirless property collecting the remainder. These two people strenuously denied all claims on the part of the foundation. However, the administrator was seconded by two witnesses to back up his claim, and if the court was indeed able to dislodge the official in charge of heirless property, the foundation should have received the house that it had been promised.

In fact, family members who considered themselves disadvantaged by the institution of a pious foundation, could cause a *vakıf* administrator almost as much trouble as the *beytülmal emini*. At least that is the impression that we gain from a case submitted to the *kadı* of Kayseri in Zilkade 1013/March–April 1604, involving the house which a certain Hasan had made into a family *vakıf* for his descendants. Fifteen years earlier, that is in 1589, the last of Hasan's direct descendants had died. According to the foundation administrator's claim, the house should then have been turned over to the *imam* of the Imam Idris mosque of Yenice town quarter, who in return was to recite portions of the Qoran. However Şahana, apparently an heir to, though not a descendant of the founder, claimed the house as her private property.[57] It seems that the case had dragged on for a very considerable time, for the document which the administrator produced, and whose validity Şahana contested, was dated 994/1586! Presumably legal steps had been undertaken in the meantime, which the document does not record. Had it been otherwise, the statute of limitations would have prevented the *kadı* from hearing the case.

Surprisingly enough, the administrator was able to counter Şahana's objections by introducing two witnesses who had signed the 1586 document, which had originally established the foundation. These men testified to the conditions stipulated by the donor Hasan, to the fact that the last of his direct descendants had died fifteen years earlier, and moreover declared that the foundation was entitled to the house. Whether this was enough to discourage the indomitable Şahana, we will never know.

Other difficulties might arise from the fact that the person establishing a pious foundation was absent from the place where the *vakıf* was to be located, and sent a legal representative (*vekil*) to conduct the transaction on his behalf.[58] Thus a certain Bekir b. Veli, who owned a house in Ankara but lived in the Ottoman capital, decided to have his Ankara house sold. The sale price was to be made over to the *avarız* foundation of Hacı Arab town quarter.[59] The house, which was at least partly in ruinous condition, was sold for the rather modest price of 2,500 *akçe* to a certain Nasuh b. Mehmed. However, the latter was little inclined to pay, giving as an excuse that he had not known that the house was being sold on behalf of the *avarız* foundation. But the court seems to have finally induced him to pay up, for the document in the *kadı*'s registers concludes that the man whom Bekir b. Veli had appointed as his representative paid over the money to the foundation administrator.

Once a *vakıf* had been legally instituted, disputes might arise out of the fact that debtors were unable or unwilling to pay back the money which they had borrowed. Under such circumstances, a court case might be necessary to determine the fate of the house that the debtor had turned over to the foundation as a security. Often the main issue was obscured by the counter-claims of the defendant, so that the case might hinge upon side issues, such as the question of whether the house had actually belonged to the person who was in debt to the foundation. As an example, one might cite the case involving the house of Deli Ibrahim b. Süleyman, of late a resident of Hasbey quarter in Kayseri.[60] When Deli Ibrahim – his nickname may well have attested to his spendthrift disposition – died, he left 28 *guruş* of debts to various pious foundations. The administrators of these foundations turned to the court when the deceased's half-sister Saliha sold the house, demand-ing repayment of the 28 *guruş*. Possibly in an attempt to safeguard not only her own inheritance, but that of Deli Ibrahim's widow as well, Saliha claimed to be the real owner of the house, which she had simply lent to Deli Ibrahim.[61] However, the foundation administrators had prepared their case very well. Not only did they produce witnesses to support their own point of view, they also submitted a *fetva* to the effect that under the conditions described, the ownership of the deceased must be presumed, rather than that of his half-sister. The court accepted the testimony, and ruled that the *fetva* was in fact applicable to the case under consideration. In consequence, Saliha was ordered to pay the 28 *guruş* which the foundation administrators demanded of her.

Things might become even more complicated if foundation administra-tors did not intervene in time to prevent the sale of a house to which they laid claim. A case of this type involved the heirs of Kör Murad, a non-Muslim formerly resident in Kayseri.[62] Kör Murad had borrowed 30 *guruş* from a foundation, and when he found himself unable to produce the money necessary for repayment, he turned over his house to the institution, thereby extinguishing his debt. For ten years, the foundation administrators enjoyed undisturbed possession. But then Osman b. Abubekir and Hanefi b. Battal appeared, and according to the administrator's assertion, forcibly ejected him and seized control of the dwelling.

When questioned by the court, the two men claimed that five years ago, they had bought the dwelling from Kör Murad's sons. That the latter lived not in Kayseri but in Tokat, the centre of caravan trade with Iran, probably explains why the *vakıf* administrators did not immediately learn about the transaction. Apparently Kör Murad's sons were no luckier in business than their late father had been; for they in turn sold the house because of debt. Not surprisingly, Osman b. Abubekir and Hanefi b. Battal denied any knowledge of the previous sale. It was only because the foundation adminis-trator could provide witnesses to support his claim that the court confirmed the *vakıf*'s title to the dwelling, leaving Osman and Hanefi to get their money back from the sellers as best they might.[63]

That disagreeable surprises of this kind were a possibility to be reckoned with, is also apparent from a case submitted to the Ankara court in Safer 1010/August 1601. In this instance, a certain Yeğen Mehmed, now deceased, had borrowed 600 *akçe* from the mosque of the Imaret town quarter, and as a result, turned over a single *oda* in his house to the foundation.[64] After Yeğen Mehmed's death, his son Hacı Nebi sold the property to a certain Mehmed Çelebi. The latter was then confronted with the foundation's claim; unfortunately, we do not know what the administrators proposed to do with the room. They may have wanted to extract a yearly rent; or else they may have planned to have Mehmed Çelebi buy out the foundation's rights. Whatever the background may have been, Mehmed Çelebi was confronted with the fact that a house which he had considered his private property was not really his at all; again, his attempts to get compensation out of Hacı Nebi must have constituted the subject of a separate court case.

Conflicts arising out of pre-emption (*şufa*)

Islamic law recognizes the right of pre-emption in case real estate is sold; in this definition of real estate, the upper floor of a house is included.[65] Co-owners, owners of rights-of-way in the property being sold, and neighbours could all exercise the right of pre-emption. The rights of a co-owner had priority, while a simple neighbour was considered to be last in line. A person wishing to make use of this right, which could not be alienated for money, had to state his intention in front of witnesses as soon as he learned of the sale. If he did not do so, it was deemed that he had abandoned his claim.

Hesitations of this type were the subject of a case submitted to the court of Ankara at the beginning of the seventeenth-century.[66] Ömer b. Mustafa claimed in court that he wished to exercise his right of pre-emption with respect to a property recently sold to a certain Hüseyin b. Mustafa. When the court asked for the latter's version of the dispute, Hüseyin answered that he had formerly asked Ömer for his consent, using what may have been a fixed formula, namely 'do you accept me for a neighbour?' Ömer had at first answered with a formula expressing consent.[67] But after having thought the matter over, he changed his mind, and declared his intention to use his right of pre-emption. Hüseyin was then asked to prove his case, which he did by producing two witnesses who confirmed his statement. The issue of the case is not known. But since Hüseyin recounted the story of Ömer's change of heart as crucial evidence to support his own case, it must be assumed that seventeenth-century Ottoman courts did not allow a person that had renounced his or her right of pre-emption to go back on their word.

Other disputes might arise from the fact that a person possessing the right to pre-emption chose to exercise it not when the property was first offered for sale, but only when the purchaser decided to dispose of the house in his turn. We may imagine that such a delayed action was due to temporary lack of funds, or else to the intention of not having a certain person for a neighbour. In the case recorded in the Ankara *kadı*'s registers under the date of Safer 1009/August–September 1600,[68] an occurrence of this type was involved. Unfortunately, in this instance as in others, the early-seventeenth-century scribe did not include the verdict in his account of the case. Therefore we do not know whether the Ankara court considered that a party that did not claim pre-emption in the first instance, renounced all further rights of intervention.

In another court case, the right to pre-emption was used as a position to fall back upon in case other, more far-reaching claims failed. According to a document which has already been analysed in a different context,[69] Abdi bey b. Abdullah, member of the *ebnai sipahiyan*, first claimed to have inherited a certain house from his father. When his opponents made it obvious that this could not possibly have been the case, Abdi bey claimed the right of pre-emption, as the son of the former owner. It is not clear how the court would have evaluated this claim if it had been submitted at the proper time. As matters stood, Abdi bey was far too late for his interests to be considered, and as a result, he lost not only his inheritance suit but also his suit for pre-emption.

Conclusion

From an analysis of the personal data concerning plaintiffs and defendants, it appears that the courts of Ankara were easily accessible to the entire urban population. Men and women, Muslims and non-Muslims, ordinary subjects of the Empire and servitors of the Ottoman central administration, all turned to the court very readily when they believed that their fellow townspeople had violated their rights. It is particularly notable that about a quarter of all plaintiffs were women, suing not only their neighbours, but also members of their families and occasionally even their own husbands for the control of real property.[70] This state of affairs is all the more remarkable since, as has been pointed out in a previous chapter, the proportion of women owning real property in seventeenth-century Ankara or Kayseri was probably not very high. Jennings' conclusion that the Ottoman courts of the seventeenth century frequently acted as the protectors of women, is thereby vindicated by the material analysed here.[71]

Equally *zimmi*s used the court without hesitation, claiming their inheritances according to the *şeriat*. In most cases, the proportion of non-Muslim plaintiffs seems to have equalled, or even surpassed, their probable percentage in the urban population. This state of affairs would seem to indicate that the acculturation of the non-Muslims of Ankara and Kayseri was already far advanced. It would be interesting to find out whether there is any evidence for the degree of activity, or lack of activity, of church courts among the non-Muslims of Anatolian towns. The documents consulted never refer to the existence of such an institution. In this context, one would like to know why non-Muslims used the *kadıs'* courts so frequently, not just in real-estate questions but in other matters as well.[72] It is known that Orthodox Christians in Rumeli sometimes recorded marriages in the *kadı's* register in order to make use of *şeriat* rules concerning divorce. Possibly similar considerations were involved when non-Muslims turned to the court in inheritance cases.

At the same time, the *askerî* of Ankara and Kayseri, or at any rate those among them which the recording conventions of the court scribes permit us to identify, can hardly be said to have overawed their neighbours with their aggressiveness in court. Obviously some of the real powers in the land, the provincial governors and major tax farmers, do not appear in the documents analysed here. The *kadıs'* records appear to deal rather with more modest people, whom only a position as a janissary, *medrese* teacher or descendant of the Prophet distinguished from their neighbours. For an analysis of the activities of the urban notables, our data concerning contested real estate transactions do not seem particularly fruitful, and other approaches must be attempted in the future.

As to the issues dividing the townsmen of seventeenth-century Ankara and Kayseri, the most frequent disputes were quite obviously connected with the right to inherit. Contested sales, or the institution and operation of pious foundations, did not occupy the minds of the townsmen to nearly the same degree. Taken by itself, this observation is not particularly surprising. But even so, it is worth making; for only when similar analyses will have been published for eighteenth- and nineteenth-century *kadı* registers, will it become possible to discern whether in the long run, there was a change in the preoccupations of Anatolian townsmen.

Conclusion

The present study has started out as a kind of 'verbal archaeology'. Since physical remains of sixteenth or seventeenth century urban houses are scarce or inaccessible, we have attempted to exploit the traces which they have left in descriptions. Apart from reconstructing the houses themselves, we have tried to place them in the urban context of which they once formed a part. These houses might be located in a public street, or else be accessible only by a private right-of-way; they might be situated close to a mosque, or built right into the town or citadel walls.[1] All these details are features which can be used in reconstructing the townscape, and thereby allow us to glimpse seventeenth-century townsmen interacting with their physical environment.

Such a reconstruction of an urban landscape may be of interest in itself, particularly where urban planners and restoration specialists are concerned. However, for the social historian, such an undertaking can only constitute a first step. If we want to understand the operation of Ottoman urban society during the seventeenth century, the houses, along with the prices paid for their purchase, provide us with evidence concerning stratification by wealth. But what was the yearly income of an urban patrician, compared to that of a weaver or a shoemaker? And more importantly, how closely did the hierarchy of wealth correspond to the locally established power structure? From the existence of extremely valuable houses, we can conclude that seventeenth-century Ankara and Kayseri contained a number of very wealthy families. Since not all the heads of these families are characterized as *askerî*, there must have been ways of enriching oneself – and maybe even of staying rich – even if one was not personally a member of the governmental apparatus of the Ottoman Empire. What were these ways and means? In the case of non-Muslims, mainly tax-farming and commerce. In the case of wealthy Muslims, the source of their fortunes are often less easy to establish.

Ways and means of making money: the urban elite

Among the possible sources of urban wealth, the most obvious ones are landholding, commerce, and political office. The problem of landholding on

202

the part of Anatolian town-dwellers has barely been touched upon. But the provisional results obtained to date do not indicate that large estates in the hands of town-dwellers were a noticeable feature of seventeenth-century Anatolian society.[2] Quite to the contrary, the land transactions entered into the kadıs' registers during the seventeenth century usually concern small pieces of land.[3] Thus the ownership of gardens, vineyards, and even occasionally of fields seems to have been both widespread and decentralized. In this respect, urban ownership of agricultural lands was comparable to the lending out of money at interest, an activity which was practised by many inhabitants of Kayseri, but which can have been the principal source of livelihood only for a very few.[4] This should not be taken to mean that some of the income available to the wealthier townsmen was not derived from their ownership of, or rights of possession over, gardens, vineyards, and fields. Obviously some of the income of these men and women must have been derived from agricultural sources; for gardens, vineyards and even fields were an important source of livelihood to the townsmen of Ankara and Kayseri in general. But we must not imagine that during the seventeenth century, a limited number of major landowners dominated central Anatolian towns. Given the political and administrative impact of provincial notables (ayan) during the eighteenth and early nineteenth centuries, the present author had expected to find landholding patrician families much more active in the urban real estate market than is apparent from the kadıs' registers.[5] Even if we make all possible allowances for the deficiencies inherent in the available documentation, it does not seem that direct ownership of, or control over, agricultural lands was the main source of wealth for the notables of seventeenth-century Ankara and Kayseri.

As a second possible source of patrician income, we must consider commerce and manufacturing. In the case of Ankara, this would have involved mainly the manufacture and distribution of mohair yarn and of the fine cloth woven out of this unusual fibre. To a lesser extent, the tanners of Kayseri must equally have provided the city with goods which could be traded outside of its immediate vicinity, so that an influx of ready cash allowed local residents to intensify their commercial exchanges. However, in order to understand the economic role of a place like Ankara or Kayseri, we need to know how much of the productive process was carried out in the city itself, and how much of it was really the work of villagers living in the vicinity. Naturally the sheep and goats providing the indispensable raw materials were bred in the countryside, and as early as the middle years of the sixteenth century, peasant women in steppe villages many kilometres away from Ankara were spinning mohair yarn for delivery to the city's merchants.[6] However, the frequent location of mohair workshops within urban residential structures indicates that townsmen had a major share in the productive process. Moreover, dyeing and finishing appear to have been largely urban activities.

At least where Ankara is concerned, the tax farmers in charge of the dye houses and presses used to finish mohair cloth, probably belonged to the urban upper class along with the merchants who organized distribution. However, we do know not to what extent these tax farmers came from established Ankara families, or whether most of them were residents of other localities, particularly İstanbul and returned to their home towns after their contracts had expired. But given the importance of the payments to which the tax farmers had pledged themselves, they must certainly, as long as they resided in Ankara, have lived in some of the best houses in town. Moreover, the more important merchants and tax farmers, with their frequent contacts to the capital, should have constituted the intermediaries through which information about new styles in house building and decoration reached the inhabitants of Ankara.

Less is known about the tanners' workshops of Kayseri, and about the manner in which urban notables were involved in this craft. But the existence of a town quarter named after the tanneries indicates that tanning was at least partly an urban activity. In the same context, one might point to the frequency of family nicknames referring to a craft among the urban notables of seventeenth-century Kayseri.[7] The popularity of such nicknames would seem to indicate that many notables were not only descended from craftsmen, but that their fellow townsmen remembered the fact. Moreover, these urban patricians themselves had probably come to terms with their ancestry, and used the nicknames in question to designate themselves and their families.

It is likely that craftsmen who enriched themselves attempted to organize the productive activities of others, and themselves specialized in the distribution of goods. In late-sixteenth-century Ankara for instance, we encounter a shoe merchant who had artisans work for him, and probably acted as a wholesaler.[8] Thus even though most craftsmen were probably poor, the industry as a whole must have contributed to the enrichment of certain members of the urban elite.

Thus it would appear that contrary to the Hellenistic and Roman towns which constituted the remote ancestors of Ottoman Ankara and Kayseri, these two cities during the seventeenth century were productive centres.[9] Not that tax-farming, state service, and other activities only remotely related to production did not constitute a source of wealth for the urban elite. But the typical townsman of Ottoman Anatolia gained his living as a craftsman or merchant. In addition, he usually owned a garden or vineyard which his family tended during the summer season, probably aided by some peasant labour. Certainly the inhabitants of the major Anatolian towns lived to a significant degree on tax grains, which were sold by tax farmers at officially controlled prices, and thus in a sense benefited from state aid. But the very prevalence of agricultural activities among the townsmen tended to limit the impact of these protective measures, which only affected those foodstuffs that were bought and sold in the market.

At the sources of urban wealth: rural landholdings

Under these circumstances, we need to explain what caused people to live in cities, and why people with agriculture as a major source of income did not prefer to live in villages. On the whole it appears that the countryside around both Ankara and Kayseri was fairly intensively cultivated, even though the seventeenth century as a whole was known as a period of rural depopulation and westward movement on the part of nomads.[10] Certainly it is easy to misconstrue reality in a context which is only very partially known, but it does seem probable that the proximity of a town market contributed to the relative density of agricultural settlement in the Ankara and Kayseri areas. During the worst stages of the late-sixteenth- and early-seventeenth-century civil wars, the cities with their walls provided a degree of protection. In a later phase of resettlement, these areas with their easy access to markets were among the first to be recuperated.

At first glance, this impression is difficult to reconcile with the observations of Tunçdilek and Hütteroth, who both agree that during the settlement contraction of the seventeenth century, the more accessible lowland villages were first to be given up.[11] In the Eskişehir area studied by Tunçdilek, peasants withdrew to inaccessible sites surrounded by water and swamps. In the province of Konya, the settlements of the hilly country to the north of the city survived much better than the lowland villages of the Hatunsaray area. However, it must be stressed that both Tunçdilek and Hütteroth were dealing with purely rural areas, open not only to the depredations of tax collectors, but of immigrating nomads as well. Living close to an urban centre brought with it the disadvantage of being close to the tax collector. But at the same time, the walls of the city provided physical protection, and the *kadı*'s court an often appreciable measure of legal protection. Market opportunities allowed the cultivation of fruit and vegetables, which should have brought the villager greater profits than grain monoculture. Most importantly, however, whenever peasant lands remained uncultivated for any length of time, there were always townsmen available who already practised agriculture to a certain extent, and who were ready to take charge. Moreover, many townsmen were in the habit of spending the summer months in their gardens and vineyards. This habit, which is well attested for seventeenth-century Kayseri, must have contributed to the intensity of cultivation in the areas immediately surrounding the cities.

Certain special features of landholding in the immediate vicinity of seventeenth-century Ankara and Kayseri are brought out when we compare the countryside surrounding these two cities with the fields and gardens recorded in the *kadı*'s registers of eighteenth-century Aleppo. Marcus has observed that the women of the latter city almost never owned agricultural land,[12] although they were often well provided with ready money and urban real property. While women owners of gardens, fields and vineyards were very much a minority phenomenon in seventeenth-century Anatolia as well, their share at least in the Kayseri area, was not, however, insignificant.[13] In the closing years of the sixteenth and the beginning of the seventeenth century, eleven per cent of all people buying agricultural lands were women, while towards the end of the century, their share had even increased to twenty per cent.

Why the women of Kayseri should have been privileged in such a fashion is difficult to determine. Possibly the phenomenon is connected with the precocious development of private property in fields (as opposed to gardens and vineyards) in this particular area, which signified the early dissolution of the Ottoman land system of the 'classical period'. Within the latter set of arrangements, fields and meadows were the property of the state,[14] with the peasants possessing only a hereditary right of usufruct; in such a context, the number of situations in which a woman could farm land was strictly limited.[15] However, from the later sixteenth century onward, legal regulations concerning the holding of what was technically state land, were progressively influenced by the provisions of the şeriat with respect to private property.[16] In the Kayseri area, the notion that fields might be private property was occasionally sanctioned by the courts even in the years around 1600;[17] by the 1690s, peasants and town-dwellers of this area sold fields much as if they had been private property. Since the şeriat placed no restrictions upon ownership of real property by a woman, one is tempted to connect the extension of freehold property with the unusually high percentage of female purchasers of land in the Kayseri area. But only when many more studies of Ottoman landholding patterns in different regions will have become available, will we be able to determine whether this interpretation is in fact the correct one.

Another aspect in which landholding patterns in seventeenth century central Anatolia differed from those prevailing in eighteenth-century Aleppo, is the relatively high percentage of non-Muslim landowners.[18] Apart from Ankara in the years around 1600, the share of non-Muslims acquiring landed property was always over twenty per cent, while non-Muslims owned no significant amounts of land in the Aleppo area. This phenomenon may be connected with the fact that in seventeenth-century Anatolian towns, every well-established family owned a garden or vineyard, while in the Aleppo area, rural landownership in the city's vicinity was concentrated in the hands of a limited number of prominent families.[19] As a result, in the area around the two Anatolian towns, a growth or decline of the non-Muslim population was readily reflected in the rural land market.

Contrasting patterns of landholding find their parallels in two different types of arrangements concerning the granting of credit. According to Jennings' findings, the number of people and pious foundations that made credit available in early-seventeenth-century Kayseri was quite large, but no lender had invested major sums of money in this business.[20] On the other hand, Marcus observes that 'the loans which they [the upper-level merchants and ulama] advanced to villagers in Aleppo's countryside were often so immense as to dwarf their real estate investments'.[21] Under these circumstances, one would expect the wealthier townsmen of Aleppo to have dominated the surrounding rural areas in a manner that had no parallel in central Anatolia, and in fact this observation has been made for more recent periods as well.[22] The townsmen of seventeenth-century Ankara and Kayseri were mostly producing on what might be considered an 'artisan' level, and this applied to their rural possessions as well as to their workshops.

An urban–rural continuum: or the validity of the town as a unit of study

These observations concerning the patterns of landholding on the part of Ankara and Kayseri townsmen may have wider implications. Here one should refer to an article by Ira M. Lapidus dealing with the limits of intra-urban solidarity in medieval Near Eastern cities, and with the closeness of town–country relations particularly in an oasis setting.[23] In a sense Lapidus carries the notion that the medieval Islamic city lacked a corporate identity to its extreme conclusion: differences between urban and non-urban settlements are de-emphasized, and in certain contexts, the oasis with its villages and towns, and not any given city, is considered the primary unit of settlement.

This approach has certain recommendable features, provided that one does not go to extremes and deny that the towns of the Islamic world were fully urban, a Weberian definition that has sometimes influenced European scholars studying non-European cities.[24] To view the town in close connection with its rural hinterland is vital if one wishes to understand how towns of the pre-industrial era functioned. Even in the present study, which focusses upon the built-up area, the impact of the countryside makes itself felt at every turn: cowsheds, barns and even facilities for stabling camels were essential parts of seventeenth-century Ankara or Kayseri. However, we must not forget that the interpenetration of urban and rural features is not a peculiarity of the Islamic or Ottoman city. As a European example, one might cite Braudel's analysis of European and particularly of Mediterranean towns.[25] Therefore it is problematic whether any amount of urban–rural interpenetration can allow us to set the 'Islamic city' apart from other forms of urban life.

At the same time, Lapidus' statements concerning the urban–rural continuum, and his references to the town as the more or less fortuitous locus of social interaction on the part of people whose main loyalties are engaged elsewhere, have parallels in rather an unexpected quarter. In his contribution to the collective volume *Towns in Societies*, Philip Abrams sketches rather a similar view of the European town – normally considered as one of the most tightly corporate urban entities in human history.[26] Obviously the social conflicts acted out in medieval or early modern Europe vastly differed from those to be observed in Syria or the Ottoman Empire. Moreover, it would seem that the two researchers in question interpret these conflicts on the basis of vastly different world views. But this makes the analogy between their views of the town all the more striking. It would thus appear that Lapidus' statements, rather than applying to the Islamic or oasis city in particular, are the expression of a research attitude towards the phenomenon 'town' in general. At the same time, this state of affairs changes the nature of the discussion, for approaches of this type are not in themselves true or false, but must be applied to concrete tasks before one can judge whether the approach in question is fruitful.

One observation which might be adduced in favour of Lapidus' urban–rural continuum is the relatively weak development of urban-dominated regional networks in seventeenth-century Rumelia and Anatolia. Braudel had assumed that any city of any importance anywhere in the world is served by a system of relay towns.[27] When one attempts to check this assumption for the sixteenth- or seventeenth-century Ottoman Empire, the 'relay towns' of İstanbul are comparatively easy to identify.[28] However, it must be admitted that considering the enormous size of İstanbul, far larger than contemporary London or Paris, one might have expected a more developed hierarchy of relay towns than has been detected to date. But when we turn to provincial towns such as Ankara, it is apparent that they possessed no or only very few relay towns.[29] Basically Ankara was surrounded by a large region inhabited only by villagers; it would appear that the Ottoman administration even curtailed the development of a rural marketing network in order to ensure that sufficient foodstuffs reached the market of the central city. One might view the lack or weak development of an urban-dominated hierarchy of settlements as evidence for the fact that the transition from 'rural' to 'urban' was gradual. In fact the present researcher, when trying to figure out whether certain settlements of the Ankara area should be classed as urban or rural has had a very direct and immediate experience of this ambiguity. However, rather than the existence of an urban–rural continuum per se, it appears that the existence or non-existence of complex urban-dominated networks may be viewed as a feature which sets certain regions of the pre-industrial world apart from others. How these networks developed at different points in time and in different parts of the world is as yet only imperfectly known, but might constitute a rewarding topic in the future.

At the sources of urban wealth: trade and the Celâlî rebellions

Mustafa Akdağ, in his study of the political and agricultural crisis known as the Celâlî uprisings, has described at length how the armed followers of former provincial administrators ravaged the Anatolian countryside, particularly under the reign of Kanuni's grandson Murad III and his immediate successors.[30] These men were a source of serious political difficulties, for as Metin Kunt has been able to demonstrate,[31] the career of a provincial administrator depended to a considerable extent on the number of servitors he was able to assemble. As long as their patron was in office, these men would be employed in the business of policing the countryside and collecting taxes; as their salaries were paid by the official who had hired them, this arrangement limited the load placed upon an already overburdened central treasury. However, once the official in question had been deposed, his armed servitors, from being an asset, could easily turn into a formidable liability to the Ottoman state. In certain cases, the band of armed retainers might pressure their former employer to rebel, so that he might retain the resources from which to pay them. In other instances, the dismissed irregular soldiers might turn to highway robbery. What is more, once conditions had become sufficiently confused, there might be little to choose between the armed men serving a governor still in office, and those associated with a rebel.[32] If several bands of this kind descended upon a village, they might easily ruin the peasants for many years to come.

Akdağ has stressed how under these circumstances, walled cities might constitute places of temporary refuge. After all, the Ankara citadel withstood two attacks by Celâlî bands, even though the unfortified town quarters were ravaged; it was this experience which induced the inhabitants of Ankara to surround their city with a wall that protected the entire settlement.[33] In the long run, however, the frequent interruption of interregional traffic and the problems of securing the necessary grain-supply should have led to a shrinkage of the towns of central Anatolia. In Konya, interregional trade suffered so badly that the covered market was abandoned, and when the Ottoman central government in 1024/1615 took steps to facilitate recuperation, extensive repairs to the building proved necessary.[34] Jennings' discussion of the taxpayer registers covering Amasya in the middle of the seventeenth century shows that the urban population was virtually halved,[35] and the same thing applies to contemporary Kayseri.

Figures are lacking for Ankara, but the tax farmers' records concerning taxes levied upon fabrics made out of mohair indicate that during the beginning of the seventeenth century, production was sagging.[36] However, the Ankara producers were at least in a position to make their complaints heard. In 1055/1645, during the darkest days of the mid-century depression, an official document prohibited the exportation of mohair thread to other provinces of the Empire, and more particularly to Europe,[37] with a view to protecting local industry and tax revenues. To what extent the Sultan's rescript prohibiting exportation was actually applied in the course of the centuries is not easy to verify. However, we do possess indirect evidence for a recovery of the mohair trade after about 1650 or 1660. One might even conclude that as the century drew to a close, raw mohair became available in abundance, and the scarcity which had caused so many difficulties to the Ankara producers about fifty years earlier had, at least for the time being, been overcome.[38]

As to the general revival of trade, in the second half of the seventeenth century we possess a document recording a fire in Ankara's covered market. This accident caused a certain amount of damage, which was promptly repaired.[39] Now at the beginning of the century, the Konya covered market had been allowed to fall in ruins when there was no business to justify the expense of maintaining it. In the nineteenth century, the same fate was to befall the Ankara *bedestan* itself: after it had been damaged by a fire, the merchant community felt that its utility no longer repaid the investment necessary for repairing it, and it was left to decay until restored for use as a museum. On the other hand, in the late seventeenth century, local merchants were apparently in a hurry to resume use of the *bedestan*. Under these circumstances, it can be assumed that business in late-seventeenth-century Ankara was again reasonably animated, and Tournefort's and Pococke's remarks only strengthen this impression.[40]

At the sources of urban wealth: patterns of Ottoman industrial development

If these assumptions are not too far removed from reality, they may have a number of implications for Ottoman textile manufacture, and Ottoman industrial history in general. Barkan once stated that after the late sixteenth century, competition on the part of imported European fabrics, and rising prices for raw materials wherever European merchants were in a position to compete for supplies, caused Ottoman manufactures to decline.[41] Or under the most fortunate circumstances, such manufactures might retain a place in the domestic market, but the impetus for expansion was permanently lost. After Barkan had written, two monographs appeared that largely confirmed his thesis. Murat Çizakça demonstrated the negative impact of rising prices for raw silk and declining profit margins upon the Bursa silk industry after about 1570.[42] According to Benjamin Braude, the manufacture of medium-quality woollen cloth in Salonica prospered for a somewhat longer period, for it was profitable until about 1650.[43] But after this time, manufacturers were losing on both ends. English merchants were bringing in woollen cloth, which they could sell at fairly low prices, since most of their profits were derived from the importation of Levantine (mainly Iranian) silk. Under these circumstances, sending the ships out with a supply even of moderately priced cloth was preferable to sending them out laden with ballast only. On the other hand, Balkan raw wool was increasingly being exported, particularly by merchants from Dubrovnik. Prices rose, and the unfortunate manufacturers of Salonica were thus being caught 'between two fires'.

At the same time, Nikolai Todorov's studies on the woollen industry of Plovdiv (Filibe) in what is today southern Bulgaria indicate a very different pattern of development.[44] The rough woollen cloth manufactured in this area first makes its appearance in Ottoman documents recorded in the *Mühimme* registers after 1560. In the course of the seventeenth century, the industry expanded into a number of towns and villages in the Plovdiv area, and its products were traded in the Balkan fairs. But the apogee of the industry came in the eighteenth and early nineteenth centuries, when pedlars not only sold Plovdiv woollen cloth to Anatolian villagers, but managed to market this material as far away as India – where it was used as elephant hangings. Given the proximity of Plovdiv and Salonica, one might almost say that one industry 'took over' from the other, following a pattern that Braudel has shown to exist in pre-industrial cloth centres of Europe as well.[45] But more importantly, it seems that the Plovdiv manufacturers produced cheap cloth (*aba*) for a low-income market, whereas the fabrics produced in Salonica, even though they were used to clothe the janissaries, were rather of medium quality. Now imported English, and at a later stage French fabrics, were not intended for a low-income market, at least not before the 1838 tariff agreement allowed the British to flood the Ottoman market with factory-produced goods. Thus the Plovdiv producers, with their well-developed marketing system, were able to expand, at a time when the better qualities of Ottoman woollen fabrics had long since succumbed to European competition.

If, as appears probable, the Ankara mohair industry recovered after the crisis of the Celâlî rebellions, and survived reasonably well throughout at least the seventeenth century, we are confronted with yet another pattern of Ottoman industrial development. In the mohair industry, a short-term crisis at the beginning of the seventeenth century was apparently followed by a recovery and subsequent long-term stability, lasting until about 1700, and probably beyond. During the sixteenth century, mohair fabrics had been classed as luxury cloths, fit to be worn by the most important men in the Ottoman state. It must be admitted that later observers do not refer to mohair cloths enjoying any particular favour at court; possibly Sultan Süleyman's gesture of always wearing mohair cloth in public should be interpreted as a gesture of 'Buy Ottoman'.[46] This is not as anachronistic as it may appear at first sight; for at least in the eighteenth century, educated Ottomans such as the court historian Naima were well aware of the losses of gold and silver occasioned by the importation of luxury fabrics, if the latter were not compensated by the exportation of goods of comparable value.[47] Be that as it may, even after mohair cloth had gone out of favour with the court, it remained a fairly expensive fabric, upon whose finishing special care was lavished. Moreover, mohair fabrics had some appeal in the European market as well, as attested by the fact that in the eighteenth century Amiens manufacturers produced what may have been a French imitation of the material woven in Ankara.[48]

Given these circumstances, and the popularity of buttons made out of mohair yarn in Europe during much of the eighteenth century, it is not surprising that Ankara continued to be a thriving place from the commercial point of view. Moreover, as late as the Napoleonic wars, the interruption of connections to Europe allowed the mohair industry a further lease on life. Certainly, in the early nineteenth century, when war had disrupted the ordinary trade routes, the masters of Ankara complained about being unable to procure the dyestuffs which they had become accustomed to use.[49] But the mohair yarn which could no longer be exported was once again being woven locally – a testimony to the industry's vitality, which only the competition of factory-produced goods was finally to extinguish.

Kayseri's tanning industry never had as prominent a place within the Ottoman economy as did the Ankara mohair manufacture. Moreover, it is probable that Kayseri was essentially a local centre of marketing and administration and, as a result, the tanning industry's conjunctural ups and downs probably had less effect upon the history of the city as a whole. From our point of view, this state of affairs might indeed be considered fortunate, as to date no close investigation has been made of Kayseri's tanners. We can assume that Kayseri did not recover nearly as rapidly from the upheavals of the Celâlî period as Ankara seems to have done. Even by the end of the seventeenth century, the city's population was quite unstable, and probably lay much below the 30,000–35,000 maximum which had characterized the closing years of the sixteenth century. On the other hand, when in the nineteenth century, Ankara was hit hard by the demise of its main industry, Kayseri came out well by comparison. The area was self-sufficient in terms of food supplies, and before the advent of synthetic dyes, the cultivation of yellowberries constituted a source of supplementary income for this semi-rural town. As to the twentieth century, the establishment of a major cotton-goods factory might be interpreted, if one is willing to stretch the point somewhat, as continuing the tradition of local seventeenth-century manufacturers using Adana cotton.

Social relations as reflected in space: the townscape

Ankara's relative prosperity in the late seventeenth century was reflected in more elaborate private dwellings than had been in use eighty or ninety years earlier. More remarkably, Kayseri houses also tended to become increasingly ornate as the century wore on. It is true that we must make allowance for the nature of the available documentation, which provides more information about houses existing around 1690 than about those which changed hands during the early years of the seventeenth century. Even so, however, the increasing number of double-courtyard houses in Kayseri, the growing number of references to houses with upper floors in Ankara, and the rising number of semi-enclosed spaces, seem to a certain extent to reflect real changes in house building. We may assume that in Ankara, increasing density within the walled perimeter was beginning to cause difficulties. Even wealthy townsmen no longer could afford double-courtyard houses, so essential an element of the setting which the wealthy Muslim families of Kayseri had created for themselves. Quite to the contrary, in Ankara even valuable houses were at times being bought and sold without any reference to a courtyard. Entries in the *kadıs'* registers occasionally allow us to visualize how a larger number of dwellings was crammed into an unchanging amount of space. Relatives more or less peaceably divided the houses which they had inherited, and then built over and adjacent to the rooms which had been assigned to them as their respective shares. As a result, it became necessary to make formal arrangements so that the different parties sharing a dwelling retained access to the public street.

However, the response of the inhabitants of Ankara to the problem of crowding differed to a certain extent from that observed with respect to eighteenth-century Aleppo. Antoine Abdel Nour has shown how when in the latter city, contracting trade opportunities coincided with a major wave of immigration from the countryside, many townsmen responded by selling shares (and quite often rather minute ones) of their dwellings.[50] The housing pattern which resulted from a cumulation of these sales must have not been too dissimilar from the *hawš*, that is the group of more or less miserable dwellings opening onto a common courtyard which was frequently observed in Syria and Egypt.[51] On the other hand, when shares in an Ankara dwelling were thrown onto the market, they were typically sold to a single person. Thus one might conclude that crowding in late seventeenth-century Ankara occurred under less difficult material circumstances than in eighteenth-century Aleppo, and this conclusion in turn might be used as another piece of evidence to show that 1690s Ankara was as yet reasonably prosperous.

In this same context (crowding under circumstances of moderate prosperity) one might also interpret the probable increase of multiple-storey buildings particularly in seventeenth-century Ankara. There is some reason to doubt whether this increase was real, and one might advance the hypothesis that the apparent increase is simply a wrong impression caused by the imperfections of our documentation. After all Ayda Arel, following the line of Emel Esin's argument, has assumed that at least one of the major traditions of house-building which the Turks brought with them from Central Asia involved a house of several storeys.[52] Under these circumstances, one might assume that in a comparatively remote area such as Central Anatolia, ancient Turkish building-traditions maintained themselves through the ages, and that the custom of building dwellings several storeys high was part of this body of building traditions.[53]

However, in spite of this and other possible objections, the present author favours the assumption that the *kadı* registers' information is correct, and that the spread of multiple-storey dwellings was in fact largely a seventeenth-century phenomenon. In this context, one might again refer to Dernschwam's account of the houses of mid-sixteenth-century Ankara. This observer described them as low structures covered with flat roofs protected by a layer of earth.[54] On the other hand, the traveller Evliya Çelebi mentions the house of several storeys as characteristic of mid-seventeenth-century Ankara, which would indicate that the transformation became visible sometime during the first half of the seventeenth century.[55] However, the traveller noted the absence of roof tiles, which would seem to indicate flat, earth-covered roofs. Certainly Evliya's account should be taken with a grain of salt, since after all, he ascribed tiled roofs to Kayseri, which the 'traditional' architecture of the city never featured in later times.[56] But at least his account is not incompatible with the transformation postulated in the present study.

At the same time, another factor apart from crowding might be considered as an explanation for the increasing popularity of the multi-storied building with a tiled roof. It does not seem unreasonable to assume that Ankara, with its close contacts to the Ottoman capital, came progressively under the influence of house types prevailing in İstanbul or Bursa. If the impact of İstanbul is viewed as the main factor, one would be inclined to see the changeover in Ankara as part of the eastward expansion of the standard Ottoman-Turkish house. According to Arel's description, Kayseri should always have remained a borderline case, as the city was located in that ill-defined area between 'Ottoman-Turkish' and 'Syrian' house types.[57] In this context, one might assume a 'moving frontier', an İstanbul or Bursa style house becoming popular first among the wealthier inhabitants of Ankara, and later with the city's inhabitants at large. But should all this be taken to mean that sixteenth-century Ankara consisted largely of village-style houses? Or else of houses resembling those of Kayseri, although of course stone was more expensive and therefore rarely used in Ankara, and mudbrick and framework construction should have been widespread as they were to be in later periods? On the basis of the limited information available in the kadıs' registers, it is impossible to be more precise.

Less difficult to interpret are the data concerning houses with a double courtyard. In late seventeenth century Kayseri, outer and interior courtyards, (muhavvata-ı dahiliye, muhavvata-ı hariciye) had become quite popular among the wealthier Muslims of the city, as indeed they were in Aleppo as well.[58] There existed a functional distinction between the two spaces: the principal inhabited rooms were invariably located in the inner courtyard, while the stable, storage sheds and other service areas were relegated to the outer court. The only doubtful case is the destination of the oda, which also formed part of most outer courtyards. In the light of Arel's observations, it would seem that by and large, the outer court of wealthier Kayseri dwellings corresponded to the largely uninhabited ground floors of typical Ottoman-Turkish houses.[59] In this context, one would imagine that the oda in the exterior court was a room for servants, which in the many-storeyed Ottoman-Turkish house was typically situated in the mezzanine.

On the other hand, this room might also be interpreted as a space in which male visitors could be received, possibly a kind of köşk. This latter term occurs very rarely in the kadı registers, but the structure so designated played an important role not just in the Ottoman-Turkish house in general, but in the Kayseri house in particular.[60] Moreover, the use of the *oda* in the outer courtyard as a visitors' room would coincide with the customs of seventeenth- and eighteenth-century Aleppines as related by Abdel Nour;[61] and while this analogy is not conclusive, it does enhance the attractiveness of such an interpretation. In addition, it is tempting to view the double courtyard as part of a Syrian tradition, which might have radiated into Central Anatolia; but that is a matter for professional historians of architecture to decide.

Another architectural feature worth bearing in mind is the fact that the *sofa* lost popularity in seventeenth-century Ankara. What is more, in this case there is no room for doubt, given the fact that the more carefully prepared descriptions of the later seventeenth century are also those which lack references to the *sofa*. This development is somewhat disquieting, since most typological studies seem to consider houses lacking a *sofa* as 'primitive' types, out of which the more developed types presumably evolved.[62] It does not seem reasonable to interpret the situation in Ankara as a case of reversion to more 'primitive' forms, presumably under the pressure of poverty; for on the whole, late-seventeenth-century Ankara houses contained a greater number of semi-enclosed spaces, and thus presumably were more elaborate, than their predecessors of the years around 1600 had been. It is possible that the problem is basically one of terminology: one might imagine that the earlier *sofa*s had been those open porches or verandas, which at a later stage, were described as *örtme*s or *çardak*s. Or else we might have to abandon the notion that the *sofa*-less house was a more primitive kind of dwelling. This again is a problem that will only be solved when we possess more urban monographs with a historical orientation.

When comparing the dwellings of Ankara and Kayseri with their counterparts in Ottoman Syria, both similarities and differences have become apparent. But even more interesting is comparison on the level of the *mahalle* and the city as a whole. Thus it would appear that the inhabitants of seventeenth-century Ankara and Kayseri had no very marked preference for house doors opening onto a semi-private *cul-de-sac* as opposed to the *tarik-i am*. After all, even though descriptions in the *kadı* registers tended to become more elaborate as the seventeenth century wore on, the number of references to *tarik-i has* remained very much limited in number. On the other hand, Aleppines of the same period never seem to have opened a doorway onto a public thoroughfare if there was a *cul-de-sac* available.[63]

On the other hand, it would appear that in Anatolian towns the number of people not living in private single family dwellings was smaller than in the 'Great Arab Cities' studied by Raymond.[64] Obviously in cities like Cairo or Aleppo, major centres of international trade, the number of transients residing in khans should have been larger than in places such as Ankara or Kayseri. Moreover, there is no evidence of any counterparts to the Cairene apartment buildings, which had been such a notable feature of the latter city ever since the Mamluk period. Nor is there any evidence of the *ḥawš* as a residential pattern at least where families are concerned. The only analogy, and that a poor one, is the existence of *bekâr odaları* in certain Anatolian towns or in İstanbul, where single workers might live in rather modest quarters until such a time as they were ready to get married or else return to their villages.

On the other hand, it would appear that segregation by income was perhaps less clearly developed in Ankara or Kayseri than it seems to have been in Mamluk or Ottoman Cairo. Certain areas in these two central Anatolian towns were wealthier or poorer than the average, and it is possible that in certain poor quarters located in the vicinity of the city gates, there existed no or almost no residences of the well-to-do. But there was nothing comparable to the luxurious quarters which could be found in Cairo.[65] Moreover, the Citadel area which, in Ankara certainly and in Kayseri probably, constituted the political centre of the town, possessed its contingent of poor dwellings. In part, this difference may be explained by the fact that agriculture was not as productive in the Anatolian steppe as it was in Egypt or in the irrigable parts of Syria. In addition, one might also assume that local administrators, particularly in Egypt, were able to retain more tax resources than their Anatolian counterparts.[66] As a result, the hierarchy of wealth in a central Anatolian town of the seventeenth century must have been less developed than in Cairo.

Family relationships and house property

But in spite of these differences in the organization of space, urban dwellers of Ankara and Kayseri had many features in common with the Aleppines that emerge from the studies of Abdel Nour and Marcus.[67] In all three places, house-ownership was fairly accessible to people of modest means, even though cheap houses were probably easier to find in central Anatolia than in the metropolis of Aleppo. To a considerable extent, access to house property was facilitated by the *şeriat* rules of partible inheritance, even though the resulting fragmentation must at the same time have made it more difficult to keep buildings in good repair.

With respect to the problem of female house ownership, Marcus' observations on Aleppo show that women of this latter city sold more properties than they bought, just as was the custom in seventeenth-century Ankara or Kayseri.[68] Thus, where women were concerned, the usual way of acquiring real property must have been through inheritance. This state of affairs is apparent even though the percentages computed by Marcus have been calculated according to somewhat different principles than those which form the basis for the present study. At the same time, participation of women in the Aleppine housing market was very impressive, since thirty-five per cent of all people purchasing houses were females. At no time was this figure ever matched in central Anatolia, not even in late seventeenth-century Kayseri, even though in this time and place, women seem to have been in a relatively advantageous position.[69] At this point it seems rather hazardous to try to explain why the women of eighteenth-century Aleppo found it so much easier to accede to urban real property than the women of seventeenth-century Ankara or Kayseri. But one might surmise that the overall level of wealth had something to do with it. After all, even though mid-eighteenth-century Aleppo had been somewhat eclipsed by İzmir as a centre of international trade, the city still dominated interregional exchange.[70] Moreover, the capital accumulated by Aleppo residents during the sixteenth and seventeenth centuries was probably not dissipated within a few decades. Where the overall level of wealth was high, many women should have had money at their disposal which permitted them to buy the homes in which they lived, or more commonly, at least a share in these homes. Possibly other factors entered into the picture as well, but those will only become apparent when more is known about the Ottoman cultural history of the seventeenth and eighteenth centuries.

To establish the changing positions of Muslim and non-Muslim homeowners, Marcus has used the same technique as has been employed in the present study.[71] When dealing with the documents in the kadıs' registers, both studies compare the shares that adherents of different religions possessed among the buyers and sellers of urban real-estate. In this way, it becomes possible to determine whether the fortunes of a given religious group were rising or declining. Where the buying and selling of residential property is concerned, differences between Aleppo on one side, and Ankara Kayseri on the other, can be explained by local causes, not excluding relatively small-scale disputes. Only eighteenth-century Aleppine history being much better documented than that of seventeenth-century central Anatolia, these localized reasons can be pinpointed in the case of Aleppo,[72] while we must often surmise what happened in Ankara or Kayseri.

On the other hand, a tantalizing problem is raised by the fact that over twenty per cent of all sales and purchases in eighteenth-century Aleppo took place between relatives,[73] while the share of such sales both in Ankara and in Kayseri was always less than ten per cent. In part this difference may be due to the nature of the documents. Particularly the material dating from the years around 1600 probably often lacks references to a family relationship between buyer and seller. Moreover, since people dealt in shares of houses much less frequently in Ankara and Kayseri than they did in Aleppo, the need for multiple deals between family members trying to sort out their respective possessions was also much reduced. But in addition, different arrangements among married couples must have also been responsible: while in eighteenth-century Aleppo it was common for a wife to own a share in the family house, this was not a very frequent occurrence in seventeenth-century Ankara or Kayseri. Last but not least, it is probable that the Celâlî rebellions may have had some impact: when population turnover was as high as it seems to have been at least in Kayseri, real estate deals among members of the same family must have declined in proportion.

One issue that has not been treated in the present context is the possibility that changing family structure may have had an impact upon the shape of urban houses both in Central Anatolia and in Syria.[74] This is due to the fact that researchers have to date usually assumed an unchanging urban family, with at most regional nuances between a Syrian-Arab and an Anatolian-Turkish tradition. But whether this is really true is a matter that needs to be investigated and not just postulated. Garcin has dwelt upon the fact that Cairene women of the Mamluk period were seen in public much more than their descendants living under Ottoman rule, and has propounded the hypothesis that the harem section in Cairene palaces is a comparatively late innovation.[75] In a different context one wonders whether the large number of female heads of households (which does not necessarily mean house-owners) which we find in the *avarız* tax register of mid-seventeenth-century Tokat was due to a passing crisis, or whether there was maybe a change in soial mores.[76] Did these women figure as heads of households because they could not either get married or return to their families, or what else was happening? Or, to tackle the problem from quite a different angle, does the fact that Ankara and Kayseri houses tended to grow in size during the seventeenth century indicate that the number of households consisting of more than a nuclear family was on the increase? At the present stage of our knowledge, we can only pose the problem. A closer study of the families documented in the *kadı*s' registers may suggest solutions in the future.

Relations between Muslims and non-Muslims

With respect to this issue, a comparison between Aleppo on the one hand, and Ankara and Kayseri on the other, can do much to further our understanding of the societies involved. In all three cities, there existed Muslim and non-Muslim town quarters, but there were no hard-and-fast barriers making it impossible for certain people to acquire real estate in certain parts of the city. As a result, Muslims and non-Muslims shared a common urban culture, based on day-to-day contacts, and while religiously based tensions were certainly not absent, they were mitigated by a common attachment to the city. In this respect, Marcus' findings agree with those of Özer Ergenç.[77] Like Ankara in the years around 1600, Aleppo in the middle years of the eighteenth century was apparently by no means a collection of semi-autonomous wards, whose inhabitants had few contacts outside of the town quarter which they inhabited. The urban culture which the townsmen shared, obviously in most respects the culture of the Muslim majority, found a modest expression in the manner in which private homes were arranged. Thus for example different configurations of rooms were preferred in the dwellings of Ankara and Kayseri at different time periods within the seventeenth century. But within a given city at a given point in time, the non-Muslims shared the preferences of their Muslim fellow townsmen.

Marcus concludes that '. . . mutually understood and accepted premises predicated upon Muslim predominance regulated tolerance . . .' and assumes that these premises, and the 'inter-confessional ties' which they made possible were not seriously challenged until the nineteenth century.[78] As the eighteenth-century social history of Anatolia is as yet very little known, we cannot be sure that the same timetable also applied to Ankara or Kayseri. But we can see how in the course of the seventeenth century, in spite of frequent ups and downs, non-Muslims were strengthening their economic position. Towards the end of the century, they could often afford to live in more expensive houses than the urban *askerî*, although it must be admitted that, particularly in Kayseri, locally resident tax-exempt families, their exemption apart, did not differ too much from ordinary townsmen. At the same time, the mutually understood and accepted premises referred to by Marcus certainly still held good in seventeenth-century Ankara and Kayseri. Moreover there is no indication, if the evidence provided by the cases contested in court is any guide, that the growing wealth of the non-Muslims was as yet straining traditional relations. Muslim townsmen, and more particularly *askeri*, do not seem to have tried to limit the accumulation of wealth on the part of non-Muslims by resorting to the court.

Thus it would seem reasonable to conclude that the assumptions governing relations between Muslims and non-Muslims, and the high degree of non-Muslim acculturation that they had resulted in, provided a rather solid framework for the conduct of everyday relationships. The cultural armature thus developed apparently could take a considerable amount of strain, that is the non-Muslims of Ankara and Kayseri could continue to enrich themselves for a considerable amount of time, before serious reactions of hostility were aroused in the Muslim majority. Only the full force of European economic penetration during the nineteenth and twentieth centuries, of which Ottoman non-Muslims were to make themselves major beneficiaries, was finally to shatter the system of Ottoman cultural assumptions, and thereby make further accommodation impossible.

Under these circumstances, the classical Ottoman system of state and society appears above all as an integrative force of considerable assimilatory power. What is particularly notable, is that the results of studies concerning sixteenth-century Jerusalem, seventeenth-century Ankara and Kayseri, and eighteenth-century Aleppo converge in so many important respects.[79] With the *kadı*'s court as an arbiter,[80] the set of arrangements whose details are slowly emerging from Ottoman archival records, made it possible for Muslims and non-Muslims to live with their differences and conflicts. Thus the present study can be seen as one of the empirical investigations that aim at 'setting the record straight', and to demolish some of the prejudices and misconceptions that, in popular and not-so-popular publications, have been accumulated around the Ottoman system of state and society.

The Islamic city – or Ottoman cities?

Finally, one might wish to ask the question how the seventeenth-century Anatolian city as analysed here can fit into a larger framework. As a first possible category, one thinks of the much discussed notion of the 'Islamic city'. This term has meant different things to different researchers; so to clarify matters, under the term 'Islamic city' we will here deal with the 'ideal type' as discussed by Gustave von Grunebaum in a famous article.[81] Von Grunebaum is concerned not with the Ottoman Empire but with the caliphal period, but given the intemporal character of his model, it is not an injustice to his work if one discusses the applicability of his ideas to the Ottoman setting.

When dealing with the notion of the Islamic city, certain researchers have been attracted by the model's power to explain similarities, while at the same time feeling dissatisfied by its inability to account for diversity both in time and space. Thus Sevgi Aktüre, when analysing the physical structure of late nineteenth-century Ankara, Tokat and Afyon, considers the 'Islamic city' as a major category for her own work,[82] but at the same time regrets that the model does not allow for any regional subtypes. Dominique Sourdel and Janine Sourdel-Thomime go several steps further when they emphasize that the physical appearance of the Islamic city, with its rejection of Roman town-planning notions, was by no means the only type of city represented in the Islamic world.[83] As a result, these authors prefer to speak of regional types, abandoning the concept of the Islamic city altogether. In a similarly empirical approach, André Raymond discusses the 'Arab city', of which he studies one specific stage, namely the much neglected Ottoman period.[84] Thus it would seem that for all these researchers, the major reason for explicit or implicit dissatisfaction with the 'Islamic city' model is that it provides insufficient scope for regional diversity.

However, there are other difficulties involved as well. One of the more obvious ones is the assumption that many if not most features of urban life in the Islamic world are directly connected with religion. Now it is certainly true that much of pre-nineteenth-century Islamic construction, just as its counterparts in the Christian world, can be explained by religious references. But certain truths stop being true once they are overstated, and it would be worth knowing what other traditions existed in, for example, Ottoman culture apart from the religious one. Oleg Grabar has pointed out this problem for the eighth to twelfth centuries, when referring to a secular palace culture and also to an urban culture, largely independent from the palace and in which secular features were equally of considerable import-ance.[85] Thus the claim that religion should have determined residential patterns to as great an extent as von Grunebaum has assumed (and what is more, in a manner which should have remained unchanged over the centuries) has made the present author very uneasy. Such an assumption would imply that there was no change in social mores, and that as a result, the manner in which people used and regarded their buildings did not change over the centuries. If this were true, then the whole notion of Ottoman social history would be all but meaningless. It would be sufficient to know, as was in fact considered satisfactory by many scholars until quite recently, what Ottoman *ulama* had to say on the subject of how people were supposed to live together in cities. Quite apart from the fact that as an Ottoman social historian, one may dislike having the ground pulled away from under one's feet in this fashion – the notion of a society without major social change seems in itself very dubious. Albert Hourani, in a lucid article, has rightly warned against the assumption that the Islamic culture of the Ottoman Safavid and Moghul empires constituted *the* traditional culture of Islam as it had continued in existence from the earliest times onward.[86] Any reasonable view of urban history must come to terms with the phenomenon of social change.

However, on the other hand, Ottoman towns and cities do have many features in common with, to name but one example, Fez in the late nineteenth or early twentieth century.[87] We do need a typology which takes account of these similarities, a simple notion of the 'preindustrial' city is not enough. Nor would one wish to deny that religion was a factor in shaping the appearance of towns; what seems dubious is the notion that before European intrusion in the nineteenth century, the impact of religion should have remained unchanged in direction and intensity. With respect to attitudes toward housing and town planning, it may be worth while to scan the *kadı* registers and *vakıf* documents surviving in different parts of what was once the Ottoman Empire, an undertaking which has already produced results in the case of Cairo.[88] It is probable that once a number of regional urban types has been developed, the time will come to re-examine the impact of Islam upon urban design. But that will be after the model has been divested of the ahistorical character which scholars such as von Grunebaum have imparted to it.

Glossary

aba	rough woollen cloth
acemi	here in the sense of 'Iranian'
ahır	stable, cowshed
ahi	organization of men, active in 14th- and 15th-century Anatolian cities
ahidname	capitulations
akçe	Ottoman silver coin, basis of the monetary system until the late 16th century, much devalued from the 1580s onward
alaca	mixed fabric of wool and silk, generally manufactured in Syria
altın	gold, gold coin
arasta	covered thoroughfare, lined with shops
askeri	servitor of the Ottoman central administration, exempt from most taxes
attar	perfume seller
avarız	tax, originally collected irregularly to finance war, later major source of revenue for the Ottoman treasury
avariz akçesi	foundation designed to help the poor pay their *avarız* taxes
avarızhane	unit upon which *avariz* taxes are levied, variable number of households constituting one *avarızhane*
avlu	courtyard
ayan	notable, patrician
bağ	garden, vineyard, orchard, etc.
bağ evi	temporary residence in the gardens or vineyards outside of a city
bahçe	garden
başoda	principal room in a dwelling

batman	unit of weight, many local variations
bedel-ı hamr	wine tax
bezazistan }	
bedestan, }	covered market
bedesten }	
bekâr odaları	temporary lodgings for single men
beşe	honorific title for military men
bey	'lord'; in the present context, a title of respect given mainly to military men
beytülmal emini	official in charge of confiscating heirless property for the benefit of the Ottoman state; often farmed his office
bezirci	oil presser
bogası	coarse cotton cloth, mainly used as lining
bostancızade	'descendants of a vegetable gardener'
cebeci	armorer
cendere	press, for the treatment of mohair cloth or the pressing of grapes
cizye	poll tax, paid by non-Muslims according to the *şeriat*
çardak	veranda
çarşı	street lined with shops
develik	camel shed
deste	parcel, bundle
devşirme	'levy of boys', mainly, from non-Muslim inhabitants of the Ottoman Empire, to supply manpower to the janissary corps and certain administrative services
dirhem	unit of weight, usually 3.2g
divanhane	reception room
ebna-ı sipahiyan	Ottoman military corps
efendi	honorific title, in this period often given to a person with a *medrese* education
fağfuri	porcelain
fahrülekran	'the pride of his equals', honorific title
fetva	decision concerning the legality of a given course of action according to the *şeriat*, made by a special official (*müfti*)
fevkanî	upper floor
fırın	baking oven
fincan	coffee cup
göncüoğlu	'descendant of a leather manufacturer'

guruş	silver coin of varying provenience and value, much used for major payments in the Ottoman Empire of the 17th century
esedi guruş	*guruş* with a lion's head stamped on it, a Dutch coin
kebir guruş	Spanish silver coin, more valuable than the *esedi*
gusulhane	small room for ablutions
hacı	person who has performed the pilgrimage to Mecca
hamam	bathing establishment
hane	unit of taxation, sometimes but not always corresponding to a household
hane-i sükena	resident household
harem odası	room for family living, mainly used by the women of the household
hassa mimarı	master builder, or architect, in the service of the Ottoman central administration
havlu	courtyard
hawš	collective dwelling built around courtyard (Syria and Egypt)
hayat	veranda, in Ankara used in the sense of 'courtyard'
hisse	share
imam	prayer leader
imaret	pious foundation; in the 16th and 17th centuries, already used in the sense of 'public kitchen'
iplikçi	thread maker
kadı	judge in the Muslim religious court; in the Ottoman Empire, a key administration official on the district level
kalaycızade	'descendants of a tinsmith'
kale	citadel
kavukçu	maker of headgear
kaysariya	covered market
kaza	administrative district, several *kaza*s make up a *sancak*
kenif	toilet
kervansaray	caravansaray
keşif	account of findings; often: estimate of the expense involved in a construction project

keyl, kile	volume unit used in measuring items such as grain, many local variations
kıyye	unit of weight, usually 1.28kg
kiler	pantry
konak	wealthy residence
köşk	pavilion, often semi-detached from the main body of the building
kuyu	well
mahalle	town quarter, ward
matbah	kitchen
mean	average, i.e. the sum of cases, a, b, c, . . ., divided by the number of cases, in this instance '3' (Compare definition in *Encyclopaedia Britannica*)
mecnun	here: mentally ill
median	a way of characterizing a series of figures which is less affected by extreme cases than the ordinary average. The cases are grouped according to their value, then the midpoint is taken. The median of a series a, b, c would thus be 'b'; the median of a series, 'a, b, c, d' would be the mean (average) of 'b' and 'c' (Compare definition in *Encyclopaedia Britannica*)
medrese	school where Muslim law and religious studies are taught
menzil	residence
mescit	local mosque, in which no Friday prayers are held
meydanevi	assembly hall in a dervish lodge
mihr-i müeccel	nuptial gift, part of which was paid when the marriage ended due to divorce or death of the husband
mihr-i müsbet	nuptial gift, the amount of which has been proved by the testimony of reliable witnesses
miskal	unit of weight, usually 4.8g
muhavvata-ı dahiliye	inner courtyard
muhavvata-ı hariciye	outer courtyard
müderris	teacher in a *medrese*
muhimme registers	registers of 'important affairs', containing copies of rescripts sent out by the Ottoman central administration
mülk	freehold property

nefer	individual taxpayer, normally an adult male
oda	room
örtme	porch
örtme sofa	porch serving as a means of access to the rooms of a house
reaya	in the present context: tax-paying inhabitants of the Ottoman Empire
rehin	an item pledged to guarantee repayment of a loan
risail-i müteferrika	various treatises
rub	divisionary coin, worth one quarter of a *guruş*
sahtiyan	Morocco leather
samanlık	barn for the storage of straw and fodder
sancak	province, several *sancak*s form a *vilayet*
sancakbeyi	administrator of a province, low-level provincial governor
sayegah, sayeban	porch, veranda
seccade	prayer rug
selamlık	room set aside for male visitors
seyyid	descendant of the Prophet Muhammad
sicil	*kadıs*' register
sikke-i hasene	Ottoman gold coin (16th century)
sipahi	member of the Sultan's household cavalry; holder of a tax grant required to provide military service
sof, sofcu	here: cloth made out of the hair of angora goats, and the manufacturer of this cloth
sof karhanesi	workshop for the manufacture of mohair cloth
sofa	hall, providing access to the remaining rooms of a dwelling
dış sofa	veranda providing access to the rooms of a dwelling
kebir sofa	large hall
suk	street lined with shops
şahnişin	veranda-like structure, balcony
şeriat	Muslim religious law
şerif	descendant of the Prophet Muhammad
şirehane	wine cellar
şikayet defteri	register of complaints
şufa	right of pre-emption

tabhane	main room of a dwelling, also 'guest room'
tahrir	tax register
tahtseki	raised seat
tarik-i am	public thoroughfare
tarik-i has	private or semi-private right-of-way
testi	jug
timar	tax assignment, granted mainly to members of Ottoman cavalry, but also to civilian officials
togana	kitchen used in winter (Kayseri parlance)
turki manzume	poetry in Turkish
tülbend	fine cotton cloth, mainly used as headgear
ulema	plural of *alim*, specialist in Muslim religious law
vakıf	pious foundation
vasi	administrator of a minor's property
vekil	person empowered to act on behalf of someone else, his rights and responsibilities are fixed by the *şeriat*
veled	son of . . .
verese	heirs
vilayet	province
yer	space, ground, piece of land
yük	load
zaviye	dervish lodge
zimmi	non-Muslim permanent resident of an Islamic state

Notes

Introduction

1. In this context it is not possible to list even the major works on Ottoman monumental architecture. As an example easily accessible to the English reader, compare Aptullah Kuran, *The Mosque in Early Ottoman Architecture* (Chicago, London, 1968). On Ottoman construction activities in the Arabic-speaking provinces, compare André Raymond, *The Great Arab Cities in the 16th–18th Centuries. An Introduction* (New York, London, 1984).

2. On the manner in which a major Ottoman mosque was constructed, and the expenses involved, the most important study is Ömer Lütfi Barkan, *Süleymaniye Camii ve Imareti İnşaatı (1550–1557)*, 2 vols. (Ankara, 1972, 1979). For comments see Michael Rogers, 'The State & the Arts in Ottoman Turkey Part 1, The Stones of Süleymaniye, Part 2 The Furniture & Decoration of Süleymaniye', *IJMES*, 14 (1982), 71–86, 283–313.

3. For an early study of the Topkapı Palace compare Barnette Miller, *Beyond the Sublime Porte, The Grand Seraglio of Stambul* (New Haven, 1931, repr. New York, 1970). On the Ibrahim Paşa Sarayı, compare Nurhan Atasoy, *Ibrahim Paşa Sarayı*, İstanbul Üniversitesi Edebiyat Fakültesi Yayını 1725 (İstanbul, 1972).

4. For the Mevlâna's dervish convent compare Ibrahim Hakkı Konyalı, *Abideleri ve Kitabeleriyle Konya Tarihi* (Konya, 1964), pp.628–91. On Seyyid Gazi, the most recent contributions, apart from Filiz Yenişehirlioğlu's as yet unpublished study, are Metin Sözen, 'Anadolu'da eyvan tipi türbeler', *Anadolu Sanatı Araştırmaları*, I (1968), 167–210; Aptullah Kuran, *Anadolu Medreseleri*, Vol. 1, Orta Doğu Teknik Üniversitesi, Yayın 9 (Ankara, 1969).

5. On the problems involved in preserving such areas, see Sevgi Aktüre, Tansı Şenyapılı, 'Safranbolu'da Mekânsal Yapının Gösterdiği Nitelikler ve 'Koruma' Önerilerinin Düşündürdükleri', [ODTÜ] *Mimarlık Fakültesi Dergisi*, 2, 1 (1976), p.93.

6. For the purposes of the present study, the most relevant books in this series are Necibe Çakıroğlu, *Kayseri Evleri* (İstanbul, 1951), and Eyüp Asim Kömürcüoğlu, *Ankara Evleri* (İstanbul, 1950).

7. Halil İnalcık, '15. Asır Türkiye İktisadî ve İctimâî Tarihi Kaynakları', *IFN*, 15, 1–4 (1953–4), 51–75.

8. Ömer Lütfi Barkan, 'Edirne Askerî Kassamına Ait Tereke Defterleri (1545–1659)', *Belgeler*, III, 5–6 (1966), 1–479.

9. Ayda Arel, *Osmanlı Konut Geleneğinde Tarihsel Sorunlar*, Ege Üniversitesi Güzel Sanatlar Fakültesi Yayınları No. 11, (İzmir, 1982).

10. Antoine Abdel Nour, *Introduction à l'histoire urbaine de la Syrie ottomane* (XVIᵉ–XVIIIᵉ siècle), Publications de l'Université Libanaise, Section des Études Historiques (Beirut, 1982). Abdel Nour has dealt with about 500 16th-century houses located in Aleppo.

11. Abdel Nour, *Introduction à l'histoire*, p. 95. Abraham Marcus, 'Men, Women, and Property: Dealers in Real Estate in 18th-Century Aleppo', *JESHO*, XXVI, II (1983), 137–163.

228

12. Bernard Maury, André Raymond, Jacques Revault, Mona Zakariya, *Palais et maisons du Caire* vol. II *Époque ottomane* (Paris, 1983). The first volume of this series: J.-C. Garcin, Bernard Maury, Jacques Revault, Mona Zakariya, *Palais et Maisons du Caire* vol. I *Époque mamelouke (XIIIᵉ–XVIᵉ – siècles)* (Paris, 1982) has also been useful in placing the present study in a wider perspective.
13. Raymond; *Great Arab Cities*, passim.
14. Raymond, *Great Arab Cities*, p.57.
15. Nikolaj Todorov, 'La différentiation de la population urbaine au XVIIIᵉ siècle d'après des régistres de cadis de Vidin, Sofia et Ruse', *La ville balkanique, XVᵉ–XIXᵉss*. Studia balkanica 3 (Sofia, 1970), pp.45–62. Nicolai Todorov, *La ville balkanique aux XVᵉ–XIXᵉ siècles, développement socio-économique et démographique* (Bucarest, 1980).
16. On the agitation of the Kadızades compare Halil İnalcık, *The Ottoman Empire, The Classical Age 1500–1600* (London, 1974), p.184 and more recently Madeline Zilfi, 'Kadızadeli Revivalism in Seventeenth-Century İstanbul', *Journal of Near Eastern Studies*, forthcoming.
17. Ronald Jennings, 'Women in Early 17th Century Judicial Records – the Sharia Court of Anatolian Kayseri', *JESHO*, XVIII, 1 (1975), 53–114.
18. Compare in this respect the article 'Husband and Wife, Laws Concerning', in *Encyclopaedia Britannica* (1971 edition) vol. 11, p.908.
19. Compare the contribution of J. C. Garcin to *Palais et Maisons du Caire*, vol. I: 'Habitat médiéval et histoire urbaine à Fusṭāṭ et au Caire', pp.212–13.
20. This uneasiness recently appears to have become quite a familiar feeling to Ottoman scholars in general. Compare I. Metin Kunt, *The Sultan's Servants, The Transformation of Ottoman Provincial Government 1550–1650* (New York, 1983), p.98.
21. Suraiya Faroqhi, *Towns and Townsmen of Ottoman Anatolia, Trade, Crafts and Food Production in an Urban setting 1520–1650* (Cambridge, Eng., 1984).
22. For a list of Turkish museums possessing holdings of *kadıs*' registers, see Halit Ongan, *Ankara'nın l Numaralı Şeriye Sicili*, (Ankara, 1958, pp. vi–vii. For scholarly work on the *kadı* registers of Ankara, compare the following articles by Özer Ergenç, '1600–1615 Yılları Arasında Ankara Iktisadî Tarihine Ait Araştırmalar', in: *Türkiye İktisat Tarihi Semineri*, ed. O. Okyar, U. Nalbantoğlu (Ankara, 1975), pp.145–68; 'XVI Yüzyılın Sonlarında Osmanlı Parası Üzerinde Yapılan Işlemlere Ilişkin Bazı Bilgiler', *Gelişme Dergisi*, special issue 1978, *Türkiye İktisat Tarihi Üzerinde Araştırmalar*, pp. 86–97; 'XVII Yüzyıl Başlarında Ankara'nin Yerleşim Durumu Üzerine Bazı Bilgiler', *Osmanlı Araştırmaları – Journal of Ottoman Studies*, II (1980), 85–108; 'Osmanlı Şehirlerindeki Yönetim Kurumlarının Niteligi Üzerinde Bazı Düşünceler' in: *VIII. Türk Tarih Kongresi, Kongreye Sunulan Bildiriler*, II (Ankara, 1981), pp.1265–1274. The author's thesis '1580–1596 Yılları Arasında Ankara ve Konya Şehirlerinin Mukayeseli Incelenmesi Yoluyla Osmanlı Şehirlerinin Kurumları ve Sosyoekonomik Yapısı Üzerine bir Deneme', doctoral thesis, Dil-Tarih-Coğrafya Fakültesi Ankara, has not been published. As to the Kayseri *sicil*s, equally located in the Ankara Etnoğrafya Müzesi, the first study to be consulted is Ronald Jennings, 'The Judicial Registers ('Şeri Mahkeme Sicilleri') of Kayseri (1590–1630) as a Source for Ottoman History', Ph.D. thesis, Univ. of California, Los Angeles, 1972. Moreover, the following articles by the same author are largely based upon the Kayseri registers: 'Loans and Credit in Early 17th Century Judicial Records, The Sharia Court of Anatolian Kayseri', *JESHO*, XVI, 2–3 (1973), 168–216; 'Women'; 'The Office of *Vekil (Wakil)* in the 17th Century Ottoman Sharia Courts', *Studia Islamica*, XLII (1975), 147–69; 'Zimmis (non-Muslims) in early 17th Century Ottoman Judicial Records; The Sharia Court of Anatolian Kayseri', *JESHO*, XXI (1978), 225–293; '*Kadı*, Court and Legal Procedure in 17th Century Ottoman Kayseri', *Studia Islamica*, XLVIII (1978), 133–72; 'Limitations of the Judicial Powers of the *Kadı* in 17th Century Ottoman Kayseri', *Studia Islamica*, L (1979), 151–84; 'Firearms, Bandits and Gun Control: some evidence on Ottoman policy toward firearms in the possession of *reaya*, from judicial records of Kayseri, 1600–1627', *Archivum Ottomanicum*, VI (1980), 339–58.

230   Notes to pages 7–14

23. The following volumes have been consulted: Ankara Kadı Sicilleri (from now on cited as AKS), 5, 6, 7, and 8, for the late sixteenth and early seventeenth centuries; AKS 67, 68, 69, 70, 71, and 72 for the closing years of the seventeenth century. For Kayseri in the years before and after 1600, the following volumes have been consulted: 7a, 8, 9, 10, 11, 12, 13, 14, 15, 16a, and 17. Concerning the later seventeenth century: 97, 98, 99, 100, and 101.
24. Halil Sahillioğlu, 'Osmanlı Para Tarihinde Dünya Para ve Maden Hareketlerinin Yeri (1300–1750)', Geslişme Dergisi, special issue 1978, Türkiye İktisat Tarihi Üzerine Araştırmalar, 1–38.
25. The Çorum register, in the possession of the Çorum Municipal Library, was studied through a microfilm graciously placed at the author's disposal through the library of Middle East Technical University, Ankara.
26. On these problems, compare Louis Stouff, 'Les registres de notaires d'Arles (début XIV^{e}s–1450), Quelques problèmes posés par l'utilization des archives notariales', Provence historique, xxv, 99 (1975), 305–24.
27. Compare note 22 for the first Ankara register. Halit Ongan also published the summaries of the second one: Ankara'nın İki Numaralı Seriye Sicili, Türk Tarih Kurumu Yayınları, xiv, 4 (Ankara, 1974).
28. On the proceedings of the Ottoman provincial courts compare: Jennings, 'Vekil'; Jennings, 'Kadı, Court and Legal Procedure'; Jennings 'Limitations'.
29. As to the rules affecting testimony by Muslims and non-Muslims, see Joseph Schacht, An Introduction to Islamic Law (Oxford, 1964), pp.82, 193. Compare also Mario Grignaschi, 'La valeur du témoignage des sujets non-musulmans (dhimmi) dans l'Empire Ottoman', in La preuve, Recueils de la Société Jean Bodin pour l'histoire comparative des institutions, xviii, 3 (1963), pp.211–324.
30. This clause was for instance part of the privileges granted to the Ottoman vassal state of Dubrovnik (Ragusa). Compare N. Biegman, The Turco-Ragusan Relationship (Paris, The Hague, 1967), p.71.
31. Ömer Lütfi Barkan, 'Edirne ve Civarındaki Bazı İmaret Tesislerinin Yıllık Muhasebe Bilançoları', Belgeler, ı, pp.1–2, 260.
32. One might object that increasing bureaucratic interference is not necessarily equivalent to competence, but the documents of the later 17th century are at any rate much more 'professional' in appearance than their 16th-century predecessors. My thanks go to Dr Michael Rogers for his comments on this section.
33. Başbakanlık Arşivi, section Maliyeden müdevver (MM) 7063, dated 1055/1645–6.
34. For the date on Tokat, see Ömer Lütfi Barkan, 'Tarihî Demografi Araştırmaları ve Osmanlı Tarihi', Türkiyat Mecmuası, x (1951–3), 1–27, and more recently the article 'Tokat' in İslam Ansiklopedisi by Tayyip Gökbilgin. On the Amasya register, see Ronald Jennings, 'Urban Population in Anatolia in the Sixteenth Century: A Study of Kayseri, Karaman, Amasya, Trabzon, and Erzurum', IJMES, vii, 1 (1976), 21–57.
35. See Bruce McGowan, Economic Life in Ottoman Europe (Cambridge, Paris, 1982), pp. 80–104. Ömer Lütfi Barkan, '894 (1488/1489) yılı Cizye Tahsilâtına ait Muhasebe Bilançolari', Belgeler ı, 1 (1964), 1–117. The most relevant cizye registers for seventeenth century Kayseri are MM 5568, p. 2 (1021/1612–13), MM 1208 (1021/1612–13), MM 3659 (1051–58/1641–48), MM 276 (1089/1678–79).
36. On the city centre of Ankara compare Özer Ergenç, 'Ankara'nın Yerleşim Dumuru'.
37. On Ankara tax registers, which are not at all abundant, see Özer Ergenç, '1600–1615 Yılları', pp. 147–50. On Kayseri, compare Jennings, 'Urban Population', pp.27–34.
38. Compare AKS 69, p.12, no. 39 (1100/1688–9).
39. The list of pious foundations concerning late-sixteenth-century Kayseri (TK584, fol 85b, 992/1584) is disappointingly scanty. Much better evidence is available for Ankara: TK 558, fol 2b (979/1571–2).
40. For the potentialities of such an approach compare David Herlihy, 'Church Property on the European Continent, 701–1208', Speculum, xxxvi, 1 (1961), 81–105.
41. Evliya Çelebi, Seyahatnamesi, vol 2, pp.430–31.

42. For architectural evidence compare Çakıroğlu, *Kayseri Evleri*; Kömürcüoğlu, *Ankara Evleri*.
43. As an example that still stands in present-day İstanbul one might mention the double *hamam* built by Mimar Sinan *vis-à-vis* the Aya Sofya.
44. Apart from Sahillioğlu, 'Osmanlı Para Tarhinide', see the same author's 'XVII Asrın Ilk Yarısında Istanbul'da Tedavüldeki Sikkelerin Raici', *Belgeler*, ı, 2 (1964), pp.227–34. For rates applied in Ankara at the end of the sixteenth century compare Özer Ergenc, 'XVI Yüzyılın Sonlarında Osmanlı Parası Üzerinde Yapılan Işlemlere Ilişkin Bazı Bilgiler', *Gelişme Dergisi*, special issue 1978: *Türkiye İktisat Tarihi Üzerine Araştırmalar*, 86–97.
45. Unfortunately, the vagueness of property descriptions in the *kadı* registers makes it impossible to follow a given property through the centuries. Thus it has not been possible to duplicate the results of certain French studies concerning medieval and early modern urban real estate. Compare, for instance, the contributions to the collective volume *Le Bâtiment, Enquête d'histoire économique XIV–XIX siècles* (Paris, La Haye, 1971).
46. Halil İnalcık, 'The Question of the Closing of the Black Sea Under the Ottomans', *Archeion Pontou*, 35 (1979), 74–110; Jennings, 'Loan and Credit', p.169.
47. Compare K. Barbir, *Ottoman Rule in Damascus, 1708–1758* (Princeton, N.J., 1980), pp.108ff.
48. Schacht, *Introduction*, p.173.
49. Compare Traian Stoianovich, 'Model and Mirror of the pre-modern Balkan City', in *La ville balkanique, XVe–XIXess*, *Studia Balcanica*, 3 (Sofia, 1970), pp.99–100 and M. Ertuğrul Düzdağ, *Ebusuud Efendi Fetvalar Işığında 16. Asır Türk Hayatı* (İstanbul. 1972), p.94.
50. Çakıroğlu, *Kayseri Evleri*, pp.38–41.
51. Compare Peter Benedict, *Ula, An Anatolian Town*, Social, Economic, and Political Studies of the Middle East (Leiden, 1974), p.151. It should be stressed that these observations are meant to apply to Ankara and Kayseri, and possibly to other seventeenth-century towns of Anatolia, not to the countryside nor to the upper classes of İstanbul.
52. Joseph Schacht, *An Introduction to Islamic Law* (Oxford, 1969), p.142.
53. M. Pitton de Tournefort, *Relation d'un voyage du Levant* (Amsterdam, 1718), vol.2, pp.180–1.
54. Richard Pococke, *Description of the East and Some Other Countries* (London, 1745), vol.2, p.89.
55. André Raymond, *Artisans et commerçants au Caire au XVIIIe siècle*, 2 vols. (Damascus, 1973–4), pp.98ff.

1. Setting the scene: two cities of central Anatolia

1. For the most recent summary, compare Sevgi Aktüre '16. Yüzyıl Öncesi Ankara'sı Üzerine Bilinenler', in: *Tarih İçinde Ankara*, Eylül 1981 Seminer Bildirileri, ed. E. Yavuz, N. Uğurel (Ankara, 1984), pp.1–49.
2. See article 'Ankara' in *EI*, 2nd edition.
3. Charles Thornton Forster, F. H. Blackburne Daniell, eds. *The Life and Letters of Ogier Ghiselin de Busbecq* . . ., 2 vols. (London, 1881), vol.1, p.143.
4. G. de Jerphanion, *Mélanges d'archéologie anatolienne*, Mélanges de l'Université St. Joseph, xııı (Beirut, 1928), pp.113–42.
5. Julio Caro Baroja, *Las brujas y su mundo* (Madrid, 1961), p.98.
6. On the medieval history of Ankara compare Paul Wittek, 'Zur Geschichte Angoras im Mittelalter', in: *Festschrift Georg Jacob* . . ., Theodor Menzel, ed. (Leipzig, 1932), pp.329–54. See also the contributions in *IA* (by Besim Darkot) and in *EI*, 2nd edition (by Franz Taeschner).
7. Franz Taeschner, 'War Murad I Grossmeister oder Mitglied des Achi-Bundes?' *Oriens*, 6

(1953), 23–31. On the *ahi*s of Anatolia during the 14th century compare also Ibn Battuta, *Voyages*, tr. C. Defrémery, B. R. Sanguinetti (Paris, 1854, repr. 1968), vol. 2, pp.260ff.

8. Compare Robert Mantran, *Istanbul dans la seconde moitié du XVIIe siècle*, Bibliothéque archéologique et historique de l'Institut français d'archéologie d'Istanbul (Paris, 1962), pp.364–5.

9. Busbecq, vol. 1, pp.152–9.

10. Franz Taeschner, *Das anatolische Wegenetz nach osmanischen Quellen*, Türkische Bibliothek, 2 vols. (Leipzig, 1924–6), map appended to vol. 1.

11. For an account of mohair production in sixteenth-century Ankara, compare Hans Dernschwam, *Tagebuch einer Reise nach Konstantinopel und Kleinasien (1553–1555) nach der Urschrift im Fugger Archiv herausgegeben und erläutert von Franz Babinger* (Munich, 1925), pp.186–7.

12. Compare Xavier de Planhol, 'Rayonnement urbain et sélection animale: une solution nouvelle du problème de la chèvre d'Angora', *Secrétariat d'État aux Universités, Comité des travaux historiques et scientifiques, Bulletin de la section de géographie*, LXXXII (1975–7), 179–96, which contains both a summary of the different solutions previously proposed and the author's own views on the subject.

13. Özer Ergenç, '1600–1615 Yılları Arasında Ankara Iktisadi Tarihine Ait Araştırmalar', in *Türkiye Iktisat Tarihi Semineri*, ed. Osman Okyar, Ünal Nalbantoğlu (Ankara, 1975), pp.145–68; David French, 'A Sixteenth Century Merchant in Ankara?' *Anatolian Studies*, XXII (1972), 241–7.

14. R. D. Barnett, 'The European Merchants in Angora', *Anatolian Studies*, 24(1974), 135–41.

15. Paul Masson, *Histoire du commerce français dans le Levant au XVIIIe siècle* (Paris, 1911), p.555.

16. Reproduced in Fernand Braudel, *Civilization matérielle et capitalisme, XVe–XVIIIe siècle*, 3 vols. (Paris, 1979), vol. III, *Le temps du monde*, pp.404, 408.

17. Semavi Eyice, 'Ankara'nın Eski bir Resmi', *Atatürk Konferanslari*, IV (1972), 61–124.

18. Suraiya Faroqhi, *Towns and Townsmen of Ottoman Anatolia, Trade, Crafts, Food Production in an Urban Setting* (Cambridge, England, 1984), p.165.

19. Ibid., p.133.

20. Ergenç, '1600–1615 Yılları', p.150.

21. On carting grain to market in general, compare Ömer Lütfi Barkan, *XV. ve XVI. Asırlarda Osmanlı Imparatorluğunda Ziraî Ekonominin Hukukî ve Malî Esasları*, vol. I, *Kanunlar* (İstanbul, 1943), p.66 (example from Erzurum).

22. Ömer Lütfi Barkan, 'Süleymaniye Camii ve İmareti Tesislerine Ait Yıllık bir Muhasebe Bilânçosu 993/994 (1585–1586)', *Vakıflar Degisi*, IX (1971), 109–162.

23. On Ottoman rice cultivation, the most recent contribution is Halil İnalcık, 'Rice Cultivation and the Çeltükci-re'ayâ System in the Ottoman Empire', *Turcica*, XIV (1982), 69–141. On donations of rice to Ottoman *zaviyes* compare Suraiya Faroqhi, 'Seyyid Gazi Revisited: The Foundation as seen through Sixteenth and Seventeenth Century Documents', *Turcica*, XIII (1981), 90–123.

24. AKS 65, p.208, no.601; p.210, no.604; p.4, no.12. On the use of Ottoman probate inventories compare Halil İnalcık, '15. Asır Türkiye İktisadî ve İctimaî Tarihi Kaynakları', *IFM*, 15, 1–4 (1953–54), 51–75, and Ömer Lüfti Barkan, 'Edirne Askerî Kassamına Ait Tereke Defterleri (1545–1659)', *Belgeler* III, 5–6, 1–479.

25. For a discussion of house prices see Chapter 3.

26. Possibly identical with the fabrics called 'Lacowries' in the accounts of the British East India Company. Company K. N. Chaudhuri, *The Trading World of Asia and the English East India Company 1660–1760* (Cambridge, England, 1978), p.476. On the whole issue of cotton imports into the Ottoman Empire from India, see Halil İnalcık, 'Osmanlı Pamuklu Pazarı, Hindistan ve İngiltere Pazar Rekabetinde Emek Maliyetinin Rolü', *ODTÜ Gelişme Dergisi*, special issue (1979–80), 1–66 and Mübahat S. Kütükoğlu, *Osmanlılarda Narh Müessesesi ve 1640 Tarihli Narh Defteri* (İstanbul, 1983), p.64.

27. On the manufacture of *alaca* in sixteenth century Syria, compare MD 52, p.238, no.622 (992/1584).
28. Dr Michael Rogers suggests that these items may have been Chinese porcelains imported by way of the Hijaz.
29. On the status of a slave woman who had borne her master a child, and which the latter had recognized, compare Joseph Schacht, *An Introduction to Islamic Law* (London, 1964), p.129.
30. On the value of different gold coins in the closing years of the seventeenth century, compare Halil Sahillioğlu, 'Osmanlı Para Tarihinde Dünya Para ve Maden Hareketlerinin Yeri (1300–1750)', *Gelişme Dergisi*, special issue (1978), pp.36, 37.
31. To date, the fullest treatment of this problem can be found in André Raymond, *Artisans et commerçants au Caire au XVIIIᵉ siècle*, 2 vols., Institut Français de Damas (Damascus, 1973–4), pp.659–770.
32. AKS 65, p.210, no.604 records 100 *guruş*, while AKS 65, no.605 has 110 *guruş-i esedî*.
33. Özer Ergenç, 'XVII Yüzyıl Başlarında Ankara'nin Yerleşim Durumu Üzerine Bazı Bilgiler' *Osmanlı Araştırmaları* ı (1980), pp.89–93 contains a listing of khans, but does not mention an Asağı Han; the same applies to Gönül Öney, *Ankara'da Türk Devri Yapıları, Turkish Period Buildings in Ankara*, AÜ Dil-Tarih ve Coğrafya Fakültesi Yayınları no.209 (Ankara, 1971), pp.135–45, and to Ömür Bakırer, Emre Madran, 'Ankara Kent Merkezinde Özellikle Hanlar ve Bedestenin Ortaya Çıkışı ve Gelişimi', in: *Tarih İçinde Ankara*, Eylül 1981 Seminer Bildirileri ed. E. Yavuz, N. Uğurel (Ankara, 1984), pp.107–30.
34. For seventeenth-century importation of European goods in the Ottoman Empire, compare Paul Masson, *Histoire du commerce français dans le Levant au XVIIᵉ siècle* (Paris, 1911; reprint New York, 1967), pp.514–18. Apart from woollen cloth, paper and ironwares were sold in sizeable quantities.
35. I owe the explanation of this term to Dr Michael Rogers.
36. Kütükoğlu, *Narh*, pp.77, 104, lists examples both of Indian and of European papers imported into the Ottoman Empire.
37. No study has been made for the spread of tea consumption in Turkey, but for North Africa compare Jean-Jacques Hémardinquer, 'Le thé à la conquête de l'Occident: le cas maghrébin' in: *Pour une histoire de l'alimentation*, J. J. Hémardinquer, ed., Cahiers des Annales 28 (Paris, 1970), pp.285–91.
38. Ömer Lütfi Barkan, *Süleymaniye Camii ve İmareti İnşaatı (1550–1557)* Türk Tarih Kurumu Yayınlarindan vı, 10 (Ankara, 1972), pp.379–80 records importation of lead for the middle of the eighteenth century.
39. On the fact that during the seventeenth and early eighteenth centuries Ottoman merchants still controlled the Ottoman market, cf. Braudel, *Civilization matérielle*, vol.3, pp.402–8.
40. A dissertation concerning this document, written at Dil-Tarih Coğrafya Fakültesi in Ankara, has never been published.
41. BA, section TT 438, pp.337ff (before 1536). In 929/1522–3, 2456 taxpayers were registered in Ankara (TT 117, pp.3ff). I owe this reference to Prof. Özer Ergenç.
42. Ömer Lütfi Barkan, 'Tarihi Demografi Araştırmaları ve Osmanlı Tarihi', *Türkiyat Mecmuası*, x (1951–2), 1–27.
43. TK 74, pp.6bff. (979–1571–2).
44. Ergenç, '1600–1615', p.148.
45. Roger Mols, *Introduction à la démographie historique des villes d'Europe du XIVᵉ au XVIIIᵉ siècle*, 3 vols. (Louvain, 1955), vol.2, pp.506–518.
46. Evliya Çelebi, *Seyahatnamesi*, vol.2, p.431.
47. M. Pitton de Tournefort, *Relation d'un voyage du Levant*, 2 vols. (Amsterdam, 1718), p.185. On p.180 the author calls Ankara one of the best cities of Turkey.
48. Richard Pococke, *A Description of the East and Some Other Countries*, 2 vols. (London, 1743), vol.2, p.89.

49. Eyice, 'Ankara'nin Eski bir Resmi', Ergenç 'Ankara'nın Yerleşim Durumu', passim.
50. Helmut von Moltke, *Briefe über Zustände und Begebenheiten in der Türkei*, 6th ed. (Berlin, 1893).
51. Ergenç, 'Ankara'nın Yerleşim Durumu', pp.87ff.
52. André Raymond, *The Great Arab Cities in the 16th–18th Centuries. An Introduction* (New York, London, 1984), p.23.
53. Ira Lapidus, *Muslim Cities in the Later Middle Ages* (Cambridge, Mass., 1967), p.185–91.
54. Ibid., p.95; however on pp.94–95 when dealing with the question of relations between *mahalle*s, the author also stresses the fact that town quarters sealed themselves off from one another only in times of unusual violence and insecurity, and were in no way isolated ghettos.
55. Özer Ergenç, 'Osmanlı Şehirlerindeki Yönetim Kurumlarının Niteliği Üzerinde Bazı Düşünceler', in *VIII. Türk Tarih Kongresi, Kongreye Sunulan Bildiriler*, 2 vols. (Ankara, 1981), vol. 2, pp.1265–1274.
56. Traian Stoianovich, 'Model and Mirror of the pre-Modern Balkan City', *La ville balkanique, XVe–XIXe ss*, Studia Balcanica 3, Académie bulgare des sciences, Institut d'Études balkaniques (Sofia, 1970), pp.83–110.
57. Fernand Braudel, *Capitalism and Material Life* (London, 1974), pp.401ff.
58. Ergenç, 'Ankara'nın Yerleşim Durumu', p.107. However, among the 84 *mahalle*s, three names (İçkale, Dışkale, and Kale) refer to larger sections of the city, and not to town quarters in the strict sense of the word.
59. Ergenç, 'Ankara'nın Yerleşim Durumu', p.107.
60. Musa Çadırcı, '1830 Genel Sayımına Göre Ankara Şehir Merkezi Nüfusu Üzerinde bir Araştırma', *Osmanlı Araştırmaları*, I (1980), p.126.
61. For the use of boundary descriptions as a source for social history compare David Herlihy, 'Church Property on the European Continent, 701–1208', *Speculum* XXXVI, 1 (1961), pp.81, 105. Also Klaus Kreiser, 'Osmanische Grenzbeschreibungen', in: *Studi preottomani e ottomani* (Napoli, 1976), pp.165–72.
62. On the *mescit* of Ankara, compare Öney, *Ankara*, pp.17–108.
63. We do not possess a list of Ankara churches for the 17th century. The map prepared by von Vincke shows two (compare Eyice, 'Ankara'nın Eski bir Resmi', pl. XXXIX, XL).
64. MD 87, p.188, no.300 (1047/1637–8).
65. Gerhart Bartsch, 'Das Gebiet des Erciyes Dağı und die Stadt Kayseri in Mittel-Anatolien', *Jahrbuch der Geographischen Gesellschaft zu Hannover* (1934–5), 89–202, gives a full discussion of the natural environment of Kayseri.
66. Albert Gabriel, *Monuments turcs d'Anatolie*, 2 vols. (1931, 1934), vol. 1 *Kayseri-Niğde*, p.21.
67. Mahmut Akok, 'Kayseri Şehri Tarihî İç Kalesi', *Türk Arkeolojisi Dergisi* (1967), 5–31.
68. Ibn Battuta, *Voyages*, Défrémery and Sanguinetti, eds., vol.2, pp.287–8.
69. For two summaries of the city's historical development, compare the articles 'Kayseri' in *IA* (by Besim Darkot) and 'Kaysariyya' in the 2nd edition of *EI* (by Ronald Jennings).
70. Compare Taeschner, *Wegenetz*, vol.I, appended map, and Naṣuhü's-Silāḥī (Maṭraḳçı), *Beyān-i Menāzil-i Sefer-i ʿIrāḳeyn*, ed. Hüseyin G. Yurdaydın Türk Tarih Kurumu Yayınları, XIV Dizi, Sa 4 (Ankara, 1974), map following p.307.
71. Faroqhi, *Towns*, p.64.
72. *IA*, article 'Evliya Çelebi' (by Cavit Baysun), p.406.
73. Faroqhi, *Towns*, p.166.
73. Faroqhi, *Towns*, p.166.
75. Huri Islamoğlu, Suraiya Faroqhi, 'Crop Patterns and Agricultural Production Trends in Sixteenth Century Anatolia,' *Review*, II, 3 (1979), 423–424.
76. Faroqhi, Towns, p.224.
77. Bartsch, 'Kayseri', p.192.
78. Ronald Jennings, 'Urban Population in Anatolia in the Sixteenth Century: A Study of Kayseri, Karaman, Amasya, Trabzon, and Erzurum', *IJMES*, VII (1976), pp.27ff.

79. Mols, *Démographie*, vol.2, pp.506–22.
80. Mols, *Démographie*, vol.2, p.516.
81. Compare Mustafa Akdağ, *Celâlî Isyanları 1550–1603*, Ankara Dil-Tarih ve Coğrafya Fakültesi Yayınları no.144 (Ankara, 1963), p.250ff., and elsewhere. For Kayseri, compare also Ronald Jennings, 'Zimmis (non-Muslims) in Early 17th Century Ottoman Judicial Records: the Sharia Court of Ottoman Kayseri', *JESHO*, xviii, 1 (1978), pp.229ff.
82. Faroqhi, *Towns*, p.284.
83. Jennings, 'Urban Population', pp.31–2.
84. Evliya Çelebi, *Seyahatnamesi*, vol.3, p.178. Compare also the article 'Evliya Çelebi' in *IA* (by Cavit Baysun).
85. BA, MM 14812, pp.1ff.
86. BA, MM 5568, p.2.
87. BA, MM 1208, pp.2–53.
88. MM 7063, pp.3ff. For the Amasya count, compare Jennings, 'Urban Population', 41. For the figures concerning Tokat see the article 'Tokat' in *IA* (by Tayyip Gökbilgin). On Samsun, see Faroqhi, *Towns*, pp.106–7.
89. The scribes preparing this count made quite a few arithmetical errors. However, the totals given by the registers have been retained, since presumably these were the figures accepted as valid by the Ottoman financial administration. The men whose actual residence in Kayseri is doubtful are those recorded as *perakende-i zimmiyân*.
90. Jennings, 'Urban Population', p.41.
91. The note is dated Safer 1052/May 1645 and has been glued in following p.2.
92. MM 3659, p.5.
93. MM 7063, p.14.
94. MM 276, pp.2ff.
95. KKS 100, pp.92–3.
96. KKS 101, p.187.
97. Cf. n. 24 above.
98. KKS 97, p.109; see also Bartsch, 'Erciyes', 192.
99. KKS 97, p.109.
100. On the Gülistan commentary by Sururî, compare the article on Sa'di in *IA*.
101. KKS 97, p.111. On the cultivation of yellowberries in the Kayseri area, compare Bartsch, 'Erciyes', p.196.
102. See Halil İnalcık, 'The Socio-Political Effects of the Diffusion of Fire-Arms in the Middle East', in: *War, Technology and Society in the Middle East*, ed V. J. Parry and M. E. Yapp (London, 1975), pp.195–217. Mücteba Ilgürel, 'Osmanlı İmparatorluğunda Ateşli Silahların Yayılışı', *Tarih Dergisi*, 32 (1979), 301–18, and Ronald Jennings, 'Firearms, Bandits, and Gun Control: Some evidence on Ottoman policy towards firearms in the possession of *reaya*, from judicial records of Kayseri, 1600–1627', *Archivum Ottomanicum*, vi (1980), 339–58.
103. KKS 97, p.102 (1101/1689–90).
104. See Barkan 'Askerî Kassam', p.50ff., for the manner in which landed property was recorded in probate inventories. On private properties granted to frontier commanders, compare Ömer Lütfi Barkan, 'Osmanlı İmparatorluğunda bir İskân ve Kolonizasyon Metodu Olarak Vakıflar ve Temlikler', *Vakıflar Dergisi*, ı (1942), pp.360–1.
105. Faroqhi, *Towns*, p.263ff.
106. Nejat Göyünç, *XVI. Yüzyılda Mardin Sancağı*, İ.Ü. Edebiyat Fakültesi Yayınları, no.1458 (İstanbul, 1969), pp.137–8.
107. KKS 98, p.172.
108. On women spinning on behalf of merchants compare Dernschwam, *Tagebuch*, p.183.
109. On practice in the Kayseri area compare: Ronald Jennings, 'Women in Early 17th Century Ottoman Judicial Records – The Sharia Court of Anatolian Kayseri', *JESHO*, xviii, I (1975), pp.75–6.

110. Gabriel, *Monuments turcs*, vol.2, pp.9, 12. Necibe Çakıroğlu, *Kayseri Evleri* (İstanbul, 1952), p.16 contains an updated version of this map.
111. Akok, 'Kayseri Şehri', p.28.
112. TK 584, fol 85bff.
113. TK 584, pp.185ff.
114. Faroqhi, *Towns*, p.148.
115. Jennings, 'Urban Development', pp.28ff.
116. MM 7063, pp.2ff.
117. MM 14812, pp.1ff.
118. Jennings, 'Urban Population', p.32.
119. Jennings, 'Zimmis', pp.278–86.
120. MD 90, p.129, no.428 (1056/1646–7).
121. For agricultural potential in the Ankara area, see S. Uslu, *Untersuchungen zum anthropogenen Charakter der zentralanatolischen Steppe*, Giessener Abhandlungen 12 (Giessen, 1960). On Kayseri, compare Barth, 'Erciyes'.
122. Paul Lucas, *Voyage du Sieur Paul Lucas fait en 1714 . . . par ordre de Louis XIV dans la Turquie* (Rouen, 1724), vol.1, p.264.
123. Vital Cuinet, *La Turquie d'Asie*, Géographie administrative, statistique, déscriptive et raisonnée de chaque province de l'Asie Mineure, 4 vols. (Paris, 1894), vol.1, pp.282 and 315.
124. At the moment of completing this study, Mrs Caroline Finkel (London) informs me that a volume called *Theatrum Europaeum, Gelehrte Anzeigen auf das Jahr 1756*, pp.189–91 has information about a major earthquake which in 1668 destroyed many buildings in Ankara, including certain sections of the fortifications. Possibly the reconstruction of many houses in the İstanbul fashion dates from that period? Unfortunately, the volume in question was not accessible to me.

2. The physical shape of urban houses

1. The generally current meaning of the term *hayat* can be found in many studies dealing with regional architecture. For one example among many, compare Xavier de Planhol, *De la plaine pamphylienne aux lacs pisidiens, nomadisme et vie paysanne*, Bibliothèque archéologique et historique de l'Institut Français d'Archéologie d'Istanbul (Paris, 1958), p.270. In the region studied by Planhol, the *sofa* itself was in the shape of a porch (*dış sofa*), and *hayat* and *sofa* were used interchangeably. The vagueness of Ottoman architectural terminology is unfortunately not remedied by the list given by Cafer Efendi in his treatise on Mimar Mehmed Ağa, the architect responsible for the Sultan Ahmed mosque in İstanbul. Compare Orhan Şaik Gökyay, 'Risale-i Mimariyye – Mehmet Ağa – Eserleri', in: *İsmail Hakkı Uzunçarşılı Armağanı*, Türk Tarih Kurumu Yayınlarından VII, 70 (Ankara, 1975), p.193. Cafer Çelebi uses *'sayeban'*, *'suffa'*, and *'çardak'* as synonyms, but also uses the term *çardak* as a synonym for *köşk*; according to this author *çardak* can even be used to describe a room with stone walls. Moreover the author seems to regard the *suffa* as basically a veranda-like structure.
2. In Konya during the 1950s *hayat* was used in the meaning of 'courtyard'. Compare Eyüp Asım Kömürcüoğlu, *Das alttürkische Wohnhaus* (Wiesbaden, 1966), p.19.
3. Necibe Çakıroğlu, *Kayseri Evleri* (İstanbul, 1952), p.22. On *tabhane* in dervish lodges, compare Semavi Eyice, 'İlk Osmanlı Devrinin Dini-İçtimai bir Müessesesi: Zaviyeler ve Zaviyeli Camiler', *IFM*, XXIII (1963), 3–80. Necdet Sakaoğlu, *Divriği'de Ev Mimarisi*, Kultur Bakanlığı Yayınları 274, Türk Sanat Eserleri Serisi 8 (Istanbul, 1978), pp.32–3, reports that in Divriği the word *toyhane* is even today employed in the sense of 'winter living-room'.
4. Fernand Braudel, *Civilisation matérielle, économie et capitalisme, XVᵉ–XVIIIᵉ siècle* (Paris, 1979), vol.I, *Les structures du quotidien, Le possible et l'impossible*, p.248, creates the mistaken impression that built-in fireplaces were a unique feature of the Sultan's

Palace. In fact, such fireplaces could often be found not only in theological schools (*medrese*), and caravansarays but also in private houses. Compare in this context Kömürcüoğlu, *Wohnhaus*, p.56.

5. For the more widespread types of traditional Turkish houses, particularly in İstanbul, compare Sedat Hakkı Eldem, *Türk Evi Plan Tipleri*, İstanbul Teknik Üniversitesi, Mimarlık Fakültesi (İstanbul, 1954).

6. For an example compare KKS 100, p.13.

7. This piece of information, and much other material concerning Kayseri vernacular architecture, I owe to Latife Bayraktar, whose study on traditional summer cottages (*bağ evi*) in the Kayseri area is shortly to appear in print. For the translation of *çardak* as trellis compare Kömürcüoğlu, *Wohnhaus*, p.5. Sakaoğlu, *Divriği*, p.134 refers to the *örtme* as a ground level veranda.

8. For an example see KKS 99, p.139. Kömürcüoğlu, *Wohnhaus*, p.6, refers to a *seyirgah* (raised seat providing a view), but it is unlikely that this could be a derivative of *sayegah*.

9. Compare Çakıroğlu, *Kayseri Evleri*, p.22, and KKS 99, p.139. For *şahniş* or *şahnişin*, compare Kömürcüoğlu, *Wohnhaus*, p.6.

10. *Hamam*s were normally constructed for public use, and only a few wealthy *konak*s contained private *hamam*s, whose glass panes (*camekân*) are often specifically mentioned. Compare KKS 100, p.13.

11. Eyüp Kömürcüoğlu, *Ankara Evleri* (İstanbul, 1950).

12. Kömürcüoğlu calls the house with a *sofa* running along the long end of a house 'Type A', while the house cut in half by a *sofa* is called 'Type B'. This nomenclature had been proposed by Eldem himself in an earlier article. However in Eldem, *Plan Tipleri*, pp.27ff the *sofa*-less house has been regarded as Type A. Since Eldem's book is more accessible than his article, the names of the types have been changed accordingly. Compare also Kömürcüoğlu, *Ankara*, pp.22ff.

13. Kömürcüoğlu, *Ankara*, pp.48–50.

14. Hans Dernschwam, *Tagebuch einer Reise mach Konstantinopel und Kleinasien (1553–55)*, ed. Franz Babinger (Munich, 1925), pp.188–9. Dernschwam describes the houses in the Kale area as low, built out of mud and 'without roofs'. A few lines later, talking about the city in general, he talks about houses built of mud and sun-dried bricks, and the roofs covered with earth only. Now the 18th- and early-19th-century houses of Ankara cannot be described as low, and moreover they all have the tiled roofs so frequently seen in İstanbul or Bursa as well. These remarks support our hypothesis that a major change of style occurred in Ankara houses, probably in the 17th and early 18th centuries.

15. Çakıroğlu, *Kayseri Evleri.*

16. Çakıroğlu, *Kayseri Evleri,* p.29.

17. Çakıroğlu, *Kayseri Evleri,* p.33.

18. Çakıroğlu, *Kayseri Evleri,* pp.23ff.

19. Çakıroğlu, *Kayseri Evleri,* pp.38ff.

20. Çakıroğlu, *Kayseri Evleri,* p.23 and elsewhere.

21. Eldem, *Plan Tipleri*, p.34.

22. Çakıroğlu, *Kayseri Evleri,* pp.23–40.

23. Çakıroğlu, *Kayseri Evleri,* p.39..

24. Çakıroğlu, *Kayseri Evleri,* pp.9–11.

25. Albert Gabriel, *Monuments turcs d'Anatolie*, 2 vols. (Paris, 1931, 1934), vol.1, *Kayseri-Niğder*, p.4. Compare also Ferdinand Bennet, ed. Kemal Karpat, 'The Social, Economic and Administrative Situation in the Sanjak of Kayseri in 1880: The Report of Lieutenant Ferdinand Bennet, British Vice-Consul of Anatolia (October, 1880)', *International Journal of Turkish Studies*, I (1980), 117.

26. Çakıroğlu, *Kayseri Evleri*, p.19.

27. Gabriel, *Monuments*, p.16.

28. Çakıroğlu, *Kayseri Evleri*, p.21.

29. Bertolt Brecht, *Gedichte*, 6 vols (Frankfurt, 1961), vol. IV, *1934–1941*, p.45: . . . 'In welchen Häusern des goldstrahlenden Lima wohnten die Bauleute? . . .'
30. It would have been desirable to differentiate between cases in which *sofa*s, *tabhane*s etc. were absent ('None') and those in which the description was manifestly incomplete ('Unknown'). However, this had been omitted in the original coding and to repair the omission by a new reading of all the documents involved would have taken so much time that the effort would have been out of all proportion to the results achieved.
31. For a recent survey of houses in the citadel area of Ankara, compare Ayşıl Tükel Yavuz, '19. Yüzyıl Ankara'sında Kale İçi, in: *Tarih İçinde Ankara*, Eylül 1981 Seminer Bildirileri, ed. E. Yavuz, N. Uğurel (Ankara, 1984), pp.155–94.
32. For a description compare KKS 100, p.13.
33. Only 17 instances of *harem odası* have been located among the 1,150 cases investigated. All of these were found in late-seventeenth-century Kayseri. However, the *harem odası* was a common feature in the large-scale dwellings examined by N. Çakıroğlu, *Kayseri Evleri*, pp.25, 30.
34. Unfortunately N. Çakıroğlu does not indicate in which *mahalle*s the mansions analysed by her are located. Moreover, since most of these mansions were rebuilt and added to many times, it is impossible to determine, by a comparison of plans with the description in the *kadı* registers, whether the mansion described in the text is, by any chance, identical with one of the buildings published by N. Çakıroğlu.
35. For Kayseri compare Çakıroğlu, *Kayseri Evleri*, passim. On Ankara compare Kömürcüoğlu, *Ankara*, passim.
36. For an example, compare KKS 97, p.3.
37. This picture, much reproduced in later times, is contained in M. Pitton de Tournefort, *Relation d'un voyage du Levant* (Amsterdam, 1718), vol.2, p.177. On the seventeenth-century city wall of Ankara compare Özer Ergenç, 'XVIII Yüzyılın Başlarında Ankara'nın Yerleşim Durumu Üzerine Bazı Bilgiler', *Osmanlı Araştırmaları – Journal of Ottoman Studies* I (1980), p.87.
38. The *Şahnişin*, a relatively elaborate balcony, seems to have been a peculiarity of Ankara domestic architecture. But even in this city, it was not a very frequent feature.
39. Çakıroğlu, *Kayseri Evleri*, pp.13, 22, 42.
40. Suraiya Faroqhi, 'Towns, Country and Regional Organization in Ottoman Anatolia'. (forthcoming, 1986).
41. On commercial bakers in late sixteenth and early seventeenth century Ankara, compare Özer Ergenç, '1600–1615 Yılları Arasında Ankara İktisadî Tarihine Ait Araştırmalar', in: *Türkiye İktisat Tarihi Semineri, Metinler-Tartışmalar*, ed. O. Okyar, Ü. Nalbantoğlu (Ankara, 1975), pp.150–1.
42. The *kadı* registers contain no information on drains, and toilets (*kenif*) are so rarely mentioned that no conclusions can be drawn from the very few references that we do have.
43. On seventeenth-century gardens and vineyards, see Suraiya Faroqhi, *Towns and Townsmen of Ottoman Anatolia, Trade, Crafts, and Food Production in an Urban Setting, 1520–1650* (Cambridge, 1984), pp.242–67.
44. For a discussion of European descriptions of the Topkapı Sarayı, compare Barnette Miller, *Beyond the Sublime Porte, The Grand Seraglio of Stambul* (New Haven, Conn., 1931), pp.157ff.
45. Hamid Zübeyr [Koşay], 'Hacı Bektaş Tekkesi', *Türkiyat Mecmuası* II (1926), 366–82; Hamit Zübeyr Koşay, 'Bektaşilik ve Hacıbektaş Türbesi', *Türk Etnografya Dergisi* (1967), 19–26.
46. Out of the 40 instances of double courtyards known to have existed in late seventeenth-century Kayseri, 11 cannot be used to determine the functions of the courtyards in question, since the documents do not record which rooms opened onto what courtyards.
47. Only one building had an *ahır* both in the outer and in the inner courtyard.

48. For a discussion of the literature concerning mohair manufacturers in Ankara compare Xavier de Planhol, 'Rayonnement urbain et sélection animale: une solution nouvelle du problème de la chèvre d'Angora', *Sécretariat d'État aux Universités, Comité des travaux historiques et scientifiques, Bulletin de la section de géographie* LXXXII (1975–7), pp.179–196.
49. Ralph Davis, *Aleppo and Devonshire Square, English Traders in the Levant in the Eighteenth Century* (London, 1969), p.28.
50. Paul Masson, *Histoire du commerce français dans le Levant au XVIIIᵉ siècle* (Paris, 1911), p.457.
51. MD 96, p.75 no.379 (1089/1678–9).
52. On *sof* manufacture in early seventeenth century Ankara, compare Ergenç, '1600–1615 Yılları', pp.152–60.
53. For a discussion of *sof* manufacture in seventeenth century Ankara, compare Suraiya Faroqhi, 'Onyedinci Yüzyıl Ankara'sında Sof İmalatı ve Sof Atölyeleri', *IFM*, 41, 1–4 (1982–3), pp.237–59.
54. Richard Pococke, *Description of the East and Some Other Countries* (London, 1745), vol. II, p.2, 90. Pococke refers not to the export of yarn, but to the export of raw mohair.
55. Ogier Ghiselin de Busbecq, *The Turkish Letters of Ogier Ghiselin de Busbecq*, tr. by Edward Seymour Forster (Oxford, 1927), p.46.
56. Ergenç, '1600–1615 Yılları', p.154.
57. Dernschwam, *Tagebuch*, p.191.
58. MD 78, p.631, no.1628 (1018/1609–10).
60. On the *dış sofa*, compare Eldem, *Plan Tipleri*, pp.31–90. Whether the needs of *sof* weavers for enclosed space had any impact upon the plans adopted in Ankara is a fascinating question; unfortunately the material available at present does not allow us to answer it.
61. Compare Kömürcüoğlu, *Wohnhaus*, pp.11ff. This study is particularly valuable because of the emphasis which is placed upon stylistic changes in Anatolian domestic architecture. If the author's conclusions do not always coincide with those expressed here, this must mainly be due to the deficiencies of the documentation available. For the houses which survive, even partially, would usually be those of wealthier families, and thereby more developed than the houses documented in the *kadıs'* registers, which have served as a basis for the present study.

3. The cost of buying a house

1. For an example compare KKS 12, p.198 (1018/1609–10).
2. Ömer Lütfi Barkan, 'The Price Revolution of the Sixteenth Century: A Turning Point in the Economic History of the Near East', *IJMES*, 6(1975), 3–28.
3. Özer Ergenç, 'XVI Yüzyılın Sonlarında Osmanlı Parası Üzerinde Yapılan İşlemlere İlişkin Bazı Bilgiler', *Türkiye İktisat Tarihi Üzerinde Araştırmalar, Gelişme Dergisi* özel sayısı (1978–9), 86–97.
4. On the different monetary units in use during the 16th and 17th centuries, compare Halil Sahillioğlu, 'Osmanlı Para Tarihinde Dünya Para ve Maden Hareketlerinin Yeri', *Türkiye İktisat Tarihi Üzerinde Araştırmalar, Gelişme Dergisi* özel sayısı (1978–9), 1–38.
5. For the later 16th and early 17th centuries, KKS records *guruş* values at 80 and at 160 *akçe*. In the present context, the average of these two figures has been taken: 1 *guruş* = 120 *akçe*.
6. Sahillioğlu, 'Osmanlı Para Tarihinde', p. 37 gives the equivalent of 1 *esedî guruş* = 120 *akçe* for 1102/1690–1 and of 1 *esedî guruş* = 160 *akçe* for 1103/1691–2. Here the average of these two figures has been used.
7. Halil Sahillioğlu, 'XVII. Asrın İlk Yarısında İstanbul'da Tedavüldeki Sikkelerin Raici', *Belgeler* I, 2 (1964), 227–34.

8. For an example see KKS 13, p.29 (1018/1609–10).
9. André Raymond, *The Great Arab Cities in the 16th–18th Centuries, An Introduction* (New York, 1984), pp.58–69 presents arguments in favour of the existence of 'rich' and 'poor' quarters in Ottoman Arab cities.
10. Besim Darkot, 'Edirne, Cografî Giriş', in: *Edirne, Edirne'nin 600. Fetih Yıldönümü Armağan Kitabı* (Ankara, 1965), p.7.
11. For late-16th-century evidence of this fact, compare TK 104, fol.10bff. (992/1584).
12. For isolation and overcrowding in the Venetian ghetto of the 16th to 18th centuries, compare Cecil Roth, *History of the Jews in Venice* (Philadelphia, 1931, reprinted New York, 1975), pp.106–12.
13. For an example compare MD 50, p.8, no.25 (991/1583).
14. Means and medians were computed by the SPSS program which takes account of 'ties' (number of cases with the same numerical value) when computing the median. This means that the figure produced by the program will generally be a few *akçe* higher than the median obtained by manual counting. When manually adjusting the medians and means to take account of data which for one reason or another needed to be included or eliminated after the basic tables had been completed, it was not possible to reproduce refinements of this type. As a result, a certain margin of error has crept into the tables. However, this state of affairs does not affect the basic conclusions of the present chapter.
15. For comparable developments in 19th-century Paris compare Adeline Daumard, *Maisons de Paris et propriétaires parisiens au XIXe siècle, 1809–1880* (Paris, 1965), pp.20–38.
16. Table 13 was lost and had to be reconstituted by hand. A certain amount of variations as to what constituted usable price data could not be avoided, so that this table is not exactly comparable to Tables 15–17. However, the general conclusions are not affected by this variation.
17. The mean price paid to houseowners of Kayseri who were both Muslims and *reaya* amounted to 15,900 *akçe*, the corresponding median to 9,800 *akçe*.
18. Raymond, *Great Arab Cities*, p.58–69. Compare also J. C. Garcin, 'Habitat médiéval et histoire urbaine à Fustāt et au Caire', p.201 and elsewhere.
19. Cengiz Orhonlu, 'İstanbul'da Kayıkçılık ve Kayık İşletmeciliği', repr. in: *Osmanlı İmparatorluğunda Şehircilik ve Ulaşım Üzerine Araştırmalar* (İzmir, 1984), pp.83–91 discusses some of the traffic problems to which these outlying quarters gave rise.
20. Traian Stoianovich, 'Model and Mirror of the pre-modern Balkan City' in: *La ville balkanique, XVe–XIX^ess*, Studia Balcanica 3 (1970), pp.83–110.

4. Urban property-owners

1. Necibe Çakıroğlu, *Kayseri Evleri* (İstanbul, 1951), pp.23ff.
2. On names in Kayseri compare Ronald Jennings, 'Urban Population in Anatolia in the Sixteenth Century: a Study of Kayseri, Karaman, Amasya, Trabzon, and Erzurum', *IJMES*, vii, 1 (1976), 21–57 and 'Zimmis (non-Muslims) in Early 17th century Ottoman Judicial Records; the Sharia court of Anatolian Kayseri', *JESHO*, xxi, 3 (1978), 225–93.
3. Halil Sahillioğlu, 'Onbeşinci Yüzyılın Sonu ile Onaltıncı Yüzyılın Başında Bursa'da Kölelerin Sosyal ve Ekonomik Hayattaki Yeri', *ODTÜ Gelişme Dergisi* (special issue, 1979–80), p.85.
4. On people who were officially considered *askerî*, compare Ömer Lütfi Barkan, 'Edirne Askerî Kassamı'na Ait Tereke Defterleri (1545–1659)', *Belgeler*, iii, 5–6 (1966), pp.7–9.
5. On joint ownership of real property in 18th-century Aleppo, compare Abraham Marcus, 'Men, Women, and Property', *JESHO*, xxvi, II (1983), p.143.
6. AKS 6, p.182, no.1189 (1008/1599–1600).
7. AKS 6, p.62, no.366 (1007/1598–9).
8. KKS 97, p.79 (1101/1689–90).
9. KKS 99, p.84 (1103/1691–2).

10. AKS 69, p.109, no.291 (1101/1689–90).
11. AKS 69, p.88, no.237 (1101/1689–90).
12. AKS 8, p.154, no.1414 (1010/1601–2).
13. Antoine Fattal, *Le statut légal des non-Musulmans en pays d'Islam*, Recherches publiées sous la direction de l'Institut de Lettres Orientales de Beyrouth (Beirut, 1958), p.140.
14. Jennings, 'Zimmis', p.251.
15. Jennings, 'Urban Population', pp.27–34.
16. Richard Pococke, *Description of the East and Some Other Countries* (London, 1745), vol. 2, p.89.
17. cf. Ch.1 above.
18. KKS 100, pp.92–3 (1104/1692–93). Compare also Jennings 'Zimmis', pp.247–50.
19. Compare in this respect MD 87, p.67, no. 168 (1047/1637–38). According to this rescript, a certain İstanbul *mahalle* had recently been settled by non-Muslims, so that the local mosque was left without a congregation. To remedy this situation, resident non-Muslims were offered the choice between conversion and removal. Those that elected to retain their faith were to be ordered to sell their houses within a certain timespan and move away. Muslim landlords were also to be ordered to evict their non-Muslim tenants, and in future, houses in this *mahalle* were only to be sold to Muslims.
20. Compare Musa Çadırcı, '1830 Genel Sayımına göre Ankara Şehir Merkezi Nüfusu Üzerinde bir Araştırma', *Osmanlı Araştırmaları* ı (1980), pp.113–14.
21. For this title, compare the article by Marcus cited in note 5.
22. On property holding among Anatolian women of the 17th century, compare Ronald Jennings, 'Women in Early 17th Century Ottoman Judicial Records – the Sharia Court of Anatolian Kayseri', *JESHO*, xvııı, ı(1975), pp.53–114; Hayim Gerber, 'Social and Economic Position of Women in an Ottoman City, Bursa 1600–1700', *IJMES*, 12 (1980), 231–44.
23. Halil İnalcık, '15. Asır Türkiye Iktisadi ve Ictimai Tarihi Kaynakları', *IFM*, 15, 1–4 (1953–4), 51–75. Since it has usually been impossible to single out women belonging to *askerî* families, all women have of necessity been classed as *reaya*.
24. Özer Ergenç, '1666–1615 Yılları Arasında Ankara Iktisadi Tarihine Ait Araştırmalar', in *Türkiye İktisat Tarihi Semineri, Metinler-Tartışmalar*, ed. Osman Okyar, Ünal Nalbantoğlu (Ankara, 1975), p.148.
25. These relationships are best known for Cairo, due to the study by André Raymond, *Artisans et commerçants du Caire au XVIIIᵉ siècle*, 2 vols. (Damascus, 1973–4), vol. 2, pp.659–770.
26. Mustafa Akdağ, *Celalî Isyanları 1550–1603* (Ankara, 1963), pp.66–7.
27. Omer Lütfi Barkan, 'Edirne ve Civarındaki Bazı Imaret Tesislerinin Yıllık Muhasebe Bilançoları', *Belgeler*, ı, 1–2 (1964), p.260.
28. On the role of the *kapu halkı* compare I. Metin Kunt, *The Sultan's Servants, The Transformation of Ottoman Provincial Government 1550–1650* (New York, 1983), passim.
29. Vital Cuinet, *La Turquie d'Asie, Géographie administrative, statistique, descriptive et raisonnée de l'Asie Mineure*, 4 vols. (Paris, 1890), vol. 1, map following p.243.
30. On the position of the descendants of the Prophet in the Ottoman Empire in general and Aleppo in particular, compare Herbert L. Bodman, *Political Factions in Aleppo 1760–1826* (Chapel Hill, N.C., 1963), pp.93 and 98–99. Bodman stresses that the tax privileges of these families were limited and ill-defined, but it appears that they were real enough to warrant the latters' inclusion among the *askerî*. Compare also Barkan, 'Askerî Kassam', p.7.
31. Such an expectation might arise from the fact that the Ottoman administration invested large amounts of money to make the road to Mecca secure, and such investments might have had a cumulative effect in the course of time. Compare Karl K. Barbir, *Ottoman Rule in Damascus 1708–1758* (Princeton, N.J., 1980), pp.108–77.
32. Çakıroğlu, *Kayseri Evleri*, pp.38–41.

33. Nurhan Atasoy, 'I. Sultan Mahmud Devrinden Bir Abide Ev', *Sanat Tarihi Yıllığı*, VI (1976), 21–43.
34. For a discussion of the relevant official figures, compare ch. 1.
35. Jennings, 'Zimmis', p.248.
36. Halil İnalcık, *The Ottoman Empire, The Classical Age 1300–1600* (London, 1974), pp.183–5, reports comparable reactions in the Muslim community during this period.
37. For sumptuary regulations concerning clothing, compare Ahmed Refik, *Onuncu Asr-ı Hicrîde İstanbul Hayatı (961–1000)*, (İstanbul, *1333//1914–15*), passim. For regulations concerning buildings compare Traian Stoianovich, 'Model and Mirror of the pre-modern Balkan City' in: *La ville balkanique XVe–XIX^ess* Studia Balkanica 3 (1970), pp.83–110.
38. As a particularly elaborate example, compare AKS 4, p.170, no.813 (1001/1592–3), also nos. 800, 801, 814, 823, 827–831.
39. Frequently it was necessary to buy off the claims of the young man or woman by paying him or her a supplementary sum of money, or goods of comparable value. As an example compare AKS 72, p.96–7, no. 206 (1103//1691–2), where a young man in this position was accorded a horse, a length of mohair, cloth and 30 *guruş* in money.
40. As examples compare AKS 5, p.95–6, no. 396 (1002/1593–7): rent fixed at 10 per cent of 'sale' price; AKS 5, p.129, no. 538 (1002/1593–94): rent fixed at 15 per cent of 'sale' price.
41. For the rate of interest collected by individuals and by pious foundations, compare Ronald Jennings, 'Loan and Credit in Early 17th Century Judicial Records, The Sharia Court of Ottoman Kayseri', *JESHO* XVI, 2–3, 168–216.
42. As an example compare AKS 6, p.9, no.49 (1007/1598–9).
43. On the legal regulation of *şufa*, see Sabri Şakir Ansay, *Hukuk Tarihinde Islam Hukuku* (Ankara, 1958), pp.99–100.
44. For an example, compare KKS 8, p.49, no. 403 (1001/1592–3).
45. AKS 6, p.16, no.97 (1007/1598–9); AKS 69, p.177, no.456 (1101/1689–90).
46. As an example compare AKS 8, p.117, no. 1065 (1010/1601–2).
47. For the principles involved in such an investigation, compare David Herlihy, 'Church Property on the European Continent, 701–1208', *Speculum*, XXXVI, 1 (1961), 81–105.
48. Only in one case were the proportions more or less the same: in the 1690s, buyers of urban dwellings in Ankara amounted to 14.9 per cent of the total; for Kayseri, the relevant figure was 14.5 per cent.
49. An interesting example of this practice is described in Roger Le Tourneau, *Fès avant le Protectorat, étude économique et sociale d'une ville de l'Occident musulman* (Casablanca, 1949), p.483.
50. Obviously, to appreciate the real extent of joint ownership, cases involving real estate held by a group of owners individually enumerated would have to be added to those concerning the *verese*. However, it seems that the instances in which joint ownership has possibly been overlooked are not numerous enough to change the conclusions outlined here. For very different patterns of real estate ownership, and the social consequences which might arise therefrom, see Jacques Heers, *Le clan familial au Moyen âge* (Paris, 1974).
51. Inalcık, '15. Asır', passim; also by the same author 'Bursa and the Commerce of the Levant', *JESHO*, III, 2, 131–147; 'Bursa I, XV. Asır Sanayi ve Ticaret Tarihine Dair Vesikalar', *Belleten*, XXIV, 93 (1960), 45–110; Gerber, 'Women of Bursa'.
52. Marcus, 'Men, Women, and Property'.
53. Jennings, 'Zimmis', pp.289–90, also considers that the relationship between Muslims and non-Muslims in early-17th-century Kayseri was quite relaxed.
54. For instance compare Vital Cuinet, *La Turquie d'Asie*, vol. I, 251, on the non-Muslims of Ankara and Kayseri.
55. Halil İnalcık, 'The Question of the Closing of the Black Sea Under the Ottomans', *Archeion Pontou*, 35 (1979), 74–110.
56. Jennings, 'Urban Population', pp.31–2.
57. Jennings, 'Women', pp.65–7.

5. The difficulties of an urban property-owner

1. On this issue compare: Ömer Lütfi Barkan, 'Türk Toprak Hukukunda Tanzimat ve 1274 (1858) Tarihli Arazi Kanunnamesi', in: *Tanzimatın 100 Yıldönümü Münasebetiyle* (Istanbul, 1940), pp.1–101, reprinted in *Türkiye'de Toprak Meselesi, Toplu Eserler,* I (Istanbul, 1980), pp.291–375 and Ömer Lütfi Barkan, 'Türk-Islam Toprak Hukuku Tatbikatının Osmanlı İmparatorluğunda Aldığı Şekiller: Imparatorluk Devrinde Toprak Mülk ve Vakıflarının Hususiyeti (I)' *Istanbul Hukuk Fakültesi Mecmuası,* 3 (1942), 906–42), reprinted in: *Türkiye'de Toprak Meselesi,* Toplu Eserler, I (Istanbul, 1980), pp.249–80.

2. However, *Şikayet defterleri* contain frequent references to people who complained to the Ottoman central administration in matters involving the ownership and the possession of houses. The authorities in İstanbul generally responded by ordering the *kadı* to investigate the case.

3. Compare Joseph Schacht, *An Introduction to Islamic Law* (Oxford, 1967, reprinted 1982), passim, and the literature cited therein.

4. '. . . *muarazadan men olmuştur*'. As one example among many, compare AKS 68, p.18, no. 46 (1099/1687–8).

5. Ronald Jennings, 'The Judicial Registers ('Şeri Mahkeme Sicilleri') of Kayseri (1590–1630) as a Source for Ottoman History', PhD dissertation, UCLA, 1972, published on demand by University Microfilms, Ann Arbor, Mich., p.57.

6. *Fetva*s by famous jurisconsults might later be collected. For a modern edition compare Ertoğrul M. Düzdağ, *Şeyhülislam Ebusuud Efendi Fetvaları Işığında 16. Asır Türk Hayatı* (Istanbul, 1972).

7. On this issue compare Mario Grignaschi, 'La valeur du témoignage des sujets non-musulmans (dhimmi) dans l'Empire Ottoman', in: *La preuve. Recueil du la Société Jean Bodin pour l'histoire comparative des institutions* XVIII, 3 (Brussels, 1963), pp.211–324.

8. Cf. Ch. 1 above.

9. The religion of three defendants could not be ascertained.

10. Compare Ch. 4, and Ronald Jennings, 'Zimmis (non-Muslims) in Early 17th Century Ottoman Judicial Records: The Sharia Court of Anatolian Kayseri', *JESHO*, XII, 3 (1978), p.285.

11. For the evidence of *kadı*s' records on the position of women in the Ottoman Empire see Ronald Jennings, 'Women in Early 17th Century Anatolian Records – The Sharia Court of Anatolian Kayseri', *JESHO*, XVIII, 1 (1975), 53–114. Haim Gerber, 'Social and Economic Position of Women in an Ottoman City, Bursa 1600–1700', *IJMES*, 12 (1980), 231–44.

12. Jennings, 'Women', p.61.

13. Jennings, 'Women', pp.99–102.

14. Ismail Hakkı Uzunçarşılı, *Osmanlı Devletinde Kapukulu Ocakları* 2 vols., Türk Tarih Kurumu Yayınlarından Seri (Ankara, 1943, 1944), vol. I, p.359.

15. Uzunçarşılı, *Kapukulu*, 1, 1–141, and the article 'Dev<u>s</u>hirme' in *EI*, 2nd edition, by Victor L. Ménage.

16. On Ottoman *askeri* in general, compare Ömer Lütfi Barkan, 'Edirne Askeri Kassamına ait Tereke Defterleri (1545–1659)', *Belgeler*, III, 5–6, 1–479.

17. *Astarı yüzünden pahalı*, cf. James W. Redhouse, *A Turkish and English Lexicon* (Istanbul, 1921), p.87.

18. Halil İnalcik, 'Adâletnâmeler', *Belgeler*, II, 3–4, (1965), pp.49–145.

19. Compare Ömer Lütfi Barkan, 'The Price Revolution of the Sixteenth Century: a Turning Point in the Economic History of the Near East', *IJMES*, 6 (1975), 3–28; and for the later seventeenth century, Robert Mantran, *Istanbul dans la seconde moitié du dix-septième siècle*, Bibliothèque archéologique et historique de l'Institut Français d'Archéologie d'Istanbul (Paris, 1962), pp.248–79.

20. Compare Schacht, *Introduction*, pp.169–74.

21. Schacht, *Introduction*, p.167.
22. Inalcık, 'Adâletnâmeler'.
23. On the functions of these architects compare Şerafettin Turan, 'Osmanlı Teşkilatında Hassa Mimarları', *Tarih Araştırmaları Dergisi*, ıı, 1 (1963), 157–202.
24. AKS 69, p.91, no. 246 (1101/1689–90).
25. KKS 101, p.116 (1107/1695–6).
26. AKS 68, p.18, no. 46 (1099/1687–8).
27. KKS 97, p.91 (1101/1689–90).
28. KKS 99, p.124 (1103/1691–2).
29. On usurpation, cf. Schacht, *Introduction*, p.160.
30. AKS 72, pp.96–7, no. 206 (1103/1691–2).
31. See for example, AKS 6, p.171, no. 1099 (1008/1599–1600).
32. *The Life and Letters of Ogier Ghiselin de Busbecq*, ed. Charles Thornton Forster, FH Blackburne Daniell, 2 vols. (London, 1881), vol. ı, p.144.
33. AKS 8, p.75, no. 706 (1009/1600–1).
34. Schacht, *Introduction*, p.132. Jennings, 'Zimmis', pp.244–5.
35. KKS 99, p.66–7 (1103/1691–2).
36. KKS 15, p.30 (1019/1610–11). On the *ebnaı sipahiyan*, compare Uzuncarşılı, *Kapukulu Ocakları*, vol. 2, pp.162–163.
37. Barkan, 'Askerî Kassam', pp.11–17.
38. The wife received one eighth of the inheritance if the deceased or one of his sons left children; one quarter if there were no direct descendants. Compare Schacht, *Introduction*, p.171.
39. KKS 15, p.75 (1019/1610–11).
40. KKS 15, p.180 (1020/1611–12).
41. For a case in which a husband gave his wife part of the family dwelling in exchange for a kaftan of purple silk, compare AKS 7, p.248, no. 1990 (1009/1600–1).
42. AKS 8, p.34, no. 334 (1009/1600–1).
43. Schacht, *Introduction*, pp.82–3, 193.
44. AKS 4, p.5, no. 8 (1002/1593–4).
45. AKS 7, p.236, no. 11 (1007/1600–1).
46. AKS 6, p.3, no.11 (1007/1598–9).
47. AKS 5, p.8, no. 34 (1002/1593–4).
48. AKS 8, p.180, no. 1630 (1601–2).
49. AKS 7, p.257, no. 2076 (1009/1600–1).
50. For the types of foundation represented in 16th-century İstanbul, compare Ömer Lütfi Barkan, Ekrem Hakkı Ayverdi, *İstanbul Vakıfları Tahrir Defterio, 953 (1546) Tarihli*, Istanbul Fetih Cemiyeti İstanbul Enstitüsü (İstanbul, 1970). For a discussion of these data, compare also Ömer Lüfti Barkan, 'Şehirlerin Teşekkül ve Inkişafi Bakımından Osmanlı İmparatorluğunda İmaret Sitelerinin Kuruluş ve İsleyiş Tarzına Ait Araştırmalar', *İFM* 23, 1–2 (1962–3), 239–296, and Jon Mandaville, 'Usurious Piety: The Cash Waqf Controversy in the Ottoman Empire', *IJMES*, x, 3 (1979), 289–308.
51. Schacht, *Introduction*, p.80.
52. KKS 69, p.97, no. 260 (1101/1689–90).
53. AKS 5, p.252, no. 1029 (1002/1593–4).
54. On complaints concerning the *beytülmal emini*, see, in quite a different context, MD 23, p.164, no. 345 (981/1573–4).
55. AKS 6, p.8, no. 42 (1007/1598–9).
56. Compare in this context Mandaville, 'Usurious Piety', passim. On the institution of *avarız* foundations, compare the article 'avarız' in *İA* by Ömer Lütfi Barkan, p.18.
57. KKS 10, p.7, no. 26 (1013/1604–5). For another case of a member of the donor's family contesting a pious foundation, compare KKS 11, p.31, no. 189 (1014/1605–6).
58. Compare Ronald Jennings, 'The Office of Vekil (Wakil) in 17th Century Ottoman Sharia Courts', *Studia Islamica*, ʟxıı, (1975), 147–169.

59. AKS 8, p.51, no. 477 (1009/1600–01).
60. KKS 99, p.2 (1103/1691–2).
61. Saliha used the term *'ariyeten'* which is employed for a loan made out of friendship and without any compensation: Schacht, *Introduction*, p. 157.
62. KKS 98, p. 148 (1103/1691–2).
63. Schacht, *Introduction*, p.139.
64. AKS 8, p.148, no. 1353 (1010/1601–2).
65. Schacht, *Introduction*, p.142.
66. AKS 8, p.136, no.1243 (1010/1601–2).
67. The question was *'Bizi konşuluğa kabul eder misin?'*, the answer *'Allah mübarek eylesin'*.
68. AKS 7, p.173, no. 1304 (1009/1600–1).
69. KKS 15, p.30 (1019/1610–11).
70. Compare AKS 72, p.156, no. 325 (1104/1692–3).
71. Jennings, 'Women', pp.65–71.
72. On the use of Ottoman courts see John C. Alexander, 'Law of the Conqueror (the Ottoman State) and Law of the Conquered (the Orthodox Church): the Case of Marriage and Divorce', in: Comité International des Sciences Historiques, *XVIe Congrès International des Sciences Historiques, Rapports*, 2 vols. (Stuttgart, 1985), vol I, pp.369–71.

Conclusion

1. On the custom of building houses on top of pre-existing walls, compare Ayda Arel, *Osmanlı Konut Geleneğinde Tarihsel Sorunlar*, Ege Üniversitesi Güzel Sanatlar Yayınları No. 11 ((İzmir, 1982), p.35.
2. For parallel observations with respect to the İzmir region, see Gilles Veinstein, '⟨Ayan⟩ de la région d'Izmir et commerce du Levant (Deuxième moitié du XVIIIe siècle)', *Études balkaniques*, XII, 3 (1976), 71–83.
3. Suraiya Faroqhi, *Towns and Townsmen of Ottoman Anatolia, Trade, Crafts and Food Production in an Urban Setting 1520–1650* (Cambridge, England, 1984), pp.256–7.
4. Ronald Jennings, 'Loan and Credit in Early 17th Century Judicial Records, The Sharia Court of Ottoman Kayseri', *JESHO*, XVI, 2–3 (1973), p.212.
5. 'Notables' and 'patricians' are here used interchangeably. I owe this latter term to Richard W. Bulliet, *The Patricians of Nishapur, A Study in Medieval Islamic Social History* (Cambridge, Mass., 1972), who, however, suggests the use of 'patrician' as a substitute for 'notable'.
6. *Vier Briefe aus der Türkei von Ogier Ghiselin von Busbeck*, tr. and commented by Wolfram von den Steinen, Der Weltkreis, 2 (Erlangen, 1926), p.53.
7. Cf. Ch. 1 above.
8. Faroqhi, *Towns*, p.165.
9. On the debate concerning the economic role of the Roman provincial town, compare Georges Duby, 'France rurale, France urbaine: confrontation', in: *Histoire de la France urbaine*, 4 vols. (Paris, 1980), vol. I, *La ville antique*, pp.14–17. Certain analysts of preindustrial societies would regard almost all towns at this stage of development as parasitic, and thus would probably disagree with the conclusion outlined here. Compare Philip Abrams, 'Towns and Economic Growth. Some Theories and Problems' in: *Towns in Societies, Essays in Economic History and Historical Sociology*, ed. Ph. Abrams and E. Wrigley (Cambridge, 1978), p.27.
10. Compare Xavier de Planhol, *Les fondements géographiques de l'histoire de l'Islam* (Paris, 1968), pp.235ff.
11. Wolf-Diether Hütteroth, *Ländliche Siedlungen im südlichen Inneranatolien in den letzten vierhundert Jahren*, Göttinger Geographische Abhandlungen (Göttingen, 1968), pp.184–5. Necdet Tunçdilek, 'Eskişehir Bölgesinde Yerleşme Tarihine Toplu Bir Bakış', *IFM*, 15, 1–4 (1953–4), 189–208.

12. Abraham Marcus, 'Men, Women, and Property: Dealers in Real Estate in 18th Century Aleppo' *JESHO*, xxvi, ii (1983), 151.

13. Faroqhi, *Towns*, p.334. Women acted as buyers of freehold property, and more rarely purchased the right of usufruct to fields and meadows.

14. For an introduction to the Ottoman land system on the 15th and 16th centuries, compare Halil İnalcık, *The Ottoman Empire, The Classical Age 1300–1600* (London, 1973), pp.107–13.

15. For examples of women who did farm peasant land in late-sixteenth- and early-seventeenth-century Ankara, compare Suraiya Faroqhi, 'Land Transfer, Land Disputes, and *askerî* Holdings in Ankara (1592–1600)', in: *Mémorial Ömer Lütfi Barkan*, ed. Robert Mantran, Bibliothèque de l'Institut Français d'Études Anatoliennes d'Istanbul, 28 (Paris, 1980), 87–99.

16. Compare Ömer Lütfi Barkan, 'Türk-İslam Toprak Hukuku Tatbikatının Osmanlı İmparatorluğunda Aldığı Şekiller: İmparatorluk Devrinde Toprak Mülk ve Vakıflarının Hususiyeti (I)', *İstanbul Hukuk Fakültesi Mecmuası*, 3 (1942), 906–42, reprinted in: *Türkiye'de Toprak Meselesi, Toplu Eserler*, vol. i (İstanbul, 1980), pp. 249–80.

17. Faroqhi, *Towns*, pp.263ff.

18. Marcus, 'Men, Women and Property', 150; Faroqhi, *Towns*, p.334.

19. Marcus, 'Men, Women and Property', 151–2.

20. Jennings, 'Loans', 178.

21. Marcus, 'Men, Women and Property', 152.

22. *Rural Politics and Social Change in the Middle East*, ed. R. T. Antoun, Ilya Harik (Bloomington, Ind., 1972).

23. Ira M. Lapidus, 'Muslim, Cities and Islamic Societies', in: *Middle Eastern Cities*, ed. I. M. Lapidus (Berkeley, Los Angeles, 1969), pp.60–9.

24. Max Weber, *The City*, tr. D. Martindale and G. Neuwirth (Glencoe, Ill., 1958), pp.65–89. I owe this reference to Albert H. Hourani, 'The Islamic City in the Light of Recent Research', in: *The Islamic City*, ed. A. H. Hourani, S. M. Stern (Oxford, 1980), p.13.

25. Fernand Braudel, *Civilisation matérielle, économie et capitalisme, XVe–XVIIIe siècle*, 3 vols. (Paris, 1979), vol. i: *Les structures du quotidien: Le possible et l'impossible*, p.428ff.

26. Abrams, 'Towns and Economic Growth', passim.

27. Braudel, *Civilisation matérielle*, vol. i, pp.444–6.

28. Robert Mantran, *Istanbul dans la seconde moitié du XVII siècle, Essai d'histoire institutionelle, économique et sociale*, Bibliothèque archéologique et historique de l'Institut Français d'Archéologie d'Istanbul, xii (Paris, 1962), pp.180–213.

29. Suraiya Faroqhi, 'Ankara ve Çevresinde Arazi Mülkiyetinin ya da İnsan-Toprak İliskilerinin Değişimi', in: *Tarih İçinde Ankara*, Eylül 1981 Seminer Bildirileri, ed. E. Yavuz, N. Uğurel (Ankara, 1984), pp.61–88.

30. Mustafa Akdağ, *Celâlî İsyanları 1550–1603*, AÜ Dil ve Tarih Coğrafya Fakültesi Yayınları, 144 (Ankara, 1963), pp.138ff. and elsewhere.

31. I. Metin Kunt, *The Sultan's Servants, The Transformation of Ottoman Provincial Government 1550–1650* (New York, 1983).

32. Michael A. Cook, *Population Pressure in Rural Anatolia 1450–1600* (London, 1972).

33. Akdağ, *Celâlî*, pp.254ff. Özer Ergenç, 'XVIII Yüzyıl Başlarında Ankara'nın Yerleşim Durumu Üzerine Bazı Bilgiler', *Osmanlı Araştırmaları – The Journal of Ottoman Studies*, 1 (1980), pp. 87–9.

34. Faroqhi, *Towns*, p. 27.

35. Ronald Jennings, 'Urban Population in Anatolia in the Sixteenth Century: A Study of Kayseri, Karaman, Amasya, Trabzon, and Erzurum', *IJMES*, vii, 1 (1976), 41.

36. Murat Çızakça, 'Impact of Free Trade on the Ottoman Textile Industry, 1550–1700', presented at the Conference on Problems and Policies of Industrialization in Opening Economics, 24–28 August, 1981. Tarabya, İstanbul. My thanks go to the author for allowing me to consult this article in manuscript.

37. Başbakanlık Arşivi, İstanbul, Maliyeden müdevver 7527, p.69 (1955/1645).
38. Compare AKS 72, p.18, no.46 (1103/1691–2).
39. AKS 69, p.33, no. 93 (1100/1688–9).
40. See Chapter 1.
41. Ömer Lütfi Barkan, 'The Price Revolution of the Sixteenth Century: A Turning Point in the Economic History of the Near East', *IJMES*, 6 (1975), 7–8.
42. Murat Çızakça, 'Price History and the Bursa Silk Industry: A Study in Ottoman Industrial Decline 1550–1650', *The Journal of Economic History*, XL, 3 (1980), 533–50.
43. Benjamin Braude, 'International Competition and Domestic Cloth in the Ottoman Empire, 1500–1650, A Study in Undevelopment', *Review*, II, 3 (1979), 437–54.
44. Nikolaj Todorov, '19. Yüzyılın İlk Yarısında Bulgaristan Esnaf Teşkilatında Bazı Karakter Değişmerleri', *IFM*, 27, 1–2 (1967–8), 1–36, and by the same author: *La ville balkanique aux XVe–XIXe siècles, développement socio-économique et démographique* (Bucarest, 1980).
45. Fernand Braudel, *Civilization matérielle, économie et capitalisme XVe–XVIIIe siècle*, 3 vols. (Paris, 1979), vol. II, *Les jeux de l'échange*, pp.268–9.
46. *Vier Briefe*, pp. 56–7.
47. Halil İnalcık, 'The Ottoman Economic Mind and Aspects of the Ottoman Economy', in: *Studies in the Economic History of the Middle East*, ed. M. A. Cook (London, 1970), p.215.
48. Pierre Deyon, *Amiens capitale provinciale, Étude sur la société urbaine au 17e siècle* (Paris, Den Haag, 1967), pp.176–8 and Paul Masson, *Histoire du commerce français dans le Levant au XVIIIe siècle* (Paris, 1911), p.457. According to this latter researcher, it was only by 1730 that the development of mohair weaving in Lille, Arras, and Amiens drove imported angora textiles from the French market.
49. Başbakanlık Arşivi, İstanbul, section Cevdet İktisat 971 (1232/1816–17).
50. Antoine Abdel Nour, *Introduction à l'histoire urbaine de la Syrie ottomane (XVIe–XVIIIe siècle)*, Publications de l'Université Libanaise, Section des Études Historiques xxv (Beirut, 1982), pp.108 and 118ff. See also Marcus, 'Men, Women and Property', 143–4.
51. On the *ḥawš*, compare Abdel Nour, *Introduction à l'histoire*, pp.134–5.
52. Arel, *Konut*, p.39.
53. These opinions have been voiced by Önder Küçükerman, *Anadolu'daki Geleneksel Türk Evinde Mekân Organizasyonu Açısından Odalar* (İstanbul, 1973). They are reflected in Arel, *Konut*, p.26.
54. Hans Dernschwam, *Tagebuch einer Reise nach Konstantinopel und Kleinasien (1553–55)*, ed. Franz Babinger (Munich, Leipzig, 1923), pp.188–9.
55. Evliya Çelebi, *Seyahatnamesi*, vol. II, p.431.
56. Evliya Çelebi, *Seyahatnamesi*, vol. III, p.178 and Albert Gabriel, *Monuments turcs d'Anatolie*, 2 vols. (Paris, 1931, 1934), vol. I, *Kayseri, Niğde*, p.16.
57. Arel, *Konut*, p.32.
58. Abdel Nour, *Introduction à l'histoire*, p.99.
59. Compare for instance Arel, *Konut*, p.34.
60. Compare the catalogue of 'secondary residences' in the Kayseri area, in Necibe Çakıroğlu, *Kayseri Evleri* (İstanbul, 1951), pp.42ff.
61. Abdel Nour, *Introduction à l'histoire*, p.99.
62. This hypothesis of Sedat Eldem's is reported in Arel, *Konut*, p.23.
63. Abdel Nour, *Introduction à l'histoire*, p.101.
64. André Raymond, *The Great Arab Cities in the 16th–18th Centuries. An Introduction*, Hagop Kevorkian Series on Near Eastern Art and Civilization (New York, London, 1984), pp.81ff.
65. J. C. Garcin, 'Habitat médiéval et histoire urbaine à Fusṭāṭ et au Caire', in: J. C. Garcin, André Raymond, Bernard Maury, Jacques Revault, Mona Zakariya, *Palais et Maisons du Caire*, vol. I, *Époque mamelouke (XIII–XVI siècles)* (Paris, 1982), pp.194ff.

66. For the procedure by which Mamluk *beys* of the 18th century managed to retain state revenues, compare Stanford J. Shaw, *The Financial and Administrative Organization and Development of Ottoman Egypt 1517–1798*. (Princeton, N.J., 1962), pp.242ff.

67. Abdelnour, *Introduction à l'histoire*, pp.91–124 and Marcus, 'Men, Women and Property', pp.138, 142.

68. Marcus, 'Men, Women, and Property', Table 1 on p.144. The total of all sellers was 2162, that of buyers 1517. Women made up 43.7% of all sellers and 35% of all buyers.

69. Compare Ch.4, Table 6.

70. On this process compare the *Histoire du commerce de Marseille*, ed. by Gaston Rambert, 6 vols. (Paris, 1949–59). vol. v, *De 1660 à 1789*, by Robert Paris, pp.421, 438–52.

71. Marcus, 'Men, Women, and Property', pp.147ff.

72. For the 18th century compare for instance Herbert L. Bodman, *Political Factions in Aleppo, 1760–1826* (Chapel Hill, N.C., 1963).

73. Marcus, 'Men, Women, and Property', pp.153ff.

74. This section owes a great deal to discussions with Dr Ferhunde Özbay (İstanbul).

75. Garcin, 'Habitat', pp.212–13.

76. BA, section Tapu Tahrir 772, pp.2ff. (1052/1642–3).

78. Özer Ergenç, 'Osmanlı Şehirlerindeki Yönetim Kurumlarının Niteliği Üzerinde Bazı Düşünceler', in: *VIII. Türk Tarih Kongresi, Kongreye Sunulan Bildiriler*, 2 vols. (Ankara, 1981), vol.2, pp.1265–74.

79. Marcus, 'Men, Women, and Property', p.158.

80. For Ottoman Jerusalem, compare Amnon Cohen, *Jewish Life under Islam; Jerusalem in the Sixteenth Century* (Cambridge, Mass., London, 1984).

81. Gustave von Grunebaum, 'The Structure of the Muslim Town', in: *Islam, Essays in the nature and growth of a cultural tradition*, 2 ed. (London, 1961), pp.141–58. I thank Dr Sevgi Aktüre (Ankara) for pointing out this article to me.

82. Sevgi Aktüre, *19. Yüzyıl Anadolu Kenti, Mekânsal Yapı Çözümlemesi* (Ankara, 1978), pp.7–9.

83. Dominique Sourdel, Janine Sourdel-[Thomime], *La civilization de l'Islam classique*, Collection Les grandes civilisations (Paris, 1968), pp.398, 420ff.

84. Raymond, *Great Arab Cities*, passim.

85. Oleg, Grabar, *The formation of Islamic Art* (New Haven, Conn., London, 1973), pp.139–82.

86. Hourani, 'Islamic City', pp.10–11.

87. Compare in this context: Roger Le Tourneau: *Fès avant le Protectorat; Étude économique et sociale d'une ville d l'Occident musulman* (Casablanca, 1949).

88. Compare Garcin, 'Habitat', and Nelly Hanna, *Construction Work in Ottoman Cairo (1517–1798)*, Supplément aux *Annales Islamologiques*, Cahier No.4 (Cairo 1984).

Bibliography

ARCHIVAL DOCUMENTS

Etnoğrafya Müzesi, Ankara
Ankara kadı sicilleri AKS 1, 2, 3, 4, 5, 6, 7, 8, 68, 69, 70, 71, 72.
Kayseri kadı sicilleri KKS 7, 7a, 8, 9, 10, 11, 12, 13, 14, 15, 16a, 16b, 96, 97, 98, 99, 100, 101.

Başbakanlık Arsivi, Istanbul
Maliyeden müdevver 276, 1208, 3659, 5568, 7063, 7527, 14812.
Tapu Tahrir 387, 438.
Cevdet Iktisat 971.

Tapu ve Kadastro Genel Müdürlüğü, Kuyudu, kadime archive, Ankara.
74, 104, 136, 558, 584.
Mühimme defteri 23, 79.

PRINTED SOURCES

Islam Ansiklopedisi, 11 vols., İstanbul, 1945–
The Encyclopedia of Islam, 4 vols and supplements, Leiden, 1955–
Abdelnour, Antoine. *Introduction à l'histoire urbaine de la Syrie ottomane* (XVIe–XVIIIe siècle), Publications de l'Université Libanaise, Section des Etudes Historiques, Beirut, 1982.
Abrams, Philip, 'Towns and Economic Growth: Some Theories and Problems', in: *Towns in Societies, Essays in Economic History and Historical Sociology*, Cambridge, 1978, pp.9–34.
Ahmed, Refik. *Onuncu Asr-ı Hicri'de İstanbul Hayatı (961–1000)*, İstanbul, 1333/ 1914–15.
Akdağ, Mustafa. *Celâlî İsyanları, 1550–1603*, Ankara, 1963.
Akok, Mahmut. 'Kayseri Şehri Tarihi İç Kalesi' *Türk Arkeolojisi Dergisi* (1976), 5–31.
Aktüre, Sevgi. '17. Yüzyıl Başından 19. Yüzyıl Ortasına Kadarki Dönemde Anadolu Osmanlı Şehrinde Şehirsel Yapının Değişme Süreci', *ODTÜ Mimarlık Fakültesi, Journal of the METU Faculty of Architecture* 1, 1 (1975), 101–28.
Aktüre, Sevgi, Şenyapılı, Tansı. 'Safranbolu'da Mekânsal Yapının Gösterdiği Nitelikler ve "koruma" Önerilerinin Düşündürdükleri', *ODTÜ Mimarlık Fakültesi Dergisi*, 2, 1 (1976), 61–96.
Aktüre, Sevgi. *19. Yüzyıl Sonunda Anadolu Kenti*, Mekânsal Yapı Çözümlemesi, Ankara, 1978.

"16. Yüzyıl Öncesi Ankara'sı Üzerine Bilinenler," in: E. Yavuz and N. Uğurel (eds.), *Tarih İçinde Ankara*, Eylül 1981 Seminer Bildirileri (Ankara, 1984), pp.1–49.

Alexander, John. 'Law of the Conqueror (the Ottoman State) and Law of the Conquered (the Orthodox Church): the Case of Marriage and Divorce', in: Comité International des Sciences Historiques, *XVIe Congrès International des Sciences Historiques, Rapports*, 2 vols, Stuttgart, 1985, vol. I, pp.369–71.

Ankara İl Yıllığı, Ankara, 1967.

Ankara İl Yıllığı, Ankara, 1973.

Ansay, Sabri Şakir. *Hukuk Tarihinde İslam Hukuku*, Ankara, 1958.

Arel, Ayda. *Osmanlı Konut Geleneğinde Tarihsel Sorunlar*, Ege Üniversitesi Güzel Sanatlar Fakültesi Yayınları, 11, İzmir, 1982.

Atasoy, Nurhan. *İbrahim Paşa Sarayı*, İstanbul Üniversitesi Edebiyat Fakültesi Yayını 1725, İstanbul, 1972.

'I. Sultan Mahmud Devrinden Bir Abide Ev', *Sanat Tarihi Yıllığı*, VI (1976), 21–43.

Ayverdi, Ekrem Hakkı. *Fatih Devri Sonlarında İstanbul Mahalleleri, Şehrin İskân ve Nüfusu*, Vakıflar Umum Müdürlüğü Neşriyatı, Ankara, 1958.

Baer, Gabriel. 'The Administrative, Economic and Social Functions of Turkish Guilds', *IJMES*, 1 (1970), 28–50.

Bakırer, Ömür., Madran, Emre. 'Ankara Kent Merkezinde Özellikle Hanlar ve Bedestenin Ortaya Çıkışı ve Gelişimi', in: E. Yavuz and N. Uğurel (eds.), *Tarih İçinde Ankara*, Eylül 1981 Seminer Bildirileri, Ankara, 1984, pp.107–30.

Bammer, Anton. *Wohnen im Vergänglichen, Traditionelle Wohnformen in der Türkei und in Griechenland*, Graz, 1982.

Barbir, Karl K. *Ottoman Rule in Damascus 1708–1758*, Princeton, N.J., 1980.

Bardet, Jean-Pierre. 'La maison rouennaise au XVIIe et XVIIIe siècles, économie et comportement', in *Le Bâtiment, Enquête d'histoire économique, XIV–XIX siècles*, 2 vols, Paris, Den Haag, 1971, vol. I, pp.315–18.

Barkan, Ömer Lütfi. 'Türk Toprak Hukukunda Tanzimat ve 1274 (1858) Tarihli Arazi Kanunnâmesi', in: *Tanzimat'ın 100. Yıldönümü Münasebetiyle* İstanbul, 1940, pp.1–101, reprinted in: *Türkiye'de Toprak Meselesi, Toplu Eserler* I, İstanbul, 1980, pp.291–375 (only one volume published).

'Türk İslam Toprak Hukuku Tatbikatının Osmanlı İmparatorluğunda Aldığı Şekiller: İmparatorluk Devrinde Toprak Mülk ve Vakıflarının Hususiyeti (I)', *İstanbul Hukuk Fakültesi Mecmuası*, 3 (1942), 906–42, reprinted in *Türkiye'de Toprak Meselesi, Toplu Eserler* I, İstanbul, 1980, pp. 249–80 (only one volume published).

'Osmanlı İmparatorluğunda bir İskân ve Kolonizasyon Metodu Olarak Vakıflar ve Temlikler', *Vakıflar Dergisi*, 1 (1942), 279–386.

XV. ve XVI. Asırlarda Osmanlı İmparatorluğunda Zirâî Ekonominin Hukuki ve Mali Esasları, vol. I, *Kanunlar* İstanbul, 1943 (only one volume published).

'Tarihî Demografi Araştırmaları ve Osmanlı Tarihi', *Türkiyat Mecmuası*, X (1951–52), 1–27.

'Şehirlerin Teşekkül ve İnkişafi Bakımından Osmanlı İmparatorluğunda İmaret Sitelerinin Kuruluş ve İşleyiş Tarzına Ait Araştırmalar', *İFM*, 23, 1–2 (1962–3), 239–96.

'894 (1488/1489) Yılı Cizye Tahsilatına Ait Muhasebe Bilânçoları', *Belgeler*, I, 1 (1964), 1–117.

'Edirne ve Civarındaki Bazı İmaret Tesislerinin Yıllık Muhasebe Bilânçoları', *Belgeler*, I, 1–2 (1864), 235–377.

'Edirne Askerî Kassamı'na Ait Tereke Defterleri (1545–1659)', *Belgeler*, III, 5–6 (1966), 1–479.

'Süleymaniye Camii ve İmareti Tesislerine Ait Yıllık bir Muhasebe Bilânçosu 993/ 994 (1585–1586)', *Vakıflar Dergisi*, ıx (1971), 109–62.

Süleymaniye Camii ve İmareti İnşaatı (1550–1557), Türk Tarih Kurumu Yayınlarından VI, 10, 2 vols., Ankara, 1972, 1979.

'The Price Revolution of the Sixteenth Century: a Turning Point in the Economic History of the Near East', *IJMES*, 6 (1975), 3–28.

Barkan, Ömer Lütfi., Ayverdi, Ekrem Hakkı. *İstanbul Vakıfları Tahrîr Defteri, 943 (1546) Târîhli*, Istanbul Fetih Cemiyeti Istanbul Enstitüsü, Istanbul, 1970.

Barnett, R. D. 'The European Merchants in Angora', *Anatolian Studies*, 24 (1974), 135–41.

Barth, Heinrich. *Reise von Trapezunt durch die nördliche Hälfte Klein-Asiens nach Scutari im Herbst 1858*, Gotha, 1860.

Bartsch, Gerhart. 'Das Gebiet des Erciyas Dağı und die Stadt Kayseri in Mittel-Anatolien', *Jahrbuch der Geographischen Gesellschaft zu Hannover* (1934–5), 89–202.

'Ankara im Wandel der Zeiten und Kulturen', *Petermanns Geographische Mitteilungen*, 98, 4 (1954), 256–66.

Beldiceanu, Nicoară, Beldiceanu-Steinherr, Irène. 'Recherches sur la province de Qaraman au XVIᵉ siècle. Étude et actes', *JESHO*, 11 (1968), 1–129.

Benedict, Peter. *Ula, An Anatolian Town*, Social, Economic, and Political Studies of the Middle East, Leiden, 1974.

Bennet, Ferdinand, ed., Karpat, Kemal. 'The Social, Economic and Administrative Situation in the Sanjak of Kayseri in 1880: The Report of Lieutenant Ferdinand Bennet, British Vice-Consul of Anatolia (October, 1880)', *International Journal of Turkish Studies*, 1, 2 (1980), 107–25.

Berk, Celile. *Konya Evleri*, İTÜ Mimarlık Fakültesi Yayınları, İstanbul, 1951.

Biegman, N. *The Turco-Ragusan Relationship*, Paris, The Hague, 1967.

Bodman, Herbert L. *Political Factions in Aleppo 1760–1826*, Chapel Hill, N.C., 1963.

Boudon, Françoise, 'Tissu urbain et architecture. L'analyse parcellaire comme base de l'histoire architecturale', *Annales ESC*, 30, 4 (1975), 773–818.

Braude, Benjamin, 'International Competition and Domestic Cloth in the Ottoman Empire, 1500–1650, A Study in Undevelopment', *Review*, ıı, 3 (1979), 437–54.

Braudel, Fernand. *Civilization matérielle, économie et capitalisme XVᵉ–XVIIIᵉ siècle*, 3 vols., Paris, 1979, vol. ı, *Les structures du quotidien; le possible et l'impossible* vol. ıı, *Les jeux de l'échange*, vol. ııı, *Le temps du monde*.

Capitalism and Material Life, 1400–1800, tr. Miriam Kochan, London, 1974.

Brentano, R. *Rome Before Avignon: A Social History of Thirteenth-Century Rome*, New York, 1974.

Bulliet, Richard W. *The Patricians of Nishapur, A Study in Medieval Islamic Social History*, Cambridge, Mass., 1972.

Busbecq, Ogier Ghiselin de. *The Life and Letters of Ogier Ghiselin de Busbecq*, ed. Charles Thornton Forster, F. H. Blackburne Daniell, 2 vols. London, 1881.

Vier Briefe aus der Türkei von Ogier Ghiselin de Busbeck, trans. and commented by Wolfgang von den Steinen, Der Weltkreis 2, Erlangen, 1926.

The Turkish Letters of Ogier Ghiselin de Busbecq, transl. by Edward Seymond Forster, Oxford, 1927.

Chaudhuri, K. N. *The Trading World of Asia and the English East India Company 1660–1760*, Cambridge, England, 1978.

Cohen, Ammon. *Jewish Life under Islam, Jerusalem in the Sixteenth Century*, Cambridge, Mass., London, 1984.

Cook, Michael A. *Population Pressure in Rural Anatolia 1450–1600*, London, 1972.

Cuinet, Vital. *La Turquie d'Asie, Géographie administrative, statistique, déscriptive et raisonnée de l'Asie Mineure*, 4 vols., Paris, 1890.

Çardırcı, Musa. '1830 Genel Sayımına Göre Ankara Şehir Merkezi Nüfusu Üzerinde bir Araştırma', *Osmanlı Araştırmaları – Journal of Ottoman Studies*, ı (1980), 109–32.

Çağatay, Neşet. 'Osmanlı İmparatorluğunda Riba-Faiz Konusu, Para Vakıfları ve Bankacılık', *Vakıflar Degisi*, ıx (1971), 39–56.

Çakıroğlu, Necibe. *Kayseri Evleri*, İstanbul, 1951.

Çızakça, Murat. 'Price History and the Bursa Silk Industry: A Study in Ottoman Industrial Decline 1550–1650', *The Journal of Economic History*, xL, 3 (1980), 533–50.

'Impact of Free Trade on Ottoman Textile Industry, 1550–1700', paper presented at the Conference on Problems and Policies of Industrialization in Opening Economies, 24–28 August 1981, Tarabya, İstanbul.

Darkot, Besim, 'Edirne, Coğrafi Giriş, in: *Edirne, Edirne'nin 600. Fetih Yıldönümü Armağan Kitabı*, Türk Tarih Kurumu Yayınlarından vıı, 43, Ankara, 1965, pp.1–12.

Daumard, Adeline. *Maisons de Paris et propriétaires parisiens au XIXᵉ siècle, 1809–1880*, Paris, 1965.

La bourgeoisie parisienne de 1815 à 1848, Paris, 1963.

Davis, Ralph. *Aleppo and Devonshire Square,* English Traders in the Levant in the Eighteenth Century, London, 1969.

Delumeau, Jean. *Vie économique et sociale de Rome, dans la seconde moitié du XVIᵉ siècle*, 2 vols., Paris, 1957, 1959.

Dernschwam, Hans. *Tagebuch einer Reise nach Konstantinopel und Kleinasien (1553–55)*, ed. Franz Babinger, Munich, Leipzig, 1923.

Desportes, P. *Reims et les Rémois aux XIIIᵉ et XIVᵉ siècles*, Paris, 1979.

Deyon, Pierre. *Étude sur la société urbaine au 17ᵉ siècle: Amiens, capitale provinciale*, Paris, 1967.

Duby, Georges. Février, Paul-Albert. Fixot, Michel. Goudineau, Christian. Kruta, Venceslas. *Histoire de la France urbaine*, vol. ı, *La ville antique des origines au IXᵉ siècle*, Paris, 1980.

Düzdağ, M. Ertuğrul. *Şeyhülislâm Ebusuud Efendi Fetvaları Işığında 16. Asır Türk Hayatı*, İstanbul, 1972.

Eldem, Sedad, H. *Köşkler ve Kasırlar, A Survey of Turkish Kiosks and Pavilions,* 2 vols., İstanbul, vol. ı, 1964, vol. 2, n.d.

Türk Evi Plan Tipleri, İstanbul Teknik Üniversitesi, Mimarlık Fakültesi, İstanbul, 1954.

Eldem Sedad H., Akozan, Feridun. *Topkapı Sarayı, Bir Mimari Araştırması*, n.p. (İstanbul, ?), n.d. (1981 ?).

Ergenç, Özer, '1580–1596 Yılları Arasında Ankara ve Konya Şehirlerinin Mukayeseli İncelenmesi Yoluyla Osmanlı Şehirlerinin Kurumları ve Sosyo-Ekonomik Yapısı Üzerine bir Deneme', unpublished Ph.D. thesis, AÜ Dil ve Tarih Coğrafya Fakültesi, Ankara, 1973.

'1600–1615 Yılları Arasında Ankara İktisadi Tarihine Ait Araştırmalar', in: Osman Okyar and Ünal Nalbantoğlu (eds.), *Türkiye İktisat Tarihi Semineri, Metinler-Tartışmalar,* Ankara, 1975, pp.145–68.

'XVI. Yüzyılın Sonlarında Osmanlı Parası Üzerinde Yapılan İşlemlere İlişkin Bazı Bilgiler', in: *Türkiye İktisat Tarihi Üzerinde Araştırmalar, Gelişme Dergisi*, (special issue, 1978–9), 86– 97.

'XVII Yüzyılın Başlarında Ankara'nın Yerleşim Durumu Üzerine Bazı Bilgiler', *Osmanlı Araştırmaları – Journal of Ottoman Studies*, ı (1980), 85–108.

'Osmanlı Şehrinde Esnaf Örgütlerinin Fizik Yapıya Etkileri', in: Osman Okyar,

Halil Inalcık (eds.), *Türkiye'nin Sosyal ve Ekonomik Tarihi (1071–1920)*, Ankara, 1980, pp.103–9.

'Osmanlı Şehirlerindeki Yönetim Kurumlarının Niteliği Üzerinde Bazı Düşünceler', in: *VIII Türk Tarih Kongresi, Kongreye Sunulan Bildiriler*, 2 vols., Ankara, 1981, vol. II, pp.1265–74.

Eser, Lami. *Kütahya Evleri*, İstanbul, 1955.

Esin, Emel. 'An Eighteenth Century "Yalı", viewed in the line of development of related form in Turkic architecture', *Atti del Secondo Congresso Internazionale di Arte Turca, Venezia 1963*, Napoli, 1965, pp.83–112.

'Sadullah Paşa'nın Bağlı Olduğu Gelenek', *Türkiyemiz*, 6, 16, (1975), 2–7.

'Sadullah Paşa Yalısı', *Türkiyemiz*, 6, 17 (1975), 22–6.

Evliya Çelebi *Seyahatnamesi*, 10 vols., İstanbul 1314/1896–7 to 1938, vols. II and III.

Eyice, Semavi, 'İlk Osmanlı Devrinin Dini-İçtimai bir Müessesesi: Zaviyeler ve Zaviyeli Camiler', *İFM*, XXIII (1963), 3–80.

'Ankara'nın Eski bir Resmi', *Atatürk Konferansları*, IV (1972), 61–124.

Faroqhi, Suraiya. 'Seyyid Gazi Revisited: the Foundation as Seen through Sixteenth and Seventeenth Century documents', *Turcica*, XIII (1981), 90–123.

'Land Transfer, Land Disputes and *askerî* Holdings in Ankara (1592–1600)', in: Robert, Mantran (ed.), *Mémorial Ömer Lütfi Barkan*, Bibliothèque de l'Institut Français d'Études Anatoliennes d'Istanbul, Paris, 1980, pp.87–99.

'Onyedinci Yüzyıl Ankara'sında Sof İmalatı ve Sof Atölyeleri', *IFM*, 41, 1–4 (1982–3), 237–59.

'Ankara ve Çevresinde Arazi Mülkiyetinin ya da İnsan-Toprak İlişkilerinin Değişmi', in: *Tarih İçinde Ankara*, Eylül 1981 Seminer Bildirileri, ed. E. Yavuz, N. Uğurel, Ankara, 1984, pp.61–88.

Towns and Townsmen of Ottoman Anatolia. Trade, Crafts and Food Production in an Urban Setting, Cambridge, Engl., 1984.

Fattal, Antoine. *Le statut légal des non-Musulmans en pays d'Islam*, Recherches publiées sous la direction de l'Institut de Lettres Orientales de Beyrouth, Beirut, 1958.

Favier, Jean. *Nouvelle Histoire de Paris, 1380–1500*, Paris, 1974.

Fekete, Lajos. 'Das Heim eines türkischen Herrn in der Provinz im XVI. Jahrhundert', *Studia Historica Academiae Scientiarum Hungaricae*, Budapest, 1960.

French, David. 'A Sixteenth Century Merchant in Ankara?', *Anatolian Studies*, 22 (1972), 241–47.

Gabriel, Albert. *Monuments turcs d'Anatolie*, 2 vols. Paris, 1931, 1934, vol. I, *Kayseri-Niğde*.

Garcin, J. C. 'Habitat médiéval et histoire urbaine à Fusṭāṭ et au Caire', in: Garcin, J. C. Maury, Bernard. Revault, Jacques. Zakarya, Mona. *Palais et maisons du Caire*, vol. I, *Époque mamelouke (XIII–XVIᵉ siècles)*, Paris, 1982.

Gerber, Haim. 'Social and Economic Position of Women in an Ottoman City, Bursa 1600–1700', *IJMES*, 12 (1890), 231–44.

Goitein, S. D. *A Mediterranean Society: The Jewish Communities of the Arab World as Portrayed in the Documents of the Cairo Geniza*, 4 vols., Berkeley, Los Angeles, 1967–, vol. IV, *Daily Life*.

'A Mansion in Fustat: A Twelfth-Century Description of a Domestic Compound in the Ancient Capital of Egypt', in : Harry A. Miskimin, David Herlihy, A. L. Udovitch, (eds.), *The Medieval City, In Honor of Robert S. Lopez*, New Haven, Conn., London, 1977, pp.163–78.

'Urban Housing in Fatimid and Ayyubid Times', *Studia Islamica*, 47 (1978), 5–24.

Goodwin, Godfrey. *A History of Ottoman Architecture*, London, 1975.

Gouhier, Pierre. 'La maison presbytérale en Normandie. Essai sur le prix de la construction dans les campagnes au XVIII. siècle', in: *Le Bâtiment, Enquête d'histoire économique, XIV–XIX. siècles*, vol. I, Paris, Den Haag, 1971, pp.123–88.

Gökbilgin, Tayyib. 'XVI. Asır Başlarında Kayseri Şehri ve Livası', *60. Doğum Yılı Münasebetiyle Zeki Velidi Togan'a Armağan, Symbolae in honorem Z. V. Togan*, İstanbul, 1950–55, pp.93–108.

Gökyay, Orhan Şaik. 'Risale-i Mimariyye–Mimar Mehmet Ağa–Eserleri', in: *İsmail Hakkı Uzunçarşılı'ya Armağan*, Türk Tarih Kurumu, 7, 70, Ankara, 1975, pp.113–215.

Göyünç, Nejat. 'Onaltıncı Yüzyılda Ankara', *Belgelerle Türk Tarihi Dergisi*, 1 (1967), 71–5.

XVI. Yüzyılda Mardin Sancağı, İU Üniversitesi Yayınları no.1458, İstanbul, 1969.

Grabar, Oleg. *The Formation of Islamic Art* (New Haven, Conn., London, 1973).

Grignaschi, Mario. 'La valeur du témoignage des sujets non-musulmans (dhimmi) dans l'Empire Ottoman', in: *La preuve. Recueil de la Société Jean Bodin pour l'histoire comparative des institutions*, XVIII, 3, Brussels, 1963, 211–324.

Güçer, Lütfi. 'Osmanlı İmparatorluğu Dahilinde Hububat Ticaretinin Tabi Olduğu Kayıtlar', *IFM*, 11, 1 (1951–2), 79–98.

Hamilton, William J. *Researches in Asia Minor, Pontus and Armenia*, with some Account of their Antiquities and Geology, 2 vols., London, 1842.

Hanna, Nelly. *Construction Work in Ottoman Cairo (1517–1798)*, Supplément aux *Annales Islamologiques* Cahier No. 4 (Cairo, 1984).

Harik, Iliya F. 'The Impact of the Domestic Market on Rural–Urban Relations in the Middle East', in: Richard T. Antoun, Iliya F. Harik (eds.), *Rural Politics and Social Change in the Middle East*. Bloomington, Ind., 1972, pp.337–63.

Heers, Jacques. *Le clan familial au Moyen âge*, Paris, 1974.

Hémardinquer, Jean-Jacques. 'Le thé à la conquête de l'Occident; le cas maghrébin', in: J. J. Hémardinquer (ed.), *Pour une histoire de l'alimentation*, Cahiers des Annales, 28, Paris, 1970, pp.285–91.

Herlihy, David. 'Church Property on the European Continent, 701–1208', *Speculum*, XXXVI, 1 (1961), 81–105.

Hild, Friedrich. *Das byzantinische Strassensystem in Kappadokien*, Vienna, 1977.

Hoepfner, Wolfgang. 'Probleme und Methode der Hausforschung', in: *Wohnungsbau im Altertum*, Berlin, n.d., pp.9–18.

Hourani, Albert H. 'Introduction: The Islamic City in the Light of Recent Research', in: A. H. Hourani, S. M. Stern (eds.), *The Islamic City*, Oxford, 1970, pp.9–24.

Hütteroth, Wolf-Diether. *Ländliche Siedlungen im südlichen Inneranatolien in den letzten vierhundert Jahren*, Göttinger Geographische Abhandlungen, Göttingen, 1968.

Türkei, Wissenschaftliche Länderkunden vol. 21, Darmstadt, 1982.

Ibn Battuta, *Voyages*, tr. C. Defrémery, B. R. Sanguinetti, Paris, 1854, repr. 1968.

Ilgürel, Mücteba. 'Osmanlı İmparatorluğunda Ateşli Silahların Yayılışı', *Tarih Dergisi*, 32 (1979), 301–18.

İnalcık, Halil. '15. Asır Türkiye İktisadi ve İctimâî Tarihi Kaynakları', *İFM*, 15, 1–4 (153–4), 51–75.

'Bursa, I. XV. Asır Sanayi ve Ticaret Tarihine Dair Vesikalar', *Belleten*, XXIV, 93 (1960), 45–110.

'Adâletnâmeler', *Belgeler*, II, 3–4 (1965), 49–145.

'The Policy of Mehmed II toward the Greek Population of Istanbul and the Byzantine Buildings of the City', *Dumbarton Oaks Papers*, 23–4 (1969–70), 230–49.

'Capital Formation in the Ottoman Empire', *The Journal of Economic History*, 29 (1969), 97–140.

'The Ottoman Economic Mind and Aspects of the Ottoman Economy', in: M. A. Cook (ed.), *Studies in the Economic History of the Middle East* (London, 1970), pp.207–18.

The Ottoman Empire, The Classical Age 1300–1600, London, 1974.

'The Socio-Political Effects of the Diffusion of Firearms in the Middle East', in: V. J. Parry and M. S. Yapp (eds.), *War, Technology and Society in the Middle East*, London, 1975, pp.195–217.

'The Question of the Closing of the Black Sea Under the Ottomans', *Archeion Pontou*, 35 (1979), 74–110.

'Osmanlı Pamuklu Pazarı, Hindistan ve İngiltere Pazar Rekabetinde Emek Maliyetinin Rolü', *ODTU Gelişme Dergisi* (special issue, 1979–80), 1–66.

'Rice Cultivation and the Çeltükçi–Re'âyâ System in the Ottoman Empire', *Turcica*, XIV (1982), 69–141.

Islamoğlu, Huri, Faroqhi, Suraiya. 'Crop Patterns and Agricultural Production Trends in Sixteenth Century Anatolia', *Review* II, 3 (1979), 401–36.

Jennings, Ronald. *The Judicial Registers ('Şerî Mahkeme Sicilleri') of Kayseri (1590–1630) as a Source for Ottoman History*, Ph.D. dissertation, UCLA, 1972 (publ. by University Microfilms, Ann Arbor, Mich.).

'Women in Early 17th Century Ottoman Judicial Records – The Sharia Court of Anatolian Kayseri', *JESHO*, XVIII, I (1975), 53–114.

'The Office of Vekil (Wakil) in the 17th Century Ottoman Sharia Courts', *Studia Islamica*, LXII (1975), 147–69.

'Urban Population in Anatolia in the Sixteenth Century: A Study of Kayseri, Karaman, Trabzon, and Erzurum', *IJMES*, VII, 1 (1976), 21–57.

'Zimmis (non-Muslims) in Early 17th Century Ottoman Judicial Records: the Sharia Court of Anatolian Kayseri', *JESHO*, XXI, 3 (1978), 225–93.

'Sakaltutan Four Centuries Ago', *IJMES*, 9 (1978), 89–98.

'Firearms, bandits, and gun control: Some evidence on Ottoman policy toward firearms in the possession of reaya, from judicial records of Kayseri, 1600–1627', *Archivum Ottomanicum*, VI (1980), 339–358.

'The Population, Society, and Economy of the Region of Erciyes Dağı in the 16th Century', in: *Contributions à l'histoire économique et sociale de l'Empire Ottoman*', Collection Turcica III Louvain, 1984, pp.149–250.

Jerphanion, G. de. *Mélanges d'archéologie anatolienne*, Mélanges de l'Université St. Joseph XIII, Beirut, 1928.

Kayseri II Yilliği, Ankara, 1968.

Kedar, Benjamin Z. 'The Genoese Notaries of 1382: The Anatomy of an Urban Occupational Group', in: *The Medieval City, In Honor of Robert S. Lopez*, New Haven, Conn., London, 1977, pp.73–94.

Keddie, Nikki R. 'Problems in the Study of Middle Eastern Women', *IJMES* 10 (1979), 225–40.

Keleş, Ruşen. *Eski Ankara'da bir Şehir Tipolojisi*, Ankara, 1971.

Kemaleddin, Kara Mehmet Ağazade. Erciyes Kayseri'si ve Tarihine bir Bakış Kayseri, 1934.

Konyalı, İbrahim Hakkı. *Abideleri ve Kitâbeleriyle Konya Tarihi*, Konya 1964.

Kostof, Spiro. *Caves of God; The Monastic Environment of Byzantine Cappadocia* Cambridge, Mass. 1972.

[Koşay] Hamid Zübeyr. 'Hacı Bektaş Tekkesi', *Türkiyat Mecmuası*, II (1926), 366–82.

'Bektaşilik ve Hacıbektaş Türbesi', *Türk Etnografya Dergisi* (1967), 19–26.

Kömürcüoğlu, Eyüp. *Ankara Evleri*, İTÜ Mimarlık Fakültesi Yayınları, İstanbul, 1950.

Kömürcüoğlu, Eyüp Asim. *Das alttürkische Wohnhaus*, Wiesbaden, 1966.

Kreiser, Klaus. 'Osmanische Grenzbeschreibungen', in: *Studi preottomani e ottomani* (Napoli, 1976), pp.165–72.

Kuban, Doğan. 'Türk Ev Geleneği Üzerine Gözlemler', in: *Sanat Tarihimizin Sorunları*, Istanbul, 1975, pp. 192–212.
'Anadolu Kentlerinin Tarihsel Gelişimi ve Yapısı Üzerine Gözlemler', in: *Sanat Tarihimizin Sorunları*, İstanbul, 1975, pp. 105–62.
'Anadolu-Türk Mimarisinde Bölgesel Etkenlerin Niteliği', in: *Sanat Tarihimizin Sorunları*, İstanbul, 1975, pp.74–93.
Kunt, I. Metin. 'Transformation of *Zimmi* into *Askeri*', in: Benjamin Braude, Bernard Lewis, (eds.), *Christians and Jews in the Ottoman Empire, The Functioning of a Plural Society*, 2 vols., New York, London, 1982, vol. I *The Central Lands*, pp.55–67.
The Sultan's Servants, The Transformation of Ottoman Provincial Government 1550–1650, New York, 1983.
Kuran, Aptullah. *The Mosque in Early Ottoman Architecture*, Chicago, London 1968.
Anadolu Medreseleri, vol. I. Orta Doğu Teknik Üniversitesi Yayın 9, Ankara, 1969.
Küçükerman, Önder. *Anadolu'daki Geleneksel Türk Evinde Mekân Organızasyonu Açısından Odalar*, Türk Turing ve Otomobil Klubü Yayınları, İstanbul.
Kütükoğlu, Mübahat S. *Osmanlılarda Narh Müessesesi ve 1640 Tarihli Narh Defteri*, Istanbul, 1983.
Lapidus, Ira. *Muslim Cities in the Later Middle Ages,* Cambridge, Mass., 1967.
'Muslim Cities and Islamic Societies', in: *Middle Eastern Cities*, ed. J. M. Lapidus, Berkeley, Los Angeles, 1969, pp.47–79.
Le Goff, Jacques. 'L'apogée de la France urbaine médiévale', in: Georges Duby (ed.), *Histoire de la France urbaine*. 4 vols., Paris, 1980, vol. II, *La ville médiévale*, by André Chédeville. Le Goff, Jacques. Jacques Rossiaud, pp. 189–407.
Le Tourneau, Roger. *Fès avant le Protectorat, Étude économique et sociale d'une ville de l'Occident musulman*, Casablanca, 1949.
Lézine, Alexandre. *Trois palais d'époque ottomane au Caire*, Institut Français d'Archéologie Orientale, Cairo, 1972.
'Influences de la Turquie sur l'architecture domestique en Égypte après la conquête ottomane', in: *IV. Congrès international d'art turc'*, Études historiques 3, Aix-en Provence, 1976, 113–15.
Lopez, Robert S. 'L'architecture civile des villes médiévales: exemples et plans de recherche', in: *Les constructions civiles d'intérêt public dans les villes d'Europe au Moyen Age et sous l'Ancien Régime et leur financement*, Brussels, 1971, pp.15–31, 201–7.
Lucas, Paul, *Voyage du Sieur Paul Lucas fait en 1714 . . . par ordre de Louis XIV dans la Turquie*, Rouen, 1724.
Mandaville, Jon. 'Usurious Piety: The Cash Waqf Controversy in the Ottoman Empire', *IJMES*, x, 3 (1979), 289–308.
Mantran, Robert. *Istanbul dans la seconde moitié du XVIIᵉ siècle*, Bibliothèque archéologique et historique de l'Institut Français d'Archéologie d'Istanbul, Paris, 1962.
Marcus, Abraham. 'Men, Women and Property', *JESHO*, XXVI, II (1983), 37–163.
Masson, Paul. *Histoire du commerce français dans le Levant au XVIIᵉ siècle*, Paris, 1911, reprint New York, 1967.
Histoire du commerce français dans le Levant au XVIIIᵉ siècle, Paris, 1911.
Maury, Bernard. Raymond, André. Revault, Jacques. Zakarya, Mona. *Palais et maisons du Caire*, vol. II, *Époque ottomane*, Paris, 1983.
McGowan, Bruce. *Economic Life in Ottoman Europe*, Cambridge, Engl., Paris, 1982.

Miller, Barnette. *Beyond the Sublime Porte, The Grand Seraglio of Stambul*, New Haven, Conn., 1931.

Mols, Roger. *Introduction à la démographie historique des villes d'Europe du XIVᵉ au XVIIIᵉ siècle*, 3 vols. Louvain, 1955.

Moltke, Helmuth v. *Briefe über Zustände und Begebenheiten in der Türkei*, 6th edition, Berlin, 1893.

Mordtmann, A. D. *Anatolien, Skizzen und Reiseberichte aus Kleinasien (1850–1859)*, Ed. Franz Babinger, Hannover, 1925.

Maṭrakçı, Naṣūhü's-Silāḥī. *Beyān-ı Menāzil-i Sefer-i 'Irakeyn*, ed. Hüseyin G. Yurdaydın, Türk 'Tarih Kurumu Yayınları, XIV Dizi, Sa 4, Ankara, 1974.

Neveux, Hugues. 'Recherches sur la construction et l'entretien des maisons à Cambrai de la fin du XIVᵉ siècle au debut du XVIIIᵉ', in: *Le Bâtiment; Enquête d'histoire économique XIV–XIX siècles*. vol. ı, Paris, Den Haag, 1971, pp.191–312.

ODTÜ Mimarlık Fakültesi Restorasyon Bölümü, *Göynük, A Town in a Timber Region,* Ankara, 1970.

Ongan, Halit. *Ankara'nın 1 Numaralı Şeriye Sicili,* AÜ Dil ve Tarih Coğrafya Fakültesi Yayınları 125, Ankara, 1958.

Ankara'nin İki Numaralı Şeriye Sicili . . . Türk Tarih Kurumu Yayınları, xıv, 4 Ankara, 1974.

Onur, Halil, 'Daday'da Eski bir Türk Evi', *Türkiyemiz* 10, 29 (1979), 11–13.

Orhonlu, Cengiz. 'Şehir Mimarları', *Osmanlı Araştırmaları – The Journal of Ottoman Studies*, ıı, (1981), 1–30.

'İstanbul'da Kayıkçılık ve Kayık İşletmeciliği', reprinted in: Salih Özbaran (ed.) *Osmanlı Imparatorluğunda Şehircilik ve Ûlaşım Uzerine Araştırmalar* (İzmir, 1984).

Owen, Diane Hughes, 'Kinsmen and Neighbors in Medieval Genoa', in: *The Medieval City. In Honor of Robert S. Lopez*, New Haven, Conn., London, 1977, pp.95–112.

Ögel, Semra. 'Eski bir Ankara Evi', *Türkiyemiz,* 3, 8 (1972), 37–43.

'Zwei Beispiele der Schleierwand im alttürkischen Wohnhaus von Ankara', in: *IV. Congrès international d'art turc*, Études historiques 3 Aix-en-Provence, 1976, pp.167–72.

Öney, Gönül. *Ankara'da Türk Devri Yapıları, Turkish Period Buildings in Ankara*, AÜ Dil-Tarih ve Coğrafya Fakültesi Yayınları, no.209, Ankara, 1971.

Özgüner, Orhan. *Köyde Mimari, Doğu Karadeniz*, Ankara, 1970.

Planhol, Xavier de. *De la plaine pamphylienne aux lacs pisidiens, nomadisme et vie paysanne,* Bibliothèque archéologique et historique de l'Institut Français d'Archéologie d'Istanbul, Paris, 1958.

Les fondements géographiques de l'histoire de l'Islam, Paris, 1968.

'Regional Diversification and Social Structure in North Africa and the Islamic Middle East: A Geographic Approach', in: Richard T. Antoun, Iliya F. Harik (eds.), *Rural Politics and Social Change in the Middle East,* (Bloomington, Ind., 1972), pp.103–17.

'Rayonnement urbain et sélection animale: une solution nouvelle du problème de la chèvre d'Angora', *Sécretariat d'État aux Universités, Comité des Travaux historiques et scientifiques, Bulletin de la section de géographie,* ᴌxxx, II (1975–77), 179–96.

Pococke, Richard. *Description of the East and Some Other Countries,* 2 vols., London, 1745.

Poujoulat, Baptistin. *Voyage dans l'Asie Mineure, en Mésopotamie, à Palmyre, en Syrie, en Palestine et en Égypte,* 2 vols., Paris 1840.

Rambert, Gaston. (ed.), *Histoire du commerce de Marseille,* 6 vols. (Paris, 1949–59), vol. v *De 1660 à 1789*, by Robert Paris.

Rath, Wolfgang. 'Die byzantinische Wohnstadt von Pergamon', in: *Wohnungsbau im Altertum*, Berlin, n.d., pp.199–223.

Raymond, André. *Artisans et commerçants du Caire au XVIIIe siècle*, 2 vols., Damascus, 1973–4.

'La conquête ottomane et le développement des grandes villes arabes. Le cas du Caire, de Damas et d'Alep', *Revue de l'Occident musulman et de la Méditerranée*, I (1979), 115–34.

The Great Arab Cities in the 16–18th Centuries. An Introduction, Hagop Kevorkian Series on Near Eastern Art and Civilization, New York, London, 1984.

Redhouse, James W. *A Turkish and English Lexicon*, İstanbul, 1921.

Renda, Günsel. 'Büyük Bürüngüz'de Eski bir Türk Evi ve III. Selim Döneminde Süsleme', *Türkiyemiz*, 7, 21 (1977), 41–4.

Batılılaşma Döneminde Türk Resim Sanatı, 1700–1850, Ankara, 1977.

Rogers, Michael. 'The State and the Arts in Ottoman Turkey. Part 1, The Stones of Süleymaniye, Part 2. The Furniture and Decoration of Süleymaniye', *IJMES*, 14 (1982), 71–86, 283–313.

Roth, Cecil. *History of the Jews in Venice*, Philadelphia, 1931; reprinted New York, 1975.

Roux, Simone. 'La construction courante à Paris, du milieu du XIVe siècle à la fin du XVe siècle', in: *La construction au MoyenAge, Histoire et archéologie*, Actes du congrès de la Société des Historiens Médiévistes de l'Enseignement Supérieur Public, Paris, 1973, pp.175–90.

'Elements quantitatifs pour une histoire urbaine: la rue St. Victor à Paris, du milieu du XIV siècle au milieu du XV siècle', in: *Économies et Sociétés au Moyen Âge*, Mélanges offerts a Édouard Perroy, Paris, 1973, pp.518–24.

Sahillioğlu, Halil. 'XVIII. Asrın İlk Yarısında İstanbul'da Tedavüldeki Sikkelerin Raici', *Belgeler*, I, 2 (1964), 227–34.

'Osmanlı Para Tarihinde Dünya Para ve Maden Hareketlerinin Yeri (1300–1750)', *ODTÜ Gelişme Dergisi* (special issue, 1978), 1–38.

'Onbeşinci Yüzyılın Sonu ile Onaltıncı Yüzyılın Başında Bursa'da Kölelerin Sosyal ve Ekonomik Hayattaki Yeri', *ODTÜ Gelişme Dergisi* (special issue, 1979–80), 67–138.

Sakaoğlu, Necdet. *Divriği'de Ev Mimarisi*, Kültür Balkanlığı Yayınları 274, Turk Sanat Eserleri Serisi 8 (İstanbul, 1978).

Schacht, Joseph. *An Introduction to Islamic Law*, Oxford, 1964, reprinted 1982.

Schneider, Jean. *La ville de Metz, aux XIIIe et XIVe siècles*, Thèse principale pour le doctorat ès lettres, Nancy, 1950.

Shaw, Stanford, J. *The Financial and Administrative Organization and Development of Ottoman Egypt 1517–1798*, Princeton, N.J. 1962.

Polonyalı Simeon, *Polonyalı Simeon'un Seyahatnamesi*, tr. ed. Hrand D. Andreasyan, Istanbul Universitesi Edebiyat Fakültesi Yayınları No.1073, İstanbul, 1964.

Sözen, Metin. 'Anadolu'daki Eyvan Tipi Türbeler', *Anadolu Sanatı Araştırmaları*, I (1968), 167–210.

Dülgerler, Osman Nuri. 'Konya Evlerinden Örnekler', *ODTÜ Mimarlık Fakültesi Dergisi*, 5, 1 (1979), 78–100.

Sourdel, Dominique. Sourdel-[Thomime], Janine. *La civilisation de l'Islam classique*, Les Grandes Civilisations, Paris, 1968.

Stirling, Paul. *Turkish Village*, London, 1965.

Stoianovich, Traian. 'Model and Mirror of the pre-modern Balkan City', in: *La ville balkanique, XVe–XIXe ss*, Studia Balcanica, 3 (1970), 83–110.

Stouff, Louis. 'Les registres de notaires d'Arles (debut XIVe s–1450). Quelques problèmes posés par l'utilization des archives notariales', *Provence historique*, xxv, 99 (1975), 305–24.

Taeschner, Franz. *Das anatolische Wegenetz nach osmanischen Quellen*, Türkische Bibliothek, 2 vols., Leipzig, 1924–6.

'Ankara bei den osmanischen Geographen des 17. Jhdts', in: *60. Doğum Yılı Münasebetiyle Zeki Velidi Togan'a Armağan, Symbolae in honorem Z.V. Togan*, Istanbul, 1950–55, pp.147–56.

'War Murad I Grossmeister oder Mitglied des Achi-Bundes?' *Oriens*, 6 (1953), 23–31.

Texier, Charles. *Asie Mineure, description géographique, historique et archéologique des provinces et des villes de la chersonnèse d'Asie*, 2 vols., Paris, 1862.

Todorov, Nikolaj. '19. Yüzyılın İlk Yarısında Bulgaristan Esnaf Teşkilatında Bazı Karakter Değişmeleri', *İFM*, 27, 1–2 (1967–68), 1–36.

'La différentiation de la population urbaine au XVIIIe siècle d'après des registres de cadis de Vidin, Sofia et Ruse', in: *La ville balkanique, XVe–XIX^{e}ss*, Studia Balcanica, 3, Sofia, 1970, 45–62.

La ville balkanique aux XVe–XIXe siècles, développement socio-économique et démographique, Bucarest, 1980.

Tomsu, Leman. *Bursa Evleri*, İTÜ Mimarlık Fakültesi Yayınları, İstanbul, 1949.

Tournefort, M. Pitton de. *Relation d'un voyage du Levant*. 2 vols., Amsterdam, 1718.

Tunçdilek, Necdet. 'Eskişehir Bölgesinde Yerleşme Tarihine Toplu bir Bakış', *İFM*, 15, 1–4 (1953–4), 189–208.

Turan, Osman. 'Les souverains seldjoukides et leurs sujets non-musulmans', *Studia Islamica* , 1 (1953), 65–100.

Turan, Şerafettin. 'Osmanlı Teşkilatında Hassa Mimarları', *Tarih Araştırmaları Dergisi*, 1, 1 (1963), 157–202.

User's Guide, SPSS, Chicago, 1981.

Uslu, S. *Untersuchungen zum anthropogenen Charakter der zentralanatolischen Steppe*, Giessener Abhandlungen 12, Giessen, 1960.

Uzunçarşılı, İsmail Hakkı. *Osmanlı Devletinde Kapukulu Ocakları*, 2 vols., Türk Tarih Kurumu Yayınlarından Seri VIII, 12, 122, Ankara, 1943, 1944.

Ünsal, Behçet. *Turkish Islamic Architecture in Seljuk and Ottoman times 1071–1923*, London, New York, 1973.

Ünver, Süheyl, Eldem, Sedad Hakkı. *Amucazade Hüseyin Paşa Yalısı*, İstanbul, 1970.

Veinstein, Gilles. '⟨Ayân⟩ de la région d'İzmir et commerce du Levant (Deuxième moitié du XVIIIe siècle)', *Études balkaniques*, XII, 3 (1976), 71–83.

Velenis, Georges. 'Wohnviertel und Wohnhausbau in den byzantinischen Städten', in: *Wohnungsbau im Altertum*, Berlin, n.d., pp.227–36.

Von Grunebaum, Gustave. 'The Structure of the Muslim Town', in: *Islam, Essays in the nature and growth of a cultural tradition*, 2nd ed. London, 1965, pp.141–58.

Wittek, Paul. 'Zur Geschichte Angoras im Mittelalter', in: Theodor Menzel, (ed.), *Festschrift Georg Jacob* . . . , Leipzig, 1932, pp.329–54.

Yavuz, Ayşıl Tükel. '19. Yüzyıl Ankara'sında Kale İçi', in: E. Yavuz and N. Uğurel (eds.), *Tarih İçinde Ankara* Eylül 1981 Seminer Bildirileri, Ankara, 1984, pp.155–94.

Zilfi, Madeline. 'Kadızadeli Revivalism in Seventeenth Century İstanbul', *Journal of Near Eastern Studies*, forthcoming.

Index of personal names and localities

Words such as 'Ankara', 'Kayseri', 'central Anatolia', 'sale' (without qualification) or 'houses', which recur on almost every page, have not been included in the indices, nor do the latter cover the tables and legends to the illustrations.

Index of technical terms

ahır, 67, 99, 100, 103, 191, 238n.47
ahi(s), 24
ahidname, 10, 31
akçe, 30, 116, 117, 122, 123, 124, 125, 127, 128, 129, 130, 135, 137, 139, 141, 144, 148, 188, 198, 240n.14
alaca, 28, 233n.27
arasta, 28
askeri, 17, 20, 32, 139, 144, 148, 150, 151, 160, 161, 162, 177, 178, 181, 187, 200, 202, 219, 240n.4, 241n.23, n.30, 243n.16
autonomy, question of urban, 37, 38
avarız (hane), 14, 46, 47, 119, 120, 196, 197, 218
avlu, see courtyard
ayan, see notables

bağ evi, 97
bahçe, see garden
baking ovens, 99
başoda, 66
bathhouses, see bath(s), public
bath(s), public, 1, 14, 15, 23, 62
bedestan, see market, covered
bekar odaları, 216
beşe, 190
bey 49, 151, 178, 187, 248n.66
beytülmal emini, 30, 196, 197, 244n.54
building, public, 14, 40
buyer(s), of houses, 8, 38, 59, 117, 152, 155, 156, 157, 158, 159, 160, 161, 162, 163, 168, 171, 173, 174, 175, 176, 178, 180, 181, 191, 194, 199, 248n.68

caravansaray(s), 13, 67, 237n.4
Celalis, 40, 43, 44, 46, 57, 62, 97, 100, 101, 106, 152, 171, 175, 208, 209, 210, 211, 212, 217
cemetaries, 33, 34
charities, see foundations, pious
child(ren), orphaned, 19, 172, 174, 190, 191

Christian(s), see also non-Muslim(s), 3, 12, 14, 24, 40, 45, 46, 59, 61, 155, 157
church(es), 14, 40, 61
city centre, 13
cizye, 12, 14, 44, 45, 46, 47, 48, 230n.35
contested cases, see dispute
co-owner, of house, 21, 174, 194, 199
courtyard, 16, 20, 30, 65, 69, 78, 100, 101, 107, 109, 111, 112, 119, 128, 129, 130, 166, 196, 213, 214
courtyard, double, 101, 102, 103, 112, 113, 114, 166, 190, 212, 238n.46, n.47
creditor(s), 152, 172
crowding, 12, 22, 111, 113, 115, 119, 125, 148, 213, 214

çardak, 66, 95, 113, 215, 236n.1, 237n.7
çarşı, 40

debt, see also mortgage, 17, 19, 29, 30, 171, 172, 174, 195, 198
defendant(s), 8, 38, 158, 185, 186, 187, 193, 198, 243n.9
dependent, city, 37, 38
develik, 67
dispute(d cases), 9, 10, 17, 39, 182, 183, 186, 187, 188, 190, 191, 194, 195, 198, 201
divanhane, 77, 104
donation, 9, 18, 194
dowry, see mihr-i müeccel

efendi, 49, 151
European(s), in Ankara, 25, 26, 31, 32, 41, 63, 104, 125, 156

female(s), see women
fetva, 182, 194, 198
fevkani, see also floor, upper, 93, 94
field(s), 52, 53, 54, 203, 205, 206, 246n.13
floor, upper, 16, 76, 94, 109, 110, 114, 212

foundation(s), pious, 9, 14, 17, 21, 40, 46, 56, 66, 104, 120, 161, 173, 195, 196, 197, 198, 199, 201, 206, 221, 242n.41, 244n.57
foundation, to help pay *avariz* taxes, 196, 197, 244n.56
foundation administrator, 196, 197, 198
fountain(s), 1, 40, 62, 76, 82, 119

garden(s), 15, 22, 54, 62, 65, 97, 99, 100, 102, 119, 203, 204, 205, 206, 238n.43
gates, Ankara city, 34
gold coins, 29, 30, 117, 118, 192
guruş, 49, 50, 51, 52, 53, 54, 93, 106, 117, 118, 148, 191, 192, 198, 239n.5, 242n.39
guruş, esedi, 28, 29, 30, 117, 118, 239n.6
guruş-ı kebir, 118
gusulhane, 76

hacı(s), 18, 49, 162, 163, 165
hamam see also bath(s) public, 67, 237n.10
harem (odası), 77, 78, 81, 93, 102, 238n.33
hassa mimarı, 190
havlu, see courtyard
ḥawš, 4, 213, 216
hayat, 65, 66, 236n.2
heir(s), 17, 20, 21, 28, 30, 32, 53, 154, 178, 179, 190, 191
hisse, see share(s)
houses, large, 93, 168
houses, small, 111, 112, 168
'housing market', 15, 16, 117, 155

imam, 49, 173, 196
imaret, 27
inheritance, 9, 17, 176, 178, 188, 190, 193, 201, 216, 244n.38
inheritances, sharing of, 12, 21, 54, 172, 178, 196, 197
inheritance, not possible between Muslims and non-Muslims, 192, 193, 194
inventories, probate, 9, 28, 29, 51, 53, 55

janissary(ies), 29, 33, 151, 160, 178, 186, 187, 201, 211
Jew(s), 3, 152

kadı(s), 7, 8, 9, 10, 12, 18, 21, 27, 35, 53, 89, 95, 116, 151, 154, 172, 176, 177, 180, 182, 183, 185, 186, 187, 190, 192, 196, 201, 205, 219, 243n.2
Karamanlı, 150, 151
kaza, 161
khan, 4, 17, 32, 233n.33
kiler, 76, 97, 99
kitchen, 15, 66, 67, 75, 76, 78, 81, 95, 97, 103
konak, 93, 102, 103, 150, 237n.10
köşk, 66, 67, 75, 78, 102, 214, 236n.1

landholding(s), rural, 203
limitations, statute of, 193, 194, 197

mahalle, see town quarter
male(s), 32, 33, 46, 47, 48, 150, 158, 166, 186
Mamluk, 4, 36, 37, 216, 218, 248n.66
market, covered, 13, 34, 56, 209, 210
matbah, see kitchen
medrese, 49, 50, 186, 187, 201, 237n.4
menzil, 65
merchant(s), 17, 25, 26, 27, 28, 29, 30, 31, 32, 54, 63, 64, 94, 105, 106, 135, 160, 204, 233n.39, 235n.108
mescit, 29, 40
mezhep, 9
mihr-i müeccel, mihr-i müsbet, 51, 55, 190, 193
minor(s), *see* child(ren) orphaned
models, impact of İstanbul, 12
mohair (industry), 22, 25, 26, 31, 62, 64, 67, 104, 105, 106, 107, 135, 148, 190, 203, 204, 209, 210, 233n.11, 239n.48, n.53, n60, 247n.48
mortgage, 15, 17, 152, 172, 195, 198
mosque(s) 1, 14, 21, 40, 42, 61, 62, 102, 119, 173, 196, 199, 202, 208n.2
mudbrick, 18, 20, 214
muhavvata, 65, 214
Muslim(s), 3, 10, 12, 16, 17, 19, 20, 37, 38, 39, 43, 47, 48, 58, 59, 60, 61, 106, 119, 120, 135, 139, 141, 144, 148, 150, 151, 154, 155, 156, 157, 158, 165, 166, 168, 169, 170, 175, 176, 179, 183, 184, 185, 192, 193, 196, 200, 202, 212, 214, 217, 218, 219, 230n.29, 249n.17, 241n.19, 242n.36, 242n.53
mülk, 65

nefer, see taxpayer
neighbour(s), 7, 14, 18, 19, 20, 21, 40, 61, 116, 173, 174, 175, 176, 177, 180, 181, 183, 199
nomad tradition, in domestic architecture, 2, 13
non-Muslim(s), *see also* Christian(s), 5, 10, 12, 14, 16, 17, 19, 20, 30, 33, 38, 39, 43, 45, 46, 47, 48, 59, 60, 61, 67, 106, 107, 119, 120, 135, 137, 139, 141, 144, 148, 150, 151, 152, 154, 156, 157, 158, 163, 165, 166, 168, 169, 170, 171, 175, 176, 179, 180, 183, 184, 187, 190, 191, 192, 193, 194, 198, 200, 201, 202, 206, 217, 218, 219, 230n.29, 240n.19, 242n.53
notables, 37, 49, 201, 202, 203, 204, 245n.5

oda, see also room(s), 15, 66, 76, 89, 93, 94, 102, 103, 104, 107, 110, 111, 113, 114, 127, 128, 166, 214, 196, 215